EUROPEAN SOCIETY OF INTERNATIONAL LAW SERIES

Secondary Rules of Primary Importance in International Law

EUROPEAN SOCIETY OF INTERNATIONAL LAW SERIES

The ESIL Book Series publishes high-quality volumes on the themes of ESIL Annual Conferences and ESIL joint events primarily. The volumes include chapters that are based on selected papers presented at ESIL events, revised to fit the theme and focus of the volume, and complemented by additional chapters that address topics that were not fully explored at the events, but that are essential for a full coverage of the theme.

Secondary Rules of Primary Importance in International Law

Attribution, Causality, Evidence, and Standards of Review in the Practice of International Courts and Tribunals

Edited by

GÁBOR KAJTÁR

ELTE Law School

BAŞAK ÇALI

Hertie School

and

MARKO MILANOVIC

University of Nottingham

OXFORD
UNIVERSITY PRESS

OXFORD
UNIVERSITY PRESS

Great Clarendon Street, Oxford, OX2 6DP,
United Kingdom

Oxford University Press is a department of the University of Oxford.
It furthers the University's objective of excellence in research, scholarship,
and education by publishing worldwide. Oxford is a registered trade mark of
Oxford University Press in the UK and in certain other countries

First Edition published in 2022

Published in the United States of America by Oxford University Press
198 Madison Avenue, New York, NY 10016, United States of America

British Library Cataloguing in Publication Data

Data available

Library of Congress Control Number: 2022938015

ISBN 978–0–19–286901–2

DOI: 10.1093/oso/9780192869012.001.0001

Printed and bound by
CPI Group (UK) Ltd, Croydon, CR0 4YY

Contents

PART III. EVIDENTIARY RULES IN INTERNATIONAL LAW

PART IV. ATTRIBUTION IN INTERNATIONAL LAW

Table of Cases

DOMESTIC AWARDS AND DECISIONS

United Kingdom

United States of America

INTERNATIONAL

European Court of Human Rights

European Commission of Human Rights

Inter-American Court of Human Rights

Court of Justice of the European Union

Permanent Court of International Justice

World Trade Organization – Dispute Settlement Body

INTERNATIONAL CRIMINAL TRIBUNALS

International Tribunal for the Law of the Sea

Iran-United States Claims Tribunal

United Nations Dispute Tribunal and United Nations Appeals Tribunal

International Arbitral Awards and Decisions

United Nations Human Rights Committee

Committee against Torture

Committee on the Elimination of Discrimination against Women

Table of Treaties

List of Abbreviations

AB	WTO Appellate Body
ACtHPR	African Court on Human and Peoples' Rights
AP I	Additional Protocol I to the Geneva Conventions
ARSIWA	International Law Commission Articles on the Responsibility of States for Internationally Wrongful Acts
BIT	Bilateral Investment Treaty
CAT	UN Convention against Torture and Other Cruel, Inhuman, or Degrading Treatment or Punishment
CEDAW	Committee on the Elimination of Discrimination Against Women
CFI	Court of First Instance
CIA	Central Intelligence Agency
CJEU	Court of Justice of the European Union
DSB	Dispute Settlement Body
DSU	Understanding on Rules and Procedures Governing the Settlement of Disputes
ECHR	European Convention on Human Rights
ECtHR	European Court of Human Rights
EEZ	Exclusive Economic Zone
EU	European Union
FAO	Food and Agriculture Organization
FCN	Nicaragua–United States Friendship, Commerce, and Navigation Treaty
FCTC	Framework Convention on Tobacco Control
FET	Fair and Equitable Treatment
FPS	Full Protection and Security
GATS	General Agreement on Trade in Services
GATT 1994	General Agreement on Tariffs and Trade 1994
HRC	UN Human Rights Committee
IAC	International Armed Conflict
IACHR	Inter-American Commission on Human Rights
IACmHR	Inter-American Commission on Human Rights
IACtHR	Inter-American Court of Human Rights
ICESCR	International Covenant of Economic, Social, and Cultural Rights
ICJ	International Court of Justice
ICRC	International Committee of the Red Cross
ICRW	International Convention on the Regulation of Whaling
ICSID	International Centre for Settlement of Investment Disputes
ICTY	International Tribunal for the Former Yugoslavia
IEL	International Economic Law

IHL	International Humanitarian Law
IHRL	International Human Rights Law
IIFFMCG	Independent International Fact-Finding Mission on the Conflict in Georgia
ILA	International Law Association
ILC	International Law Commission
IMT	International Military Tribunal
ISDS	Investor-State Dispute Settlement
ISIL	Islamic State
IT	International Tribunal
ITLOS	International Tribunal for the Law of the Sea
IUU	Illegal, Unreported, and Unregulated
IWA	International Wrongful Act
IWC	International Whaling
JARPA II	ICRW Japanese Whale Research Program under Special Permit in the Antarctic: Phase II
LRM	Least Restrictive Measure
MoA	Margin of Appreciation
NGO	Non-Governmental Organization
NIAC	Non-International Armed Conflict
PCA	Permanent Court of Arbitration
PCIJ	Permanent Court of International Justice
PLO	Palestinian Liberation Organization
SCM Agreement	Agreement on Subsidies and Countervailing Measures
SPR	Single Presentation Requirement
SPS	Sanitary and Phytosanitary Measures
STL	Special Tribunal for Lebanon
STS	Science and Technology Studies
TBT Agreement	Agreement on Technical Barriers to Trade
TNC	Transnational Corporation
TPD	Tobacco Products Directive 2014/40 (EU)
TRIPS Agreement	Agreement on Trade-Related Aspects of Intellectual Property Rights
TRNC	Turkish Republic of Northern Cyprus
UK	United Kingdom
UN	United Nations
UNAT	United Nations Appeals Tribunal
UNCh	Charter of the United Nations
UNCITRAL	United Nations Commission on International Trade Law
UNCLOS	United Nations Convention on the Law of the Sea
UNCTAD	United Nations Conference on Trade and Development
UNGA	United Nations General Assembly
UNSC	United Nations Security Council
US	United States

VCDR	Vienna Convention on Diplomatic Relations
VCLT	Vienna Convention on the Law of Treaties
VRS	Bosnian Serb Army
WHO	World Health Organization
WTO	World Trade Organization

List of Contributors

Tilmann Altwicker is Swiss National Science Foundation (SNSF) Professor for Public Law, International Law, Legal Philosophy and Empirical Legal Research at University of Zurich, Law Faculty. He is a Review Panel Expert for the European Cooperation in Science and Technology (EU COST). Previously, he has been head of the SNSF-Research Group on Transnational Public Security Law at the University of Basel (2013–2017) and Lecturer (German Academic Exchange Service) at Eötvös Loránd University and at the Andrassy University, Budapest.

Eyal Benvenisti is Whewell Professor of International Law (Cambridge), University of Cambridge, Director of the Lauterpacht Centre for International Law, CC Ng Fellow of Jesus College, Cambridge. He is Samuel Rubin Visiting Professor of Law, Columbia Law School (2022) and Visiting Professor, The Hebrew University of Jerusalem. Eyal Benvenisti was Anny and Paul Yanowicz Professor of Human Rights, Tel Aviv University Faculty of Law (from 2002) and Hersch Lauterpacht Professor of Law at the Hebrew University (from 1990). He was Global Professor of Law at New York University School of Law (since 2003). He was Visiting Professor at Yale, Harvard, Toronto, Columbia, Pennsylvania, and Michigan, and gave a special course at The Hague Academy of International Law (2013). Eyal's areas of research and teaching are international law, constitutional law, and administrative law. He is a member of the Institut de Droit International and of the Israeli Academy of Sciences. He is a co-editor of the British Yearbook for International Law and was on the Editorial Board of the American Journal of International Law.

Christina Binder, EMA, holds the Chair for International Law and International Human Rights Law at the Bundeswehr University, Munich since April 2017. Previously, she was University Professor of International Law at the Department of European, International and Comparative Law at the University of Vienna and Deputy Director of the interdisciplinary Research Centre "Human Rights." She is a member of the ILA Committee on Human Rights in Times of Emergency. Christina is member of the Executive Board and former Vice-President of the European Society of International Law (ESIL) and a member of the Council of the Global Campus of Human Rights since 2019.

Başak Çalı is Professor of International Law at the Hertie School and Co-Director of the School's Centre for Fundamental Rights. She is an expert in international law and institutions, international human rights law and policy. She has authored publications on theories of international law, the relationship between international law and domestic law, standards of review in international law, interpretation of human rights law, legitimacy of human rights courts, and implementation of human rights judgments. She is the Chair of European Implementation Network and a Fellow of the Human Rights Centre of the University of Essex. She has acted as a Council of Europe expert on the European Convention on Human Rights since 2002. She has extensive experience in training members of the judiciary and lawyers across Europe in the field of human rights law. She received her PhD in international law from the University of Essex in 2003.

Catherine Gascoigne is a Research Affiliate at the University of Sydney. Catherine holds a Bachelor of Arts (Honours Class I) and a Bachelor of Laws (Honours Class I) from the University of Sydney, a Bachelor of Civil Law (Distinction) from the University of Oxford, and a Doctor of Philosophy in Law from the University of Cambridge, where she studied as both a Gates Cambridge Scholar and a WM Tapp Scholar. Catherine is admitted as a Lawyer in New South Wales and practiced as an associate at a major international commercial law firm for three years.

Lukasz Gruszczynski (dr. habil.) is Associate Professor of International Law at Kozminski University (Poland) and Research Fellow at the CSS Institute for Legal Studies (Hungary). He specializes in WTO law, global health law, and risk regulation. Lukasz is a Managing Co-Editor of the Polish Yearbook of International Law and a EJRR Board member. His scientific portfolio includes two monographs with OUP and an edited volume with Edward Elgar. His forthcoming book discusses the crisis of multilateralism (*The Crisis of Multilateral Legal Order: Causes, Dynamics and Implications*, co-edited with M. Menkes, V. Bilkova, and P. Farah, Routledge, London-New York, 2022).

Alexandra Ellen Hansen recently completed her PhD thesis at the law faculty at the University of Zurich and was a recipient of the Candoc research grant (2021–2022). She studied Swiss Law at the University of Basel (BLaw) and Transnational Law at the Universities of Basel and Geneva (MLaw) before completing her MSc in Philosophy and Public Policy at the London School of Economics and Political Science. As of September 2022 she will be leading the NGO humanrights.ch's independent counselling centre for people deprived of their liberty.

Martin Jarrett is a Senior Research Fellow at the Max Planck Institute for Comparative Public Law and International Law and an adjunct lecturer at the University of Heidelberg. He formerly worked as a Senior Lecturer at the University of Mannheim, Germany. He is qualified as a solicitor and barrister (New South Wales, Australia) and holds a Bachelor of Arts, Bachelor of Laws (with first class honors), Graduate Diploma of Legal Practice, and Doctor of Laws (*summa cum laude*). His research profile is focused on international investment law and the law of international responsibility. His publication record is headlined by his Cambridge University Press-published monograph, *Contributory Fault and Investor Misconduct in Investment Arbitration*. The complete record of his research activities can be accessed at: martin-jarrett.com<http://martin-jarrett.com>.

Gábor Kajtár LLM (Cantab) is Associate Professor of International Law and vice-dean for science and research at ELTE Law School Budapest. He holds a Law degree, an MA in Political Sciences, and an LLM from the University of Cambridge (2007). His PhD dissertation concerned the self-defense against non-state actors and was awarded the Pro Dissertatione Iuridica Excellentissima Award, given to the best legal PhD dissertation in 2013–2014 by the Hungarian Academy of Sciences. Dr Kajtár was a Visiting Researcher at Harvard Law School in the academic year 2015/2016, a Leibniz Fellow at the Max Planck Institute in Heidelberg in 2017, and a Visiting Fellow at the Lauterpacht Centre in 2019. Dr

Kajtár is the coach of ELTE Jessup and Telders mooting teams since 2009, his teams won the Jessup World Championship in 2019 and the Telders Finals in 2019 and 2022.

Vladyslav Lanovoy is Assistant Professor of Public International Law at the Faculty of Law, Université Laval, in Quebec City, Canada. He was formerly an Associate Legal Officer at the International Court of Justice and an Assistant Legal Counsel at the Permanent Court of Arbitration. He also held visiting academic positions at Lille Catholic University and Queen Mary University of London. He received his PhD in international law from the Graduate Institute of International and Development Studies in Geneva and is the author of *Complicity and its Limits in the Law of International Responsibility* (Hart 2016), which was awarded the 2017 Paul Guggenheim Prize in International Law. His research interests include the law of international responsibility, international dispute settlement, international economic law, law of the sea, and human rights law.

Christopher Lentz has worked for more than a dozen years in international tribunals, where he has gained experience in international criminal law and procedure, public international law and diplomacy, and related fields of international law. Currently, he serves as a Legal Officer in the Office of the President of the United Nations International Residual Mechanism for Criminal Tribunals. In addition, he is Lecturer in Law at the University of Chicago Law School. He holds a Doctor of Law degree from the University of Chicago.

Marko Milanovic is Professor of Public International Law at the University of Reading School of Law. He is co-editor of EJIL: Talk!, the blog of the European Journal of International Law, as well as a member of the EJIL's Editorial Board. Professor Milanovic was formerly Vice-President and member of the Executive Board of the European Society of International Law. He held visiting professorships at Michigan Law School, Columbia Law School, Deakin Law School, the University of the Philippines College of Law, and the Geneva Academy of International Humanitarian Law and Human Rights, and was previously Professor of Public International Law at the University of Nottingham.

Alice Ollino (PhD, LLM) is a post-doctoral fellow in public international law at the University of Milano-Bicocca. She is the author of *Due Diligence Obligations in International Law* (CUP 2022). In 2019, she was awarded the ESIL Young Scholar Prize. Alice undertook her doctoral studies at the University of Milano-Bicocca and has published on public international law issues in national and international peer-reviewed journals. Her research interests include general public international law, international responsibility, and international human rights.

Katalin Sulyok is Lecturer in International Law and Environmental Law at ELTE Eötvös Lorand University, Budapest. She holds a PhD in law, a BSc in Biology from ELTE University, and an LLM from Harvard Law School. Her dissertation on the role of science in the judicial reasoning of international fora was awarded the Wheaton (JB Scott) Prize by the Institut de Droit international and was published by Cambridge University Press in 2021 entitled "*Science and Judicial Reasoning: The Legitimacy of International Environmental Adjudication.*" Dr. Sulyok also works as chief legal advisor to the Ombudsman for Future Generations of Hungary. Dr Sulyok has been a Leibniz Fellow at the Max Planck Institute in Heidelberg, a Visiting Researcher in the Lauterpacht Centre, a Visiting Scholar in the Center for the Environment, Energy and Natural Resource Governance of Cambridge University, and a re:constitution fellow at Sorbonne and Aarhus University.

Stephan Wittich is Professor of International Law at the University of Vienna Law School. He also teaches at the Vienna School of International Studies. He obtained his doctoral degree from the University of Vienna and was a visiting professor at the University of Bologna. His research interests include international responsibility, international procedural law, sources, immunities, and international law in domestic courts. Professor Wittich was legal advisor to the Principality of Liechtenstein in the *Certain Property* case before the ICJ (2001–2004). He is a member of the International Law Association and a convener of the ESIL IG on International Courts and Tribunals. He is a co-editor of the *Austrian Review of International and European Law* (Nijhoff/Brill) and co-editor of the forthcoming *Research Handbook on International Procedural Law* (Edward Elgar, together with Joanna Gomula).

Jure Zrilič is a Senior Lecturer at the City Law School, City, University of London. He holds PhD in law from the University of Cambridge. His research interests are principally in international law, in particular international investment law and international arbitration. Jure is the sole author of *The Protection of Foreign Investment in Times of Armed Conflict* (OUP 2019).

1

Introduction

Secondary Rules of Primary Importance

Gábor Kajtár, Başak Çalı, and Marko Milanovic

1. Introduction

The role of secondary rules in international law is an often overlooked, yet crucially important, aspect of international adjudication. Most international courts and tribunals do not have clear, consistent, and coherent approaches to issues such as standards of review, causation, evidentiary rules, or attribution. Yet, they employ these rules routinely in their everyday work by attaching divergent meanings and normative contents to these notions.[1]

In its codification efforts regarding the law of international responsibility,[2] the International Law Commission (ILC) aimed to elaborate on a set of generally applicable secondary rules, in particular those concerning the attribution of conduct. But, even so, inconsistencies and ambiguities in employing the secondary rules terminology[3] and their scope abound.[4] Of the issues that concern us here, the ILC dealt with causality sporadically and superficially in its project.[5] Standards of review and evidentiary standards have been omitted, in their entirety, from the ILC's

[1] See eg Charles Brower, "Evidence before International Tribunals: The Need for Some Standard Rules" (1994) 28 International Lawyer 47–58; Ilias Plakokefalos, "Causation in the Law of State Responsibility and the Problem of Overdetermination: In Search of Clarity" (2015) 26 European Journal of International Law 471–92; Lukasz Gruszczynski and Wouter Werner (eds), *Deference in International Courts and Tribunals: Standard of Review and Margin of Appreciation* (OUP 2014).

[2] ILC, Articles on Responsibility of States for Internationally Wrongful Acts (ARSIWA), UN Doc A/56/83 (3 August 2001); Draft Articles on the Responsibility of International Organizations (2011) II/2 Yearbook of the International Law Commission.

[3] See eg J Combacau and D Alland, "'Primary' and 'Secondary' Rules in the Law of State Responsibility Categorizing International Obligations" (1985) 16 Netherlands Yearbook of International Law 81–109; Ulf Linderfalk, "State Responsibility and the Primary-Secondary Rules Terminology: The Role of Language for an Understanding of the International Legal System" (2009) 78 Nordic Journal of International Law 53–72; Anastasios Gourgourinis, "General/Particular International Law and Primary/Secondary Rules: Unitary Terminology of a Fragmented System" (2011) 22 European Journal of International Law 993–1026.

[4] See eg André Nollkaemper, "Attribution of Forcible Acts to States: Connections Between the Law on the Use of Force and the Law of State Responsibility" in Niels M Blokker and Nico J Schrijver (eds), *The Security Council and the Use of Force: Theory and Reality—A Need for Change?* (Martinus Nijhoff 2005) 133–71; Csaba Kovacs, *Attribution in International Investment Law* (Kluwer 2018).

[5] ARSIWA Commentary (n 2) 81, 93.

Gábor Kajtár, Başak Çalı, and Marko Milanovic, *Introduction* In: *Secondary Rules of Primary Importance in International Law.* Edited by: Gábor Kajtár, Başak Çalı, and Marko Milanovic, Oxford University Press. DOI: 10.1093/oso/9780192869012.003.0001

consideration due to the ILC's focus on codification of rules that apply outside the courtroom.

Yet, recent decades have seen much judicial use, development, and interpretation of the secondary rules across different branches of international law. International courts have had to address substantially similar issues that are not covered by the ILC Articles. They have articulated or revised their standards of review.[6] They have laid out and adjusted their rules of evidence and assessments of causality.[7] All of these developments make a deeper theoretical scrutiny and comparative analysis of the judicial and doctrinal treatment of secondary rules in international law timely. This edited volume responds to this need.

This volume focuses on four domains of secondary rules that fundamentally shape international adjudication, namely evidentiary rules, standards of review, causation, and attribution. The contributions in this volume investigate how various international courts have, in many different contexts, grappled with these four domains of secondary rules and identify lessons that can be learned therefrom. The different courts covered in the volume range from the International Court of Justice (ICJ), arbitration tribunals, the European Court of Human Rights (ECtHR), the Court of Justice of the European Union (CJEU), UN quasi-judicial bodies, and World Trade Organization (WTO) dispute settlement. Legal contexts span from law of immunity to human rights, trade, investment, and environmental law. This broad coverage allows for detailed observations on the operation of secondary rules, including their methodological dimensions and normative effects on primary rules, legitimacy of judicial decision-making, and systemic coherence. In this introductory chapter, we start by defining secondary rules in international law for the purposes of this study (see section 2). We then lay out the book's approach to the comparative analysis of secondary rules across different domains of international law undertaken in the book (see section 3). We subsequently introduce the contributions to the volume (see section 4) and outline some of the key findings of the book as a whole (see section 5).

[6] Andrew T Guzman, "Determining the Appropriate Standard of Review in WTO Disputes" (2009) 42 Cornell International Law Journal 45–76; J Gerards and E Brems (eds), *Procedural Review in European Fundamental Cases* (CUP 2017) 17–39; Başak Çalı, "Coping with Crisis: Whither the Variable Geometry in the Jurisprudence of the European Court of Human Rights" (2018) 35(2) Wisconsin International Law Journal 237–76.

[7] R Teitelbaum, "Recent Fact-Finding Developments at the International Court of Justice" (2007) 6 Law and Practice of International Courts and Tribunals 119–58; J Kokoff, *The Burden of Proof in Comparative and International Human Rights Law* (Kluwer 1998); M Vagias and J Ferencz, "Burden and Standard of Proof in Defence Challenges to the Jurisdiction of the International Criminal Court" (2015) 28 Leiden Journal of International Law 133–55; PA Nollkaemper and I Plakokefalos (eds), *Principles of Shared Responsibility in International Law: An Appraisal of the State of the Art* (CUP 2014).

2. Defining Secondary Rules in International Law

The distinction between primary and secondary rules was introduced into the language of international law by Robert Ago when he worked as the ILC's Special Rapporteur on state responsibility, and was then taken up by the ILC as a whole in its codification project.[8] The adoption of the distinction clearly served an instrumental purpose: it allowed the ILC to move away from the substantive area of the treatment of aliens, which had previously led it to an impasse. The ILC had found itself seriously divided, for example, over issues such as the minimum international standard of protection that foreigners should enjoy in the territory of other states, including the protection of their investments.[9]

Ago's, and the ILC's, idea of a secondary rule was simple—a secondary rule is one which has *general applicability* across all or many different sub-areas of international law. Codifying such rules would thus allow the ILC to transcend (and avoid) the various specific subject matter areas of international law, which was the whole point of the distinction in the context of the impasse in which the ILC had found itself in regarding the treatment of aliens. The label has no other theoretical basis. As explained by Bodansky and Crook:

> To some degree, classifying an issue as part of the rule of conduct (the primary rule) or as part of the determination of whether that rule has been violated (the secondary rule) is arbitrary. What defines the scope of the articles is not their "secondary" status but their generality: the articles represent those areas where the ILC could identify and reach consensus on general propositions that can be applied more or less comprehensively across the entire range of international law.[10]

The ILC's conception of secondary rules was, therefore: (1) that they operated in the area of state responsibility for wrongful acts; (2) were of a general character; but (3) were also *residual* in character, in the sense that their generality did not prevent states from opting out of them if they so wished. This is not only expressly affirmed in article 55 (*lex specialis*) of the ILC's Articles on the Responsibility of States for Internationally Wrongful Acts (ARSIWA), but is also a consequence of the fact

[8] International Law Commission (ILC), "Second Report on State Responsibility, by Roberto Ago, Special Rapporteur: The Origin of International Responsibility" (1970) II Yearbook of the International Law Commission 179.

[9] See J Crawford, *State Responsibility: The General Part* (CUP 2013) 64.

[10] D Bodansky and R Crook, "Symposium on the ILC's State Responsibility Articles: Introduction and Overview" (2002) 96 Journal of International Law 773, 780–81. See also A Nollkaemper and D Jacobs, "Shared Responsibility in International Law: A Conceptual Framework" (2013) 34 Michigan Journal of International Law 359, 408–12.

that the ILC's rules are conceived as being customary in character, and that most custom is *jus dispositivum* and can be displaced by other rules if states so desire.[11]

It is not clear, however, where Ago and the ILC took the terminology of secondary rules from.[12] The likeliest, and certainly the most famous candidate, is HLA Hart's, *The Concept of Law*.[13] But, in fact, the ILC's distinction between primary and secondary rules is of a very different kind, even if Hart may have inspired it. For Hart, primary rules govern conduct, while secondary rules govern three interrelated sets of issues in a legal system: (1) the criteria for the validity of a rule, (2) the ways in which rules can change, and (3) the creation and powers of authoritative mechanisms of adjudication.[14] The ILC's secondary rules are none of these.[15] In Hart's scheme they would squarely fall within the primary rule category, for example, in specifying the consequences (say reparation) of a state's failure to comply with a duty of conduct, or in specifying who gets to act on behalf of the state (attribution). The same goes for causation, that is, legal criteria that determine whether the state's conduct caused some event or consequence, because only through those rules can we know that the state is *doing* or *not doing* something that the law regards as wrongful.

In short, it is clear that the ILC's secondary rules are not Hartian secondary rules. In particular, they are not Hartian rules of adjudication. In the vast majority of cases, the Articles will be applied, and were designed to apply, outside any courtroom, since international law does not possess a system of compulsory adjudication. This is not to say that there are no Hartian secondary rules sense in international law—indeed, we do have such rules, and many of them are also of a general applicability. Think, for example, of the many customary rules codified in the Vienna Convention on the Law of Treaties (VCLT) that regulate how states can conclude new treaties, modify them, or denounce them.[16]

What then of the four different types of rules that we examine in this volume: on causation, attribution, standards of review, and evidentiary standards? Of these, only attribution features as a secondary rule in the ILC scheme, even if—as explained—it is not a secondary rule in the Hartian sense. Rules on causation would be regarded as primary both by the ILC and by Hart. Rules on evidence and standards of review would, on the other hand, be Hartian rules of adjudication, that is, part of the package of power-conferring rules that enable international

[11] ILC Study Group, "Fragmentation of International Law: Difficulties Arising from the Diversification and Expansion of International Law," UN Doc A/CN.4/L.682 (13 April 2006) (finalized by Martti Koskenniemi), para 79ff.

[12] Crawford, *State Responsibility: The General Part* (n 9) 64.

[13] HLA Hart, *The Concept of Law* (2nd edn, OUP 1994).

[14] ibid 79–99.

[15] See R Sloane, "On the Use and Abuse of Necessity in the Law of State Responsibility" (2012) 106 American Journal of International Law 447, 491.

[16] Vienna Convention on the Law of Treaties (adopted 23 May 1969, entered into force 27 January 1980) 1155 UNTS 331 (VCLT).

courts and tribunals to authoritatively decide cases before them, yet the ILC has not addressed them as secondary rules.

Our conception of secondary rules does not, therefore, neatly align either with the ILC's or with Hart's. But, like the ILC's, it is purely instrumental or functional. Here, we try to capture rules that operate in the background of any international dispute, yet are often determinative of the outcome—think, for example, of how the ICJ's insistence in the *Bosnian Genocide* case on a high standard of evidence and its rigorous approach to attribution meant that Serbia escaped responsibility for the commission of the Srebrenica genocide at the hands of the Bosnian Serb forces.[17] Equally, consider how the outcomes in human rights adjudication alter based on whether the courts or quasi-judicial bodies use a deferential or non-deferential standard of review.[18] Our focus on questions of proof, causality, standards of review, and attribution, therefore, is justified due to their general application and common features as background rules with which international courts grapple. They are also all broadly concerned with establishing international responsibility for a wrongful act.

3. Overview of the Approach of the Book

A comparative study of standards of review, causality, evidentiary standards, and attribution in international law is no easy task. Whilst some of these secondary rules have not received any attention in general international law and by the ILC, those that have received attention remain under-developed and contested. The ILC's set of generally applicable secondary rules was and remains contingent, depending on what that particular composition of the ILC believed, at the time, to reflect a general consensus. It is also perfectly possible for the set of secondary rules, if these are to be defined by their general applicability, to vary over time. In addition, there are diverse practices across international courts and tribunals, employing and developing secondary rules in relation to a diverse range of primary, substantive rules in different fields of international law. Given the under development of the scholarly field of secondary rules and their wide-ranging use in diverse contexts, the starting point of this book is to take the divergence in secondary rules of international law seriously. This requires recognizing that such divergence may have conceptual, empirical, and normative dimensions.

At the conceptual level, this means that there can be reasonable disagreement as to what types of rules qualify as secondary rules as a matter of international

[17] *Application of the Convention on the Prevention and Punishment of the Crime of Genocide (Bosnia and Herzegovina v Serbia and Montenegro)* [2007] ICJ Rep 43.

[18] Stephanie E Berry, "A 'Good Faith' Interpretation of the Right to Manifest Religion? The Diverging Approaches of the European Court of Human Rights and the UN Human Rights Committee" (2017) 37(4) Legal Studies 672–94.

law, understood as rules of general applicability employed for establishing state responsibility. Our conceptualization is broad enough to include rules of adjudication in the wider sense, covering how international courts and tribunals apply international law to facts, as well as the means and methods of establishing responsibility and fault through doctrines of attribution and causation. At the level of the identification of secondary rules, we recognize the work of the ILC where relevant, but also the diversity with respect to the emergence and development of secondary rules and in particular through judicial decisions.

At the empirical level, chapters in the book focus on standards of review, causality, evidentiary standards, or attribution in a single judicial setting or in a comparative context. In studies that focus on a single judicial setting,[19] authors trace the development of secondary rules over time and ask whether developments that take place in such individual settings are part of self-contained, special secondary rules. In chapters that have a comparative scope, authors seek to identify whether the practices of international courts and tribunals develop *sui generis*, context-specific secondary rules, or whether more general trends for the identification and employment of secondary rules can be gleaned from judicial practice and doctrine across different fields of international law.[20] Of particular concern, both over time and in cross sectional analysis, is the interaction between primary rules, understood as substantive rules of international law such as those in the fields of trade, investment, human rights, and secondary rules developed in these fields. This enables us to investigate whether and how secondary rules are colored by the primary rules in respective fields and whether and to what extent they are capable of remaining general.

Normatively, the chapters in the book are interested both in the justifications for the employment of different secondary rules in various fields of international law and in the substantive outcomes generated by the employment of one set of secondary rules over others. Whilst some of the authors argue that the interpretation of primary norms warrant variation in the establishment of secondary rules,[21] others identify more systemic reasons as to why secondary rules should diverge.[22] In terms of outcomes, contributors point to the important link between the types of secondary rules employed and the perceived legitimacy of the rulings in the eyes of their constituencies. These outcomes, for example, may strengthen or weaken substantive norms or can make the judgments appear more or less legitimate. Finally, and inevitably, the divergent uses of secondary rules across different fields of international law may foster fragmentation in international law, whilst convergence in such rules may have the effect of fostering coherence.

[19] See Chapters 7, 8, 10, and 12.
[20] See Chapters 2, 3, 4, 5, 9, 11, 13, 14, and 15.
[21] See Chapters 7, 8, 10, and 12.
[22] See Chapter 2.

4. Contributions to the Book

The volume consists of four main parts focusing on one set of secondary rules under investigation in the book. We start with standards of review in international law, followed by causation, evidentiary standards, and attribution.

4.1 Part I: Standard of Review in International Law

Standards of review have arguably been part of secondary rules of adjudication of international law since the establishment of the Permanent Court of Arbitration (PCA) in 1899. Yet, this is also one of the least developed areas of international law as a matter of settled principles, let alone hard rules. In the context of domestic legal systems, standards of review are an aspect of the power of a court to review the facts or laws as established or held by another court or another organ of the state. The standard of review is a spectrum concept, ranging from a *de novo* review of facts or laws, to varying degrees of deference to another court or body. In the context of international law, standards of review typically engage the degree to which international courts and tribunals defer to sovereign states on matters of law and fact.

A central debate in the field of standards of review for international law is whether such standards can be generalizable. First, there are a diverse range of courts and tribunals on the international plane. They range from those tasked with traditional inter-state despite resolution to those that routinely carry judicial review-like functions similar to those of domestic (administrative) courts, as in the case of regional human rights courts and quasi-judicial United Nations (UN) human rights treaty bodies. Second, international adjudication increasingly addresses highly technical issues or risk assessment based on scientific expertise, raising questions about the epistemic legitimacy of international courts to employ *de novo* forms of review. Third, the democratic legitimacy of international courts is suspect, in particular, when they encroach on matters of domestic public interests weighed and balanced by deliberative domestic legislative or judicial processes. In response to these issues, contributions in this part take stock of the contemporary trends regarding the standard of review in international law.

Part I starts with Chapter 2 by Eyal Benvenisti, who analyses the seemingly different standards of review employed by international courts and tribunals through the prism of the "problem of the disregard" relying on Richard Stewart's work which defines this problem as "structures and practices of [...] regulatory governance [that] often generate unjustified disregard of and consequent harm to the interests and concerns of weaker groups and targeted individuals."[23] Policymakers on

[23] Richard B Stewart, "Remedying Disregard in Global Regulatory Governance: Accountability, Participation, and Responsiveness" (2014) 108 American Journal of International Law 211.

both the domestic and international levels disregard certain less powerful actors, and international adjudicators may fight this by setting more intrusive standards of review in cases where disregarded interests are at stake. International courts encounter those disregarded by state action, but, increasingly, also those affected by global bodies. The chapter provides a typology for different problems of disregard faced by international courts, distinguishing between domestic, external, and global disregarded interests. It identifies these types of disregard in the jurisprudence of international courts and seeks to discern a consistent pattern in the jurisprudence and to provide an analytic narrative that explains the varying extent of deference granted to states by international courts and tribunals.

In Chapter 3, Vladyslav Lanovoy shows that the textual silence on the standards of review in international law has led to much variety in practice. International courts and tribunals apply a variety of standards to such review exercises, either expressly or impliedly, which range from the most intrusive (*de novo*) to the most deferential (clearly erroneous or manifest lack of reasons), with many in between (reasonableness, good faith, or abuse of discretion). Given this variety, the chapter enquires into whether the selection of the standard of review in the practice of international courts and tribunals are based on coherent and consistent criteria. It discusses the normative repercussions that the use of a diversity of standards of review, coupled with the failure of international courts and tribunals by and large to justify their selection, may have on the international dispute settlement system.

In Chapter 4, Lukasz Gruszczynski looks at the latest case law of WTO panels and the Appellate Body, investment tribunals, and the CJEU relating to tobacco control measures. In this context, the chapter analyzes the use of standard of review by international economic law (IEL) dispute settlement bodies (DSBs) when dealing with complex factual determinations that form the basis for national regulatory measures. It argues that IEL DSBs have applied deferential standard of review when analyzing national tobacco control measures. While the approaches taken by different IEL DSBs are not identical, all of them seem to aim at guaranteeing a considerable margin of discretion to national regulators, thus promoting unity in the IEL field and reinforcing legitimacy of DSBs' decisions. This also means that the DSBs have actually broadened, rather than undermined, the regulatory space available to states.

In Chapter 5, Katalin Sulyok comparatively assesses the various standards of review that major international courts and tribunals apply in science-intensive environmental adjudication to scrutinize the scientific claims submitted by litigants. The overview of the recent case law suggests that the relevant fora have become inclined to apply relatively intrusive standards to assess the science-based positions of the parties. The chapter evaluates the reasonableness assessment of the ICJ, the coherence review of the WTO, and the consistency test of the European Union (EU) judiciary as part of this trend. It argues that these standards of review are structurally similar and have shared epistemic characteristics. The chapter then challenges the view that international judges ought to grant wide measure of deference to states in making scientific claims. It concludes with providing normative justifications for setting intrusive and science-intensive standards of review from the point of view of epistemic legitimacy.

4.2 Part II: Causation in International Law

Legal theorists of causation have suggested that "[c]ausation in the law is less a concept to be analyzed than a ghost to be exorcised."[24] Indeed, searching for consistent and clear causal requirements in international law is a daunting exercise. Causal links are legally relevant in several specialized primary rules of international law, ranging from WTO law, through investment arbitration and environmental law, to human rights law. Yet causal requirements are not necessarily the same in relation to every breach but vary across different fields of international law.[25] Causality is certainly a topic that the ILC chose to avoid in its codification project,[26] even if its implicit in most, if not all, inquiries into the existence of an internationally wrongful act. That said, causation may come into play at several stages of the judicial analysis a given dispute. Besides being a necessary condition to allocate liability and to delineate the scope thereof, causality may also become relevant for the calculation of damages. Notably, exact causal requirements may often vary at each of these stages. Furthermore, causal inquiry is routinely disrupted by complex causal scenarios arising both in terms of facts and law.[27] Consider, for example, how difficult it would be to exactly determine who or what *caused* any given loss of human life during the COVID-19 pandemic, with any loss of life being at the end of a very long chain of decisions by various state and non-state actors. International and domestic courts and tribunals have all struggled with apportioning liability for causing a particular harm among multiple causes when competing causes are present, or in the case of causal overdetermination.[28] In terms of factual intricacies, highly technical causal evidence complicates the causal assessment of international dispute settlement mechanisms.

All the considerations discussed above translate into a high level of diversity in terms of causal requirements in international law; the variety of causal standards is hardly just terminological. Not surprisingly, international adjudicators often handle causal concepts and devise new causal tests in an opaque and inconsistent

[24] HLA Hart and Tony Honoré, *Causation in the Law* (2nd edn, OUP 1985) 3.
[25] ARSIWA Commentary, art 31.
[26] Crawford, *State Responsibility: The General Part* (n 9) 493.
[27] Dinah Shelton, "Righting Wrongs: Reparations in the Articles on State Responsibility" (2002) 96 American Journal of International Law 833, 846.
[28] Ilias Plakokefalos, "Causation in the Law of State Responsibility and the Problem of Overdetermination: In Search of Clarity" (2015) 26 European Journal of International Law 471.

manner. This partly explains why the question of causality in international law has thus far remained relatively understudied and undertheorized compared to other secondary norms of international law.[29] Contributions in this part of the book address several causal standards that are at play in international law and explore the theoretical justifications and practical implications of the fragmented application of causation. They also point to the various roles that the causal nexus can play in international adjudication and address the need for improvement in respective causal doctrines of courts.

Part II starts with Chapter 6, the contribution of Alice Ollino, discussing the appropriate the role of causation in establishing wrongfulness. This chapter argues that causality is a missed "secondary" element for assessing the breach of certain categories of international obligations. Specifically, causal queries come to play whenever adjudicators need to evaluate the extent of state responsibility for failing to comply with preventive and other due diligence obligations. The chapter focusses on the normative function of causality in tailoring the scope of states' due diligence obligations and critically appraises the hitherto inconsistent case law of international courts in this regard.

In Chapter 7, Martin Jarret investigates the applicable causal standards in the field of investor-state arbitration. In this context, the causal question interrogates whether the state conduct at hand caused the investor's loss. The chapter provides a critical reading of the currently prevailing causal standard in investment arbitration and argues that it is flawed methodologically. This chapter takes issue with the solution of arbitral panels to borrow the ILC's causal approach instead of discerning investment law's own causal standards based on the growing corpus of investment arbitral decisions. Jarret argues that the attempts by arbitral tribunals to test for legal causality is likely to adversely impact the legitimacy of investor-state arbitration, and the reasons for undertaking this process in domestic law disputes are not applicable to investor-state disputes.

Part II concludes with Chapter 8 by Catherine Gascoigne, dealing with causal requirements in WTO law, specifically with certain provisions of the Agreement on Subsidies and Countervailing Measures (SCM Agreement) and the general exceptions under the GATT 1994 and the GATS. This contribution detects a causal fallacy in the case-practice of WTO dispute resolution bodies and points out a methodologically erroneous approach to causation, in which causation is established based on *a priori* inferences about the nature of the cause. Gascoigne offers an alternative, and doctrinally appropriate, solution to employ a causal model that relies on econometric tests in order to reveal real-world effects in such disputes.

[29] Andrea Gattini, "Breach of International Obligations" in André Nollkaemper and Ilias Plakokefalos (eds), *Principles of Shared Responsibility in International Law: An Appraisal of the State of the Art* (CUP 2014); A Gattini, "Breach of the Obligation to Prevent and Reparation Thereof in the ICJ's Genocide Judgment" (2007) 18 European Journal of International Law 695; Michael Straus, "Causation as an Element of State Responsibility" (1984) 16 Law and Policy in International Business 893.

4.3 Part III: Evidentiary Rules in International Law

Evidentiary rules, governing the judicial assessment of evidence, are normally regarded as technical rules of procedure, yet they have a central role in shaping prospects for success of substantive claims. Therefore, the theoretical foundations and the convergence or divergence of these judicial tools merit closer examination. International courts and tribunals are faced with a multilayered problem in their evidentiary assessments. Not only can the presence of highly technical party-submitted evidence pose difficulties, but the absence of relevant factual evidence also calls for employing specific judicial tools. Permanently missing information may be bridged by courts through applying presumptions or drawing inferences, while doing so also raises specific legitimacy questions about the proper constraints of judicial discretion. Similar concerns arise as to how the bad faith or ulterior motivations of respondent states should be appraised by international courts as a matter of evidence. Finally, a party's non-participation in international proceedings raises specific questions as to the fact-finding obligations of international courts, as well as the appropriate limits to their obligation to reconstruct the facts of a dispute.

The first contribution in Part III is Chapter 9 by Tilmann Altwicker and Alexandra Ellen Hansen, and it deals with the role and legitimacy of applying presumptions in international human rights law (IHRL). Presumptions constitute secondary rules designed to manage specific situations of doubt arising in adjudicatory settings. They guide the interpretation of legal rules in cases of factual, practical, or legal uncertainty. Presumptions serve as evidentiary tools inasmuch as they enable courts to announce legal judgments despite gaps in the factual knowledge. In human rights adjudication specifically, drawing presumption-based inferences assists adjudicators in overcoming situations of information asymmetry, in reducing the complexity of the legal argument or in avoiding normative conflicts with other actors. This chapter examines in particular the conditions under which employing presumptions in international human rights adjudication can be considered legitimate.

In Chapter 10, Başak Çalı addresses the specific questions of evidence surrounding proving bad faith in international law. By way of a close reading of the case law of the ECtHR between 2004, when it found its first violation of the convention in bad faith under article 18 of the European Convention on Human Rights (ECHR), until 2020, the chapter investigates how the Court has come to treat good faith as a rebuttable presumption, how the secondary rules of evidence concerning bad faith violations have developed in the case law of the Court over time, and what the consequences of these developments are for the primary rule provided in article 18 of the Convention. The chapter argues that the development of secondary rules of evidence to prove bad faith violations of the Convention is closely interrelated with the recent developments in the interpretation of the primary rules of the Convention under its article 18. The Court's bad faith case law has, over time, evolved away from a direct and subjective evidence paradigm to a circumstantial and indirect evidence paradigm. At the same time, the substantive interpretation of article 18 of the Convention has too evolved, to signal that the use of domestic laws and judicial proceedings in the service of anti-rule of law and antidemocratic agendas constitutes a violation of the Convention. These developments make the Court an *avant-garde* adjudicatory body in developing secondary rules of evidence for deciding whether states violate their international law obligations in bad faith.

The analysis of evidentiary rules concludes with Chapter 11 by Christopher Lentz, addressing the evidentiary implications of a party's non-participation in the proceedings before international courts. Such non-participation raises fundamental evidentiary questions, since adjudicators need to decide whether they will look beyond the record to take into account additional evidence and the views of the absent party expressed elsewhere. The survey of relevant jurisdictions includes the inter-state practice of the ICJ, the PCA, the International Tribunal for the Law of the Sea (ITLOS), decisions of international human rights bodies based on select conventions such as the Covenant on Civil and Political Rights (CCPR), Convention against Torture (CAT) and the Convention on the Elimination of All Forms of Discrimination Against Women (CEDAW), as well as practice concerning international administrative law, for example, as developed by the United Nations Administrative Tribunal (UNAT). The comparative overview reveals some differences between the handling of non-participation, which the chapter traces back to differences in the precise language used in the foundational texts providing jurisdiction to the respective institutions.

4.4 Part IV: Attribution in International Law

The concept of attribution features as a secondary rule in the ILC's ARSIWA, yet the inquiry pursued by chapters in this part does not end at discussing attribution within a state responsibility context, also looking at it as a broader notion than it is generally perceived in the scholarly literature as well as in the practice of international courts.

For this reason, the chapters distinguish between attribution understood in a traditional, narrow sense in a state responsibility context and attribution used in a broader context, wherever the nexus between the conduct of a human being or a legal entity and a state ought to be established for purposes of the legal inquiry. As the state can act only through its agents, fields like the law of treaties, law of immunities, *jus ad bellum*, international humanitarian law (IHL), investment law, or IHRL all feature attributive or ascriptives rules, which begs the question whether these specialized subfields have developed their own attribution norms or the same attribution test may be employed on several fields. Putting the choice of appropriate attribution standard under doctrinal scrutiny gains more and more importance in light of the significant number of international legal disputes that appear to turn on the question of attribution rather than on substantive law. Well known examples include the *Nicaragua*, *Loizidou*, and *Tadić* decisions, which were allegedly, or in fact, decided based on various attribution standards. Properly distinguishing between distinct attribution standards applicable in specific regimes is also important with a view to the fact that they serve different purposes and hence that they ought not to be transferred to other fields in an interchangeable manner, at least without an articulated and coherent justification for doing so.

The discussion on attribution issues in this volume starts with Chapter 12 by Marko Milanovic, who examines the jurisprudence of the ECtHR with regard to the acquiescence or connivance of states parties to the ECHR in the wrongful conduct of third states or non-state actors. The chapter discusses the origins of the acquiescence or connivance test in the Court's case law, and its legal nature. It argues that the conceptual basis for this test remains unclear, and that the current state of the case law could support two theories. First, that acquiescence or connivance, as applied in the Court's most recent cases, is a Convention-specific rule of attribution of conduct, which deviates from the general rules of attribution in international law. Secondly, and alternatively, that the Court's acquiescence or connivance jurisprudence would best be conceptually framed as a Convention-specific theory of state complicity. Such a conceptual framing would accommodate human rights-specific needs while maintaining coherence with general international law. Even under such a framing, however, there are many aspects of the acquiescence or connivance test that require further clarification by the Court.

In Chapter 13, Christina Binder and Stephan Wittich compare the rules of attribution in the law of state responsibility, state immunity, and customary international law. They examine the commonalities, as well as the distinctions, between the different rules of attribution in these three fields. While it seems tempting to use the same, or at least similar, rules of attribution across the board, a more detailed analysis reveals that the different nature and rationale of attributive rules in each field under scrutiny have a varying impact on their scope and application. Unsurprisingly, structural and functional elements of attribution are similar in their application to state responsibility, state immunity, and customary law, whereas the differences are palpable in the context of more specific aspects, such as attribution of conduct of private persons or entities, the attributability of *ultra vires* acts, or the categorization of presumably attributive acts as either *acta iure imperii* or *acta iure gestionis*.

In Chapter 14, Jure Zrilič raises the question of whether the due diligence standard can be utilized to determine state responsibility when the injury was not caused at the hands of private actors. In international investment law, states have an obligation to protect foreign investors against certain interferences of their own organs as well as private actors. In the first case, state responsibility emerges from breach of the obligation to refrain from a wrongful activity and is attached to the state through the attribution of the acts of its organs. By contrast, when the harm is caused by non-state actors, a state can incur responsibility if it fails to exercise due diligence in protecting investors. Departing from doctrine, this chapter argues that due diligence standard can be utilized also to determine state responsibility when the injury was not caused at the hands of private actors, articulating legal, policy, and theoretical justifications for this proposition, and relying in particular on the concept of risk. The chapter shows how this approach converges with other areas of international law, especially IHL and IHRL.

Finally, in Chapter 15, Gábor Kajtár examines the practice of international courts and tribunals and contends that adjudicators, consciously or unconsciously, use the notion of attribution in both a narrow and a broad sense, without however properly distinguishing between the applicable nuanced attribution standards. Attribution tests in the narrow sense are drawn from the ARSIWA and are applied in the context of establishing the international responsibility of states. In the broad sense, however, attribution concepts serve a variety of other legal purposes. This phenomenon is termed as the "fragmentation of attribution" in the chapter, which maps out various attribution concepts used in the field of *jus ad bellum*, *jus in bello*, and international investment law. It concludes by raising judicial and scholarly awareness about the doctrinal inconsistencies that arise from the judicial use of different attribution tests in an interchangeable way, and about the corresponding need for doctrinal scrutiny and methodological consistency in dealing with the secondary rules of international law.

5. Secondary Rules: Heart of the Matter

The volume as a whole offers a survey of the diverse ways in which standards of review, causality, evidentiary rules, and attribution manifest themselves as secondary rules of international law, and in the practice of international courts and tribunals. Contributors to this volume find, however, that the diversity of the secondary rule is not a problem in and of itself. Rather, the problem is usually the lack of a properly articulated justification for a judicial choice with regard to secondary rules, with such choices frequently remaining opaque. A lack of justification often raises question of the fit of the secondary rule. A key finding of the book in this regard is that secondary rules are central not only to international adjudication and judicial outcomes, but also for our very understanding of the purpose and function of international law as a whole. In particular, unreflective transplants of concepts and doctrines of secondary rules borrowed from domestic law do not succeed in the field of international law. These concepts either need to be tailored to be responsive to the purposes of different fields of international law or secondary rules have to be created anew for the specific contexts in international law.

Despite this diversity, across fields of international as well as courts and tribunals, the contributors also find some converging trends. This, for example, is most pronounced in the field of standards of review across different courts and tribunals, as well as with regard to the non-participation of parties in proceedings. Contributors also point to convergence around secondary rules within individual branches of international law, such as IHRL for example, with regard to the use of presumptions. Yet, different secondary rules also accentuate distinct theoretical and practical challenges.

As to the standards of review, choosing the proper degree of stringency for judicial scrutiny remains a matter of balancing between deference and intrusive review, a balancing which should be carried out by adequately considering the legitimacy implications of setting any particular standard of review. Undoubtedly, international courts and tribunals often ought to exercise caution and grant deference to the domestic decision-maker,[30] owing to the fact that they are dealing with complex factual determinations that form the basis for national regulatory measures reflecting sovereign policy choices. However, exercising the international judicial function may also call for exerting a certain measure of control over states' room for maneuver in making factual allegations, or in devising legal policies that are under review before international jurisdictions. In this context, judges need to be aware of the policy implications of setting too lenient standards of review in respective disputes, as this, in turn, may impact their perceived legitimacy. In particular, by adopting more intrusive review standards, international adjudicators may effectively fight against state choices to disregard less powerful actors on the domestic level,[31] which may be a legitimate aim for exercising judicial power. Similarly, adopting a more intrusive scrutiny into the factual bases of science-based measures through judicial reasoning that more directly reflects on the scientific aspects of disputes can enhance the epistemic legitimacy of the relevant judgments.[32] On the other hand, in regimes experiencing legitimacy deficits—particularly with regard to perceived interferences with sovereign regulatory measures—respect for the policy choices of states may warrant more deferential standards. The chapters in this volume further find that standards may vary based on the specificities of the nature of the issue at stake.[33] The choice of particular secondary rules also appears to be context-dependent in the sense that distinct subfields and specialized regimes of international law may experience differing standards of review in dispute resolution processes.[34] International adjudicators, therefore, ought to carefully choose

[30] See Chapters 3 and 4.
[31] See Chapter 2.
[32] See Chapter 5.
[33] See Chapters 4 and 5.
[34] See Chapters 4 and 5 investigating IEL and international environmental disputes and finding divergent trends in the scrutiny.

the appropriate level of their scrutiny in order to accommodate these conflicting considerations underlying standards of review.

In the arena of causation, the absence of doctrinal clarity and settled practice is especially striking on the international stage. Against this background, international judicial bodies tend to extensively rely on domestic causal concepts, which confuses conceptual and methodological clarity even further.[35] Given that the ILC expressly declined to systemize the different causal concepts as a matter of secondary rule of international law, the task of developing a coherent causal doctrine necessarily falls upon international courts and tribunals which, however, often avoid to address causal standards in a nuanced way.[36] The current landscape of international adjudication attests that causality issues related to wrongful acts are still very much uncertain.

The interplay between primary and secondary rules is manifest in the field of evidentiary rules. The growing frequency of international adjudicatory dispute settlement renders the political–legal stakes higher for litigating states and judges alike with respect to deciding contested primary rules through binding judicial decisions. In particular, states may increasingly decide to stay away from international judicial proceedings in order to evade litigating politically sensitive issues. This, in turn, warrants international courts to develop novel evidentiary rules for producing and evaluating evidence in such situations.[37] At the same time, deciding international disputes revolving around nuanced primary rules is a considerable driver for devising new evidentiary tools, such as those governing the process of proving bad faith motivations of states.[38] Similarly, the use of presumptions can also be traced back to the commitment of international judges to discharging their duty, even in disputes burdened with the lack of evidence.[39] All of these dynamics illustrate the ways in which the rising significance of deciding disputes creates a heightened strategic role for secondary rules that are necessarily at play in the adjudicative process.

As to attribution, contributors to this volume emphasized the doctrinal and practical significance of distinguishing and delineating the notion of attribution from neighboring concepts.[40] They stress that attribution is not a monolithic term, as it covers various actual legal notions that operate for various distinct purposes, whenever the connection between a state and an act needs to be established for purposes of the international legal inquiry. They also pointed out that acknowledging the heterogeneity of attribution cautions against applying the ILC's well known attribution standards across distinct subfields of international law, when

[35] See Chapters 7 and 8.
[36] See Chapter 6.
[37] See Chapter 11.
[38] See Chapter 10.
[39] See Chapter 9.
[40] See Chapters 12 and 14.

the purpose of the relevant rules is not the establishment of state responsibility for an internationally wrongful act.[41]

The above discussion ultimately points to a single conclusion. We must take secondary rules of international law seriously—from methodological, system consistency, and legitimacy points of view. Yet, it is also clear that secondary rules will continue to develop in response to the primary norms they address, particularly judicial contexts. The volume as a whole, however, shows that developments of secondary norms in one judicial context may also influence their development in other contexts or their development as a matter of general international law.

As to methodology, international courts and tribunals ought to be ready to justify their choices between various alternative standards. The survey of judicial practice in this volume suggests that the nuanced legal content of secondary rules of international law is far from being self-evident. On the one hand, courts and tribunals should demonstrate in their reasoning the origin and adequate foundations of their chosen standard within the respective field of international law. On the other hand, they also have to clarify the precise content of the preferred standard they apply.

Preserving the consistency of international law also warrants a more coherent and conscious judicial handling of secondary rules of international law. The undeniable absence of doctrinal clarity with respect to certain secondary rules does not in itself justify borrowing similar concepts operating in domestic law. The high level of specialization and sophistication of specialized subsystems within international law also caution against transferring specific secondary rule standards from their original legal context to other fields of international law.

Ultimately, concerns for preserving the legitimacy of decisions and international courts and other mechanisms of dispute settlement also underline the importance of treating and applying secondary rules in practice with proper foundations and in a transparent manner. International adjudicators ought to be aware of the far-reaching consequences that the selection between secondary rules has on the substantive outcome of the dispute resolution process, and on how that outcome will be perceived by external audiences. The primary importance of secondary rules hence necessitates that international judges be open about their choices as to different secondary rules and ready to justify them in light of the implications for the legitimacy of their judgments.

41 See Chapters 13 and 15.

PART I

STANDARD OF REVIEW IN INTERNATIONAL LAW

2

Explaining Variations in Standards of Review in International Adjudication

*Eyal Benvenisti**

1. Introduction

How much deference should international tribunals (IT) grant states when reviewing the compatibility of their policies with their international obligations? The obvious answer is: the deference provided for by the relevant international norm, be it a specific treaty obligation or a general rule or standard of customary international law. But this still leaves us with the following question: what is the *scope* of deference, often referred-to as the "standard of review," that the specific obligation or context calls for? Much like in domestic constitutional law scholarship,[1] this question has attracted much debate among observers of ITs, who have tended to focus on specific types of courts (in particular, on the role of private arbitrators reviewing host states' regulation of foreign investments),[2] on specific areas of law (human rights, trade, etc), and on specific types of considerations (economic, cultural, national security, etc).[3] Several scholars have pointed out the distinction between epistemic considerations (whether the reviewed decision was rendered by an adequately skillful and impartial actor, especially in matters requiring non-legal expertise) versus legitimacy concerns (such as whether the reviewed decision was reached following a sufficiently inclusive process by accountable actors, or whether it promoted certain values, such as global justice).[4] But these considerations often

[1] See, most recently, Stephen Gardbaum, "Comparative Political Process Theory" (2020) 8 I-CON 1.

[2] See Lisa Diependaele, Ferdi De Ville, and Sigrid Sterckx, "Assessing the Normative Legitimacy of Investment Arbitration: The EU's Investment Court System" (2019) 24 New Political Economy 37.

[3] For recent scholarship on this subject, see Julian Arato, "The Margin of Appreciation in International Investment Law" (2014) 54 Virginia Journal of International Law 545; Lukasz Gruszczynski and Wouter Werner (eds), *Deference in International Courts and Tribunals: Standard of Review and Margin of Appreciation* (OUP 2014); Robert Howse, "The World Trade Organization 20 Years On: Global Governance by Judiciary" (2016) 27 European Journal of International Law 9; Andrew Lang, "The Judicial Sensibility of the WTO Appellate Body" (2016) 27 European Journal of International Law 1095; Maria Weimer, "Reconciling Regulatory Space with External Accountability through WTO Adjudication: Trade, Environment and Development" (2017) 30 Leiden Journal of International Law 901; J Benton Heath, "The New National Security Challenge to the Economic Order" (2019) 129 Yale Law Journal 1020.

[4] On the distinction between these two dimensions, see Paul Daly, *A Theory of Deference in Administrative Law: Basis, Application and Scope* (CUP 2012) 7–10; Mark Elliott, "Proportionality and Deference: The Importance of a Structured Approach" in Christopher Forsyth and others (eds),

Eyal Benvenisti, *Explaining Variations in Standards of Review in International Adjudication* In: *Secondary Rules of Primary Importance in International Law.* Edited by: Gábor Kajtár, Başak Çalı, and Marko Milanovic, Oxford University Press.
 DOI: 10.1093/oso/9780192869012.003.0002

beget new questions as they rarely provide a simple response to the question of the proper standard of review, especially when issues of relative expertise and relative legitimacy point to different directions. In an attempt to connect the judicial dots and offer a general and coherent rationale for shaping the appropriate standards of review for ITs, this chapter argues that the standards of review employed by ITs often reflect their ability (if not the explicit authority) to resolve "the problem of disregard"—a term articulated by Richard Stewart, referring to "structures and practices of […] regulatory governance [that] often generate unjustified disregard of and consequent harm to the interests and concerns of weaker groups and targeted individuals."[5] Similar to administrative and constitutional courts, ITs are often uniquely positioned to remedy the problem of disregard and take action to do so, albeit without official authorization. As a result, what may ostensibly appear to be incongruent and even contradictory applications of the standards of review are, in many cases, internally consistent and motivated by entirely coherent sensitivities: as I show in this chapter, ITs often deliberately shape the standards of review they apply in response to "the problem of disregard."[6] In other words, this problem may act as an organizing principle that shapes the ITs' attitude toward the level of scrutiny they apply in international adjudication and may offer a rationale and justification for variations among standards of review.

Of course, ITs, like other courts, are political actors themselves, constantly adjusting and reconstructing their space for action[7]—in our context, the space for responding to the "problem of disregard." Faced with states parties that can react to "unruly" courts by modifying their jurisdiction[8] or the composition of the judges,[9] ITs are aware of their limitations when it comes to protecting the disregarded. When facing majorities bent on burdening minorities, or complex political arrangements among certain groups in society, arguments in favor of the rights of

Effective Judicial Review: A Cornerstone of Good Governance (OUP 2010) 272–77; Andreas von Staden, "The Democratic Legitimacy of Judicial Review Beyond the State: Normative Subsidiarity and Judicial Standards of Review" (2012) 10 I-CON 1023, 1026; Benedikt Pirker, *Democracy and Distrust in International Law: The Procedural Democracy Doctrine and the Standard of Review Used by International Courts and Tribunals* (OUP 2014) ch 4; Caroline Henckels, *Proportionality and Deference in Investor-State Arbitration: Balancing Investment Protection and Regulatory Autonomy* (CUP 2015) 35–37.

[5] Richard B Stewart, "Remedying Disregard in Global Regulatory Governance: Accountability, Participation, and Responsiveness" (2014) 108 American Journal of International Law 211 (Stewart refers to global regimes, while this chapter addresses domestic regimes).

[6] For an earlier version of this observation, with respect to the ECtHR's jurisprudence, see Eyal Benvenisti, "Margin of Appreciation, Consensus, and Universal Standards" (1999) 31 New York University Journal of International Law and Politics 843.

[7] Eyal Benvenisti and George W Downs, "The Empire's New Clothes: Political Economy and the Fragmentation of International Law" (2007) 60 Stanford Law Review 595.

[8] See eg Convention for the Protection of Human Rights and Fundamental Freedoms (European Convention on Human Rights, as amended), Protocol No 15 amending the Convention for the Protection of Human Rights and Fundamental Freedoms (24 June 2013).

[9] Gregory Shaffer, "A Tragedy in the Making? The Decline of Law and the Return of Power in International Trade Relations" (2019) 44 Yale Journal of International Law (Online) 37.

majority interests and values will weigh more heavily. Consequently, the standards of review ITs would adopt might reflect these constraints.

To set the context for the standard of review question, section 2 elaborates on the types of disregard that arise in the context of international adjudication. It explains how the "problem of disregard" plays out variously in contemporary national and global politics, distinguishing between three typical situations where this problem arises. It then explores the respective practices of several ITs vis-à-vis each of these situations and assesses the extent to which these tribunals have shown sensitivity to each of them. The findings presented in this chapter suggest that ITs have indeed attempted to respond to these three types of problems of disregard, even if they have done so "under the radar," without explicitly acknowledging this concern. Section 3 argues that, despite the ITs being coy about their sensitivity to disregard, such mindfulness provides a consistent explanation for the variations in the standards of review that they have adopted: from granting wide margins of appreciation to exercising strict scrutiny. Section 4 concludes.

2. Background: The "Problem of Disregard" in International Adjudication

Stewart uses the term "the problem of disregard" to describe the practice of global regulatory authorities whereby they give "inadequate regard to the interests and concerns of vulnerable and politically weak groups, diffuse and less well-organized and resourced societal interests, and vulnerable individuals."[10] This practice, he argues, causes "unjustified harm or disadvantage" to the interests of those groups and individuals.[11] Stewart notes that the "problem of disregard" implies also that there are "normative principles of regard" that:

> [S]erve to identify which affected groups, interests and individuals are entitled to have their interests and concerns considered ... by particular global regulatory bodies with specialized missions and taken into account in their decisions.[12]

How, then, to respond to the "problem of disregard"? The insight for this chapter is derived from constitutional law scholarship—more specifically, from John Hart Ely's famous suggestion, in *Democracy and Distrust*,[13] that the role of judicial review of legislation is to correct the inherent failures of the democratic system when those failures are exploited by majorities to limit the voice of politically weak

[10] Stewart, "Remedying Disregard in Global Regulatory Governance" (n 5) 220.
[11] ibid.
[12] ibid.
[13] John Hart Ely, *Democracy and Distrust* (Harvard UP 1981).

minorities (the "domestic" problem of disregard, to use Stewart's terminology). Accordingly, Ely proposes, the constitutional court should focus on ensuring an inclusive political process that is open for all to weigh in and shape public policies.

The same approach was then transferred to the international plane by scholars who regarded international or regional human rights litigation as yet another quasi-constitutional judicial response to the inherent problems of democratic decision-making.[14] Vague concepts such as "subsidiarity" and "margin of appreciation" (MoA) were accordingly explained as allowing ITs to defer to domestic democratic processes when and if these were proven sufficiently inclusive and responsive to problems of domestic disregard. This, it was argued, incentivized national actors to clear up the political channels and thereby avoid litigation.[15]

ITs have demonstrated their awareness of the problem of disregard in several ways, beyond the "standard of review" context. They have opened their doors to disregarded constituencies by asserting their own jurisdiction to adjudicate disputes involving such constituencies—be it by granting standing for disregarded litigants or encouraging others to submit amicus briefs, or even by interpreting relevant norms as requiring attention to the disregarded. Indeed, some of these responses can be seen as facilitating the function of the IT as provider of remedies to the problem of disregard by providing the court concerned with the necessary information to weigh the interests of the disregarded.

There are three typical situations of disregard that tend to arise in international litigations, which reflect three distinct groups of potentially disregarded individuals and groups, specifically: (1) the internally disregarded—individuals or communities that are part of the state's body politic but have limited political voice; (2) the externally disregarded—foreign individuals or communities that are specifically impacted by the reviewed national decision; or (3) global disregard—humanity at large.

First, *the internally disregarded* are those whose rights or interests have not been adequately addressed by their own government (be it a national regulator, a legislator, or a court). Such situations typically arise in human rights litigation before regional human rights tribunals, but they can also be the subject of claims regarding treaty conclusion or implementation (such as peace agreements[16] or boundary-delimitation agreements[17]), when the treaty adversely affects individuals or groups

[14] Benvenisti, "Margin of Appreciation, Consensus, and Universal Standards" (n 6); Robert O Keohane, Stephen Macedo, and Andrew Moravcsik, "Democracy-Enhancing Multilateralism" (2009) 63 International Organization 1.

[15] Eyal Benvenisti, "The Margin of Appreciation, Subsidiarity and Global Challenges to Democracy" (2018) 9 Journal of International Dispute Settlement 240. On subsidiarity and international litigation, see Markus Jachtenfuchs and Nico Krisch, "Subsidiarity in Global Governance" (2016) 79 Law and Contemporary Problems 1; Andreas Føllesdal, "Subsidiarity and International Human-Rights Courts: Respecting Self-Governance and Protecting Human Rights—Or Neither?" (2016) 79 Law and Contemporary Problems 147.

[16] Michal Saliternik, "Perpetuating Democratic Peace: Procedural Justice in Peace Negotiations" (2016) 27 European Journal of International Law 617.

[17] See section 2.1.

within the state's territory. Second, the *externally disregarded* are foreign individuals or groups whose rights or interests are harmed by a certain government. We encounter this type of claim in litigation concerning harms done to individuals situated outside the state during international armed conflicts, or otherwise as a response to the extraterritorial exercise of authority that harms human rights. Refugees and other asylum seekers, foreign investors, and foreign exporters who do business in a certain country may also find themselves among the externally disregarded. Finally, there is the situation of *global disregard*, where a national decision affects global concerns. Examples of this third type include national acts and omissions that contribute to climate change or harm to biodiversity.

In what follows, I briefly discuss these three types of disregard and how ITs have responded to them. These observations demonstrate that, while questions of relative institutional competence remain relevant to ITs' decision to intervene, by and large, they pay attention to these types of disregard and respond by improving their informational tools to be able to identify the disregarded and address their concerns, and also to adjust their level of scrutiny of the impugned national decision.

2.1 International Tribunals and the Internally Disregarded

There are two systemic flaws in the democratic process that generate problems of disregard. The first flaw lies in the inherent difficulties of the democratic process within the state when translating voters' preferences to public decisions. This is the well-known problem of voters' suppression of minority preferences—the so-called "tyranny of the majority." The second systemic flaw is its less widely discussed but no less endemic opposite—the "tyranny of the minority"—when minority groups[18] or special interests, such as the powerful industries or major private service providers, "capture" politicians.[19] The theory on collective action explains why at least some minorities and interest groups within society can engage so effectively in national politics, become highly influential, and even outweigh the votes of diffuse majorities.[20] Besides policies and norms that are not sufficiently inclusive of all members of the polity, these two inherent political problems can

[18] Bruce A Ackerman, "Beyond 'Carolene Products'" (1985) 98 Harvard Law Review 713, 714; Michael Klarman, "An Interpretive History of Modern Equal Protection" (1991) 90 Michigan Law Review 213, 222–26. For a general critique, see Brian Barry, *Culture and Equality: An Egalitarian Critique of Multiculturalism* (Harvard UP 2002).

[19] Mancur Olson, *The Logic of Collective Action* (Harvard UP 1965). See also Eyal Benvenisti and George W Downs, *Between Fragmentation and Democracy: The Role of National and International Courts* (CUP 2017) ch 3.

[20] Olson, The Logic of Collective Action (n 19); Benvenisti and Downs, *Between Fragmentation and Democracy* (n 19). See also Eyal Benvenisti, "Exit and Voice in the Age of Globalization" (1999) 98 Michigan Law Review 167 (arguing that, by employing international organizations as venues for policymaking, state executives and interest groups manage to reduce the impact of domestic checks and balances).

also beget institutional flaws—when regulators and courts are not granted sufficient independence to correct these endemic failures. National courts or regulators that are not adequately insulated from those two sources of political failure will be incapable of offering corrections to these problems.

Naturally, these democratic failures are often reflected in international law. State executives representing majorities or special interests have often succeeded in securing their preferences in international agreements and ensuring that ITs remain "compliant."[21] But there are situations in which the international arena is more conducive to civil society efforts to counter such problems, such as the singular success of the campaign to curtail, by means of a multilateral treaty, the access of tobacco companies to domestic regulatory processes.[22] Through the resolution of disputes, ITs can also respond to, and correct, internal democratic failures at least in some member states. In fact, ITs have sought to intervene in and respond to the problem of the internally disregarded in various ways. For instance, they have

[21] See, in general, Benvenisti and Downs, *Between Fragmentation and Democracy* (n 19). On the impact of special interests, see eg Ruth Lopert and Deborah Gleeson, "The High Price of 'Free' Trade: US Trade Agreements and Access to Medicines" (2013) 41 Journal of Law, Medicine and Ethics 199; Frederick M Abbott, "The Evolution of Public Health Provisions in Preferential Trade and Investment Agreements of the United States" in Pedro Roffe and Xavier Seuba (eds), *Current Alliances in International Intellectual Property Lawmaking: The Emergence and Impact of Mega-Regionals, Global Perspectives for the IP System* (CEIPI-ICTSD 2017). See also Melissa J Durkee, "Astroturf Activism" (2017) 69 Stanford Law Review 201. On the involvement of special interests in Notice and Comment proceedings related to the Montreal Protocol, see Ayelet Berman, "The Role of Domestic Administrative Law in the Accountability of Transnational Regulatory Networks: The Case of the ICH" (2012) 22 IILJ Emerging Scholars Paper <http://iilj.org/wp-content/uploads/2016/08/Berman-The-Role-of-Domestic-Administrative-Law-in-the-Accountability-of-Transnational-Regulatory-Networks-2012.pdf> accessed 30 January 2021.

[22] World Health Organization (WHO), Framework Convention on Tobacco Control (adopted 21 May 2003, entered into force 27 February 2005) 2302 UNTS 166 (Framework Convention on Tobacco Control). The preamble of the Convention refers to "the need to be alert to any efforts by the tobacco industry to undermine or subvert tobacco control efforts and the need to be informed of activities of the tobacco industry that have a negative impact on tobacco control efforts." On the motivation for the convention, see generally Hadii M Mamudu, Ross Hammond, and Stanton Glantz, "Tobacco Industry Attempts to Counter the World Bank Report Curbing the Epidemic and Obstruct the WHO Framework Convention on Tobacco Control" (2008) 67 Social Science and Medicine 1690; Hadii M Mamudu and Stanton Glantz, "Civil Society and the Negotiation of the Framework Convention on Tobacco Control" (2009) 4 Global Public Health 150; Paul Cairney, Donley Studlar, and Hadii M Mamudu, *Global Tobacco Control: Power, Policy, Governance and Transfer* (Palgrave McMillan 2012); Tatiana Andia and Nitsan Chorev, "Making Knowledge Legitimate: Transnational Advocacy Networks' Campaigns Against Tobacco, Infant Formula and Pharmaceuticals" (2017) 17 Global Networks 255. See also Hadii M Mamudu, Ross Hammond, and Stanton A Glantz, "Project Cerberus: Tobacco Industry Strategy to Create an Alternative to the Framework Convention on Tobacco Control" (2008) 98 American Journal of Public Health 1630; Thilo Grüning and others, "Tobacco Industry Attempts to Influence and Use the German Government to Undermine the WHO Framework Convention on Tobacco Control" (2012) 21 Tobacco Control 30; Derek Yach, "The Origins, Development, Effects, and Future of the WHO Framework Convention on Tobacco Control: A Personal Perspective" (2014) 383 Lancet 1771. On tobacco companies blocking domestic regulation, see Andrew D Mitchell and Tania Voon, "Someone to Watch Over Me: Use of FOI Requests by the Tobacco Industry" (2014) 22 Australian Journal of Administrative Law 18; Georgina Dimopoulos, Andrew D Mitchell, and Tania Voon, "The Tobacco Industry's Strategic Use of Freedom of Information Laws: A Comparative Analysis" (2016) Oxford University Comparative Law Forum 2 <https://ouclf.law.ox.ac.uk/the-tobacco-industrys-strategic-use-of-freedom-of-information-laws-a-comparative-analysis/> accessed 30 January 2021.

given voice to disregarded constituencies by exercising jurisdiction to adjudicate disputes involving such constituencies or by giving standing to otherwise disregarded litigants. The exercising by the International Court of Justice (ICJ) of its advisory jurisdiction is perhaps the clearest example of this.[23] In its *South West Africa* opinions[24] and, most recently, its opinion concerning the *Separation of the Chagos Archipelago from Mauritius in 1965*,[25] the ICJ arguably interpreted its advisory jurisdiction expansively to give voice to those otherwise disregarded constituencies seeking self-determination. In its *Wall* advisory opinion,[26] the ICJ included the Palestinian Liberation Organization (PLO) alongside the states entitled to provide the Court with information, thus giving voice to the occupied population, arguably disregarded by Israel's decision to construct a wall in the occupied territory. Similarly, in the *Kosovo* advisory opinion[27] concerning Kosovo's declaration of independence, the ICJ, in the exercise of its advisory jurisdiction, provided a voice to Kosovars. The fact that ITs seek to respond to the problem of internal disregard can also explain the selective permission they give to submit amicus curiae. In circumstances where individuals do not or cannot challenge the relevant domestic decision by themselves, ITs have also addressed the problem of the internally disregarded by allowing the submission of amicus briefs in the proceedings. An amicus can give a voice to the otherwise disregarded, though whether these briefs are, in fact, ultimately taken into account varies from case to case. In the *Canada–US Softwood Lumber* dispute,[28] for example, the World Trade Organization (WTO) Panel permitted Interior Alliance (a representative organization of indigenous nations) to submit an amicus brief. The domestic decision at issue was Canada's charging Canadian timber producers stumpage fees at below market value. Interior Alliance's position was that competitive advantage did not stem from the fact that there were more trees in Canada but, rather, from the lack of due financial compensation paid to indigenous peoples. Its position thus supported the United States (US) position, and the US cited the amicus submission in its responses to the Panel.[29] The Panel, which ultimately agreed with the US position, did "accept

[23] On the jurisprudence of the ICJ in this context, see also Chiara Ragni, "Standard of Review and the Margin of Appreciation before the International Court of Justice" in Lukasz Gruszczynski and Wouter Werner (eds), *Deference in International Courts and Tribunals: Standard of Review and Margin of Appreciation* (OUP 2014).

[24] *Legal Consequences for States of the Continued Presence of South Africa in Namibia (South West Africa) notwithstanding Security Council Resolution 276 (1970)* (Advisory Opinion) [1971] ICJ Rep 16.

[25] *Legal Consequences of the Separation of the Chagos Archipelago from Mauritius in 1965* (Advisory Opinion) [2019] ICJ Rep 95.

[26] *Legal Consequences of the Construction of a Wall in the Occupied Palestinian Territory* (Advisory Opinion) [2004] ICJ Rep 136.

[27] *Accordance of International Law of the Unilateral Declaration of Independence in respect of Kosovo* (Advisory Opinion) [2010] ICJ Rep 403.

[28] WTO, *United States—Preliminary Determinations with Respect to Certain Softwood Lumber from Canada—Report of the Panel* (1 November 2002) WT/DS236/R (*Canada—US Softwood Lumber*).

[29] See Megan Davis, "Identity, Power, and Rights: The State, International Institutions, and Indigenous Peoples in Canada" in Suzana Sawyer and Edmund T Gomez (eds), *The Politics of Resource Extraction* (Palgrave Macmillan 2012) 247.

for consideration" Interior Alliance's amicus brief, albeit without commenting substantively on the issues raised therein.[30]

ITs have similarly accepted the submission of amicus briefs giving voice to the otherwise internally disregarded in the arbitration context. In *Glamis Gold v United States*,[31] for instance (a dispute concerning a proposed open-pit mine), the Quechan Indian Nation (QIN) successfully applied for amicus status, apparently on the basis that their arguments differed from those of the disputing parties. While primarily objecting to the claimant's case, the QIN's arguments did not align with the claims of the US either. Rather, the QIN argued that it had its own "significant interest" in the issue to present. It contended that the arbitration "could affect the integrity of the sacred area and the Tribe's relation to it,"[32] and that an amicus brief could "assist the tribunal in the determination of factual and legal issues by bringing the perspective, particular knowledge and insight that is unique to American tribal sovereign governments."[33]

Where amicus participation is requested by a person or group that has not been "disregarded" at the domestic level, as such, there are instances of ITs refusing the submission of those briefs. For example, in *Chevron and Texaco v Ecuador*,[34] while citing reasons such as the fact that neither party favored amicus participation, arguably the Permanent Court of Arbitration (PCA) saw no reason to accept amicus participation by a non-governmental organization (NGO) purporting to represent the indigenous voice because the parties to the dispute had already covered the issues raised by the submission,[35] and thus the indigenous voice had already been represented. Similarly, in *Von Pezold/Border Timbers v Zimbabwe*, an International Centre for Settlement of Investment Disputes (ICSID) tribunal rejected amicus participation by indigenous groups in Zimbabwe, in part, because their views were

30 *Canada—US Softwood Lumber* (n 28) [7.2].

31 *Glamis Gold Ltd v United States* (Award) (NAFTA Ch 11 Arbitral Tribunal) (8 June 2009) (*Glamis Gold v United States*).

32 *Glamis Gold Ltd v United States* (Quechan Indian Nation Application for Leave to File a Non-Party Submission) (NAFTA Ch 11 Arbitral Tribunal) (19 August 2005) [2].

33 ibid [3]. See discussion in Brigitte Stern, "Civil Society's Voice in the Settlement of International Economic Disputes" (2007) 22 ICSID Review: Foreign Investment Law Journal 280, 302–05; Sergio Puig, "The Role of Procedure in the Development of Investment Law: The Case of Section B of Chapter 11 of NAFTA" in Chester Brown and Kate Miles (eds), *Evolution in Investment Treaty Law and Arbitration* (CUP 2011) 361.

34 *Chevron Corp and Texaco Petroleum Co v Ecuador* PCA Case No 2009-23 (Procedural Order No 8) (11 April 2011) [17]–[20].

35 There are, however, instances where ITs might still allow participation as amicus to those who were not necessarily disregarded in domestic proceedings. In *Bear Creek Mining Corp v Republic of Peru*, for example, Peru had revoked a mining concession following strong opposition from the Aymara indigenous people, a decision that was then challenged by Bear Creek. An NGO purporting to represent the Aymara people successfully applied to participate as amicus. The Aymara people arguably had not been disregarded, indeed it was because of their protests that the decision was made, but the IT also allowed them voice. See *Bear Creek Mining Corp v Republic of Peru* ICSID Case No ARB/14/21 (Procedural Order No 5) (21 July 2016) (*Bear Creek v Peru*).

represented in—and supportive of—Zimbabwe's land reform policies, challenged by the foreign investor.[36]

The problem of the internally disregarded can also arise in the context of international agreements, such as boundary demarcation disputes. In these situations, ITs might be in a position to intervene on their behalf. Such was the case in a boundary delimitation dispute between Niger and Burkina Faso, where the ICJ offered constructive insights on how to integrate the human factor into states' boundary delimitation agreements to facilitate cross-border movement of a semi-nomad community affected by the anticipated border regime. Whereas in 2002, in *Land and Maritime Boundary between Cameroon and Nigeria (Cameroon v Nigeria: Equatorial Guinea Intervening)*,[37] the ICJ found that it had no authority to modify the course of the boundary as established by colonial-era instruments to safeguard the interests of a village that had spread into the other state's territory,[38] in 2013 it demonstrated greater sensitivity to the plight of those disregarded. In its April 2013 judgment, the ICJ demonstrated greater sensitivity toward the human factor. In *Frontier Dispute (Burkina Faso v Niger)*,[39] the Court was tasked with resolving a boundary delimitation dispute arising from different interpretations of pre-independence documents that had delineated the boundaries between the then-French colonies (Niger and Upper Volta). In their pleadings, both parties consistently invoked either the principle of the intangibility of boundaries inherited from colonization or the *uti possidetis juris* principle, neither of which offered room for considering affected populations. But, in response to requests from the bench, the parties also furnished information about the populations potentially affected by the delimitation and expressed willingness to take their interests into account. The ICJ stopped short of imposing a transit regime on the parties. Such a matter was clearly outside its jurisdiction. Nevertheless, it expressed its wish:

> [T]hat each Party, in exercising its authority over the portion of the territory under its sovereignty, should have due regard to the needs of the populations concerned, in particular those of the nomadic or semi-nomadic populations, and to the necessity to overcome difficulties that may arise for them because of the frontier.[40]

[36] *Bernhard Von Pezold v Zimbabwe* ICSID Case No ARB/10/15 (Procedural Order No 2) (26 June 2012); *Border Timbers Ltd, Border Timbers International (Private) Ltd, and Hangani Development Co (Private) Ltd v Zimbabwe* ICSID Case No ARB/10/25 (Procedural Order No 2) (26 June 2012) [55]ff.

[37] *Land and Maritime Boundary between Cameroon and Nigeria (Cameroon v Nigeria: Equatorial Guinea Intervening)* (Judgment) [2002] ICJ Rep 303.

[38] ibid [107], [123]. This position was rightly criticized by Gbenga Oduntan as "not [in] accord with the demands of natural justice and only lead[ing] to the creation of future conflicts and severe hardship on native populations": see Gbenga Oduntan, "The Demarcation of Straddling Villages in Accordance with the International Court of Justice Jurisprudence: The Cameroon—Nigeria Experience" (2006) 5 Chinese Journal of International Law 79, 87.

[39] *Frontier Dispute (Burkina Faso/Niger)* (Judgment) [2013] ICJ Rep 44.

[40] ibid [112].

The Court also "note[d] the co-operation that ha[d] already been established on a regional and bilateral basis between the Parties in this regard," and "encourage[d] them to develop it further."[41]

This expansive understanding of the Court's jurisdiction is in line with its 2011 Order of Provisional Measures of Protection in the *Temple of Preah Vihear* case,[42] where, clearly concerned about threats to life and the historical importance of the temple, which is a cultural heritage site, it went beyond the request to stop cross-border incursions and indeed beyond the subject matter of the dispute (see the dissents by President Owada, Judge Xue, and Judge Donoghue), by creating a de-militarized zone around the temple. The Order simply stated: "[I]t is for the Court to ensure [...] that no irreparable damage is caused to persons or property in that area pending the delivery of its Judgment on the request for interpretation."[43]

2.2 International Tribunals and the Externally Disregarded

The "externally disregarded" category includes the foreigners whose human rights are violated, whose opportunities to export to an importing state are limited despite trade agreements designed to protect them,[44] whose fishing opportunities in a foreign state's exclusive economic zones (EEZ) are limited, in breach of the provisions of the United Nations Convention on the Law of the Sea (UNCLOS),[45] whose investments are exposed to expropriation, in violation of bilateral investment treaties (BITs),[46] and so on. While these typical cases involve unilateral state action, the externally disregarded may include victims of inter-state agreements, such as bilateral treaties allocating shares in a transboundary river that has many more riparian states whose rights are *not* acknowledged.[47] In such situations, ITs may take into consideration the rights and interests of these externally disregarded individuals and groups when applying the relevant international legal norm.

[41] ibid. This effort to "humanise" the delimitation of boundaries is even more pronounced in the opinions of some of the judges, especially Judge Cançado-Trindade and Judge Bennouna.

[42] *Request for Interpretation of the Judgment of 15 June 1962 in the Case Concerning the Temple of Preah Vihear (Cambodia v Thailand)* (Order of 18 July 2011: Request for the Indication of Provisional Measures) [2011] ICJ Rep 537.

[43] ibid [61].

[44] The paradigmatic case is WTO Appellate Body Report, *United States—Import Prohibition of Certain Shrimp and Shrimp Products*, WT/DS58/AB/R (adopted 12 October 1998).

[45] The *"Juno Trader" Case (Saint Vincent and the Grenadines v Guinea-Bissau)* (Judgment of 18 December 2004) [2004] ITLOS Rep 17 (*Juno Trader*).

[46] See *James v United Kingdom* App no 8793/79 (ECtHR, 21 February 1986), para 63; Kassi Tallent, "The Tractor in the Jungle: Why Investment Arbitration Tribunals Should Reject a Margin of Appreciation Doctrine" in Ian Laird and Todd Weiler (eds), *Investment Treaty Arbitration and International Law* (Jurisnet 2010); Sarah Vasani, "Bowing to the Queen: Rejecting the Margin of Appreciation Doctrine in International Investment Arbitration" in Ian Laird and Todd Weiler (eds), *Investment Treaty Arbitration and International Law* (Jurisnet 2010) 167.

[47] Saliternik, "Perpetuating Democratic Peace" (n 16) 626.

An example of an IT enabling the voice of the externally disregarded might be found in the *Juno Trader* decision[48] taken by the International Tribunal for the Law of the Sea (ITLOS). Coastal states are permitted to manage the activity of fishing fleets within their EEZ and can detain foreign vessels and crews for the purpose of securing compliance with their laws and policies in that area. In *Juno Trader*, the ITLOS gave voice to the externally disregarded (namely, foreign crew members), finding that the coastal state must not discriminate between domestic versus foreign vessels or crews and must provide *all* those detained and sanctioned with a voice.

Of course, the problem of disregard must also be addressed in the proper legal context. The text of the relevant treaty is a significant starting point determining the permitted extent to which the disregarded may be taken into account. A treaty obligation that requires states to extend equal treatment to foreign parties (under human rights law or WTO law, for instance) will call for stricter judicial scrutiny of states' policies that affect foreigners. In contrast, a treaty text that requires states to give foreigners' interests "due regard" may call for more deference by the IT.[49]

The jurisprudence of the WTO Appellate Body is a case in point. In our analysis of its jurisprudence, Sivan Shlomo-Agon and I observed that the Appellate Body was conscious of the need to balance space for domestic policymaking with the duty to take into account the interests of third parties.[50] We found that the Appellate Body "seems to have walked a fine line ... respecting members' policy space, 'but with a warning not to abuse this policy space for protectionist ends' "[51] or to project the costs of their policies on foreigners. The Appellate Body construed the necessity test (enshrined in several policy exceptions in article XX of the GATT 1994 and article XIV of the GATS) as entailing a process of weighing and balancing a series of factors, including the importance of the policy objective pursued by the regulating member and "the restrictive effect of the measure on international commerce" and on the interests of other stakeholders in the multilateral trade system.[52]

[48] *Juno Trader* (n 45).

[49] See Michael Ioannidis, "Beyond the Standard of Review: Deference Criteria in WTO Law and the Case for a Procedural Approach" in Lukasz Gruszczynski and Wouter Werner (eds), *Deference in International Courts and Tribunals: Standard of Review and Margin of Appreciation* (OUP 2014). The WTO Appellate Body has stated, "[t]he standard of review ... must reflect the balance established ... between the jurisdictional competences conceded by the Members to the WTO and the jurisdictional competences retained by the Members for themselves": WTO Appellate Body Report, *European Communities—Measures Concerning Meat and Meat Products (Hormones)*, WT/DS26/AB/R and WT/DS48/AB/R (adopted 16 January 1998) [115].

[50] Sivan Shlomo-Agon and Eyal Benvenisti, "The Law of Strangers: The Form and Substance of Other-Regarding International Adjudication" (2018) 68 University of Toronto Law Journal 598, 610.

[51] ibid, citing Howse, "The World Trade Organization 20 Years On" (n 3) 53.

[52] WTO Appellate Body Report, *China—Measures Affecting Trading Rights and Distribution Services for Certain Publications and Audiovisual Entertainment Products*, WT/DS363/AB/R (adopted 21 December 2009) [240], [251], [306]–[307] (*China—Publications*); WTO Appellate Body Report, *Korea—Measures Affecting Imports of Fresh, Chilled and Frozen Beef*, WT/DS161/AB/R and WT/DS169/AB/R (adopted 11 December 2000) [164], [166]; WTO Appellate Body Report, *United States—Measures Affecting the Cross-Border Supply of Gambling and Betting Services*, WT/DS285/AB/R [304]–[308] (adopted 20 April 2005) (*US—Gambling*); WTO Appellate Body Report, *Brazil—Measures*

It later developed the notion of even-handedness to indicate members' duty to reconcile their legitimate regulatory interests with their obligation to treat foreigners in an even-handed manner.[53] The even-handedness test seems to convey an idea resembling, if not identical to, equal concern and respect for all affected stakeholders, requiring sovereigns not merely to abstain from inefficient protectionism but to positively pay regard to the interests of foreign constituencies and ensure that national regulations treat foreign and domestic producers equitably, if not with strict equality.

This notion of even-handedness was relevant in the *Seal Products* dispute,[54] for instance. The case concerned the general prohibition on exporting seal products into the EU when these resulted from hunts conducted by Inuit and other indigenous communities. The prohibition was found by the WTO Panel not to be designed and applied in an even-handed manner because it was not, according to the Panel, "equally available to all Inuit or indigenous communities." The Panel concluded that it disproportionately benefitted Inuit communities in Greenland, while those in Canada were incapable of benefitting from the exception.[55] Thus, while the Panel considered the general purpose-based distinction between commercial and indigenous hunts justifiable in light of the benefits for the Inuit indigenous communities, it considered its design and application to have failed the even-handedness test.[56] No doubt, the Canadian Inuit were "externally disregarded" and

Affecting Imports of Re-treaded Tyres, WT/DS332/AB/R (adopted 3 December 2007) [178], [182], [210] (*Brazil—Tyres*); WTO Appellate Body Report, *European Communities—Measures Prohibiting the Importation and Marketing of Seal Products*, (22 May 2014) WT/DS400/AB/R and WT/DS401/AB/R [5.169], [5.214] (*Seal Products (Report of the Appellate Body)*; WTO Appellate Body Report, *European Communities—Measures Affecting Asbestos and Asbestos-Containing Products*, WT/DS135/AB/R (adopted 12 March 2001) [172].

[53] Robert Howse and Philip I Levy, "The TBT Panels: US-Cloves, US-Tuna, US-COOL" (2013) 12 World Trade Review 327. Thus, in *US–Clove Cigarettes*, the Appellate Body understood the TBT preamble as suggesting that "Members have a right to use technical regulations in pursuit of their legitimate objectives, provided that they do so in an even-handed manner" in addressing foreign and domestic interests: WTO Appellate Body Report, *United States—Measures Affecting the Production and Sale of Clove Cigarettes*, WT/DS406/AB/R (adopted 24 April 2012) [95].

[54] WTO Panel Report, *European Communities—Measures Prohibiting the Importation and Marketing of Seal Products*, WT/DS400/R (adopted 25 November 2013) [7.301]ff (*Seal Products (Report of the Panel)*).

[55] ibid [7.318]. Exception: Council Regulation (EC) 1007/2009 on trade in seal products [2009] OJ L286/36, art 3(1).

[56] Ultimately, both the Dispute Settlement Body and the Appellate Body ruled in favor of the EU Seal Regime and considered the measure provisionally justified under the public morals exception within the meaning of art XX(a) of the General Agreement on Tariffs and Trade 1994 (adopted 5 April 1994, entered into force 1 January 1995) 1867 UNTS 190 (GATT 1994), although, regarding the potentially discriminatory effects of the IC exception, the Appellate Body found that the EU Seal Regime was not yet designed and applied in a manner that met the requirements of the chapeau of art XX of the GATT 1994 (*Seal Products (Report of the Appellate Body)* (n 52) [5.338]). In order to be permanently justified under art XX(a) of the GATT 1994, the EU had to make some adjustments, such as facilitating the access of the Canadian Inuit population to the exception: *Seal Products (Report of the Panel)* (n 54) [7.639]; *Seal Products (Report of the Appellate Body)* (n 52) [5.326]–[6].

the Appellate Body was able to remedy this political shortcoming by interfering in the importer's policy.

2.3 International Tribunals and the Globally Disregarded

While international litigation tends to be a bilateral exercise, there are often disputes whose resolution indirectly affects the interests and rights of third parties or of the international community more generally. ITs, aware of their role in setting global expectations,[57] have shown an appetite for developing and imposing other-regarding obligations on states. Often expressing their commitment to a systemic vision of the law, these tribunals are not typically shy about their self-perceived role as guardians of the international legal system rather than as resolvers of specific, bilateral interstate disputes,[58] even when the institutional structure is clearly bilateral (as is the case in investment arbitrations).[59] Many examples, and in many contexts, can be cited. In some cases, international tribunals have unilaterally decided to take into account global welfare and global justice concerns, such as environmental protection.[60] When it has made no economic sense to assign full sovereignty rights to one country over what are essentially shared resources (eg rivers or fisheries), ITs have redefined the relevant property as shared, despite scant treaty language to that effect.[61] The WTO Appellate Body has also lowered the burden of proof

[57] See Eyal Benvenisti, "Community Interests in International Adjudication" in Eyal Benvenisti and Georg Nolte (eds), *Community Interests Across International Law* (OUP 2018).

[58] See Armin von Bogdandy and Ingo Venzke, "On the Functions of International Courts: An Appraisal in Light of Their Burgeoning Public Authority" (2013) 26 Leiden Journal of International Law 49, 63–67.

[59] Despite the discrete nature of their activity, these ad hoc panels, whose task is to interpret and apply bilateral obligations under bilateral treaties, strive to converge on common principles and collectively develop a systemic vision of "investment law." As recently stated in one arbitral award (among many), every panel must adopt a global vision: "A case-specific mandate is not license to ignore systemic implications. To the contrary, it arguably makes it all the more important that each tribunal renders its case-specific decision with sensitivity to the position of future tribunals and an awareness of other systemic implications": *Glamis Gold v United States* (n 31) [6].

[60] *Southern Bluefin Tuna (New Zealand v Japan; Australia v Japan)* (Provisional Measures) (Order of 27 August 1999) [1999] ITLOS Rep 280 [70]–[80]: "Considering that the conservation of the living resources of the sea is an element in the protection and preservation of the marine environment . . . [and] that, although the Tribunal cannot conclusively assess the scientific evidence presented by the parties, it finds that measures should be taken as a matter of urgency to preserve the rights of the parties and to avert further deterioration of the southern bluefin tuna stock." See Markus Benzing, "Community Interests in the Procedure of International Courts and Tribunals" (2006) 5 The Law and Practice of International Courts and Tribunals 369, 382. See also Thomas A Mensah, "Provisional Measures in the International Tribunal for the Law of the Sea (ITLOS)" (2002) 62 Zaörv 43, 53. Both point out that the ITLOS considered this aspect of the case on its own initiative, even though it had not been raised by the parties.

[61] Eyal Benvenisti, *Sharing Transboundary Resources: International Law and Optimal Resource Use* (CUP 2002) 44–46; Eyal Benvenisti, "Customary International Law as a Judicial Tool for Promoting Efficiency" in Eyal Benvenisti and Moshe Hirsch (eds), *The Impact of International Law on International Cooperation* (CUP 2004); Lucius Caflisch, "Règles générales du droit des cours d'eau internationaux" (1989) 219 Recueil Des Cours 9, 32–33, 109–10.

for justifying preferences given to imports from developing countries, in order to "provide developing countries with increasing returns from their growing exports, which returns are critical for those countries' economic development."[62]

Moreover, the WTO Appellate Body might be understood as having extended the notion of even-handedness beyond requiring the balancing of foreign interests, to requiring the balancing of interests of "global others" more generally. As Sivan Shlomo-Agon and I observed in relation to the *China-Rare Earths* dispute,[63] the Panel recognized that WTO members must exercise their rights with respect to natural resources in a manner consistent with the WTO obligations they have taken up as sovereigns. The Appellate Body further interpreted article XX(g) as not requiring a member to demonstrate that its proposed trade-restrictive measure "evenly" distributes the conservation burden between foreigners and domestic consumers,[64] but it added:

> [I]t would be difficult to conceive of a measure that would impose a significantly more onerous burden on foreign consumers or producers and that could still be shown to satisfy all of the requirements of Article XX(g).[65]

As we proposed in that article, the statement appears to articulate a duty among exporting members to consider global others broadly "who in an interconnected economy are dependent on their exports."[66] But, perhaps most remarkably of all, the statement also, "brings to the fore a broader notion of burden-sharing in a world of limited natural resources, thereby expressing a more demanding conception of members' other-regarding duty—not only the negative duty to 'do no harm,' but also the positive duty to 'do good,' by respecting dependency and considering the continued supply of their own resources."[67]

3. Adapting Standards of Review to Accommodate the Disregarded

In light of the general observation that ITs, like national courts, are sensitive to the "problem of disregard" and are known to actively respond to it, it is the thesis

[62] WTO Appellate Body Report, *European Communities—Conditions for the Granting of Tariff Preferences to Developing Countries*, WT/DS246/AB/R (adopted 20 April 2004) [106].

[63] WTO Panel Report, *China–Measures Related to the Exportation of Rare Earths, Tungsten and Molybdenum*, WT/DS431/R, WT/DS432/R, and WT/DS433/R (adopted 29 August 2014) [7.266]–[7.270] (China—Rare Earths); WTO Appellate Body Report, *China-Measures Related to the Exportation of Various Raw Materials*, (adopted 22 February 2012) WT/DS394/AB/R, W/TDS395/AB/R, and WT/DS398/AB/R (adopted 22 February 2012) [7.380]–[7.381].

[64] *China—Rare Earths* (n 63) [5.128]–[5.136].

[65] ibid [5.134].

[66] Shlomo-Agon and Benvenisti, "The Law of Strangers" (n 50) 617.

[67] ibid 617–18.

of this chapter that ITs also often adjust the standard of review that they adopt to remedy the disregard that they identify –even if they do not acknowledge this practice. Of course, in any litigation, there may be more than one type of disregard pitted against another—for example, a foreign investor challenging a policy that favors an indigenous people. In such cases, the IT may be able to assess which side has, in fact, disproportionally influenced the impugned decision. Such willingness to support the disregarded is obviously constrained by circumstance. Thus, for example, the European Court of Human Rights (ECtHR) has not always been willing to challenge complex political bargains within society. In the *Belgian Linguistic* case, for instance, despite concerns about discrimination on the basis of ethnicity, the Court stated that it could not "disregard those legal and factual features which characterize[d] the life of the society in the State which, as a Contracting Party, ha[d] to answer for the measure in dispute."[68] In cases such as *Lautsi v Italy*,[69] concerning the legal requirement to display crucifixes in Italian classrooms, and *SAS v France*,[70] which centered around a French law prohibiting the concealing of the face in public, the ECtHR confirmed the state's autonomy to define public spaces and culture. These examples mark the limits of the ability—or the perceived ability—of ITs to offer correction to the problem of disregard.

Let us now turn to the potential of ITs to correct the problem of disregard, taking into account the different types of disregard: the internal, the external, and the global.

3.1 The Standard of Review and the Internally Disregarded

Concerns about the inherent failures of the domestic political process and the potential inability of national courts to remedy those failures inform the (self-appointed) task of the ITs to intervene by adopting a stricter standard of review to remedy those failures.[71] Among the various ITs, the ECtHR stands out for its willingness to address the issue directly in its jurisprudence. While it recognizes the need to protect minorities by exercising strict scrutiny of national decisions,

[68] *Case Relating to Certain Aspects of the Laws on the Use of Languages in Education in Belgium, European Commission of Human Rights v Belgium* (1968) 1 EHRR 252, para 10.

[69] *Lautsi v Italy* App no 30814/06 (ECtHR, 18 March 2011).

[70] *SAS v France* App no 43835/11 (ECtHR, 1 July 2014).

[71] Benvenisti, "The Margin of Appreciation, Subsidiarity and Global Challenges to Democracy" (n 15); Benvenisti, "Margin of Appreciation, Consensus, and Universal Standards" (n 6); Eyal Benvenisti, "National Courts and the International Law on Minority Rights" (1997) 2 Austrian Review of International and European Law 1. For a more recent reiteration of this point, see Keohane, Macedo, and Moravcsik, "Democracy-Enhancing Multilateralism" (n 14); Daniel Halberstam, "Constitutional Heterarchy: The Centrality of Conflict in the European Union and the United States" in Jeffery L Dunoff and Joel P Trachtman (eds), *Ruling the World?: Constitutionalism, International Law, and Global Governance* (CUP 2009) 338–44; Stephen W Schill, "Deference in Investment Treaty Arbitration: Re-conceptualizing the Standard of Review" (2012) 3 Journal of International Dispute Settlement 577.

even in highly sensitive political scenarios,[72] it has been known to grant a wide MoA when the political process was robust and inclusive enough.[73] For example, in *MSS v Belgium and Greece*, which concerned the expulsion of asylum seekers by Belgian authorities, the ECtHR found Convention violations—partly on the basis of the applicant's asylum seeker status, pointing out that they were a "member of a particularly underprivileged and vulnerable population group in need of special protection."[74] The Court has also offered robust protection to the Roma minority[75] and, more recently, identified HIV-positive individuals who were seeking residence permits in the context of family unification among those "particularly vulnerable group[s] in society that ha[ve] suffered significant discrimination in the past," thereby narrowing the state's MoA.[76]

The MoA doctrine is grounded in the premise that open and inclusive democratic processes are likely to resolve internal tensions that might affect individual and group rights. Hence, any impugned domestic policy can be assumed to have benefited from meaningful democratic deliberations at the national level or at least from effective judicial scrutiny by an independent and impartial national court.[77] In other words, the MoA doctrine serves as an inducement for state regulators and national courts to ensure open and inclusive domestic democratic processes and effective judicial review and thereby enhance protection of rights and reduce the workload of the IT.

As noted earlier, the problem of disregard affects not only, and not always, minorities. There is another systemic failure in democracies that arises when minorities or—more commonly—special interest groups turn their numerical inferiority into a political asset. Responding to this type of disregard is thus another

[72] *Sejdić and Finci v Bosnia and Herzegovina* App nos 27996/06 and 34836/06 (ECtHR, 22 December 2009). For a critique, see Christopher McCrudden and Brendan O'Leary, "Courts and Consociations, or How Human Rights Courts May De-stabilize Power-sharing Settlements" (2013) 24 European Journal of International Law 477. See also Dominic McGoldrick, "A Defence of the Margin of Appreciation and an Argument for its Application by the Human Rights Committee" (2016) 65 International and Comparative Law Quarterly 21, 24–25.

[73] On the MoA from this perspective, see Benvenisti, "The Margin of Appreciation, Subsidiarity and Global Challenges to Democracy" (n 15).

[74] *MSS v Belgium and Greece* App no 30696/09 (ECtHR, 21 January 2011), para 251. See also *Chahal v United Kingdom* App no 22414/93 (ECtHR, 15 November 1996).

[75] *Orsus v Croatia* (2010) 52 EHRR 7.

[76] *Novruk v Russia* App nos 31039/11, 48511/11, 76810/12, 14618/13, and 13817/14 (ECtHR, 15 June 2016), para 100.

[77] See von Staden, "The Democratic Legitimacy of Judicial Review Beyond the State" (n 4) 1039–42; Andrew Legg, *The Margin of Appreciation in International Human Rights Law: Deference and Proportionality* (OUP 2012) 38: "The strength of reasons for a margin of appreciation on the basis of external factors depends on one's view of the role of the Tribunals. If one regards the Tribunals as having the primary role of establishing human rights standards, then it is plausible that there ought to be very little scope for a margin of appreciation to states. However, if states are important participants in the interpretation of international human rights standards and their application within their jurisdiction, then there may be reasons to give the state a margin of appreciation." Hence, the limited margin for measures that suppress political freedoms. See Dean Spielmann, "Allowing the Right Margin: the European Court of Human Rights and the National Margin of Appreciation Doctrine: Waiver or Subsidiarity of European Review?" (2012) 14 Cambridge Yearbook of European Legal Studies 381.

challenge and an opportunity for courts, including ITs, to offer remedies to limit the possibilities or consequences of such special interests dominating the domestic political process. Applying strict scrutiny to policies preferring special interests (or, conversely, allowing a wide MoA when domestic decision-makers have managed to avoid capture) helps minimize any distortion of the domestic democratic processes.[78]

Such sensitivity to the state's decision-making process may explain what, on the face of it, might appear to be inconsistent application of the standard of review by the investment tribunals in the *Philip Morris v Uruguay* case[79] and that of *Tecmed v Mexico*.[80] In both cases, the assertion of "public health" was the stated motivation for the impugned domestic regulation. But whereas, in *Tecmed*, the tribunal dismissed the significance of health concerns, applying strict scrutiny of the decision, the *Philip Morris* tribunal granted the same concerns "great deference," stating:

> The responsibility for public health measures rests with the government and investment tribunals should pay great deference to governmental judgments of national needs in matters such as the protection of public health. In such cases respect is due to the "discretionary exercise of sovereign power, not made irrationally and not exercised in bad faith ... involving many complex factors."[81]

Viewed from the perspective of the "problem of disregard," it is possible to reconcile these two apparently conflicting approaches. Before leaping to conclude that *Philip Morris* proposes a change of course with respect to the proper standard of review employed by investment tribunals, it is useful to recall that, in *Tecmed*, the tribunal was concerned with the foreign investor—"the externally disregarded" whose interests were upended by vocal domestic opposition. The *Tecmed* tribunal was evidently attentive to "the existence of community or political pressure ... as made public by the local mass media," which led it to "consider [...] whether community pressure and its consequences ... were so great as to lead to a serious emergency situation, social crisis or public unrest."[82]

While *Tecmed*, therefore, represented the paradigmatic case in which the externally disregarded needed judicial protection, in *Philip Morris*, it was the foreign investor that enjoyed political leverage. Tobacco companies famously exert significant political power by lobbying governments both at home and in host states.[83]

[78] On minorities as wielding undue influence in politics, see Ackerman, "Beyond 'Carolene Products'" (n 18).

[79] *Philip Morris Brand Sarl (Switzerland), Philip Morris Products SA (Switzerland) and Abal Hermanos SA (Uruguay) v Uruguay* ICSID Case No ARB/10/7 (Award) (6 July 2016) (*Philip Morris*).

[80] *Técnicas Medioambientales Tecmed, SA v United Mexican States* ICSID Case No ARB(AF)/00/02 (Award) (29 May 2003) (*Tecmed*).

[81] *Philip Morris* (n 79) [399].

[82] *Tecmed* (n 80) [133].

[83] The Framework Convention on Tobacco Control, negotiated under the auspices of the WHO, sought to limit the opportunities of tobacco companies to intervene in national regulation concerning

Given the tobacco industry's strong influence, particularly in developing countries, the tribunal's granting of "great deference" must be understood as support for national regulation that successfully withstood the inordinate pressures exerted by the foreign investor.[84]

3.2 The Standard of Review and the Externally Disregarded

While there is a robust political justification for remedying the problem of the internally disregarded, there may be more divergent attitudes toward the level of state commitment to foreigners, both within and outside its territory. To what extent should national decisions accommodate the sometimes-conflicting interests of foreigners?[85] This divergence can be expected to be reflected in varied judicial attitudes toward the proper level of scrutiny to which the ITs resort.

For example, the ECtHR has exercised strict scrutiny of decisions related to migrants in dire situations seeking entry to Europe, such as in the case of *Hirsi Jamaa v Italy*.[86] By contrast, the General Court of the European Union,[87] while recognizing the "wide discretion" that the EU Council had in the field of external economic relations, still required the Council to:

> [E]xamine, carefully and impartially, all the relevant facts in order to ensure that the production of goods for export [was] not conducted to the detriment of the population of the territory concerned, or entail[ed] infringements of fundamental rights, including, in particular, [their human rights].[88]

Note that this was a unique case in which it was quite obvious that a specific foreign community, the inhabitants of occupied Western Sahara, would be subject to a trade agreement between Morocco and the EU without their interests and rights being allowed to have any impact on the outcome. The judgment required the EU Council to remedy this disregard.

The typical cases of the externally disregarded who are situated outside state jurisdictions relate to foreign investors and foreign trading partners. ITs have

the sale and branding of tobacco products. See Mamudu and Glantz, "Civil Society and the Negotiation of the Framework Convention on Tobacco Control" (n 22).

[84] For a close analysis of such pressures, see Tim Dorlach and Paul Mertenskötter, "Interpreters of International Economic Law: Corporations and Bureaucrats in Contest over Chile's Nutrition Label" (2020) 57 Law and Society Review 571.

[85] See Eyal Benvenisti, "Sovereigns as Trustees of Humanity: On the Accountability of States to Foreign Stakeholders" (2013) 107 American Journal of International Law 295.

[86] *Hirsi Jamaa v Italy* App no 27765/09 (ECtHR, 22 February 2012).

[87] Case T-512/12 *Front populaire pour la libération de la saguia-el-hamra et du rio de oro (Front Polisario) v Council of the European Union* [2015] EU:T:2015:953.

[88] ibid para 228.

acknowledged the often-fragile position of the investor, to which the host state has a duty to secure its rights and interests against a possibly hostile domestic public.[89] As noted earlier, the WTO Appellate Body has offered similar protection to foreign exporters and importers affected by national trade policies.[90]

3.3 The Standard of Review and Global Disregard

A paradigmatic case to demonstrate the strength of the *global* aspect of the problem of disregard is the ICJ judgment in the *Whaling* case.[91] The dispute focused on Japan's discretion to issue "special permits" for killing whales, ostensibly for scientific research, as provided by article 8(1) of the International Convention for the Regulation of Whaling.[92] The said article allows a member state to issue permits and impose conditions "as the Contracting Government thinks fit."[93] The question that defined the dispute hinged on the proper standard of review of Japan's discretion under that article. Japan interpreted this as a "good faith" obligation, arguing that neither the International Whaling Commission (IWC) nor the ICJ has the "power to approve or disapprove the issue of a special permit."[94] Australia argued for a strict scrutiny approach, according to which Japan would have to demonstrate the scientific value of the permits. What is the principle that the Court should have adopted in interpreting the level of scrutiny under article 8(1)?

The principle that arguably informed the Court was not articulated but can be gleaned from the arguments made by the parties. Australia's claim for strict scrutiny was based on the concept of globally shared ownership of the whales. As stated by James Crawford, arguing for Australia: "In respect of resources in the international public domain, to recognize a wide margin of appreciation is, in effect, to allocate those resources to the exploiting State."[95] However, he continues, "Japan does not 'own' the whales it catches."[96] Therefore, the Convention requires "a

[89] See section 3.1 of this chapter.

[90] See section 2.2 of this chapter.

[91] *Whaling in the Antarctic (Australia v Japan: New Zealand intervening)* (Judgment) [2014] ICJ Rep 226 (*Whaling*).

[92] International Convention for the Regulation of Whaling (adopted 2 December 1946, entered into force 10 November 1948) 161 UNTS 72.

[93] ibid art 8: "Notwithstanding anything contained in this Convention any Contracting Government may grant to any of its nationals a special permit authorizing that national to kill, take and treat whales for purposes of scientific research subject to such restrictions as to number and subject to such other conditions as the Contracting Government thinks fit, and the killing, taking, and treating of whales in accordance with the provisions of this Article shall be exempt from the operation of this Convention. Each Contracting Government shall report at once to the Commission all such authorizations which it has granted. Each Contracting Government may at any time revoke any such special permit which it has granted."

[94] *Whaling in the Antarctic (Australia v Japan: New Zealand intervening)* Verbatim Record 2013/16 (4 July 2013), 36 [23]–[24].

[95] ibid [22].

[96] *Whaling in the Antarctic (Australia v Japan: New Zealand intervening)* Verbatim Record 2013/19 (10 July 2013), 65 [23].

proper showing ... that [research] proposals are genuinely motivated by scientific considerations and adapted appropriately to achieve scientific goals."[97] Moreover, Japan must "consider seriously" the views of the IWC and its subsidiary organs, otherwise, the conclusion will be "that the project is not being carried out for the purposes of scientific research, but for some other purpose inconsistent with the Convention."[98]

Although the Court did not expand on the theory behind its interpretation, it would seem that, in subjecting Japan's discretion to strict scrutiny, the Court was inspired by the need to respect *global* concerns about conservation of common resources, realizing that its support could be crucial.[99] The *Whaling* judgment shows that ITs might prefer to adjust the standard of review they employ without expressly acknowledging the justification for choosing more (or less) rigor. This allows them to navigate less-chartered territory with respect to the level of commitment that states make toward the disregarded. The decision also demonstrates that ITs have their own capacity and inclination to identify the interests of the disregarded and give them voice through a heightened level of scrutiny.

4. Conclusion

In this chapter, I argued that, explicitly or implicitly, ITs often adjust their standard of review of national decisions in ways that seek to remedy "the problem of disregard" in its three manifestations. The chapter did not venture to discuss questions regarding the factors that may render the IT in question more or less capable of remedying disregard (eg whether it is an established court like the ICJ or an ad hoc investment tribunal). Nor did it attempt to delve into the normative questions concerning the appropriateness of such intervention, including the matter of how much weight states should give to foreign stakeholders to correct the problem of the "externally disregarded" or "global disregard." These are especially acute issues for ITs that obtain their legitimacy from their claim to merely settle inter-state disputes according to specific treaties rather than engaging in global governance and the promotion of democracy and individual rights.

Beyond the variance in the standards of review, the chapter has hinted at other judicial doctrines and policies, such as standing and the availability of amicus briefs, that may be motivated by the same concern, namely to allow those disregarded in the political decision-making process to have their day in court (and,

[97] ibid [26].
[98] ibid.
[99] *Whaling* (n 91) [67] (requiring Japan to show that its program involved scientific research, and that the killing of whales is "for purposes of" scientific research, and the program's design and implementation are reasonable and not to a greater extent than is necessary in relation to achieving a given program's stated research objectives).

indirectly, their say through the court). This analysis, which suggests that ITs, as a matter of fact, tend to be sensitive to the disregarded, also demonstrates the resilience of the doctrinal approach that conceals its purpose behind the rhetoric of treaty interpretation etc and, hence, enabling the ITs to evade accountability for their attitude. Regardless of the legal rhetoric employed by ITs, identifying the disregard contained in a certain judgment could be a key, if not *the* key, to anticipating the IT's level of scrutiny.

3

Standards of Review in the Practice of International Courts and Tribunals

Vladyslav Lanovoy[*]

1. Introduction

As disputes increasingly involve complex relationships between the domestic and international, between the state and the individual, and between competing public and private interests, international courts and tribunals frequently face a dilemma. How far should they go in their review of the decisions of domestic state authorities under an international norm which affords them discretion? International courts and tribunals apply a variety of standards of review. The term "standards of review" in this context is used to describe the intensity of the scrutiny that an international adjudicator will apply to the domestic decision-maker's assessment of the facts, the law, or a combination thereof.[1] This scrutiny ranges from the most intrusive *de novo* review, whereby the dispute settlement mechanism substitutes its own findings for those of the earlier decision-maker, to the least intrusive or most deferential review where the dispute settlement mechanism will interfere only where the earlier decision is clearly erroneous or there is a manifest lack of reasons. In adopting the least intrusive or most deferential standard of review, the dispute settlement mechanism will not re-examine the findings of the domestic decision-maker or the process it followed in making those findings. The selection of the standard of review is important as it touches upon the balance of power in the international legal order and the proper distribution of competencies between sovereign states and international courts and tribunals.

Much of the vast literature in this area can be summed up by the following proposition: a standard of review should "strike an appropriate balance between

[*] The author would like to thank the editors of this volume, the organizers and participants of the ESIL Workshop held in Budapest in May 2019, the anonymous peer-reviewers, as well as Heather Clark and Massimo Lando for their helpful comments on earlier drafts. This chapter was completed in January 2021 and does not consider any subsequent developments in case law.

[1] See Chiara Ragni, "Standard of Review and the Margin of Appreciation before the International Court of Justice" in Lukasz Gruszczynski and Wouter G Werner (eds), *Deference in International Courts and Tribunals* (OUP 2014) 319 (the standard of review "can indicate whether, and to what extent, an international court may assess factual or legal findings made by a State . . . as regards the adoption of domestic measures, when their compliance with international law is at issue").

Vladyslav Lanovoy, *Standards of Review in the Practice of International Courts and Tribunals* In: *Secondary Rules of Primary Importance in International Law.* Edited by: Gábor Kajtár, Başak Çalı, and Marko Milanovic, Oxford University Press.
 DOI: 10.1093/oso/9780192869012.003.0003

oversight of compliance with a state's international obligations and respect for national autonomy."[2] The following questions thus arise. Is there—or should there be—a one-size-fits-all standard of review across different areas of international law and in respect of different types of domestic decisions (eg public health and environmental protection measures, a new tax regime, or judgments of domestic courts, etc)? If not, what possible criteria should be taken into account by an international court or tribunal in making that selection? What are the potential normative repercussions of a variety of standards of review being used and the failure of courts and tribunals by and large to explain and justify their selection?

This chapter examines the practice of the International Court of Justice (ICJ), the World Trade Organization (WTO), the European Court of Human Rights (ECtHR) and investor-state arbitral tribunals, with a view to identifying whether there are any trans-systemic trends relating to the manner in which international courts and tribunals approach standards of review.[3] It aims to identify criteria that may assist courts and tribunals in selecting the appropriate standard of review. These include the nature of obligation in question, the type of proceedings and of the decision under review, the question of expertise and resources, and the degree of institutional or systemic integration of a particular dispute settlement mechanism. This chapter argues that the selection by international courts and tribunals of a standard of review should be adequately reasoned, which in turn may increase the perceived legitimacy of their decision in the eyes of states and other stakeholders.[4] This is particularly important today in light of a growing tension of "governance powers between States and international courts and tribunals,"[5] and calls for the reform of many of the institutions that deal with standards of review

[2] Caroline Henckels, *Proportionality and Deference in Investor-State Arbitration* (CUP 2015) 30. For the most recent and thorough analysis of deference and standards of review in international adjudication, see Johannes Hendrik Fahner, *Judicial Deference in International Adjudication: A Comparative Analysis* (Hart 2020); Esmé Shirlow, *Judging at the Interface: Deference to State Decision-Making Authority in International Adjudication* (CUP 2021).

[3] The choice of dispute settlement mechanisms reflects the frequency with which they have dealt with the issue of the standard of review. That does not mean that other dispute settlement mechanisms have not considered the issue. For example, in the context of the International Tribunal for the Law of the Sea (ITLOS), see Rosemary Rayfuse, "Standard of Review in the International Tribunal for the Law of the Sea" in Lukasz Gruszczynski and G Wouter Werner (eds), *Deference in International Courts and Tribunals* (OUP 2014); Jean-Pierre Cot, "The Law of the Sea and the Margin of Appreciation" in Tafsir Malick Ndiaye and Rüdiger Wolfrum (eds), *Law of the Sea, Environmental Law and Settlement of Disputes: Liber Amicorum Judge Thomas A Mensah* (Martinus Nijhoff 2007). For the practice of the Inter-American Court of Human Rights (IACtHR) and the African Court on Human and Peoples' Rights (ACtHPR), see Fahner, *Judicial Deference in International Adjudication* (n 2) 47–58.

[4] See Yuval Shany, "Toward a General Margin of Appreciation Doctrine in International Law?" (2005) 16 European Journal of International Law 907, 916 (arguing that a proper balance between oversight and deference in selecting the standard of review may contribute to the "legitimacy and effectiveness of international judicial supervision").

[5] Anthea Roberts, "The Next Battleground: Standards of Review in Investment Treaty Arbitration" (2011) 16 International Council for Commercial Arbitration Congress Series 170.

on a regular basis, including the ECtHR, the WTO, and the investor-state dispute settlement system.[6]

The chapter proceeds as follows: Section 2 examines how different international courts and tribunals approach standards of review. Section 3 seeks to identify the criteria that may inform their selection of a standard of review. Section 4 contains some preliminary conclusions.

2. Standards of Review in the Practice of International Courts and Tribunals

Primary rules in international law rarely set out a standard of review. Article 17.6 of the WTO Anti-Dumping Agreement is a well-known exception, but thousands of other bilateral and multilateral treaties are silent on the subject of standards of review.[7] Similarly, the statutes or rules of procedure that govern how international courts and tribunals are to reach their decisions are generally silent on this issue. The determination of what standard of review should be applied is thus normally an exercise of the dispute settlement body's (DSB) inherent powers,[8] and often resembles a policy choice between activism and self-restraint.

The practice of international courts and tribunals discussed below shows several general features underlying the application of standards of review. First, standards of review have been considered both in inter-state proceedings as well as in proceedings brought by individuals against the state. The fact that some mechanisms have a more developed case law on the subject may be explained by the types of disputes and obligations the compliance with which they have been called to assess. Second, their depth of experience is varied ranging from the ICJ that has explicitly ruled on the applicable standard of review in a limited set of cases to the ECtHR which has elaborated an overarching doctrine—that of the margin of appreciation—as the applicable standard of review. Finally, while some like the ICJ have by and large adopted fairly deferential standards of review, none of the

[6] See eg "Copenhagen Declaration on the Reform of the European Convention of Human Rights System" (13 April 2018) <https://rm.coe.int/copenhagen-declaration/16807b915c>; UNCITRAL, "Possible Reform of Investor-State Dispute Settlement (ISDS): Note by the Secretariat", UN Doc A/CN.9/WG.III/WP.166 (30 July 2019); Chang-Fa Lo, Junji Nakagawa, and Tsai-Fang Chen, *The Appellate Body of the WTO and Its Reform* (Springer 2020).

[7] Article 17.6 of the WTO Anti-Dumping Agreement reads: "[I]n its assessment of the facts of the matter, the panel shall determine whether the authorities' establishment of the facts was proper and whether their evaluation of those facts was unbiased and objective. If the establishment of the facts was proper and the evaluation was unbiased and objective, even though the panel might have reached a different conclusion, the evaluation shall not be overturned."

[8] For the notion of inherent powers in international adjudication, see eg Chester Brown, "Inherent Powers in International Adjudication" in Cesare PR Romano, Karen J Alter, and Yuval Shany (eds), *The Oxford Handbook of International Adjudication* (OUP 2014); Chester Brown, "The Inherent Powers of International Courts and Tribunals" (2005) 76 British Yearbook of International Law 195.

international courts and tribunals examined below can be said to have afforded total deference to domestic decision-makers, even in cases of clauses concerning essential security interests, as can be seen from a review of the case law of the ICJ, investor-state arbitral tribunals and a recent review of measures purportedly covered by the general security exception in article XXI of the GATT 1994.

2.1 International Court of Justice

As noted above, the ICJ has rarely made an express reference to the standard it has applied when reviewing whether a decision taken by domestic authorities complied with a particular obligation under international law. The existing jurisprudence as analyzed below shows that the consideration of standards of review by the Court has thus far principally arisen in respect of the so-called "standard-type norms" that allow the state a certain level of discretion and that may "resort to concepts like proportionality, necessity, security, public policy or public concerns."[9]

The Court's decision in the *Whaling in the Antarctic* case is the closest it came to making an express pronouncement on the applicable standard of review, even if this case must be considered in its factual context and in light of the particularities of the relevant legal instrument, the International Convention for the Regulation of Whaling (ICRW). The case concerned a dispute between Australia and Japan concerning the Second Phase of its Japanese Whale Research Program under Special Permit in the Antarctic (JARPA II), and whether specific permits granted by Japan for this program were or were not for purposes of scientific research within the meaning of article VIII(1) of the ICRW.[10] The Court found that that provision gave "discretion to a State party to the ICRW to reject the request for a special permit or to specify the conditions under which a permit will be granted."[11] It noted, however, that "whether the killing, taking and treating of whales pursuant to a requested special permit is for purposes of scientific research cannot depend simply on that State's perception."[12] Thus, in reviewing the grant of special permits by the Japanese authorities for this program, the Court adopted a two-pronged standard of review: first, examining whether the program involved scientific research and,

[9] Ragni, "Standard of Review" (n 1) 322.

[10] ICRW, art VIII(1) reads as follows: "Notwithstanding anything contained in this Convention any Contracting Government may grant to any of its nationals a special permit authorizing that national to kill, take and treat whales for purposes of scientific research subject to such restrictions as to number and subject to such other conditions as the Contracting Government thinks fit, and the killing, taking, and treating of whales in accordance with the provisions of this Article shall be exempt from the operation of this Convention. Each Contracting Government shall report at once to the Commission all such authorizations which it has granted. Each Contracting Government may at any time revoke any such special permit which it has granted."

[11] *Whaling in the Antarctic (Australia v Japan; New Zealand intervening)* (Judgment) [2014] ICJ Rep 226, 253 [61].

[12] Ibid.

second, assessing whether the program's design and implementation were reasonable in relation to achieving its stated objectives.[13] While the Court did not consider it necessary to define "scientific research," thereby largely deferring to Japan's qualification of JARPA II as a scientific research project, the second limb of its standard of review was more exacting. As a result, having taken into account the use of lethal methods by Japan, the scale of the use of lethal sampling, the methodology used to select sample sizes, and other aspects of the program, the Court concluded that its design and implementation were not "reasonable in relation to achieving its stated objectives" and that the special permits thus granted were not "for purposes of scientific research."[14]

The Court has also considered the question of the standard of review in a few cases that involved the invocation of purportedly self-judging clauses in a treaty.[15] As explained by Schill and Robyn, "[b]y means of these clauses states reserve to themselves the right to unilaterally declare such obligations to be non-binding if the state in question determines that its essential interests are at stake and, according to its determination, should take precedence over international law."[16] The terms of any such clause are of course very important. For instance, when considering article XXI of the Treaty of Friendship, Commerce and Navigation (FCN) between Nicaragua and the United States in the *Military and Paramilitary Activities* case, the Court held that "whether a measure is necessary to protect the essential interests of a party is not ... purely a question for the subjective judgment of the party."[17] In other words, the Court held that the clause in question was a not a genuine self-judging clause and did not preclude the Court from reviewing the United States' actions. The ICJ has consistently held that the presence of similarly

[13] ibid [67], [178]ff.

[14] ibid [88], [227]. For further analysis of the standard of review applied in the *Whaling* case, see eg Enzo Cannizzaro, "Margin of Appreciation and Reasonableness in the ICJ's Decision in the *Whaling* Case" in Pierre d'Argent, Beatrice Bonafé, and Jean Combacau (eds), *The Limits of International Law: Essays in Honour of Joe Verhoeven* (Bruylant 2015); Enzo Cannizzaro, "Proportionality and Margin of Appreciation in the *Whaling* Case: Reconciling Antithetical Doctrines?" (2016) 27 European Journal of International Law 1061; Asier Garrido-Muñoz, "Managing Uncertainty: The International Court of Justice, 'Objective Reasonableness' and the Judicial Function" (2017) 30 Leiden Journal of International Law 457; Caroline E Foster, "Methodologies and Motivations: Was Japan's Whaling Programme for Purposes of Scientific Research?" in Malgosia Fitzmaurice and Dai Tamada (eds), *Whaling in the Antarctic: The Significance and the Implications of the ICJ Judgment* (Brill Nijhoff 2016); Shotaro Hamamoto, "From the Requirement of Reasonableness to a 'Comply and Explain' Rule: The Standard of Review in the *Whaling* Judgment" in Malgosia Fitzmaurice and Dai Tamada (eds), *Whaling in the Antarctic: Significance and Implications of the ICJ Judgment* (Brill Nijhoff 2016).

[15] See Stephan W Schill and Robyn Briese, "'If the State Considers': Self-Judging Clauses in International Dispute Settlement" (2009) 13 Max Planck Yearbook of United Nations Law 61, 67 (defining these clauses as having the "function of allowing a state to enter into international cooperation on the basis of binding international obligations, while at the same time retaining the power to escape from such obligations in certain circumstances, most frequently if the state determines that it would harm its sovereignty, security, public policy, or more generally, its essential interests").

[16] ibid 64.

[17] *Military and Paramilitary Activities in and against Nicaragua (Nicaragua v United States of America)* (Merits) [1986] ICJ Rep 14, 141 [282]. See similarly, *Oil Platforms (Islamic Republic of Iran v United States of America)* (Merits) [2003] ICJ Rep 161, 183 [43].

drafted clauses and reliance upon them by one of the parties does not restrict its jurisdiction, but it may constitute a defense on the merits and affect the standard of review applied by the Court.[18]

The wording of the relevant clause in the *Military and Paramilitary Activities* case, which referred to measures "necessary to protect its essential security interests," can be contrasted with that of article 2(c) of the Mutual Assistance Convention between Djibouti and France in the *Mutual Assistance* case.[19] The latter provision sets out that assistance in proceedings relating to criminal offences "may be refused [. . .] *if the requested State considers* that execution of the request is likely to prejudice its sovereignty, security, public policy or other of essential interests."[20] While that provision allowed France a wide measure of discretion, the Court held that the exercise of that discretion remained "subject to the obligation of good faith".[21] In particular, the Court considered that France had to show that the reasons for its refusal to execute the letter rogatory fell within those allowed for in article 2(c). The Court held that the existence of declassified "defense secret" documents fell within the scope of that provision.[22] This case shows that even in the presence of terms such as "if the State considers/determines" or "in the State's opinion," the Court has not construed them to oust its jurisdiction and has interpreted such terms as requiring states to provide reasons, subject to a rather deferential standard of good faith review.[23] The Court failed, however, to provide any further guidance in terms of the actual application of such standard, a point addressed in some detail in Judge Keith's declaration.[24]

That said, the standard of a good faith review, which is closely intertwined with the notion of reasonableness, has resurfaced with some frequency in the Court's jurisprudence.[25] In a recent judgment in the *Immunities and Criminal Proceedings*

[18] See eg *Alleged Violations of the 1955 Treaty of Amity, Economic Relations, and Consular Rights (Islamic Republic of Iran v United States of America)* (Preliminary Objections) [2021] ICJ Rep 9, 40 [109]; *Certain Iranian Assets (Islamic Republic of Iran v United States of America)* (Preliminary Objections) [2019] ICJ Rep 7, 25 [45]; *Oil Platforms (Islamic Republic of Iran v United States of America)* (Preliminary Objections) [1996] ICJ Rep 803, 811 [20].

[19] *Certain Questions of Mutual Assistance in Criminal Matters (Djibouti v France)* (Judgment) [2008] ICJ Rep 177.

[20] Convention Concerning Judicial Assistance in Criminal Matters, 1695 UNTS 297 (signed 27 September 1986, entered into force 1 August 1992) (emphasis added).

[21] *Certain Questions of Mutual Assistance in Criminal Matters (Djibouti v France)* (Judgment) [2008] ICJ Rep 177, 229 [145].

[22] ibid 230 [148].

[23] ibid 230–32 [149]–[156], 245 [203]–[204].

[24] See ibid Declaration of Judge Keith, 279–80 [6] (opining that the Court should have first assessed "the reasons given by the judge in her *soit-transmis* against the principles of good faith, abuse of rights and *détournement de pouvoir*. Those principles require the state agency in question to exercise the power for the purposes for which it was conferred and without regard to improper purposes or irrelevant factors").

[25] See *Gabčíkovo-Nagymaros (Hungary/Slovakia)* (Judgment) [1997] ICJ Rep 7, 79 [142] (where the Court explained that the principle of good faith, as enshrined in Article 26 of the Vienna Convention on the Law of Treaties (VCLT), implies that a state party should apply the treaty "in a reasonable way and in such a manner that its purpose can be realized"); *Dispute regarding Navigational and Related Rights (Costa Rica v Nicaragua)* (Judgment) [2009] ICJ Rep 213, 253 [101] ("a court examining the

case, the Court applied a standard of review said to be based on notions of reasonableness and good faith in the context of a different treaty regime, namely the Vienna Convention on Diplomatic Relations (VCDR). The Court had to identify and justify the standard of review in relation to the exercise of the power by the receiving state to object to a sending state's designation of the premises of its diplomatic mission. It noted that "where a State possesses a discretionary power under a treaty, such a power must be exercised reasonably and in good faith."[26] In the context of the VCDR and in light of its object and purpose, that meant that the Court had to examine "whether any such objection was communicated in a timely manner, and was neither arbitrary nor discriminatory in character."[27] In applying this standard of review in respect of the French objection to the Equatorial Guinea's designation of the building at 42 Avenue Foch as its premises of the mission, the Court made an important contribution to the understanding of the balance of rights and obligations of the sending and receiving states under the VCDR. The Court's standard of review, which finds only partial support in the text of the VCDR itself,[28] may well be of broader application and transposable to other treaties that provide for the exercise of similar discretionary powers.

Finally, the Court has considered the question of the standard of review when dealing with defenses or justifications such as necessity and self-defense. For instance, in the *Gabčikovo-Nagymaros* case, when evaluating the lawfulness of Hungary's non-performance of its treaty obligations on the basis of certain environmental concerns, the ICJ held that: "[T]he state of necessity can only be invoked under certain strictly defined conditions which must be cumulatively satisfied; and the State concerned *is not the sole judge* of whether those conditions have been met."[29] Similarly, in the *Oil Platforms* case, the United States argued that the Court should afford the United States some margin of discretion in determining whether its decision to resort to force, in response to armed attacks by Iran, was necessary and proportionate. The Court rejected that argument, highlighting that "the requirement of international law that measures taken avowedly in self-defence

reasonableness of a regulation must recognize that the regulator, in this case the State with sovereignty over the river, has the primary responsibility for assessing the need for regulation and for choosing, on the basis of its knowledge of the situation, the measure that it deems most appropriate to meet that need. It will not be enough in a challenge to a regulation simply to assert in a general way that it is unreasonable. Concrete and specific facts will be required to persuade a court to come to that conclusion").

[26] *Immunities and Criminal Proceedings (Equatorial Guinea v France)* (Judgment) [2020] ICJ Rep 300, 323 [73]. See also *Rights of Nationals of the United States of America in Morocco (France v United States of America)* (Judgment) [1952] ICJ Rep 17, 212.

[27] *Immunities and Criminal Proceedings* (n 26) 324 [74].

[28] See ibid, Separate Opinion of President Yusuf 354 [36]. Indeed, for example, the arbitrariness criterion as part of the standard applied by the Court is nowhere expressly reflected in the VCDR itself. On this point, cf eg *ELSI Elettronica Sicula SpA (ELSI) (United States of America v Italy)* (Judgment) [1989] ICJ Rep 15, 73–76 [123]–[128]; *Ahmadou Sadio Diallo (Republic of Guinea v Democratic Republic of the Congo)* (Merits) [2010] ICJ Rep 639, 663–69 [65]–[82].

[29] *Gabčíkovo-Nagymaros Project* (n 25) 40 [51] (emphasis added).

must have been necessary for that purpose is *strict and objective*, leaving *no room for any 'measure of discretion'*."[30] While the Court appeared to move in the direction of a stricter standard of review in situations of purported necessity and self-defense, it failed again to elaborate on the precise standard.[31]

In sum, the jurisprudence of the Court shows that the standard of review is rarely, if ever, spelled out and depends on the terms and character of the obligation, the object and purpose of the treaty and the surrounding context.[32] In the cases discussed above, the Court appears to have adopted a fairly deferential approach to states' decisions taken pursuant to obligations that allow them some discretion, provided that such decisions are reasoned and consistent with the stated objectives. The Court has resorted to concepts of good faith and reasonableness when reviewing decisions of domestic authorities, including decisions concerning essential security interest and self-judging clauses. However, it has failed to spell out the exact parameters of any such standard of review. Nor has the Court set out a general standard of review that would apply in all circumstances, thus preserving its flexibility for future cases. This is understandable. By contrast to other specialized dispute settlement mechanisms such as the ECtHR, which operates within a single treaty and may fine-tune a uniform standard of review, the Court considers cases arising in a great variety of areas of international law and under a host of treaties, which may justify the adoption of different standards of review depending on the nature of the obligation and the object and purpose of the treaty in question.

2.2 World Trade Organization

By contrast to the ICJ, where the issue has arisen only in select instances, standards of review are applied in almost every case before the WTO panels and the Appellate Body.[33] As explained by Oesch, "[w]hen the examination of a domestic measure

30 *Oil Platforms* (Merits) (n 17) 196 [73] (emphasis added).

31 For express criticism on this point, see *Oil Platforms* (Merits) (n 17), Separate Opinion of Judge Higgins at 238 [48] ("The Court should, in my view, have itself first assessed whether there were essential security interests at risk [...] The Court should next have examined—without any need to afford a 'margin of appreciation'—the meaning of 'necessary' "). See also ibid, Separate Opinion of Judge Buergenthal at 285 [37] ("while a Government's determination is ultimately subject to review by the Court, it may not substitute its judgment completely for that of the Government which, in assessing whether the disputed measures were necessary, must be given the opportunity to demonstrate that its assessment of the perceived threat to its essential security interests was reasonable under the circumstances"). cf ibid, Separate Opinion of Judge Kooijmans at 260 [44] ("The evaluation of what essential security interests are and whether they are in jeopardy is first and foremost a political question and can hardly be replaced by a judicial assessment. Only when the political evaluation is patently unreasonable (which might bring us close to an 'abuse of authority' is a judicial ban appropriate").

32 Ragni, "Standard of Review" (n 1) 335 (concluding on the basis of the review of the Court's jurisprudence that "uniform standards may be difficult to identify and establish").

33 See Dispute Settlement Understanding (DSU), art 1, Annex 1. See also Ross Becroft, *The Standard of Review in WTO Dispute Settlement* (Edward Elgar 2012).

falls within the jurisdiction of panels and the Appellate Body, the question arises to what depth and with what intensity the national policy determination should be reviewed."[34] Standards of review were, in fact, a key issue during the Uruguay Round that led to the establishment of the WTO and have been described as "one of three or four issues that could have broken apart the WTO negotiations."[35]

From the beginning, the WTO panels and the Appellate Body have recognized that the question of the standard of review "goes to the very core of the integrity of the WTO dispute settlement process itself."[36] However, with the exception of article 17.6 of the Anti-Dumping Agreement, the rules set out in the Dispute Settlement Understanding (DSU) do not expressly mention the standards of review, apart from a general requirement that the panels must conduct an "objective assessment of the facts of the case and the applicability of and conformity with the relevant covered agreements."[37] That provision alone, however, does not settle the question of what deference, if any, must be afforded to the domestic authorities of the state that adopted a given measure nor the specific standard of review to be applied.[38] According to the Appellate Body, "the applicable standard is neither *de novo* review as such, nor 'total deference.'"[39]

While the above approach that resembles a sliding scale between *de novo* review and total deference applies in respect of factual determinations made by the domestic authorities, any legal interpretation of WTO law performed by domestic authorities is subject to a *de novo* review by the WTO panels and the Appellate Body.[40] That is justifiable in an institutional framework in which panels and the Appellate Body are entrusted with interpreting and clarifying the WTO agreements and in which the DSB seeks to guarantee "security and predictability to the multilateral trading system".[41] Conversely, panels and the Appellate Body have on balance been more reluctant to apply a *de novo* or any other intrusive standard of review when examining domestic legal provisions that may be at issue. Questions relating to the meaning and construction of domestic laws call for a "considerable

[34] Matthias Oesch, *Standards of Review in WTO Dispute Resolution* (OUP 2003) 13. See also Steven P Croley and John H Jackson, "WTO Dispute Procedures, Standard of Review and Deference to National Governments" (1996) 90 American Journal of International Law 193.

[35] John H Jackson, "Remarks by John H Jackson" (1994) 88 Proceedings of the ASIL Annual Meeting 136, 139.

[36] WTO Appellate Body Report, *European Communities—Measures Affecting the Importation of Certain Poultry Products*, WT/DS69/AB/R (adopted 23 July 1998) [133].

[37] DSU, art 11.

[38] Jan Bohanes and Nicolas Lockhart, "Standard of Review in WTO Law" in Daniel Bethlehem and others (eds), *The Oxford Handbook of International Trade Law* (OUP 2010) 383 (suggesting that "[a]ny assessment, whether highly deferential, marginally deferential, or not deferential at all, can be an 'objective assessment'").

[39] WTO Appellate Body Report, *European Communities—Measures Concerning Meat and Meat Products (EC—Hormones)*, WT/DS26/AB/R (adopted 13 February 1998) [117].

[40] Bohanes and Lockhart, "Standard of Review in WTO Law" (n 38) 385 ("they perform a *de novo* review of the law").

[41] DSU, art 3.2.

deference" to the views of the member states concerned.[42] Finally, complex issues may arise in situations where the panel is addressing mixed determinations of fact and law, as these often arise for instance in the context of trade remedy agreements. In such cases, it would appear that "the more purely factual a question, the more deference is afforded; in contrast, the more legal a question is, the more a panel and the Appellate Body are inclined to intervene to ensure that the legal characterization meets the requirements of WTO law."[43]

The question of what standard of review should be applied has arisen with greatest frequency in respect of the panels' examination of the factual determinations made by domestic authorities. As noted by the Appellate Body, when selecting the standard of review, the requirement of "an 'objective assessment' under Article 11 DSU must be understood in the light of the obligations of the particular covered agreement at issue in order to derive the more specific contours of the appropriate standard of review."[44] The diversity of approaches taken to the selection of the standard of review can de demonstrated in three categories of cases: (1) measures imposed as a result of safeguards investigations, (2) sanitary and phytosanitary (SPS) measures imposed by member states, and (3) measures purportedly covered by the general security exception in article XXI of the GATT 1994.

When examining whether the safeguards determinations conducted by domestic authorities are WTO-consistent, "panels must not conduct a *de novo* review of the evidence nor substitute their judgement for that of the competent authority."[45] In *United States—Softwood Lumber VI (Article 21.5—Canada)*, the Appellate Body clarified that, even though a panel "must take care not to assume itself the role of initial trier of facts, nor to be passive by 'simply accept(ing) the conclusions of the competent authority,'" the panel in that case had "failed to engage in the type of critical and searching analysis called for by Article 11 of the DSU."[46] In particular, the Appellate Body ruled that article 11 of the DSU requires the adjudicating bodies to satisfy themselves that two criteria are fulfilled. While the formal criterion requires domestic authorities to evaluate all relevant factors, the

[42] WTO Panel Report, *United States—Section 301–310 of the Trade Act of 1974*, WT/DS152/R (adopted 27 January 2000) [7.19], [7.122]–[7.123]. See also WTO Panel Report, *Canada—Patent Protection of Pharmaceutical* Products, WT/DS114/R (adopted 7 April 2000) [7.99]. cf WTO Appellate Body Report, *India—Patent Protection for Pharmaceutical and Agricultural Chemical Products*, WT/DS50/AB/R (adopted 16 January 1998) [67]–[69].

[43] Bohanes and Lockhart, "Standard of Review in WTO Law" (n 38) 392.

[44] WTO Appellate Body Report, *United States—Countervailing Duty Investigation on Dynamic Random Access Memory Semiconductors (DRAMS) from Korea*, WT/DS296/AB/R (adopted 20 July 2005) [184].

[45] WTO Appellate Body Report, *United States—Transitional Safeguard Measure on Combed Cotton Yarn from Pakistan*, WT/DS192/AB/R (adopted 5 November 2001) [74].

[46] WTO Appellate Body Report, *United States—Investigation of the International Trade Commission in Softwood Lumber from Canada (United States—Softwood Lumber VI (Article 21.5—Canada))*, WT/DS277/AB/RW (adopted 9 May 2006) [113].

substantive one requires them to provide "a reasoned and adequate explanation" of how the facts support their determination.[47]

The standard of review is quite different when reviewing whether an SPS measure is WTO-consistent. In such cases, a panel should verify whether the scientific basis underlying such measures "comes from a respected and qualified source" and has "the necessary scientific and methodological rigour to be considered reputable science."[48] In *United States—Continued Suspension*, the Appellate Body found that instead of determining whether the risk assessment was supported by coherent reasoning and reputable scientific evidence, the panel had wrongly sought to determine whether the risk assessment relied upon by the EU was based on correct scientific evidence.[49] In other words, the test is that of whether the "reasoning articulated on the basis of the scientific evidence is objective and coherent" and not of substituting its own risk assessment for that performed by the WTO Member state.[50] There are two aspects to a panel's review of such a risk assessment, namely "scrutiny of the underlying scientific basis and scrutiny of the reasoning of the risk assessor based upon such underlying science."[51] In respect of the former, the panel's task is limited to reviewing whether the scientific basis constitutes "legitimate science according to the standards of the relevant scientific community."[52] In respect of the latter, the panel's task involves the assessment of whether the reasoning of the risk assessor is objective and coherent, that is, whether "the conclusions find sufficient support in the scientific evidence relied upon".[53] Such a two-part review is consistent with the relevant provisions of the SPS Agreement requiring "that there be a 'rational or objective relationship' between the SPS measures and the scientific evidence."[54]

Finally, in a recent decision, a WTO Panel has for the first time ruled on the standard of review applicable in the context of the general security exception in article XXI of the GATT 1994. In *Russia—Measures Concerning Traffic in Transit*, the WTO Panel held that it was vested with "the power to review whether the requirements of the enumerated subparagraphs [of article XXI(b) of the GATT 1994] are met, rather than leaving it to the unfettered discretion of the invoking Member' and that this provision 'is not totally "self-judging."'[55] The panel proceeded to examine

[47] WTO Appellate Body Report, *United States—Safeguard Measures on Imports of Fresh, Chilled or Frozen Lamb Meat from New Zealand and Australia*, WT/DS177/AB/R, WT/DS178/AB/R (adopted 16 May 2001) [103].

[48] WTO Appellate Body Report, *United States—Continued Suspension of Obligations in the EC—Hormones Dispute*, WT/DS320/AB/R (adopted 14 November 2008) [591].

[49] ibid [590].

[50] ibid [591].

[51] WTO Appellate Body Report, *Australia—Measures Affecting the Importation of Apples from New Zealand*, WT/DS367/AB/R (adopted 17 December 2010) [215].

[52] ibid.

[53] ibid.

[54] ibid.

[55] WTO Panel Report, *Russia—Measures Concerning Traffic in Transit*, WT/DS512/R (adopted 26 April 2019) [7.102].

the Russian measures at issue applying the standard of a good faith review. It held that this standard applied both in respect of "the Member's definition of the essential security interests ... and most importantly, to their connection with the measures at issue."[56] Thus, in interpreting article XXI(b)(iii), the Panel ruled that this provision demands "that the measures at issue meet a minimum requirement of plausibility in relation to the proffered essential security interests, i.e. that they are not implausible as measures protective of these interests."[57] As a result, the panel found that it had to "review whether the measures are so remote from, or unrelated to, the 2014 emergency that it is implausible that Russia implemented the measures for the protection of its essential security interests arising out of the emergency."[58]

An interesting takeaway from this brief overview of WTO case law is that even within a rather self-contained system there is no uniform standard of review, and the selection of an applicable standard depends first and foremost on whether the review concern a purely factual determination, legal interpretation, or mixed. Beyond the general requirement for the panels to conduct an objective assessment of the facts, the exact standard of review depends on the obligation at issue, the covered agreement and the nature of the underlying domestic decision-making process. Thus, for instance, an investigation conducted into whether a given product is causing injury to the domestic producers will be subject to a different standard of review from the risk assessment underlying a public health measure under the SPS Agreement. Moreover, the decision-making process by which a measure was adopted directly influences the intensity of review by the WTO panel.[59] Accordingly, "if a measure results from a treaty mandated investigative procedure, conducted at national level [such as in the context of covered agreements on trade remedies], that dictates a more lenient level of review than applies to a measure where no similar national procedure is required under WTO law."[60]

2.3 European Court of Human Rights

The European Court of Human Rights (ECtHR) has developed the well-known doctrine of the margin of appreciation, which is an expression of qualified deference

[56] ibid [7.138].
[57] ibid.
[58] ibid [7.139]. Three other cases are currently pending, involving art XXI of the GATT 1994: WTO, *Ukraine—Measures Related to Trade in Goods and Services* (Request for consultations made by Russia on 19 May 2017), WT/DS525/1; WTO, *Russia—Measures Concerning Importation and Transit of Certain Ukrainian Products* (Request for Consultation made by Ukraine on 13 October 2017), WT/DS532/1; WTO, *United Arab Emirates—Measures Relating to Trade in Goods and Services, and Trade-Related Aspects of Intellectual Property Rights* (Request for consultations made by Qatar on 31 July 2017), WT/DS526/1 [suspended].
[59] Bohanes and Lockhart, "Standard of Review in WTO Law" (n 38) 384.
[60] ibid 384, 390–409.

to domestic decision-makers.[61] Inspired by French (*marge d'appréciation*) and German (*Ermessensspielraum*) administrative law,[62] this doctrine is well-suited to the structure of the human rights system in Europe, which has to reconcile concerns with subsidiarity and the effective protection and promotion of human rights.[63] In essence, the doctrine entails two elements: (1) deference owed to states in fulfilling their obligations under the European Convention on Human Rights (ECHR) and (2) normative flexibility, particularly in respect of norms with relatively open-ended content.[64] Domestic authorities are generally regarded as best placed to determine the means necessary to comply with human rights obligations under the ECHR, and the ECtHR generally refrains from substituting its own assessment for that of national authorities.[65] However, the doctrine has also been characterized as indeterminate or "contentless," as it does not attempt to circumscribe the scope and degree of deference in the abstract, nor has it led to any concrete standard of review.[66] At the same time, this flexibility has worked well for the so-called "inward-looking" norms that are applied where a deliberative procedure has taken place at the domestic level.[67] In this context, the following considerations have influenced the deference afforded to the national authorities: (1) comparative advantage of local authorities, (2) indeterminacy of the applicable standard, and (3) nature of the contested interests.[68]

Over the years, the ECtHR has set limits to the scope of the margin of appreciation doctrine in practice. The extent of deference afforded depends on the "nature of the Convention right in issue, its importance for the individual, the nature of

[61] See *Leyla Sahin v Turkey* (2007) 44 EHRR 5, Dissenting Opinion of Judge Tulkens at [2] ("the Court must seek to reconcile universality and diversity"). See also Eyal Benvenisti, "Margin of Appreciation, Consensus, and Universal Standards" (1999) 31 New York Journal of International Law and Policy 843, 844 (arguing that the margin of appreciation may undermine the universality of human rights and the very authority of the ECtHR as a judicial institution).

[62] See Yutaka Arai-Takahashi, *The Margin of Appreciation Doctrine and the Principle of Proportionality in the Jurisprudence of the ECHR* (Intersentia 2002) 2–3; cf Eirik Bjorge, "Been There, Done That: The Margin of Appreciation and International Law" (2015) 4 Cambridge International Law Journal 181, 182–85 (arguing that the doctrine finds its roots in international law itself).

[63] Andrew Legg, *The Margin of Appreciation in International Human Rights Law: Deference and Proportionality* (OUP 2012) 61; Michael R Hutchinson, "The Margin of Appreciation Doctrine in the European Court of Human Rights" (1999) 48 International and Comparative Law Quarterly 638, 642–43.

[64] See eg Shany, "Toward a General Margin of Appreciation Doctrine in International Law?" (n 4) 910.

[65] See eg *Handyside v United Kingdom* (1976) 1 EHRR 737, para 49. See also *United Communist Party of Turkey v Turkey* (1998) 26 EHRR 121, para 47; *Goodwin v United Kingdom* (2002) 35 EHRR 447, para 85.

[66] Julian Arato, "The Margin of Appreciation in International Investment Law" (2014) 54 Virginia Journal of International Law 545, 558 ("unlike review for good faith, reasonableness, LRM [least restrictive measure], and proportionality, the margin does not inherently imply any particular level of deference to the decisions of national authorities"). See also Gary Born, Danielle Morris, and Stephanie Forrest, "'A Margin of Appreciation': Appreciating Its Irrelevance in International Law" (2020) 61 Harvard Journal of International Law 65.

[67] Shany, "Toward a General Margin of Appreciation Doctrine in International Law?" (n 4) 920.

[68] ibid 927.

the interference and the object pursued by the interference."[69] Many other factors may come into play, including the importance of the policy aims pursued by national authorities,[70] the availability of adequate procedural safeguards at the domestic level,[71] and the existence of European consensus on the right in question.[72] The margin of appreciation may be narrower if the right at stake is "crucial to the individual's effective enjoyment of intimate or key rights"[73] or where "a particularly important facet of an individual's existence or identity is at stake"[74] or yet where the right is absolute and fundamental, such as for instance the prohibition of torture and ill treatment.[75] The margin of appreciation may be wider in cases involving interference with rights in furtherance of important objectives such as national security, the protection of public morals or the environment, or the implementation of international obligations.[76] In recent years, the ECtHR appears to have moved towards a greater degree of subsidiarity, which emphasizes a direct connection between the quality of the domestic parliamentary process and the breadth of the margin of appreciation.[77] In sum, the margin of appreciation has become "an elaborate framework listing a variety of factors that determine the intensity of the [ECtHR] review."[78]

2.4 Investor-State Arbitration

Standards of review also feature prominently in the practice of investor-state arbitral tribunals. Compared to WTO or ECtHR, disputes arise before ad hoc arbitral tribunals under thousands of bilateral and multilateral treaties which do not

[69] *S and Marper v United Kingdom* (2009) 48 EHRR 50, para 102; *Buckley v United Kingdom* (1996) 23 EHRR 101, para 74; *Ireland v United Kingdom* (1979–80) 2 EHRR 25, para 48; *Nada v Switzerland* (2013) 56 EHRR 18, para 184.

[70] *Jahn v Germany* (2004) 42 EHRR 49, para 80.

[71] *Camenzind v Switzerland* (1997) 28 EHRR 458, para 45.

[72] *X, Y, and Z v United Kingdom* (1997) 24 EHRR 143, para 44.

[73] *Connors v United Kingdom* (2005) 40 EHRR 189, para 82; *Dudgeon v United Kingdom* (1982) 4 EHRR 149, para 52.

[74] *Evans v United Kingdom* (2008) 46 EHRR 34, para 77.

[75] *Chahal v United Kingdom* (1996) 23 EHRR 413, para 96.

[76] See eg *CG v Bulgaria* (2008) 47 EHRR 1117, para 43; *Depalle v France* (2012) 54 EHRR 17, para 84; *Lawless v Ireland* (1961) 1 EHRR 15, paras 39–47; *Klass v Germany* (1979) 2 EHRR 214, paras 42–43; *Brannigan and McBride v United Kingdom* (1993) 17 EHRR 539, paras 40–43; *James v United Kingdom* (1986) 8 EHRR 123, para 46.

[77] See eg *Animal Defenders International v United Kingdom* (2013) 57 EHRR 21, para 108; *Shindler v United Kingdom* (2013) 58 EHRR 5, paras 112, 115–17; *SAS v France* (2015) 60 EHRR 255, para 154ff; *Hirst v United Kingdom (No 2)* (2006) 42 EHRR 41, paras 78–80; *Sukhovetskyy v Ukraine* (2007) 44 EHRR 1185, para 65. See also Matthew Saul, "The European Court of Human Rights' Margin of Appreciation and the Processes of National Parliaments" (2015) 15 Human Rights Law Review 745, 746; Thomas Kleinlein, "The Procedural Approach of the European Court of Human Rights: Between Subsidiarity and Dynamic Evolution" (2019) 68 International and Comparative Law Quarterly 91, 93.

[78] Fahner, *Judicial Deference in International Adjudication* (n 2) 46 (arguing that "this development has obscured rather than clarified the [ECtHR's] approach").

specify the standard of review to be applied in respect of governmental measures that may aim to regulate issues such as access to water, public health, the protection of the environment and cultural heritage. The measures at issue often involve complex factual and legal determinations, and the immediate question arises as to whether arbitral tribunals have the capacity to review such measures and, if so, pursuant to which benchmarks. Some authors have sought to conceptualize investor-state arbitration as a form of "global administrative law" framework.[79] As prior recourse to domestic courts is usually not required, Schill has rightly pointed out that "investment treaty tribunals functionally assume the role of, and to a large extent replace, domestic courts in public law disputes."[80] In doing so, arbitral tribunals review the legality of the government's conduct both in law and in fact against the obligations subscribed by the state on an international level, and it is in that context that they need to balance their role as the first and last instance of potential relief for an investor with the need to accord sufficient leverage to government regulatory powers.

The importance of standards of review in this context is that they "determine how interventionist or deferential tribunals will be in assessing the actions and decisions of respondent States."[81] As explained by Schill, deference "can refer to the respect an arbitral tribunal pays to the determination of facts by a domestic agency or a domestic court, to the state's substantive policy choices, including the weight attributed to non-investment interests, and to the interpretation of law, both domestic and international, by the decision-making whose decision is under review."[82] As noted by the tribunal in *SD Myers v Canada*, investment treaty tribunals "d[o] not have an open-ended mandate to second-guess governmental decision-making" as governments have to make potentially controversial choices and the "ordinary remedy . . . for errors in modern governments is through internal political and legal processes, including elections."[83]

Investor-state tribunals have taken very different approaches to the degree of deference owed to domestic decision-makers. For instance, in cases such as *CMS v Argentina*, *BG v Argentina*, *Sempra v Argentina*, or *Enron v Argentina*, the tribunals accorded limited deference to Argentina in respect of whether its emergency

[79] See eg Gus van Harten and Martin Loughlin, "Investment Treaty Arbitration as a Species of Global Administrative Law" (2006) 17 European Journal of International Law 121. See also Santiago Montt, *State Liability in Investment Treaty Arbitration: Global Constitutional Law and Administrative Law in the BIT Generation* (Hart 2009).

[80] Stephan W Schill, "Deference in Investment Treaty Arbitration: Re-Conceptualizing the Standard of Review" (2012) 3 Journal of International Dispute Settlement 577, 588. See also WW Burke-White and A von Staden, "Private Litigation in a Public Law Sphere: The Standard of Review in Investor-State Arbitrations" (2010) 35 Yale Journal of International Law 283, 287 (arguing that the investment arbitration regime has transitioned into a form of public law litigation, in which foreign investors regularly challenge host states' fundamental regulatory policy).

[81] Roberts, "The Next Battleground" (n 5) 172.

[82] Schill, "Deference in Investment Treaty Arbitration" (n 80) 582.

[83] *SD Myers Inc v Canada* UNCITRAL (Partial Award) (13 November 2000) [261].

legislation constituted the "only way" to react to its economic and financial crisis under the necessity clause in the respective treaties.[84] Other tribunals, such as *LG&E v Argentina*, *Continental Casualty v Argentina*, or *Total v Argentina* appeared to show more deference to the respondent, considering that its regulatory measures were one of several possible permissible responses in the circumstances and were justified as a matter of necessity.[85]

Tribunals also appear to have applied different standards of review, depending on the specific substantive obligation that is claimed to have been breached. For instance, in *Tecmed v Mexico*, the tribunal, in determining whether a regulatory act constituted an indirect expropriation, held that it could examine whether the measures in question were "reasonable with respect to their goals."[86] By comparison, the *SD Myers v Canada* tribunal ruled, in respect of the standard of fair and equitable treatment, that the determination of whether such standard has been breached "must be made in the light of the *high measure of deference* that international law generally extends to the right of domestic authorities to regulate matters within their own borders."[87] What is more, the applicable standard of review may fluctuate even in the context of the same obligation. Thus, for instance, on *Chevron v Ecuador*, the tribunal acknowledged that two different standards of review could apply to different aspects of a claim based on a denial of justice.[88]

One area where investor-state tribunals appear to have been more consistent is in determining whether host State measures are scientifically or technically well-founded. In this context, arbitral tribunals have generally avoided substituting their "own judgment of underlying factual material ... for that of a qualified agency."[89]

[84] *CMS Gas Transmission Co v Argentina* ICSID Case No ARB/01/8 (Award) (12 May 2005) [304]–[394]; *BG Group plc v Argentina* UNCITRAL (Award) (24 December 2007 [381]–[387], [407]–[412] (subsequently set aside by a court in the United States); *Sempra Energy International v Argentina* ICSID Case No ARB/02/16 (Award) (28 September 2007) [325]–[397] (subsequently annulled); *Enron Corp and Ponderosa Assets LP v Argentina* ICSID Case No ARB/01/3 (Award) (22 May 2007) [288]–[345] (subsequently annulled).

[85] See eg *LG&E Energy Corp v Argentina* ICSID Case No ARB/02/1 (Decision on Liability) (3 October 2006) [201]–[236]; *Continental Casualty Co v Argentina* ICSID Case No ARB/03/9 (Award) (5 September 2008) [160]–[236]; *Total SA v Argentina* ICSID Case No ARB/04/1 (Decision on Liability) (27 December 2010) [135]–[184], [219]–[231]. Cf José Alvarez, "The Public International Law Regime Governing International Investment" (2011) 344 Recueil des cours 197, 454 ("[i]ronically, the decision that arguably interferes the most with the sovereign right to regulate is the one that on the surface appears to be the most deferential to it, namely *Continental Casualty*").

[86] *Técnicas Medioambientales Tecmed SA v Mexico* ICSID Case No ARB(AF)/00/2 (Award) (29 May 2003) [122].

[87] *SD Myers Inc v Canada* UNCITRAL (Partial Award) (13 November 2000) [263] (emphasis added). See also *Saluka Investments BV (The Netherlands) v Czech Republic* UNCITRAL (Partial Award) (17 March 2006) [304]ff; *Joseph Charles Lemire v Ukraine* ICSID Case No ARB/06/18 (Decision on Jurisdiction and Liability) (14 January 2010) [505]; *Gemplus SA, SLP SA, Gemplus Industrial SA de CV and Talsud SA v Mexico* ICSID Case Nos ARB(AF)/04/3 and ARB(AF)/04/4 (Award) (16 June 2010) [6]–[26]; *Marion Unglaube and Reinhard Unglaube v Costa Rica* ICSID Case Nos ARB/08/1 and ARB/09/20 (Award) (16 May 2012) [246]–[247], [258].

[88] *Chevron Corp and Texaco Petroleum Co v Ecuador* UNCITRAL PCA Case No 34877 (Partial Award on the Merits) (30 March 2010) [379].

[89] *Glamis Gold v United States* UNCITRAL (Award) (8 June 2009) [779].

Instead, they have focused on the process followed by domestic regulators.[90] For instance, in *Crystallex v Venezuela*, the tribunal noted that governmental authorities making technical decisions should enjoy a high level of deference because of their expertise and competence. As a result, the tribunal refrained from making findings as to whether or not the concerns expressed by the government had been adequately addressed by the claimant, or whether the reasons put forward by the respondent when denying the permit were substantively valid. Instead, the tribunal focused on whether there had been serious procedural flaws which have resulted in the permit being arbitrarily denied, or in the investor being treated non-transparently or inconsistently throughout the process.[91]

In recent years, a question that has gained some momentum in the practice and scholarship is whether the doctrine of the margin of appreciation should be transposed to other areas of international law, in particular whether it could bring some discipline to the determination of the appropriate degree of deference owed to domestic competent authorities in international economic law.[92] A few arbitral tribunals, including most recently in *Philip Morris v Uruguay*, have applied this doctrine in international investment context.[93] Of course, as noted by another tribunal, state's "margin of appreciation cannot be unlimited: otherwise there would be nothing to arbitrate and the Respondent's decisions would be unchallengeable; 'discretionary' cannot be equated with 'arbitrary'; margin of appreciation is different from unfettered discretion."[94] There are, however, several key differences between the ECHR and the substantive provisions typically found in investment treaties, which make the adoption of this doctrine in the latter context a dubious exercise. First, subsidiarity is embedded in the ECHR which has been incrementally interpreted by a standing court, which is not the case of the investment law dispute settlement system. Second, the subject matter of disputes under the ECHR

[90] Joshua Paine, "Standard of Review (Investment Arbitration)" in Hélène Ruiz Fabri (ed), *Max Planck Encyclopedia of International Procedural Law* (OUP 2019) 11; Yuka Fukunaga, "Standard of Review and 'Scientific Truths' in the WTO Dispute Settlement System and Investment Arbitration" (2012) 3 Journal of International Dispute Settlement 559, 573.

[91] *Crystallex International Corp v Venezuela* ICSID Case No ARB (AF)/11/2 (Award) (4 April 2016) [583]–[585].

[92] Yuka Fukunaga, "Margin of Appreciation as an Indicator of Judicial Deference: Is It Applicable to Investment Arbitration?" (2019) 10 Journal of International Dispute Settlement 69; Shany, "Toward a General Margin of Appreciation Doctrine in International Law?" (n 4); Jeanrique Fahner, "The Margin of Appreciation in Investor-State Arbitration: The Prevalence and Desirability of Discretion and Deference" in Nikos Lavranos and Ruth Kok (eds), *Hague Yearbook of International Law 2013* (Brill 2014); Arato, "The Margin of Appreciation in International Investment Law" (n 66); WW Burke-White and A von Staden, "The Need for Public Law Standards of Review in Investor-State Arbitrations" in SW Schill (ed), *International Investment Law and Comparative Public Law* (OUP 2010) 717–20.

[93] See eg *Philip Morris Brands Sarl v Uruguay* ICSID Case No ARB/10/7 (Award) (8 July 2016) [388], [399]; *Continental Casualty Co v Argentina* ICSID Case No ARB/03/9 (Award) (5 September 2008) [181]; *Micula v Romania* ICSID Case No ARB/05/20 (Decision on Jurisdiction and Admissibility) (24 September 2008) [94].

[94] *RREEF Infrastructure (GP) Ltd and RREEF Pan-European Infrastructure Two Lux Sarl v Spain* ICSID Case No ARB/13/30 (Decision on Responsibility and on the Principles of Quantum) (30 November 2018) [468].

is fundamentally different from investment law disputes, as the former often involve the appreciation of evolving morals or the level of consensus among member states, fundamental civil and political rights, religious and other freedoms, etc. Thus, the majority of authors appear to agree that the doctrine of the margin of appreciation is an "empty proxy for any real analysis" of how to determine the appropriate level of deference, and provides no certainty as to which standard of review to adopt, contrary for instance to review for good faith, reasonableness, least restrictive measures, and proportionality.[95]

In sum, investor-state arbitral tribunals have adopted a great variety of standards of review, which shows the difficulties in "the distribution of powers that must inevitably exist between those tribunals and the national bodies under [their] control."[96] As rightly pointed out by Schill, this approach not only compromises "the predictability in decision-making of arbitral tribunals but indicates a more general insecurity as to the conceptual foundations of deference and the appropriate standard of review to be applied in investment treaty arbitration." It may be difficult then, if not impossible, to adopt a uniform standard of review, taking into account the diversity of situations and international obligations that were at issue in these cases.[97] However, tribunals should be conscious of the subject matter of the decisions they review, and the public nature of many disputes brought before them, which should call for them to allow states a sufficient margin to determine and implement various policy goals.[98] Such increasing awareness when selecting the appropriate standard of review is likely to contribute to mitigating the ongoing legitimacy crisis in the investment treaty system, by better "calibrating the balance of governance powers between States and tribunals."[99]

3. Criteria That Appear to Inform the Selection of the Standard of Review

The above review of how international courts and tribunals approach standards of review shows that there are significant differences not only in distinct areas of law, but also within a particular area of law, and often even within the same dispute settlement system and in respect of similar obligations or fact patterns. Of course, it is not surprising that international law, a horizontal and an inherently

[95] Arato, "The Margin of Appreciation in International Investment Law" (n 66) 558; Born, Morris, and Forrest, "A Margin of Appreciation" (n 66).

[96] Montt, *State Liability in Investment Treaty Arbitration* (n 79) 15.

[97] Valentina Vadi, *Proportionality, Reasonableness and Standards of Review in International Investment Law and Arbitration* (Elgar 2018) 195 (arguing that it would be difficult and perhaps ultimately undesirable to attempt devising a unified standard of review to be applied in investor-state arbitration).

[98] Roberts, "The Next Battleground" (n 5) 173.

[99] ibid.

heterogeneous system, has failed to achieve some degree of consistency in this area. Nor is it necessarily a problem that there is a variety of standards, depending on a specific field of international law or different sets of institutional constraints that one or the other dispute settlement mechanism may face when adopting a particular standard of review. The experience of domestic legal systems shows that the adoption of different standards of review in administrative law does not necessarily undermine legal certainty. Rather, it is the lack of reasoned and justified explanation for the selection of a particular standard of review that may have serious normative repercussions on the international dispute settlement system.

For the international dispute settlement system to thrive, the reasoning underlying the selection of an appropriate standard of review should be clear and consistent. Instead, we appear to be facing a "broader problem of legal certainty arising out of fragmented approaches to the standard of review."[100] Without such clarity and consistency, there is a risk that an adjudicator may either undermine the effectiveness of its function or undermine the legitimacy of its decisions, or worse the very object and purpose of a given rule and continuing compliance with that rule in the future. When we speak of legitimacy in this context, it is not limited to the legitimacy of a given decision, a court or tribunal, but the system of international dispute settlement as a whole. This is particularly visible in the context of investor-state arbitration, where the growing number of arbitral awards finding against states has generated a backlash, founded on the perception that unelected arbitrators are interfering too much with the sovereign regulatory space of states and in particular on sensitive issues such as public health or the environment.[101] It is not difficult to analogize certain of these critiques to other international dispute settlement bodies as well. Of course, too much intrusiveness does not automatically cast doubt on the legitimacy of the adjudicators, so long as there is consistency in the standards applied. Thus, the clarification of the rules to be applied when selecting the standard of review is at the core of any future resolution of this tension, regardless of whether the investor-state dispute settlement system will retain its ad hoc character or whether it will go through significant institutional reforms.[102]

This section seeks to outline criteria that may assist a court or tribunal in selecting a standard of review which, if applied, could mitigate some of the concerns noted above. These criteria can be classified in two categories, those featuring at the macro or systemic level, and those at the micro or operational level.

[100] Arato, "The Margin of Appreciation in International Investment Law" (n 66) 553.

[101] Roberts, "The Next Battleground" (n 5) 173 (arguing that "the failure of some arbitral tribunals to recognize the public nature of investment treaty arbitration, and to allow States a sufficient margin to determine and implement various policy goals, has contributed to the legitimacy crisis in which the investment treaty system currently finds itself").

[102] Burke-White and von Staden, "Private Litigation in a Public Law Sphere" (n 80) 283–346. See also Schill, "Deference in Investment Treaty Arbitration" (n 80); Caroline Henckels, "The Role of the Standard of Review and the Importance of Deference in Investor-State Arbitration" in Lukasz Gruszczynski and Wouter G Werner (eds), *Deference in International Courts and Tribunals* (OUP 2014).

3.1 Systemic Criteria

At the systemic level, there appear to be three primary criteria that may inform the selection of the standard of review. These criteria resemble those employed in many domestic legal systems.[103]

First, the regulatory autonomy and proximity of national authorities warrant, in principle, the selection of a more deferential standard of review. This is so because national authorities are, in general, better placed to "discern and evaluate local conditions, as they are usually more closely acquainted with local issues, sensitivities and traditions."[104] In showing a degree of deference to any domestic determinations that involve objectives of public interest, international courts and tribunals are likely to avoid any direct normative clash that would risk unduly encroaching upon states' regulatory autonomy in areas of key importance to their constituencies. As the various cases analyzed above demonstrate, the adoption of more deferential standards of review such as good faith or reasonableness does not necessarily entail the finding that the State did not incur responsibility for applying the relevant measure.[105]

Second, the greater knowledge of local circumstances of domestic decision-makers militates, in principle, in favor of greater degree of deference and thus the adoption of a less intrusive standard of review, along the lines of good faith, reasonableness, or rational basis review.[106] The greater expertise of domestic decision-makers may be related to the resources available to them and arguably their greater legitimacy and accountability in relation to the type of decision being made.[107] Burke-White and von Staden argue, for example, that investment tribunals should exercise deference because arbitrators rarely have public law expertise, lack any such institutional capacity, and are not embedded within the national environment in which these decisions are made.[108] In this context, Fahner proposes

[103] Vadi, *Proportionality, Reasonableness and Standards of Review in International Investment Law and Arbitration* (n 97) 186–87 (suggesting that the following aspects determine the selection of the standard of review: self-determination, subsidiarity, and judicial economy). See also Lukasz Gruszczynski and Wouter G Werner, "Introduction" in Lukasz Gruszczynski and Wouter G Werner (eds), *Deference in International Courts and Tribunals* (OUP 2014) 2 (speaking of the separation of powers, the epistemic superiority, and judicial economy).

[104] Caroline Henckels, "Balancing Investment Protection and the Public Interest: The Role of the Standard of Review and the Importance of Deference in Investor-State Arbitration" (2013) 4 Journal of International Dispute Settlement 197, 205; Shany, "Toward a General Margin of Appreciation Doctrine in International Law?" (n 4) 919; George Letsas, *A Theory of Interpretation of the European Convention on Human Rights* (OUP 2007) 80–84.

[105] See similarly Roberts, "The Next Battleground" (n 5) 172.

[106] Henckels, "Balancing Investment Protection and the Public Interest" (n 104) 205–13.

[107] Paine, "Standard of Review (Investment Arbitration)" (n 90) 6–11; Anna T Katselas, "A Comparative Analysis of the US Administrative Procedure Act's Arbitrary and Capricious Standard of Review and the Fair and Equitable Treatment and Arbitrary or Discriminatory Measures Treaty Standards" (2012) 34 Michigan Journal of International Law 87, 142ff; Andrew T Guzman, "Determining the Appropriate Standard of Review in WTO Disputes" (2009) 42 Cornell International Law Journal 45, 54.

[108] Burke-White and von Staden, "Private Litigation in a Public Law Sphere" (n 80) 329–33.

to "distinguish between epistemic deference, based on the superior capacity of domestic-makers to make factual and technical assessments, and constitutional deference, based on the democratic legitimacy of domestic decision-making."[109] Of course, where domestic authorities, despite their superior competence and expertise, have not fully addressed the relevant issues underlying the adoption of a given measure or decision, courts and tribunals should not shy away from undertaking a more intrusive scrutiny of decision-making process.[110]

Third, the greater the institutional integration of a dispute settlement system in a given sphere of activity, the greater the proclivity of an adjudicator to opt for a more intrusive standard of review. For example, the conception of a standard of review in the WTO system is naturally more sophisticated than that in an investor-state arbitration, which lacks the same level of institutional integration as the WTO. A predisposition on the part of ad hoc tribunals to afford deference to states in the performance of some of their obligations may also send a positive signal for the trust and confidence of states in international dispute settlement process and facilitate the enforcement of that decision.[111] For example, in the WTO context, panels exercise greater scrutiny over certain science-based determinations conducted by member states when compared to similar determinations being made by an *ad hoc* investor-state arbitral tribunal.

3.2 Operational Criteria

At the operational level, two criteria may inform the selection of the standard of review by an international court or tribunal. First, the nature of the underlying obligation is of paramount importance. Shany, for example, has identified three categories of norms, which may prompt the selection of a more deferential standard of review. These are: (1) standard-type norms (eg necessity, proportionality); (2) discretionary norms (eg national security exceptions); and (3) result-oriented norms (eg those obligations that require a particular result but leave the choice of means to implement it to the state).[112] As demonstrated in section 2, the question of the standard of review often arises in the context of rules with flexible or normatively less determinate content, essential security interests or self-judging clauses. In such cases, depending on the terms of the obligation at issue, as well as its context and object and purpose of the treaty regime in which it is set out, international courts and tribunals may opt for a more deferential standard of review, such as for instance good faith review. The actual expression of that standard

[109] Fahner, *Judicial Deference in International Adjudication* (n 2) 22.
[110] Schill, "Deference in Investment Treaty Arbitration" (n 80) 603; Fukunaga, "Standard of Review" (n 90) 576; Henckels, "Balancing Investment Protection and the Public Interest" (n 106) 212.
[111] See Shany, "Toward a General Margin of Appreciation Doctrine in International Law?" (n 4) 922.
[112] ibid 912–18.

may entail verifying whether the measure was applied in a non-arbitrary and non-discriminatory manner. In this context, the adoption of a more deferential standard of review would bolster the proper separation of powers and competencies between States and international courts and tribunals.

Second, the selection of the standard of review is determined by the nature of the decision under consideration. International courts and tribunals will frequently consider whether the underlying decision is one relating to the factual, legal, or technical/scientific assessment undertaken by the domestic authorities. For instance, the ECtHR has often faced the dilemma of whether the threats to public safety or order posed by a certain security challenge amounted to a "public emergency threatening the life of the nation," which could justify a derogation from the ECHR pursuant to its article 15. In the ECtHR's view, this is a fact-based risk-assessment and the ECtHR itself has consistently recognized a broad margin of appreciation to the domestic authorities in making such factual determinations by reason of their proximity to local conditions and their superior fact-finding capacity.[113] On the other hand, legal determinations made by domestic authorities are more open to an intrusive or *de novo* review by international courts and tribunals, as can be seen from the practice of the WTO panels and the Appellate Body. Finally, in terms of scientific or technical determinations, international courts and tribunals tend to avoid second-guessing domestic authorities, even if they review the objective character and coherence of any scientific information on the basis of which risk assessment had been conducted.

4. Conclusion

The basic notion that states enjoy "a wide measure of discretion which is only limited in certain cases by prohibitive rules"[114] has progressively given way to a much more complex international legal order, in which courts and tribunals play an important role in the oversight of states' decisions and their compliance with international obligations. The ever-increasing activity of international dispute settlement mechanisms has limited, but has certainly not done away with, the discretion that states enjoy in many spheres of national and transnational activity. Over the years, we have witnessed the application of a wide variety of standards of review by international courts and tribunals to decisions and measures taken by domestic decision-makers, many of which touch upon fundamental aspects of the regulatory space of sovereign states and the needs of their constituencies. On the one hand, the multiplication of standards of review thus employed by international courts and tribunals may be regarded as a product of the expansion of the

[113] *A v United Kingdom* (2009) 49 EHRR 29, para 173.
[114] *The Case of the SS "Lotus"* (Judgment) 1927 PCIJ Series A no 10 at 19 (7 September 1927).

international legal system. On the other hand, the effect of this multiplication "is a state of general uncertainty as to what the standard of review might be from one case to the next."[115] That uncertainty is not only apparent when comparing different dispute settlement mechanisms, but it is also visible with the confines of a single system of dispute settlement.

Unless there is clarity and consistency in the approach of international courts and tribunals in respect of standards of review, there is a risk that it could undermine the legitimacy of adjudicators and the balance that has been struck between their functions and the prerogatives of sovereign states, particularly in sensitive matters, such as national security, public health, or the environment that may affect the constituencies of different states in different ways, depending on a set of complex economic, development, and social considerations. As the standard of review may have a decisive impact on the outcome of a given dispute, courts and tribunals should fully explain and justify their selection. This chapter has identified certain systemic and operational criteria that appear to inform the selection of the relevant standard of review by dispute settlement mechanisms.

[115] Arato, "The Margin of Appreciation in International Investment Law" (n 66) 556.

4

Saving Regulatory Space for States through the Standard of Review

A Case Study of Tobacco Control-Related International Disputes

*Lukasz Gruszczynski**

1. Introduction

International economic law (IEL) is perceived by some scholars as imposing excessive constraints on the regulatory freedom enjoyed by states.[1] For example, it is argued that IEL rules may force countries to abandon, or refrain from implementing, certain societally important policies if they collide—actually or potentially—with the free trade principles or legal protections provided to foreign investors. According to this view, IEL is seen as an expression of the hegemonic neoliberal international order that currently organizes the economic relationships among states.

This chapter looks at the latest case law of World Trade Organization (WTO) Panels and the Appellate Body, investment tribunals, and the Court of Justice of the European Union (the Court or CJEU) relating to tobacco control measures. In this context, the chapter analyzes the standard of review used by dispute settlement bodies (DSB) in the field of IEL when dealing with complex factual determinations that form the basis for national regulatory measures. Such a narrow focus is justified for three reasons. First, disputes over tobacco control measures are at the heart of the debate over the proper relationship between IEL and the regulatory autonomy of states (ie promotion of economic interests versus protection of public health), and allows for testing the wider claims of excessive constraints imposed by those rules. Second, they are relatively frequent, thus providing necessary normative material for the legal analysis. Third, these disputes are also decided in different international fora, which in turn allows for comparison of applied methodologies in various adjudication processes.

* This research has been financed by the National Science Centre (Poland) pursuant to Grant No UMO-2018/31/B/HS5/03556.

[1] For a more detailed review of the relevant literature, see section 2 of this chapter.

Lukasz Gruszczynski, *Saving Regulatory Space for States through the Standard of Review* In: *Secondary Rules of Primary Importance in International Law.* Edited by: Gábor Kajtár, Başak Çalı, and Marko Milanovic, Oxford University Press.
 DOI: 10.1093/oso/9780192869012.003.0004

This chapter argues that IEL DSBs apply a relatively deferential standard of review when analyzing national tobacco control regulations.[2] While the approaches taken by different IEL DSBs are not identical, all of them appear to aim at guaranteeing a considerable margin of discretion to national regulators, thus promoting unity in the IEL field and reinforcing the legitimacy of their decisions. This also means that the DSBs have actually preserved, in the analyzed category of cases, rather than undermined, the regulatory space available to states. Interestingly, this result has been achieved not so much through reinterpretation of relevant treaty provisions but through the application of a specific category of the secondary rules of international law pertaining to the intensity of the judicial review.

Before going into details, it is worth defining the central concept of this chapter. Standard of review is understood here as "the degree of deference or discretion that the court accords to legislator or regulator"[3] with respect to questions of facts, of law, or mixed questions of facts and law. Standard of review as such does not call for any specific level of deference, it is simply a neutral framework that can be used to measure and describe the intensity of the review applied by a reviewing body. Such review may fall somewhere between two extremes—full deference and *de novo*. Under the first one, a court/tribunal is barred from reviewing the substance of a contested decision/action except in extreme cases of unreasonableness. This means that procedural aspects play a particularly important role in the deferential forms of review (eg "Have specific designated procedures been followed?" "Have all stakeholders participated in the process?" "Has all available evidence been considered?"). On the other hand, under a *de novo* review, the reviewing body examines the merits of a contested decision/action, reassesses available evidence, and may substitute prior factual (legal or mixed) determinations with its own.[4]

This chapter proceeds as follows: Part II briefly describes the tension between international trade and investment obligations and the regulatory activities of states. Against this background, Part III looks at the recent tobacco control-related disputes and analyzes how various IEL DSBs have used the mechanism of standard of review to strike a balance between IEL obligations and the sovereign prerogatives of states in the area of public health protection. Part IV offers conclusions.

[2] Describing the level of applied scrutiny as more or less deferential is a relational task and depends on one's perspective. The progressive scientization of dispute settlement processes result in a broader engagement of both the parties and DSBs with scientific evidence. In this sense the approach taken by the DSBs appears to be more intrusive than in the international disputes of the past. At the same time, however, IEL DSBs (at least in the tobacco-related disputes) greatly defer to the scientific findings relied on by regulators. If one compares such approaches with the hard look doctrine of the US Supreme Court, they clearly can be labeled as deferential. See, in this context, Chapter 5.

[3] Jan Bohanes and Nicolas Lockhart, "Standard of Review in WTO Law" in Daniel Bethlehem and others (eds), *The Oxford Handbook of International Trade Law* (OUP 2009) 379. For a general introduction to the subject, see Lukasz Gruszczynski and Wouter Werner (eds), *Deference in International Courts and Tribunals: Standard of Review and Margin of Appreciation* (OUP 2014) 1–15.

[4] Stefan Schill, "Deference in Investment Treaty Arbitration: Re-conceptualizing the Standard of Review" (2012) 3(3) Journal of International Dispute Settlement 577.

2. IEL Rules and Domestic Regulatory Space

States, as sovereign entities, enjoy a very broad, but not unlimited, authority over their internal affairs. This means that they possess, at least in theory, powers to govern themselves, free from external interferences. The power to regulate forms an important part of this authority. At the same time, states' powers can be constrained by international rules. In particular, states can agree to comply with certain international obligations (eg included in treaties), thus restricting the extent of their regulatory freedom. In principle, these restrictions have a limited scope, which is determined by the consent of states, as reflected in the language of the relevant treaty or any other applicable source of international law.[5]

IEL is frequently identified in the literature as a branch of international law that is particularly intrusive when it comes to the exercise of domestic regulatory powers.[6] This should not come as a surprise—trade rules, which were first concerned with border restrictions, over time have shifted their focus to internal regulations that impact international trade (so-called "behind the border restrictions").[7] The same is true for the protection of investments and investors. While at the beginning protection against traditional forms of expropriation was a central issue, over time indirect forms (ie "regulatory expropriations") and defense of the "legitimate expectations" of investors within the fair and equitable treatment (FET) clause have become more important.[8] Consequently, a great array of national regulations relating to various public policies—such as consumer, environmental, or public health protection—have gradually come under the purview of the IEL rules.

In the above context, some scholars argue that IEL, by its nature, is biased towards non-economic considerations and promotes a free trade agenda and the interests of foreign investors at the expense of other socially important values.[9] According to them, the structural bias is reflected in the substance of the relevant IEL provisions (ie pro-trade and pro-investment), while the flexibilities provided

[5] See Samantha Besson, "Sovereignty" in *Max Planck Encyclopaedia of Public International Law* (OUP 2011). Of course, not all restrictions can be derived from the states' consent (expressed either in a direct or indirect form). In particular, peremptory norms have an independent status and cannot be derogated by states.

[6] In the more recent literature, see generally Gillian Moon and Lisa Toohey (eds), *The Future of International Economic Integration: The Embedded Liberalism Compromise Revisited* (CUP 2018); Andrew Mitchell, Elizabeth Sheargold, and Tania Voon (eds), *Regulatory Autonomy in International Economic Law: The Evolution of Australian Policy on Trade and Investment* (Edward Elgar 2017); Bradly J Condon, "Treaty Structure and Public Interest Regulation in International Economic Law" (2014) 17(2) Journal International Economic Law 333.

[7] See eg Robert W Steiger, "Non-Tariff Measures and the WTO" (WTO Staff Working Paper ERSD-2012-01).

[8] See eg Andrew Newcombe, "The Boundaries of Regulatory Expropriation in International Law" (2005) 20(1) ICSID Review: Foreign Investment Law Journal 1.

[9] See eg Martin Kohr, "Rethinking Liberalization and Reforming the WTO" in Jane Kelsey, *International Economic Regulation* (Routledge 2017); Ellen Shaffer and others, "International Trade Agreements: A Threat to Tobacco Control Policy" (2005) 14 Tobacco Control ii19.

in the form of exceptions have been construed by IEL DSBs too narrowly to guarantee the necessary freedom for states to pursue various domestic policies.[10] Equally problematic is the institutional architecture behind IEL rules (eg access to dispute settlement mechanisms only for investors) and the profiles of individuals managing the system (eg IEL experts who are embedded in a specific type of institutional culture and may place a greater value upon economic rather than other interests).[11] More recent literature, while admitting that IEL rules do not necessarily prevent states from pursuing legitimate policies, also highlights that those rules can still be problematic because they can produce a regulatory "chilling effect."[12] In other words, states may choose not to enact certain regulatory measures due to a fear that proposed regulations would conflict with their international trade and investment obligations. The costs of potential IEL proceedings may also be a factor here as they are prohibitively high for many smaller and less developed nations.[13]

The above arguments are often raised in the context of public health protection and, in particular, tobacco control policies. A number of scholars argue that IEL rules may prevent countries in certain situations from implementing effective and comprehensive tobacco control measures.[14] In addition to the arguments referred to above, it is also submitted that the regulatory chilling effect may be strengthened by an aggressive litigation strategy on the part of the multinational tobacco companies,[15] and the fact that the potential uncertainties are higher in this specific regulatory field because innovation and experimentation in the field of tobacco control is essential for developing effective policies.[16] While some of the these

[10] See eg Ben Baumberg and Peter Andreson, "Trade and Health: How World Trade Organization (WTO) Law Affects Alcohol and Public Health" (2008) 103(12) Addiction 1952; Donald W Ziegler, "International Trade Agreements Challenge Tobacco and Alcohol Control Policies" (2006) 25(6) Drug and Alcohol Review 567.

[11] See eg Matthew Rimmer, "Plain Packaging for the Pacific Rim: Tobacco Control and the Trans-Pacific Partnership" in Tania Voon (ed), *Trade Liberalisation and International Co-operation: A Legal Analysis of the Trans-Pacific Partnership Agreement* (Edward Elgar 2013); Jonathan Liberman and Andrew Mitchell, "In Search of Coherence Between Trade and Health: Inter-Institutional Opportunities" (2010) 25 Maryland Journal of International Law 143.

[12] See eg Kyla Tienhaara, "Regulatory Chill in a Warming World: The Threat to Climate Policy Posed by Investor-State Dispute Settlement" (2018) 7(2) Transnational Environmental Law 229; Lukasz Gruszczynski, "Australia Plain Packaging Law, International Litigations and Regulatory Chilling Effect" (2014) 5(2) European Journal of Risk Regulation 160.

[13] Kyla Tienhaara, "Regulatory Chill and the Threat of Arbitration: A View from Political Science" in Chester Brown and Kate Miles (eds), *Evolution in Investment Treaty Law and Arbitration* (CUP 2011) 627.

[14] Robert Wiessman, *International Trade Agreements and Tobacco Control: Threats to Public Health and the Case for Excluding Tobacco from Trade Agreements* (Essential Action 2003).

[15] Eric Crosbie and George Thomson, "Regulatory Chills: Tobacco Industry Legal Threats and the Politics of Tobacco Standardised Packaging in New Zealand" (2018) 131(1473) New Zealand Medical Journal 25.

[16] Cynthia Callard, Hatai Chitanondh, and Robert Weissman, "Why Trade and Investment Liberalization May Threaten Effective Tobacco Control Efforts" (2001) 10 Tobacco Control 68.

concerns are arguably overstated,[17] there seems to be a broad consensus that IEL may indeed pose certain challenges for those countries, particularly less developed ones, that decide to adopt ambitious tobacco control measures, notably because of its regulatory chilling effect.[18]

3. Using the Standard of Review to Preserve Regulatory Space for States

IEL DSBs use different strategies to reaffirm the regulatory freedom of states in the area of tobacco control.[19] In particular, they explicitly refer to states' sovereign right to regulate in this policy space (which may be relevant in the context of various balancing tests performed by DSBs). Second, courts and tribunals interpret and apply the IEL rules in a manner that is sympathetic to public health considerations, for example, by extending the scope of relevant exceptions or nuancing some of the obligations. Third, DSBs also use the Framework Convention on Tobacco Control (FCTC)[20]—a major treaty in the field of tobacco control—as a point of reference for the determination of certain factual issues that are relevant to a given dispute, which in turn helps in establishing that a particular measure is necessary or based on sufficient scientific evidence. Fourth, IEL DSBs also highlight the limited scope of their review in examining complex health-related measures and adopt a relatively deferential approach in their assessment. This means that DSBs tend to defer to the factual determinations (predominantly of scientific character) made at the national level by a defendant/host state that form the basis for a contested measure, assessing their rationality, but not their correctness. The subsequent three parts of this section (3.1—3.3) will analyze this aspect in more detail.

Of course, the strategies outlined above are not fully disjunctive as there are certain overlaps between them. For example, a deferential standard can be strengthened by reliance on the FCTC, or justified through reference to state sovereignty. Similarly, when performing one of the balancing tests (eg under the proportionality requirements), a deferential standard of review may be as important as reference to the FCTC. Nevertheless, for conceptual clarity, it is still useful to distinguish all four strategies.

[17] cf Jeffrey Drope and Raphael Lencucha, "Tobacco Control and Trade Policy: Proactive Strategies For Integrating Policy Norms" (2013) 34(1) Journal of Public Health Policy 153; Libermann and Mitchell, "In Search of Coherence Between Trade and Health" (n 11).

[18] Holly Jarman, *The Politics of Trade and Tobacco Control* (Palgrave Macmillan 2015) 22–23.

[19] See Lukasz Gruszczynski, "The Role of IEL Dispute Settlement Bodies in Reinforcing the Sovereign Rights of the States in the Field of Tobacco Control" in Marie EC Gispen and Brigit Toebes (eds), *Human Rights and Tobacco Control* (Edward Elgar 2020).

[20] Framework Convention on Tobacco Control (opened for signature 16 June 2003, entered into force 27 February 2005) 2302 UNTS 166 (FCTC).

3.1 International Investment Arbitration Practice and Tobacco Control Measures

Probably the clearest example of a deferential approach can be found in *Philip Morris v Uruguay*.[21] The complaint filed by Phillip Morris subsidiaries related to two regulatory measures enacted by Uruguay: (1) the so-called single presentation requirement (SPR), which prohibited multiple variants of one cigarettes brand (the prohibition also covered use of the same design elements with a mere change of colors); and (2) the new health warnings requirements for tobacco products, which increased their size from 50% to 80% of the surface of a package. The objective of the first measure was to prevent consumers from being misled into believing that some variants of tobacco products were associated with less harm (ie "eliminating the ability of tobacco companies to use color contrast within a brand family to promote the misimpression that there are differences in healthiness"[22]). The second one was aimed at improving the overall visibility of health warnings. The complainant alleged, among other things, that these two measures violated various provisions of the bilateral investment treaty (BIT) between Switzerland and Uruguay,[23] in particular the expropriation and FET clauses.

In the above context, it should be noted that the SPR was of an experimental character, as Uruguay was the first country to introduce such a measure. The SPR is neither contemplated by the FCTC nor contained in its guidelines. The Convention only provides a general obligation to prevent the packaging of tobacco products from creating a "false impression that a particular tobacco product is less harmful than other tobacco products" (article 11(1)(a) of the FCTC). On the other hand, health warnings on tobacco products were already common, but the size required by Uruguay went well above the average (although currently there are countries with even stricter rules[24]). The FCTC and its guidelines require health warnings of at least 30% of the principal display areas, but also recommend 50% or more as a preferable regulatory option.[25]

The investment tribunal highlighted in its analysis that due deference had to be granted to Uruguay and went so far as to recognize the doctrine of margin of appreciation[26] as relevant in the IEL field, at least as far as public health-related measures

[21] *Philip Morris Brands Sarl, Philip Morris Products SA and Abal Hermanos SA v Oriental Republic of Uruguay* ICSID Case No ARB/10/7 (Award) (8 July 2016) (*Philip Morris*).

[22] ibid [406].

[23] Agreement between the Swiss Confederation and the Oriental Republic of Uruguay on the Reciprocal Promotion and Protection of Investments (adopted 7 October 1988, entered into force 22 April 1991) 1976 UNTS 389.

[24] cf Canadian Cancer Society, *Cigarette Package Health Warnings: International Status Report* (7th edn, September 2021).

[25] See art 11(1)(b)(iv) of the FCTC and the guidelines for implementation of art 11 of the WHO FCTC (Packaging and Labelling of Tobacco Products) [12]–[13].

[26] On the distinction between standard of review and the margin of appreciation, see Gruszczynski and Werner (eds), *Deference in International Courts and Tribunals* (n 3) 2–5.

were concerned.[27] The tribunal justified taking the deferential approach by three reasons. First, deference was required in order to respect national sovereignty and the discretionary exercise of sovereign powers. Second, the need for deference was reinforced by the subject matter of the regulation (ie protection of public health), which is a particularly sensitive area.[28] Third, the tribunal also referred to the epistemic superiority of national regulators when confronted with situations that involve complex scientific and social considerations.[29] This general pronouncement was subsequently reflected in the nature of the examination undertaken by the tribunal in the context of the FET clause. The tribunal concentrated only on the overall rationality of the contested measures rather than their correctness. For example, the tribunal concluded that, despite the fact that the SPR had not been subject to any detailed research concerning its actual effects, it could be regarded as a legitimate measure. In this context, the tribunal explained that "it [was not] necessary to decide whether the SPR actually had the effects that were intended by the State, what matter[ed] being rather whether it was a 'reasonable' measure when it was adopted."[30] In order to establish reasonableness it was enough to show that the measure: (1) attempted to address a real public concern, (2) was not disproportionate, and (3) was adopted in good faith.[31] On that basis, and without any in-depth analysis, the tribunal concluded that the SPR did not violate the FET clause. This conclusion seems to rely, at least partially, on the testimonies of respondent's witnesses interrogated in the course of the proceeding, as well as the WHO amicus brief.[32]

A similar approach was taken when analyzing the increased size of the health warnings. The tribunal was interested in the reasonableness of the measure, which could be established by reference to general evidence (ie tobacco consumption had lethal effects), and without the need to show any actual causality between the size of health warnings and the behavior of smokers.[33] The tribunal again confirmed that "substantial deference [was] due in that regard to national authorities' decisions as to the measures which should [have been] taken to address an acknowledged and major public health problem."[34] It also added that "[t]he fair and equitable treatment standard is not a justiciable standard of good government."[35] In this specific context, this meant that "how a government require[d] the acknowledged health risks of products, such as tobacco, to be communicated to the persons at risk, [was] a matter of public policy, to be left to the appreciation of the regulatory authority."[36]

27 *Philip Morris* (n 21) [399].
28 ibid.
29 ibid [400] (referring to the *Chemtura v Canada* award).
30 ibid [409].
31 ibid.
32 ibid fns 585, 586.
33 ibid [417].
34 ibid [418].
35 ibid.
36 ibid [419].

Overall, the approach of the arbitration tribunal was very deferential, but as a matter of principle it was not unprecedented. A number of investment tribunals in the past have granted a considerable level of deference to governments regulating in the areas of public health and environmental protection. Such an approach has been justified, as with the *Philip Morris v Uruguay* case, by the epistemic reasons, the limited scope of international investment obligations, or the general regulatory freedom enjoyed by states as sovereign actors. For example, the tribunal in *SD Myers v Canada* noted that one had to recognize the "high measure of deference that international law generally extends to the right of domestic authorities to regulate matters within their own borders,"[37] and the assessment of the measure had to take into account the fact "that certain agencies manage highly specialized domains involving scientific and public policy determinations."[38] A similar approach was taken by tribunals in other cases.[39] All these tribunals saw the scope of their examination as primarily aimed at the detection of a manifest lack of reason.[40] Having said this, it also needs to be stressed that the investment arbitration case law is not fully consistent as some tribunals have engaged in a more intrusive review of national regulatory measures with varied levels of intensity.[41] For example, the *Tecmed* tribunal in the dispute concerning non-renewal of the license necessary to operate the waste landfill in Mexico, while recognizing a need for deference, also noted that this "does not prevent the Arbitral Tribunal . . . from examining . . . whether [regulatory] measures are reasonable with respect to their goals, the deprivation of economic rights and the legitimate expectations of who suffered such deprivation."[42] Such a formulation clearly invites a more intrusive review, including the assessment of relevant scientific evidence (eg relating to environmental impact of the waste landfill).

3.2 WTO Practice and Tobacco Control Measures

On its face a different approach has been adopted by the WTO panels, which have decided to look more closely at the science underlying the national regulatory measures. At the same time, more detailed examination of their reports reveals that

[37] *SD Myers Inc v Government of Canada* NAFTA/UNCITRAL (Partial Award) (13 November 2000) [263].

[38] ibid [123].

[39] See eg *Electrabel SA v Republic of Hungary* ICSID Case No ARB/07/19 (Decision on Jurisdiction, Applicability and Liability) (30 November 2012) [8.35]; *Saluka Investments BV (The Netherlands) v The Czech Republic* UNCITRAL (Partial Award) (17 March 2006) [272]–[273].

[40] *Glamis Gold v United States* NAFTA/UNCITRAL (Award) (8 June 2009) [805].

[41] See eg *Metalclad Corp v United Mexican States* ICSID Case No ARB(AF)/97/1 (Award) (30 August 2000); *Suez, Sociedad General de Aguas de Barcelona SA and Vivendi Universal SA Argentina and AWG v The Argentine Republic* ICSID Case No ARB/03/17 (Decision on Liability) (30 July 2010).

[42] *Tecnicas Medioambientales Tecmed SA v The United Mexican States* ICSID Case No ARB(AF)/00/2 (Award) (29 May 2003) [122].

deferential elements were strongly present in their analysis, albeit hidden behind the formal strict scrutiny.

The first dispute (*US—Clove Cigarettes*[43]) concerned the US measure that prohibited the manufacture and sale of cigarettes with characterizing flavors other than tobacco or menthol, with the aim of reducing the prevalence of smoking among children and adolescents. Indonesia, which was the major producer and exporter to the US of clove cigarettes, argued that the ban was incompatible with several provision of the Agreement on Technical Barriers to Trade (TBT Agreement),[44] in particular because it was discriminatory (ie menthol cigarettes, which were mainly of domestic origin, were exempted from the ban) and more trade restrictive than necessary to achieve the regulatory objective of the US. The panel did not explicitly address the problem of applicable standard of review. In one of the passages, it only noted that under the TBT Agreement deference was warranted for assessment of the policy objectives pursued by WTO Members, but not the means used to achieve those objectives.[45]

The above passage could be read as opening the door to a rather intrusive review of the evidence behind the US measure. In the subsequent analysis, however, the panel referred to the standard developed by the Appellate Body under the Agreement on the Application of Sanitary and Phytosanitary Measures (SPS Agreement),[46] which may be regarded as being quasi deferential. According to this standard, a panel must: (1) identify the scientific basis underlying a measure; (2) verify that the scientific basis comes from a respected and qualified source; (3) assess whether the reasoning articulated on the basis of the scientific evidence is objective and coherent; and (4) determine whether the results of the risk assessment sufficiently warrant the measure at issue.[47] Such a standard does not require a panel to determine whether the evidence is correct, but only whether it is supported by coherent reasoning and respectable scientific evidence. This shifts, at least in theory, the focus of the analysis from the substance of the evidence to formal and methodological aspects, and leaves WTO Members with a relatively broad degree of discretion as to how to assess scientific data and what kind of inferences to derive from them.[48]

[43] WTO Panel Report, *United States—Measures Affecting the Production and Sale of Clove Cigarettes*, WT/DS406/R (adopted 24 April 2012) (*US—Clove Cigarettes*).

[44] Agreement on Technical Barriers to Trade (15 April 1994), Marrakesh Agreement Establishing the World Trade Organization, Annex 1A, 1868 UNTS 120 (1994).

[45] *US—Clove Cigarettes* (n 43) [7.329].

[46] Agreement on the Application of Sanitary and Phytosanitary Measures (15 April 1994), Marrakesh Agreement Establishing the World Trade Organization, Annex 1A, 1867 UNTS 493 (1994) (SPS Agreement).

[47] *US—Clove Cigarettes* (n 43) fn 715 (the Panel referred to WTO Appellate Body Report, *United States—Continued Suspension of Obligations in the EC—Hormones Dispute*, WT/DS320/AB/R (adopted 14 November 2008)).

[48] See also Lukasz Gruszczynski, "Standard of Review of Health/Environmental Regulation by WTO Panels" in Geert Van Calster and Denise Prévost (eds), *Research Handbook on Environment, Health and the WTO* (Edward Elgar 2013).

The Panel, however, after pronouncing its methodological approach, did not actually follow it and simply referred to a number of articles and reports submitted by the US. In this context, it observed the "evidence before the Panel provides a solid basis for reaching a definite conclusion. The evidence ... squarely contradicts Indonesia's assertion that there is no scientific evidence to support the United States ban on clove cigarettes."[49] Although such an approach blurred the whole picture, it seemed understandable in this specific case, as the relevant aspect of the dispute (ie the contribution of the ban to the prevention of youth smoking) did not raise any special scientific controversies. This fact obviously made the task of the Panel much easier.

This was not a case for the more recent dispute (*Australia—Plain Packaging*[50]), which arose in the context of the Australian measure[51] that set strict restrictions on the color, size, and format of tobacco products' packaging and established the rules applicable to the appearance of brand, company, and variant names on packs. At the time of its adoption, Australia was the first country to introduce such a regulatory solution. Plain packaging is not mentioned in the FCTC as one of the available regulatory solutions and only appears in one of the Convention guidelines. The measure was eventually contested by several WTO Members, which claimed that it violated several provisions of the TBT Agreement and the Agreement on Trade-Related Aspects of Intellectual Property Rights (TRIPS Agreement).[52]

Regrettably, the panel remained silent on the applicable standard or review and only stated that its assessment should have been objective.[53] This obviously provides little guidance as to the required level of scrutiny, as both deferential and *de novo* review can be objective.[54] Throughout the report no reference was made to the notions of deference, deferential standard of review, or margin of appreciation. Nor does a brief review of the report provide any clear answers. On one hand, a dense, 888-page document—with a considerable portion of the text dedicated to a discussion of the scientific evidence—gives the impression of a quite intrusive assessment

[49] *US—Clove Cigarettes* (n 43) [7.401].

[50] WTO Panel Report, *Australia—Certain Measures concerning Trademarks, Geographical Indications and other Plain Packaging Requirements applicable to Tobacco Products and Packaging*, WT/DS435/R (Honduras), WT/DS441/R (Dominican Republic) (both adopted 29 June 2020); WT/DS458/R (Cuba), WT/DS467/R (Indonesia) (both adopted 27 August 2018) (*Australia—Plain Packaging*).

[51] Tobacco Plain Packaging Act 2011, No 148, 2011, An Act to discourage the use of tobacco products, and for related purposes.

[52] Agreement on Trade-Related Aspects of Intellectual Property Rights (15 April 1994), Marrakesh Agreement Establishing the World Trade Organization, Annex 1C, 1869 UNTS 299 (1994) (TRIPS Agreement).

[53] *Australia—Plain Packaging* (n 50) [7.514]. The parameters of the "objective assessment" were pronounced by the Appellate Body in the *EC—Hormones* case. The applicable standard was defined as neither *de novo* nor total deference: see WTO Appellate Body Report, *EC Measures Concerning Meat and Meat Products*, WT/DS26/AB/R, WT/DS48/AB/R (adopted 13 February 1998) [117] (*EC—Hormones*).

[54] For an additional discussion of this aspect, see Michael Ioannidis, "Beyond the Standard of Review: Deference Criteria in WTO Law and the Case for a Procedural Approach" in Lukasz Gruszczynski and Wouter Werner (eds), *Deference in International Courts and Tribunals: Standard of Review and Margin of Appreciation* (OUP 2014) 91–112.

of the science behind the measure. Indeed, the panel, at least on its face, engaged with the evidence submitted by the parties and carried out a very detailed analysis. On the other hand however, the panel was explicit in stating that "[i]n assessing the probative value of . . . evidence, [its] role [was] not to make scientific determinations or otherwise seek to resolve scientific debates."[55] It also explained that such an assessment had to concentrate on the following three elements: (1) whether the relevant evidence comes from qualified and respected sources; (2) whether it has the necessary scientific and methodological rigor to be considered reputable science or reflects legitimate science according to the standards of the relevant scientific community; and (3) whether the reasoning articulated on the basis of the scientific evidence is objective and coherent.[56]

The first criterion is a formal one and relates to the reputation of the authors (ie scientists or institutions) or the reputation of the journals where the results have been published. The second one is of a methodological rather than substantive character, and can be assessed using the methodological parameters of the relevant scientific community. As noted above, it calls not so much for an assessment of correctness, but rather the defensibility of scientific claims. For the sake of consistency, the third criterion should also be conceptualized narrowly. This means that it would only call for establishing whether the specific interferences based on the evidence are defensible in the light of a particular methodology that may be described as scientific, and whether an interference is objective.[57] Consequently, the Panel would not be required to assess whether a particular reasoning is the best or preferred one.

As noted above, both panels were inspired by the methodological model developed under the SPS Agreement. What is less clear however is why they decided to adopt this approach. The SPS Agreement is a unique part of WTO law. Contrary to other WTO agreements, it makes science a central point of reference for assessing the legality of national measures, by explicitly requiring Members to base their measures on risk assessment. On the other hand, the TBT Agreement is less demanding in this respect, as it simply mandates consideration of the scientific evidence as part of an assessment of the rationale standing behind a technical regulation, while the TRIPS Agreement remains completely silent on this issue. This suggests that the task of a panel under both agreements should be somehow limited, without any need for it to deeply engage with the scientific evidence. Such an approach would not be an unprecedented, as there are a number of WTO cases dealing with health and environmental risks where a deferential review of scientific evidence—much closer to what we saw in *Philip Morris v Uruguay*—has

[55] *Australia—Plain Packaging* (n 50) [7.514].

[56] ibid [7.516].

[57] But see WTO Appellate Body Report, *Australia—Measures Affecting the Importation of Apples from New Zealand*, WT/DS367/AB/R (adopted 17 December 2010) [231].

been adopted. For example, the Panel in *EC—Asbestos* noted under the General Agreement on Tariffs and Trade (GATT 1994) that "it is not its function to settle a scientific debate, not being composed of experts in the field of the possible human health risks posed by asbestos. Consequently, the Panel does not intend to set itself up as an arbiter of the opinions expressed by the scientific community."[58] This limited role only required assessing whether the evidence was sufficient to conclude that there was a human health risk and whether the measure was necessary to achieve the domestic regulatory goal. In *Brazil—Retreaded Tyres*, the Panel was satisfied with the evidence, which merely suggested a correlation between the spread of different diseases and the improper accumulation of waste tyres.[59] Similarly, under the TBT Agreement, the panel in another case only required Mexico to prove that a certain methodology used by the US was unscientific or non-objective, rather than that there were some better methodologies.[60]

So how does the detailed examination of scientific evidence by the Panel in *Australia—Plain Packaging* fit into the parameters of the review? A closer look reveals that the Panel's use of science was quite superficial and, in practice, its analysis expressed a considerable level of deference. Let us look at four different techniques that were used by the Panel in the course of its analysis. It should be noted that these techniques—similarly as the strategies described at the beginning of section 3—are not fully disjunctive and, in some instances, the Panel used a combination of them to deal with specific scientific issues.[61]

First, the Panel frequently concentrated on the objectivity of the evidence (eg lack of bias) and its methodological rigor. In particular, the Panel noted that "in [our] assessment, to the extent that scientific evidence is being relied upon, we must determine whether such evidence has the necessary scientific and methodological rigor to be considered 'reputable science' according to the standards of the relevant scientific community."[62] In the specific circumstances of the dispute, this meant that the Panel tended to defer to various systemic literature reviews and their assessment of reviewed studies (as well as the quality ratings that they assigned to specific pieces of research).[63] The affiliation of the authors, as well as the reputation of the journals where research results were published (ie peer-reviewed publications), also played a role in the Panel's assessment.

[58] WTO Panel Report, *European Communities—Measures Affecting Asbestos and Asbestos-Containing Products*, WT/DS135/R (adopted 5 April 2001) [8.181].

[59] WTO Panel Report, *Brazil—Measures Affecting Imports of Retreaded Tyres*, WT/DS332/R (adopted 17 December 2007) [7.61], [7.68], fn 1118.

[60] WTO Panel Report, *United States—Measures Concerning the Importation, Marketing and Sale of Tuna and Tuna Products—Second Recourse to Article 21.5 of the DSU by Mexico*, WT/DS381/RW2 (adopted 11 January 2019) [7.151].

[61] Note that the Appellate Body confirmed the correctness of the Panel's approach: see WTO Appellate Body Reports, *Australia—Certain Measures Concerning Trademarks, Geographical Indications and Other Plain Packaging Requirements Applicable to Tobacco Products and Packaging*, WTO/DS435/AB/R, WTO/DS441/AB/R (adopted 29 June 2020).

[62] *Australia—Plain Packaging* (n 50) [7.627].

[63] ibid [7.638], [7.674]–[7.675].

For example, the Panel observed that "studies reviewed by the complainants were authored by a total of more than 110 individuals, affiliated with a number of different institutions, including University College London, the University of Surrey, the University of Melbourne, Sydney Medical School, the University of Paris 1–Sorbonne, Pennsylvania State University, the University of Calgary, and the University of Ottawa. These elements support the view that these studies 'come from ... qualified and respected source[s]'."[64] Both elements clearly relate to formal rather than substantive criteria.

Second, on other occasions the Panel spent a considerable amount of time describing the evidence submitted by the parties and explaining the character of specific scientific controversies (and thus creating the impression of conducting an in-depth re-examination that is close to *de novo* review), but after doing this it simply referred to the evidence *as a whole* and drew some general conclusions instead of addressing each scientific claim and assigning it with certain probative value. For example, when assessing the methodological strength of the plain packaging literature, following a detailed discussion of its various technical and scientific nuances, the Panel simply stated that

> we do not consider that we are in a position to draw definitive conclusions on the methodological merits of each individual study referred to in relation to the impact of plain packaging on various relevant measured outcomes, or that it would be appropriate for us to do so. Rather ... what we must consider is the extent to which the body of evidence before us, *as a whole*, provides a reasonable basis in support of the proposition that it is being invoked for.[65]

This strategy allowed the panel to avoid addressing each piece of the evidence or deciding on every specific point that was contested between the parties to the dispute (thus moving the Panel away from an intrusive form of review). When combined with the high probative threshold required by the Panel (see below in the next paragraph), such a technique also made the whole review more deferential.

Third, the Panel also introduced a high evidentiary threshold for the complainants by requiring them to adduce evidence that would *fundamentally* undermine the probative value, and the evidentiary base, underlying the adoption of the plain packaging measure.[66] This obviously went beyond the traditional preponderance of evidence approach and implied a certain trust in the scientific and factual findings of the defendant (ie Australia). This approach led the Panel to conclude, *inter*

[64] ibid [7.549]. See also [7.628] ("This research gave rise to a number of publications, emanating from a range of recognized institutions conducting research on tobacco control") and [7.570] ("we find it implausible that flaws of such a fundamental and pervasive character as to render each and every reviewed study unworthy of publication *would have entirely escaped the attention of researchers and reviewers* in the relevant field of study" [emphasis added]).

[65] ibid [7.627] (emphasis added). See also [7.673], [7.747], [7.825], [7.1025].

[66] See eg ibid [7.562], [7.570].

alia, that the complainants failed to establish that the plain packaging did not contribute to the achievement of Australia's objectives. This conclusion was reached despite a number of shortcomings in individual studies relied on by Australia and loopholes in the existing plain packaging literature.[67]

Last but not least, the Panel recognized that the Australian measure had to be assessed taking into account the broader system of tobacco control in that country (with the Plain Packaging Act as being a part of it). In this context, the panel referred to the Appellate Body Report in *Brazil—Tyres*, which observed that "certain complex public health or environmental problems may be tackled only with a comprehensive policy comprising a multiplicity of interacting measures. In the short-term, it may prove difficult to isolate the contribution to public health or environmental objectives of one specific measure from those attributable to the other measures that are part of the same comprehensive policy."[68] This meant that there was no need to establish clear and direct causality between the measure and the realization of specific regulatory objectives.[69] For example, when analyzing the relationship between plain packaging and smoking cessation (as well as smoking relapse), the panel recognized that plain packaging was an element of a broader policy, which in turn facilitated the conclusion that the measure was rationally related to the specific regulatory objective. It was not necessary to show that the plain packaging requirements were expected to be generally effective in changing smoking behaviors, and it was enough to substantiate that only some consumers might be influenced.[70]

3.3 EU Law Practice and Tobacco Control Measures

The CJEU has also taken a deferential approach in its tobacco control-related disputes. In a relatively recent judgment (*Philip Morris v Secretary of State*), the Court, in its examination of the proportionality of the specific provisions of the Tobacco Products Directive (TPD),[71] clearly deferred to the assessment made by the EU regulators. Under EU law, proportionality requires that acts of the EU institutions be appropriate for attaining legitimate objectives, without exceeding the limits of what is necessary, in order to achieve those objectives.[72]

[67] ibid [7.1027] ("we are not persuaded that the complainants have established that the largely convergent conclusions reflected in the body of studies at issue, and the overall conclusions drawn from them, should be considered to be so fundamentally flawed as to provide no support for the proposition that the TPP measures are capable of contributing to their objective through these mechanisms").

[68] ibid [7.981] (quoting WTO Appellate Body Report, *Brazil—Measures Affecting Imports of Retreaded Tyres*, WT/DS332/AB/R (adopted 17 December 2007) [151]).

[69] See eg *Australia—Plain Packaging* (n 50) [7.983]. See also [7.756], [7.776], [7.1043].

[70] ibid [7.776].

[71] Directive 2014/40 (EU) of the European Parliament and of the Council on the approximation of the laws, regulations and administrative provisions of the member states concerning the manufacture, presentation and sale of tobacco and related products [2014] OJ L127/1.

[72] Moreover, whenever there is a choice between several measures, regulators must choose the least onerous one, and the disadvantages caused cannot be disproportionate to the aims pursued.

In the above context, the CJEU confirmed its limited role in making assessments of political, economic, and social choices, which is the domain of the EU regulators who are called upon to undertake complex evaluations.[73] Note that discretion was conceptualized here more broadly and was not limited to scientific determinations only, but also extended to various trade-offs and other normative judgments made by the EU regulators. Consequently, according to the Court, the contested provisions could be struck down only if they would be "manifestly inappropriate having regard to the objective which the competent institutions [were] seeking to pursue."[74] This also meant, as noted by the Advocate General in the same case, that "it is irrelevant, on the other hand, whether the measure adopted in the legislative act is the only conceivable measure or even only the most appropriate."[75]

Applying this standard, the CJEU found that it was not manifestly inappropriate to ban tobacco products containing menthol (the complainant argued that such a ban would not contribute to the achievement of the objective because menthol was not attractive to young people). The Court came to this conclusion by simply finding that, in general, tobacco products containing characterizing flavors "have certain similar, objective characteristics and similar effects as regards initiating tobacco consumption and sustaining tobacco use."[76] It was not necessary to show that menthols indeed facilitate such an initiation.[77] The same conclusion was reached in the context of the claims of arbitrariness relating to the size of health warnings. In particular, the Court found that requiring warnings that cover 65% of the package surface could not have been regarded as an arbitrary decision, partially due to the discretion granted to the EU regulators.[78]

In the other recent tobacco control case (*Pillbox 38 v The Secretary of State for Health*[79]), the Court upheld the provision of the TPD which set the maximum nicotine limits for e-liquids. The Court did not examine in detail the science standing behind this requirement (which was actually disputed between the parties). Instead, it was satisfied with some general data, for example, relating to the structure of the market and general equivalency between the intake of nicotine by traditional and e-cigarettes users. Such a deferential approach was justified by reference to the broad discretion enjoyed by the EU regulators.[80]

[73] Case C-547/14 *Philip Morris Brands SARL v Secretary of State for Health* ECLI:EU:C:2016:325 [166].
[74] ibid.
[75] Opinion of Advocate General Kokkot delivered on 23 December 2015: see Case C-547/14 *Philip Morris Brands SARL v Secretary of State for Health*, ECLI:EU:C:2015:853 [150].
[76] *Phillip Morris v Secretary of State for Health* (n 73) [115].
[77] ibid [179].
[78] ibid [208]. The Court also referred in this context to the relevant FCTC guidelines.
[79] Case C-477/14 *Pillbox 38 (UK) Ltd, trading as Totally Wicked v Secretary of State for Health* ECLI:EU:C:2016:324.
[80] ibid [96].

The approach taken by the Court in these two disputes was consistent with the existing case law[81] (if not even more deferential). The CJEU normally grants a broad discretion to the EU regulators (but sometimes is more intrusive with respect to measures adopted by EU member states) when assessing policies that involve complex scientific and technical determinations. As noted by the Court in one of the leading cases, "that broad discretion and those complex assessments imply a limited power of review on the part of the courts of the European Union."[82] In principle, under such a standard of review the Court is interested in the plausibility of the evidence and "it is not [its] role to substitute its assessment of complex facts for that of the institution which adopted the decision."[83] The extent of discretion is additionally reinforced whenever there are some external technical standards/documents that are prepared by international expert bodies. In both cases discussed above these were the non-binding guidelines adopted by the Conference of the Parties of the FCTC, while in other cases the relevant group also included the Food and Agriculture Organization (FAO), the World Health Organization (WHO), or the Codex Alimentarius Commission.[84]

4. Conclusion

A comparative review of the relevant IEL case law clearly shows that DSBs operating in this field afford a considerable degree of deference to domestic regulators when assessing the scientific determinations that form the basis for a contested tobacco control measure. In particular, the IEL DSBs tend to look at the formal criteria, such the defensibility of evidence, the coherence of the reasoning, and general reasonableness of contested measures rather than assessing their substance (eg correctness of science behind such measures or merits of specific mitigation strategy). By doing so, they have not only preserved—rather than undermined as worried by some experts—the regulatory space available to states in this specific policy area, but also strengthened the legitimacy of the regime within which they operate, that is, by recognizing the importance of non-economic values and ensuring that domestic regulatory measures are protected against legal challenges. While the decisions of the CJEU and WTO Panels are generally illustrative of the

[81] For additional details, see Patrycja Dąbrowska-Kłosińska, "Risk, Precaution and Scientific Complexity Before the Court of Justice of the European Union" in Lukasz Gruszczynski and Wouter Werner (eds), *Deference in International Courts and Tribunals: Standard of Review and Margin of Appreciation* (OUP 2014) 196ff. See also Case C-233/94 *Germany v Parliament and Council* (13 May 1997) ECLI:EU:C:1997:231; Case C-491/01 *The Queen v Secretary of State for Health, ex p British American Tobacco (Investments) Ltd and Imperial Tobacco Ltd* (10 December 2002) ECLI:EU:C:2002:741.

[82] Case T-257/07 *French Republic v European Commission* (9 September 2011) ECLI:EU:T:2011:444 [85].

[83] ibid [86].

[84] Case C-236/01 *Monsanto Agricoltura Italia SpA v Presidenza del Consiglio dei Ministri* (9 September 2011) ECLI:EU:T:2011:444.

approach taken by the respective IEL DSB when confronted with the review of health regulatory measures, the arbitral award discussed here only represents one of the competing lines of jurisprudence in international investment law, with some tribunals actually engaging more deeply with the rationality of domestic decisions. Having said this, the decision in *Philip Morris v Uruguay* can be seen as a sign of the evolution of the whole field (at least with respect to tobacco control-related disputes) in a similar direction to WTO case law.

The analyzed case law also serves as a proof that the applicable standard of review matters and may have a real impact on the outcome of a specific dispute. In this context, the award in *Philip Morris v Uruguay* is particularly instructive. More intrusive review, as evidenced by the dissenting opinion of one arbitrator, would result in finding a violation of the FET clause for the SPR measure.[85] Uruguay only won the dispute because the tribunal decided to take an extremely deferential approach.

One also needs to admit that the degree of deference expressed by the different IEL DSBs varies. Both the CJEU and the investment tribunal in *Philip Morris v Uruguay* were highly deferential towards the relevant regulators. The same is true for the WTO panel in *US—Clove Cigarettes*, although it has to be acknowledged that that panel was not really confronted with any controversial scientific or complex factual issue (so any generalization is not possible here). Comparatively, the most intrusive approach was taken by the *Plain Packaging* Panel, which spent a considerable part of its analysis on its detailed assessment of the scientific claims made by the parties. However, a closer look at its analysis reveals that deferential elements were also strongly present in the panel's examination. While the review model was more intrusive than the one that was pronounced in *Philip Morris v Uruguay*, the epistemic value of the evidence and the internal coherence of the reasoning still remained at the center of its analysis. When one adds to this the high evidentiary threshold for complainants and the lack of a requirement of strict causality, this approach may be labelled as qualified form of deference. One may only speculate why the WTO panel decided to engage (even if superficially) with the scientific evidence submitted by the parties. Perhaps this was a reflection of the progressive scientification of the WTO dispute settlement process influenced by the standards developed under the SPS Agreement,[86] and the need to ensure overall consistency across the whole WTO body of law. Since the SPS jurisprudence provides the most elaborate set of rules (while the parties tend to build their litigation strategies in scientific terms), it was only natural to consider its standards as a kind of general guideline on how to properly handle the dispute.

85 *Philip Morris* (n 21) Annex A [157], [163].

86 The Panel noted, for example, that the nature of its task was similar to the one required under the SPS Agreement: see *Australia—Plain Packaging* (n 50) [7.517].

All the IEL DSBs discussed in this chapter have referred to the comparative epistemic superiority of domestic regulators in situations that involve assessment of complex scientific questions (and this element can perhaps explain emerging convergences across different IEL subfields). This is in line with their general practice. At the same time, it was only the investment tribunal in *Philip Morris v Uruguay* that explicitly identified the national sovereignty and the subject matter of the regulation (ie protection of public health) as elements that are relevant in determining the required level of deference. Lack of such justification is understandable in the context of the relevant CJEU case law as the acts under review were adopted at the European rather than national level, while their main objective was creation and maintenance of the internal market within the EU (rather than protection of public health). On the other hand, it is unclear why the *Plain Packaging* Panel avoided using one of such rationales, particularly when one considers the conceptual similarities between trade and investment rules and the general WTO case law.[87]

One might expect that the problem of applicable standard of review will remain highly relevant in the future in all disputes relating to national measures that involve assessment of complex facts. The cases analyzed here indicate that the IEL DSBs do recognize the significance of this issue and are willing to accord states with a wide degree of discretion. It remains to be seen whether a similar approach will be taken by other international adjudicating bodies.

[87] cf eg *EC—Hormones* (n 53) [124] ("a panel . . . should . . . bear in mind that responsible, representative governments commonly act from perspectives of prudence and precaution where risks of irreversible, eg life-terminating, damage to human health are concerned").

5

Science, Legitimacy, and the Judicial Function

A Need for More Intrusive Standards of Review

Katalin Sulyok

1. Introduction

An increasing number of international judicial fora adjudicate environmental disputes, where parties raise competing and conflicting science-based arguments. Facing complex scientific evidence and highly technical science-backed arguments prompts adjudicative bodies to decide about the extent and ways in which they are willing to consider and engage with the scientific facts underlying such disputes. This chapter will focus on the standards of review international courts set in hearing science-intensive legal disputes that have manifest scientific dimensions. Standard of review will be understood here as a judicial tool marking the intensity of scrutiny with which international fora review the scientific merits of the parties' factual allegations. On a more abstract level, the standard of review understood in this sense also serves as a judicial mechanism for demarcating issues of judicial competence from factual evaluations reserved for the experts, and thereby it determines the scope of the adjudicatory purview and the essence of judicial function in legal disputes.

These questions will be examined against the background of environmental dispute resolution before the International Court of Justice (ICJ), the dispute settlement mechanism of the World Trade Organization (WTO), and the judiciary of the European Union (EU courts), where judges routinely confront cases, where science and law are closely intertwined in the underlying legal dilemmas and the parties' arguments. Environmental disputes are defined for present purposes in a broad sense as encompassing all "disputes with environmental components."[1] The reason for focusing on these jurisdictions for the comparative assessment is essentially twofold. On the one hand, these adjudicative bodies are permanent fora that

[1] Pierre-Marie Dupuy and Jorge E Vinuales argue that instead of "environmental disputes" the more exact definition would be "disputes with environmental components." See Pierre-Marie Dupuy and Jorge E Vinuales, *International Environmental Law* (CUP 2018) 247.

Katalin Sulyok, *Science, Legitimacy, and the Judicial Function* In: *Secondary Rules of Primary Importance in International Law.* Edited by: Gábor Kajtár, Başak Çalı, and Marko Milanovic, Oxford University Press.
DOI: 10.1093/oso/9780192869012.003.0005

seek to maintain a consistent case law in applying their standards of review. On the other hand, these adjudicative fora have been oscillating between deferential and more intrusive standards of review, which provides a fertile ground for a doctrinal analysis. This contribution will put forth the following argument. First, there is an observable trend before the ICJ, WTO, and the EU courts of moving away from strictly deferential to more intrusive standards of review when interrogating scientific claims in environmental disputes.[2] Second, this is a welcome development because more intrusive standards of review towards scientific allegations of the parties are warranted in international adjudication for reasons of epistemic legitimacy.

In this chapter, section 2 discusses the strategic importance for parties and adjudicators of choosing particular standards of review in science-intensive cases. Section 3 will conduct a comparative overview of the recent practice of major permanent international judicial fora in terms of the depth of their scrutiny applied in science-heavy environmental cases. This part of the analysis will focus on the nuanced legal tests with which relevant jurisdictions operationalize the standards of review. The ICJ's reasonableness review, the coherence requirement of WTO law, and the consistency analysis of EU courts will be discussed in more detail. This is followed by section 4, which discusses the normative justifiability of these standards from the viewpoint of epistemic legitimacy. Section 5 concludes by summing up the main challenges courts face in the twenty-first century in conducting their analysis in ever more complex and scientized disputes and the requirements of conducting an epistemically legitimate scrutiny of the litigants' factual claims.

2. Setting the Standard of Review in Science-Intensive Cases: A Strategic Tool of Litigants and Judges

The standard of review is understood in this study as being a procedural mechanism, which determines the intensity of judicial scrutiny[3] and, thus, delineates

[2] This proposition holds true with respect to a narrowly defined arena, that is, environmental case law of the chosen jurisdictions. Importantly, the present analysis did not encompass the environmental case practice of investment arbitration panels, which notably apply much more deferential standards of review towards science-backed claims of states: see Katalin Sulyok, *Science and Judicial Reasoning: The Legitimacy of International Environmental Adjudication* (CUP 2021) 232–34. Furthermore, the prevailing standard of review may also be informed by sector specific factors such as the perceived legitimacy capital of the adjudicatory body, the scope of the mandate conferred on the adjudicative fora, the formulation of underlying substantive laws and legal principles, the complexity of scientific issues, and the state of scientific knowledge regularly featured in respective disputes, as well as the extent to which controversies surround the technical questions on which legal claims depend in the litigious process. The prevailing adjudicatory approach towards setting the standard of review therefore may be different across different fields of international law. See Chapter 4 finding more intrusive standards of review in tobacco control litigation of certain international jurisdictions.

[3] Caroline E Foster, *Science and the Precautionary Principle in International Courts and Tribunals* (CUP 2011) 14.

the extent to which national authorities enjoy unfettered discretion in making scientific factual allegations. Put differently, the standard of review distributes powers between supranational judicial organs and states by striking a balance between the competences afforded to international bodies against those retained by sovereigns.[4]

In the specific context of science-intensive disputes, the controversy before the court typically concerns a factual determination, for example, whether domestic authorities enacted the contested measure based on sufficient scientific evidence. The answer to that question largely hinges upon the chosen standard of review. The applicable standard may spread across a theoretical spectrum between two extremes: *de novo* review and total deference. The *de novo* standard of review entrusts a judicial organ with reviewing the initial determinations of national level decision-making authorities.[5] Total deference implies a quasi-automatic acceptance of the determination offered by the primary risk assessor. Between these two extremes, there are many possible formulations ranging from more intrusive standards of review to less intrusive, and thus, more deferential ones. The appropriate extent of deference in terms of making scientific evaluations is extensively debated among scholars[6] and international judges alike.[7]

It is to be underlined that the standard of review vis-à-vis making factual claims—which is the focus of this study—is an analytically distinct issue from the deference afforded to states' policy choices. The former rests upon epistemic grounds, while the latter can be justified by the democratic legitimacy of sovereign policy makers. Despite this analytical distinction, the two aspects of scrutiny are closely intertwined in the adjudicatory process. To take an example, states usually defend their public health or environmental policy decisions before a court

[4] Lukasz Gruszczynski, "Standard of Review of Health and Environmental Regulations by WTO Panels" in G Van Calster and D Prévost (eds), *Research Handbook on Environment, Health and the WTO* (Edward Elgar 2014) 734.

[5] Lukasz Gruszczynski and Wouter Werner, "Introduction" in Lukasz Gruszczynski and Wouter Werner (eds), *Deference in International Courts and Tribunals: Standard of Review and Margin of Appreciation* (OUP 2014) 2.

[6] Esmé Shirlow, *Judging at the Interface: Deference to State Decision-Making Authority in International Adjudication* (CUP 2021); Michael Ioannidis, "Beyond the Standard of Review: Deference Criteria in WTO Law and the Case for a Procedural Approach" in Lukasz Gruszczynski and Wouter Werner (eds), *Deference in International Courts and Tribunals: Standard of Review and Margin of Appreciation* (OUP 2014); CE Foster, "Adjudication, Arbitration and the Turn to Public Law 'Standards of Review': Putting the Precautionary Principle in the Crucible" (2012) 3 Journal of International Dispute Settlement 525; Stephan W Schill, "Deference in Investment Treaty Arbitration: Re-Conceptualizing the Standard of Review" (2012) 3 Journal of International Dispute Settlement 577; Shotaro Hamamoto, "From the Requirement of Reasonableness to a 'Comply and Explain' Rule: The Standard of Review in the *Whaling* Judgment" in Malgosia Fitzmaurice and Dai Tamada (eds), *Whaling in the Antarctic Significance and Implications of the ICJ Judgment* (Brill Nijhoff 2016) vol 23; Caroline E Foster, "International Adjudication—Standards of Review and Burden of Proof: *Australia—Apples* and *Whaling in the Antarctic*" [2012] Review of European Community and International Environmental Law 80–91; Yuka Fukunaga, "Standard of Review and 'Scientific Truths' in the WTO Dispute Settlement System and Investment Arbitration" (2012) 3 Journal of International Dispute Settlement 559.

[7] See eg the separate opinions in *Whaling in the Antarctic* case discussed in section 3.3.

by reference to scientific reasons and evidence. Moreover, sovereigns may also appeal to science in order to mask their economic or other policy choices. Yet, making a distinction between these grounds of deference (ie scientific expertise on the one hand, and the competence of making sovereign policy choices, on the other hand) is nevertheless necessary in order to conduct a fine-grained analysis of adjudicatory scrutiny afforded to scientific claims. The ensuing analysis will therefore interrogate the proper extent of deference to be afforded to factual assessment of states on epistemic grounds.

As alluded to above, the chosen standard may substantially impact the outcome of science-heavy litigation. This makes the degree of deference afforded to states' factual claims of strategic importance for litigants. Notably, arguments cloaked in science may carry strong persuasive force in the eyes of judges, as they may appeal to ideals of "objectivity" and describing the factual "truth." Science may also be suitable for disguising the economic and political interests of states[8] and thereby insulating such interests from judicial review. In short, the chosen standard fundamentally impacts the extent to which states can get away with making flawed scientific assessments disguising the non-scientific motivations underlying their contested measures.

The prevailing standard of review is also consequential for international judges themselves, as it impacts the science-intensity of their tasks and shapes the scope of the adjudicatory purview. By choosing between various levels of scrutiny, judges, in fact, adjust the level of science they must grapple with in their inquiry. In other words, the chosen standard of review will determine the extent to which they ought to directly interact with scientific facts and arguments in their assessments. Setting deferential standards saves the bench from the arduous task of interpreting contradicting pieces of technical evidence submitted by the parties. In turn, choosing more intrusive scrutiny will result in a need to develop epistemic capacities for the bench in order to provide sound justifications for rejecting a particular piece of partisan scientific evidence.

Finally, before delving into the comparative analysis of various standards of review it is to be emphasized that "intrusive" and "deferential" scrutiny are essentially relative terms, as their meaning depends on which hypothetical extreme one compares the depth of applicable scrutiny to. Judicial review, in fact, covers a host of legal benchmarks with which adjudicators scrutinize scientific claims of states. The devil, as usual, lies in the detail. More specifically, the intensity of a judicial scrutiny depends upon the nuanced legal test, with which adjudicators choose to fill their announced standard of review. For this reason, the following comparative analysis

[8] For an argument made in the context of WTO law concerning scientific narratives used as a tool for masking economic policy objectives, see Anne Orford, "Trade, Human Rights and the Economy of Sacrifice" in Anne Orford (ed), *International Law and Its Others* (CUP 2006) 166–73.

will focus on the exact legal tests that have been developed and applied by international courts and tribunals under the aegis of various standards of review.

3. Comparative Overview of the Standards of Review in Science-Intensive Adjudication

The international fora of interest in this study conduct their scrutiny of states' scientific claims in diverse legal contexts. Nevertheless, they face essentially similar dilemmas in deciding about the depth of science they are willing to interrogate. WTO panels and EU courts set the standard of review while reviewing the legality of scientific risk assessment measures. Whereas the ICJ devised a standard of review[9] in a scientific context for the first time in the *Whaling in the Antarctic* case,[10] where the concept of "scientific research" had to be interpreted for purposes of international law. The ensuing sections will discuss the evolution of the applicable standards of review before these adjudicative bodies. It will be argued that most recent formulations of the standard of review often foster a close and direct adjudicatory engagement with the underlying scientific knowledge and these tests bear some structural resemblance to each other.

3.1 The Consistency Review of the EU Judicature

Several EU directives and regulations set forth risk assessment obligations, which are subject to the scrutiny of the EU judiciary to ensure that EU institutions and member states (MS) have respected their discretion in making scientific evaluations. Initially, EU courts were known for affording total deference in such cases to regulatory measures concerning environmental and health risks involving complex scientific evidence. This resulted in a simplified judicial task in deciding such disputes. Hence, not surprisingly, EU courts handed down relatively short judgments in cases, where the contested decisions or legislations were based on complex scientific data.[11]

[9] Shotaro Hamamoto, "From the Requirement of Reasonableness to a 'Comply and Explain' Rule: The Standard of Review in the *Whaling* Judgment" in Malgosia Fitzmaurice and Dai Tamada, *Whaling in the Antarctic Significance and Implications of the ICJ Judgment* vol 23 (Brill Nijhoff 2016) 39.

[10] *Whaling in the Antarctic (Australia v Japan: New Zealand intervening)* (Judgment of 31 March 2014) [2014] ICJ Rep 226.

[11] Eg for the practice of the EU judiciary, see: Case C-180/96 *United Kingdom v Commission of the European Communities* [1998] ECR I–2265; Case C-331/88 *R v Ministry of Agriculture, Fisheries and Food, ex p Federation Europeene de la Sante Animale (FEDESA)* [1990] ECR I–4023; Case C-405/92 *Establissements A Mondiet v Armement Islais* [1993] ECR I–6133.

However, since the beginning of 2000s, they have started to develop a more thorough approach to reviewing the validity of scientific arguments.[12] *Technische Universität München*[13] marks a departure from the previous deferential approach. The Court broadened the scope of its assessment and did not refrain from scrutinizing the composition of an expert body that made the scientific evaluation underlying the contested decision. The Court articulated that EU institutions have a duty "to examine carefully and impartially all the relevant aspects of the individual case, the right of the person concerned to make his views known and to have an adequately reasoned decision."[14] It ruled that the Commission has exceeded the limits of its discretion when it announced the scientific equivalence of certain microscopes without securing sufficient scientific expertise. Ever since, EU courts have started to scrutinize whether primary risk assessors have exercised due care in understanding and appraising the scientific questions and risks involved.[15]

The high-water mark of conducting such an intrusive scrutiny into the scientific basis of risk assessment decisions is perhaps best illustrated by the *Pfizer*[16] and *Alpharma*[17] judgments. In both decisions, the Court of First Instance (CFI) still spoke in deferential language,[18] but was nevertheless willing to have a closer look at the informational basis on which the Commission has made its assessment. The CFI emphasized that it would scrutinize whether the expert opinion relied on by MS was "consistent."[19]

As to the factual background in *Pfizer*, the CFI had to engage with the expert report of SCAN, the Commission's expert body. SCAN concluded that the use of virginiamycin, an antibiotic produced by Pfizer and used as growth promoter in feedingstuffs, did not constitute an immediate risk to public health. The existence of a link between the use of antibiotics and the development of antibiotics resistance in humans was to a large extent recognized by the scientific community.[20] However, according to Pfizer, the transfer of such resistance from animals to humans had not yet been scientifically established with respect to the specific

[12] Ellen Vos, "The European Court of Justice in the Face of Scientific Uncertainty and Complexity" in Mark Dawson, Bruno De Witte, and Elise Muir (eds), *Judicial Activism at the European Court of Justice* (Edward Elgar 2013) 143; Patrycja Dąbrowska-Kłosińska, "Risk, Precaution and Scientific Complexity before the Court of Justice of the European Union" in Lukasz Gruszczynski and Wouter Werner (eds), *Deference in International Courts and Tribunals: Standard of Review and Margin of Appreciation* (OUP 2014) 195.

[13] Case C-269/90 *Technische Universität München v Hauptzollamt München-Mitte* [1991] ECR I-5469.

[14] ibid para 14.

[15] Vos, "The European Court of Justice in the Face of Scientific Uncertainty and Complexity" (n 12) 151.

[16] Case T-13/99 *Pfizer Animal Health SA v Council of the European Union* [1999] ECR II-1961.

[17] Case T-70/99 *Alpharma Inc v Council of the European Union* [2002] ECR II-3495.

[18] Case T-13/99 *Pfizer Animal Health SA v Council of the European Union* (Judgment of the Court of First Instance of 11 September 2002) [2002] ECR II-3305, paras 166–69.

[19] ibid para 198.

[20] ibid para 35.

antibiotic in question.[21] Even though Pfizer's position was expressly countered by reports of the UK House of Lords, Sweden, Denmark, and the World Health Organization (WHO), SCAN disputed the relevance of these pieces of evidence. In spite of that, the Commission recommended the withdrawal of virginiamycin, and the Council acted accordingly.

Against this background, the CFI had to rule whether the Commission made a manifest error of assessment when interpreted the expert evidence contained in the SCAN report. Specifically, Pfizer alleged that the Commission distorted the expert findings submitted to it. In order to ascertain these allegations, the Court had to look at the scientific facts contained in the experts' report. During such a "more interventionist"[22] review, the CFI emphasized that Community institutions were not bound to accept the conclusion reached in the opinion of its expert consultant bodies.[23] If they were to rely on such opinion, they must "assess the probative value of the [expert] opinion delivered" in which regard they must ensure that "the reasoning in the opinion is full, consistent and relevant."[24] Should the Commission disregard the expert opinion, it must provide specific reasons for doing so and "its statement of reasons must be of a scientific level at least commensurate with that of the opinion in question."[25]

Such a judicial review ultimately engendered a thirty-five-paragraph long assessment in the judgment interrogating the *logical consistency* of the SCAN report with the contested regulation's preamble. This exercise necessarily included looking at the scientific subject matter of the evaluation. Importantly, the CFI has managed to carefully meander along the border of a legal and scientific inquiry in order not to substitute the experts' assessment with its own view on the hazards involved, since such a decision is emphatically reserved for the legislature.

This approach resulted in a surprisingly science-intensive judicial inquiry for the EU judicature. For instance, the CFI had to decide whether the Council correctly interpreted the SCAN report's findings that "resistance to pristinamycin amongst staphylococci remains low at around 5% of isolates" and the fact that from "1000 MRSA collected from hospitals, 98.5% were found susceptible to both pristinamycin and Synercid,"[26] as "virginiamycin-resistance enterococci and staphylococci isolated from poultry and pigs all had cross-resistance to pristinamycin used in human medicine."[27] It may not warrant further illustration that such a legal assessment on the consistency of the opinion requires a basic understanding of the technicalities of the relevant scientific field. It is submitted

21 ibid para 41.
22 Vos, "The European Court of Justice in the Face of Scientific Uncertainty and Complexity" (n 12) 145.
23 Case T-13/99 *Pfizer Animal Health SA v Council of the European Union* (Judgment of the Court of First Instance of 11 September 2002) (n 18) para 196.
24 ibid para 198.
25 ibid para 199.
26 ibid para 240.
27 ibid para 237.

here that the logical and scientific consistency are closely tied aspects of the analysis. Therefore, the dividing line between logical consistency (which the CFI says it is reviewing) and scientific consistency (which the Court emphatically does not want to review) becomes ever more blurred upon closer examination.

The consistency analysis introduced in *Pfizer* was further elaborated on in *Artegodan*[28] and *Olivieri v Commission and EMEA*.[29] The CFI emphasized that its task only encompassed reviewing "the internal consistency of the opinion and the statement of reasons contained therein,"[30] and it was only empowered to examine "whether the opinion contains a statement of reasons from which it is possible to ascertain the considerations on which the opinion is based, and whether it establishes a comprehensible link between the medical and/or scientific findings and its conclusions."[31]

What is noteworthy for the purposes of the present analysis is that the CFI could hardly form an opinion on the existence of a comprehensible link between the applicable scientific facts and a risk assessor's conclusion—that is, about the consistency of the opinion—without engaging directly with the merits of scientific arguments. By setting such an intrusive standard of review, the CFI has, in fact, extended the scope of its judicial review, allowing it to consider the underlying scientific arguments when drawing its legal conclusions. This marks a significant departure from the EU judiciary's initial default deferential approach. Such a more interventionist review signaled that the EU judicature has become willing to touch upon "the adequacy and quality of the informational basis of science-based measures"[32] and thereby to restrict the discretion granted to MS and EU institutions.

The above line of cases notwithstanding, the discretion granted to primary decision-makers appears to be more limited in other decisions.[33] Science-intensive judgments in *Hitachi*,[34] *Gowan*,[35] *Afton*,[36] and *Bayer*

[28] Case T-74/00 *Artegodan GmbH v Commission of the European Communities* (Judgment of the Court of First Instance of 26 November 2002) ECLI:EU:T:2006:286.

[29] Case T-326/99 *Nancy Fern Olivieri v Commission of the European Communities and European Agency for the Evaluation of Medicinal Products* (Judgment of the Court of First Instance of 18 December 2003) [2003] ECR II-6053, for the scientific assessment, see paras 83–92 of the judgment.

[30] Case T-74/00 *Artegodan GmbH v Commission of the European Communities* (Judgment of the Court of First Instance of 26 November 2002) (n 28) para 200.

[31] ibid para 200.

[32] Vos, "The European Court of Justice in the Face of Scientific Uncertainty and Complexity" (n 12) 144.

[33] Alberto Alemanno, "EU Risk Regulation and Science: The Role of Experts in Decision-Making and Judicial Review" in Ellen Vos (ed), *European Risk Governance Its Science, Its Inclusiveness and Its Effectiveness* (Connex 2008); E Madalina Busuioc, "Blurred Areas of Responsibility: European Agencies' Scientific 'Opinions' under Scrutiny" in Monika Ambrus and others (eds), *The Role of "Experts" in International and European Decision-Making Processes* (CUP 2014); Dąbrowska-Kłosińska, "Risk, Precaution and Scientific Complexity before the Court of Justice of the European Union" (n 12).

[34] Case T-135/13 *Hitachi Chemical Europe GmbH v European Chemicals Agency* (Judgment of the General Court of 30 April 2015) ECLI:EU:T:2015:253, para 57.

[35] Case C-77/09 *Gowan Comércio International e Services L v Ministero della Salute*, Judgment of the Court, 22 December 2010, paras 56–67.

[36] Case C-343/09 *Afton Chemical Ltd v Secretary of State for Transport* (Judgment of the Court of 8 July 2010) [2010] ECR I-7027, paras 28–42.

CropScience[37] returned to shorter and less substantive assessments not revealing the fine-grained legal contents of the applicable review. In these scientific risk assessment cases, EU courts reiterated their deferential language and only conducted a formalistic manifest error assessment, which did not reach the depth of the consistency of the risk assessor's reasoning. It remains to be seen whether and in what ways the EU judicature would be willing to return to the approach showcased in *Pfizer* and accompanying decisions, or whether these judgments should rather be viewed as the exception and not the rule of an intrusive review.

3.2 The Coherence Review of the WTO Dispute Settlement System

The Agreement on Sanitary and Phytosanitary Measures (SPS Agreement) sets forth a most elaborate scientific risk assessment criteria in WTO law, where the defining question is whether a given SPS trade restrictive measure can be justified on scientific grounds. This dilemma has been put before a WTO panel in an especially heated atmosphere in the *EC–Hormones* dispute. The case concerned an import ban instituted by the EC on meat and meat products derived from cattle to which certain natural hormones were administered for growth promoter purposes. The EC imposed the ban with reference to an alleged risk of conferring carcinogenic effects on consumers of hormone-treated beef meat.

In their quest for the appropriate standard of review, WTO panels first embarked on scrutinizing whether the ban was "sufficiently supported or reasonably warranted"[38] by scientific evidence. Such an intrusive standard of review resulted in a finding of inconsistency regarding the EC's measure. The Panel and the WTO Appellate Body (AB) both found that the scientific research cited by the EC was too general, and therefore the measure was inconsistent with the SPS Agreement.[39] The scientific reports relied on by the EC all concluded that the consumption of meat, to which growth hormones were administered was safe, albeit studies indeed "show[ed] the existence of a general risk of cancer."[40] However, these studies did not specifically address the risks imposed by hormone residues found in meat,[41] but referred to much higher dosages.[42] The AB stressed that for this reason the ban lacked a "rational relationship"[43] with scientific opinions describing carcinogenic

[37] Case T-75/06 *Bayer CropScience AG v Commission of the European Communities* (Judgment of the Court of First Instance of 9 September 2008) [2008] ECR II-2081, paras 141–42.
[38] WTO Appellate Body Report, *EC–Hormones*, WT/DS26/AB/R, WT/DS48/AB/R (adopted 16 January 1998) [186].
[39] ibid [199]–[200].
[40] ibid [200].
[41] ibid [199]–[200].
[42] Jacqueline Peel, *Science and Risk Regulation in International Law* (CUP 2010) 206.
[43] *EC–Hormones* (n 38) [192].

risks of growth promoters, as the latter were not "sufficiently specific to the case at hand."[44]

The harsh criticism triggered by the decision prompted the AB to intervene in *Continued Suspension of Obligations*, the sequel to the *EC—Hormones* dispute, in order to mandate a more deferential approach towards members' regulatory autonomy, where "genuine and legitimate scientific controversy"[45] existed concerning the health risks of certain products. This new, thus far prevailing standard of review comprises two stages: (1) the first being a scrutiny as to the underlying scientific basis of SPS measures. This is a more deferential review as in order to become accepted, scientific evidence must only come from a legitimate scientific source respecting necessary methodological rigor. Importantly, this test is also met if the evidence represents only a minority view within the scientific community. Whereas (2) the second stage of the review is a scrutiny of the reasons provided by the risk assessor. This latter step is more intrusive and entails an assessment as to whether the reasoning "is objective and coherent in which the conclusions find sufficient support in the evidence."[46]

It is argued here that the wording of this second arm of the review entails that WTO panels remain able to conduct a relatively intrusive review into science-based regulatory measures, in case they wish to do so. The "coherence analysis" enables WTO panelists to couch their reasoning in legal terms, given that they should emphatically not address the correctness of the underlying science,[47] or resolve longstanding scientific controversies[48] but to review whether intermediate steps were revealed and adequately documented in a transparent and coherent manner in light of the scientific evidence. The epistemic nature of such an assessment allows adjudicators to form their own reading of the "coherency" of the risk assessor's reasoning, and hence it makes possible for WTO panels to find a given trade measure inconsistent with WTO law even if the same measure could pass the avowedly deferential first arm of the review.

This coherence review has been applied, mutatis mutandis in the panel report in *Australia—Tobacco Plain Packaging*.[49] The Panel here again reviewed in depth the

[44] ibid [200].

[45] EC's appellant submission, cited by the AB in WTO Appellate Body Report, *US—Continued Suspension of Obligations in the EC—Hormones Dispute*, WT/DS320/AB/R (adopted 16 October 2018) [585].

[46] WTO Appellate Body Report, *Australia—Measures Affecting the Importation of Apples from New Zealand*, WT/DS367/AB/R (adopted 29 November 2010) [215].

[47] Lukasz Gruszczynski, "How Deep Should We Go?—Searching for an Appropriate Standard of Review in the SPS Cases" (2011) 2 European Journal of Risk Regulation 111, 114.

[48] The EC raised such an argument in favor of a least intrusive review before the Panel in *Continued Suspension of Obligations*: see WTO Panel Report, *US—Continued Suspension of Obligations*, WT/DS320/R (adopted 31 March 2008) [4.377].

[49] WTO Panel Report, *Australia—Certain Measures concerning Trademarks, Geographical Indications and other Plain Packaging Requirements applicable to Tobacco Products and Packaging*, WT/DS435/R (Honduras), WT/DS441/R (Dominican Republic), WT/DS458/R (Cuba), WT/DS467/R (Indonesia) (adopted 28 June 2018) [7.516].

scientific studies supporting Australia's measure in order to appraise whether the design, structure and application of tobacco plain packaging requirement was consistent with the scientific results concerning smoking behavior. The Panel found that Australia's reliance on the evidence was "objective and coherent."[50] The scientific assessment, which was more than a hundred pages long, has led to a conclusion that Australia rightly instituted the measure based on scientific studies showing that such policies reduce the attractiveness of tobacco products for smokers.[51]

3.3 The Reasonableness Assessment of the ICJ

The ICJ has only recently started to engage in a meaningful scrutiny of the parties' appeals to scientific authority. The Court first defined its standard of review in *Whaling in the Antarctic*, where the Court had to scrutinize whether Japan legitimately claimed that it was pursuing whaling "for purposes of scientific research" under the special permit procedure of the International Convention on the Regulation of Whaling (ICRW) in its state-run whaling program, called JARPA II.

Against this background, the Court had to devise a tool to distinguish claims of "genuine science" from "non-science" in light of the parties' arguments justifying and challenging respectively the "scientific" nature of JARPA II. Japan claimed that its whaling program, JARPA II, pursued "scientific objectives" and therefore fulfilled this criterion; while Australia argued that Japan relied on science only as a pretext. The applicant claimed that JARPA II was essentially commercial whaling, which produced poor data from a scientific point of view, while generated huge volumes of whale meat to be sold on the Japanese food market.

The Court consciously avoided providing a general definition of "science" for purposes of international law, instead, it announced an objective test of reasonableness to assess whether JARPA's "design and implementation [were] reasonable in relation to its stated scientific objectives."[52] The application of this standard of review amounted to an eighty-paragraph long substantive inquiry into the research items of JARPA II, its stated objectives, and its implementation scheme. Notably, the Court refused to accept the definition of science as provided by Australia's expert witness neither did it come up with its own definition on the defining characteristics of science. Instead, it created the yardstick of "reasonableness," which was intended to function as an objective standard of review. Judge Owada suggests that its genesis can be traced back to the standard devised by the WTO AB in *Continued Suspension of Obligations*.[53]

[50] ibid [7.677].
[51] ibid [7.518]–[7.931].
[52] *Whaling in the Antarctic* (n 10) [88].
[53] The dissenting opinion of Judge Owada refers to WTO Appellate Body Report, *US—Continued Suspension of Obligations in the EC—Hormones Dispute*, WT/DS320/AB/R (adopted 16 October 2018).

The reasonableness test is an ambitious and intrusive standard of review, especially compared to the competing possibilities furthered by the parties and by some members of the bench. Notably, Japan offered a much narrower reading, according to which reasonableness can only be relevant in examining whether "a State [could] reasonably regard this [JARPA II] as scientific research."[54] In contrast, Australia submitted a broader notion of reasonableness, inherent in states' obligation of good faith.[55] Australia argued that good faith implementation required Japan in the material case to "have due regard to and respond to the views of the [International Whaling Commission], particularly those urging the cessation of the lethal elements of any program."[56] New Zealand proposed a slightly different reading on reasonableness, one akin to that which was provided in *Gabcikovo-Nagymaros*, compelling states "to apply a treaty provision in a reasonable way and in such a manner that its purpose can be realised."[57] Judge Owada dissenting would have preferred yet another reading under which reasonableness was to be conceived as a "yardstick for ascertaining whether a decision or an action is or is not 'arbitrary' or patently 'out of bounds.'"[58]

These alternative standards are more lenient and deferential compared to the test ultimately set by the ICJ interrogating the reasonable nature of the JARPA II program. This is also reflected in the outcome of the litigation. Notably, the Court did not accept Japan's appeal to "scientific research" and found that JARPA II was in violation of the ICRW in light of the design and implementation of the program. The reasonableness test is therefore seen here as facilitating an in-depth, substantive review of Japan's scientific claim, which by certain accounts came even close to a "*de novo*"[59] judicial review.

The Court's majority has been criticized for using the reasonableness test as its standard of review by four dissenting judges[60] and by several publicists.[61] Their criticism specifically aimed at the reasonableness standard for not being "grounded in law or in the practice of the Court,"[62] and for taking a "magic formula ... out

[54] Statement of Mr Vaughan Lowe KC (verbatim record, public sitting on Monday 15 July 2013, at 3pm, at the Peace Palace, CR/2013/22, p 60, paras 19–20).

[55] *Whaling in the Antarctic (Australia v Japan: New Zealand intervening)*, Memorial of Australia [4.61].

[56] *Whaling in the Antarctic (Australia v Japan: New Zealand intervening)*, Memorial of Australia [5.126].

[57] *Whaling in the Antarctic (Australia v Japan: New Zealand intervening)*, Written observations of New Zealand [12].

[58] *Whaling in the Antarctic* (Dissenting Opinion of Judge Owada) (n 10) [39].

[59] Judge Owada described the Court's approach as "making a *de novo* assessment," though he criticized the Court for this: see *Whaling in the Antarctic* (Dissenting Opinion of Judge Owada) (n 10) [38].

[60] Judge Abraham, Judge Yusuf, Judge Owada, and Judge Xue criticized the reasonableness test on diverse grounds.

[61] Gogarty and Lawrence dismiss the judgment for using the reasonableness standard without providing a satisfactory explanation as to its basis in the Court's case law. See Brendan Gogarty and Peter Lawrence, "The ICJ *Whaling* Case: Missed Opportunity to Advance the Rule of Law in Resolving Science-Related Disputes in Global Commons?" (2016) 77 Heidelberg Journal of International Law 161, 178–79.

[62] *Whaling in the Antarctic* (Dissenting Opinion of Judge Yusuf) (n 10) [15].

of the context",[63] or suggested that assessing reasonableness of a research scheme simply falls outside judicial purview.[64] However, others suggested that the reasonableness standard was as an objective criterion flowing from states' general obligation of good faith,[65] as it is rooted in the assumption that one cannot rely on an argument in good faith unless its position is reasonable. Viewed from this perspective, the reasonableness standard is, in fact, nothing other than an appeal to rationality,[66] and it is not at all alien to the ICJ's prior jurisprudence.[67] The reasonableness assessment was also praised for being a "loose limit,"[68]which at the same time prevents states from defining scientific research in a way as to encroach upon the sovereign interests of others.

3.4 Variations on a Theme of Intrusive Judicial Scrutiny

The above survey suggests that international fora have recently opened the door for standards of review that allow judges to assess scientific claims from a substantive point of view. The coherence assessment of WTO dispute settlement bodies, the consistency review of EU courts, and the reasonableness test of the ICJ are couched in somewhat different words, nevertheless their epistemic characteristics are similar to a surprising extent. In short, these standards of review all demarcate scientific questions—which legal adjudicators ought not to review—from legal issues—which judges are entitled to appraise—in a remarkably similar fashion. They are conducive to a judicial inquiry, which prompts judges to closely consider scientific arguments in drawing legal conclusions.

First, these standards of review all meander along the border of a scientific and a legal analysis. Their key concepts are rooted in scientific facts, but their primary focus remains on the *reasoning* of the party appealing to scientific authority. Concepts such as the consistency, coherence, and reasonableness of a reasoning are positioned on the boundary of the legal and the scientific realm. That is to say, they are legal qualities that can be appraised based on legal logic, but their application to a given scenario necessitates looking at the scientific facts of the case. In this sense, they are essentially "hybrid" in nature.[69] The hybridity of these standards of

[63] *Whaling in the Antarctic* (Dissenting Opinion of Judge Owada) (n 10) [34].

[64] *Whaling in the Antarctic* (Separate Opinion of Judge Xue) (n 10) [15].

[65] Asier Garrido-Munoz, "Managing Uncertainty: The International Court of Justice, 'Objective Reasonableness' and the Judicial Function" (2017) 30 Leiden Journal of International Law 457, 467.

[66] ibid 461.

[67] ibid 463.

[68] Enzo Cannizzaro, "Proportionality and Margin of Appreciation in the *Whaling* Case: Reconciling Antithetical Doctrines?" (2016) 27 European Journal of International Law 1061, 1068.

[69] This terminology draws on philosophy of science literature, more particularly the field of Science and Technology Studies (STS). The term "hybrid" has been used by Bruno Latour in STS to describe hybrid constructs in which the scientific and the social aspects are inextricably entangled with each other. Also, Peter M Haas distinguished "hybrid" facts from brute and social facts. Just like hybrid standards

review[70] will be used here to underline that although the above tests are justified by legal rationality, reasoners cannot apply them without directly reflecting on and engaging with the scientific evidence involved in the case. Such hybrid standards of review hence enable legal adjudicators to craft a persuasive argumentation in questions including interlinked issues of science and law while still speaking the language of a legalistic assessment.

Indeed, any attempt to strictly separate the scientific and the legal dimensions of the reasonableness, coherence, and consistency reviews is a somewhat perplexing exercise. Judge Owada's rhetorical question, posed in *Whaling*, points rather emblematically to the peculiarity of such tests: "is it the legal or the scientific context that the Court claims to be engaged in?"[71] This study proposes that the answer to this query is "both," as the reasonableness standard prompted the ICJ to evaluate a feature of the research scheme, which had close ties to both legal and scientific analysis. As will be argued later on, legal tests with such an epistemic characteristic should not disrupt the judicial inquiry; but should rather be seen as a virtue of the courts' analysis and reasoning.

Moreover, these converging standards of review promote an intrusive scrutiny into the scientific bases of claims instead of confining the judicial review to a formalistic assessment of the strictly legalistic aspects of applicable dilemmas. These standards of review therefore invite and necessitate an in-depth judicial engagement with scientific knowledge, given that courts and tribunals can hardly form a solid opinion on the existence of a comprehensible link between scientific facts and risk assessors' conclusions, or on the reasonableness of a research scheme's implementation without forming a basic understanding of the scientific issues implicated in the legal controversy.

4. Justifications for Setting Intrusive and Science-Intensive Hybrid Standards of Review

The proliferation of intrusive tests for reviewing the scientific allegations of litigants is somewhat striking given that affording deference to primary risk assessors and science-based legislators has been an established practice of international

of review, hybrid facts also "stretch the reach" of a given expert community. See Bruno Latour, *We Have Never Been Modern* (Harvester Wheatsheaf 1993) 3; Peter M Haas, "Ideas, Experts and Governance" in Mónika Ambrus and others (eds), *The Role of Experts in International and European Decision-Making Processes* (CUP 2014) 25.

[70] For a more detailed analysis of the epistemic benefits and perils of using such a hybrid standard of review, see Sulyok, *Science and Judicial Reasoning* (n 2) 323–28, 351–57.

[71] *Whaling in the Antarctic* (Dissenting Opinion of Judge Owada) (n 10) [25].

courts and tribunals.[72] The ensuing analysis will defend the application of this less deferential standard of review on epistemic legitimacy grounds.

It deems appropriate to first clarify the concept of epistemic legitimacy, from the angle of which this contribution evaluates the different standards of review. Legitimacy, in its broadest sense means the right to pass authoritative judgments, and is traditionally measured from a normative and sociological standpoint.[73] However, the persuasive and thus, legitimate nature of a judgment is also dependent upon the quality of the judicial reasoning.[74] Epistemic legitimacy posits that the presence of science has implications for the legitimate and persuasive nature of the reasoning,[75] because inadequate ways of reflecting on the scientific dimensions of disputes results in "inaccurate, opaque" and altogether "unconvincing"[76] decisions.

The ways in which judges treat scientific arguments in their analysis impact the legitimacy of their judgments in idiosyncratic ways.[77] On the one hand, science is seen as a necessary prerequisite of legitimate decision-making in a democratic society, which favors making rational choices involving questions of scientific risks.[78] In the context of judicial review, this translates into requiring states to substantiate the objective factual bases of their allegedly science-based policies and measures. On the other hand, preserving the effectiveness of judicial review also militates against applying automatic deference to the scientific allegations of the parties. Granting total deference tolerates the litigants' abuse of scientific authority for concealing value choices not rooted in scientific facts. In sum, judgments that disregard the factual realities in disputes with manifest scientific dimensions prove unconvincing from an epistemic point of view. Only those judicial findings are seen as objective and unbiased that are based on a "careful consideration of relevant facts."[79]

At the same time, as soon as courts are willing to conduct a substantive assessment into scientific allegations another set of legitimacy challenges arise. If judges do not properly account for relevant scientific knowledge in their intrusive scrutiny,

[72] Gruszczynski and Werner (eds), *Deference in International Courts and Tribunals: Standard of Review and Margin of Appreciation* (n 6) 2.

[73] Harlan Grant Cohen and others, "Legitimacy and International Courts: A Framework" in Harlan Grant Cohen and others (eds), *Legitimacy and International Courts* (CUP 2018).

[74] Yuval Shany, *Assessing the Effectiveness of International Courts* (OUP 2014) 37.

[75] For a similar inquiry in the context of WTO law, see CA Thomas, "Of Facts and Phantoms: Economics, Epistemic Legitimacy, and WTO Dispute Settlement" (2011) 14 Journal of International Economic Law 295.

[76] ibid 288.

[77] For a detailed analysis of the impact of scientific arguments on the legitimacy of judicial reasoning, see Sulyok, *Science and Judicial Reasoning* (n 2) chs 2, 10.

[78] Robert Howse, "Democracy, Science, and Free Trade: Risk Regulation on Trial at the World Trade Organization" (1999) 98 Michigan Law Review 2329, 2330.

[79] Daniel C Esty, "Good Governance at the World Trade Organization: Building a Foundation of Administrative Law" (2007) 10 Journal of International Economic Law 509, 517.

the decision would be arbitrary from an epistemic point of view. The ability of a judicial bench to integrate scientific authority into their inquiry much depends on their scientific fact-finding powers, which shape their epistemic competence to evaluate the scientific arguments of the parties. A major risk in this respect lies in making epistemically arbitrary judgments, where a scientific knowledge claim is judged by standards alien to scientific knowledge, for instance, according to legalistic logic. Such arbitrary decisions are viewed as illegitimate from an epistemic point of view.[80] To guard against such failures, judicial fora usually seek expert advice to evaluate the parties' factual claims. Yet, this may result in outsourcing the appraisal of science-intensive questions entirely to experts, which threatens with delegating or even eroding the judicial function.[81] This again would give rise to understandable legitimacy concerns.

Against the background of such a legitimacy conundrum, setting more science-intensive, hybrid standards of review yields an epistemically legitimate judicial approach in science-heavy adjudication. Respect for epistemic legitimacy requires that adjudicators retain epistemic control over scientific expertise, and their scrutiny adequately reflect on the scientific profile of cases. A number of reasons suggest that judges need not shy away from setting less deferential standards of review that enable them to directly engage with the scientific evidence in their inquiry.

First of all, a significant benefit of drawing on hybrid standards of review lies in retaining epistemic judicial control over scientific expertise. Putting it differently, legally trained reasoners can easily form an opinion about qualities such as reasonableness, consistency, or coherence autonomously from the expert submissions. Such hybrid concepts function as points of translation on the law-science interface, about which lawyers can well formulate their own reading. For instance, "incoherent" reasoning can be comfortably detected from a *legal point of view*, in cases where the inferences drawn are not logical, the uncertainties are not revealed or left out of the analysis, or conclusions suffer from serious inconsistencies or gaps in the underlying facts. Doing so ensures that scientific opinions put forth by experts do not dictate the judicial decision in a dispute.

Importantly, this is not to suggest that scientific evidence is, or let alone should be, irrelevant to the legal interpretation of these translation points. These concepts do have a scientific grounding. The advantage of such standards of review is that they enable courts to assume full responsibility for the adjudicatory process by not delegating the judicial function to experts. This feature is aptly illustrated by the

[80] Nathan Ballantyne, "Epistemic Trespassing" (2019) 128 Mind 367; Scott Brewer, "Scientific Expert Testimony and Intellectual Due Process" (1998) 107 Yale Law Journal 1535; Jean D'Aspremont and Makane Moïse Mbengue, "Strategies of Engagement with Scientific Fact-Finding in International Adjudication" (2014) 5 Journal of International Dispute Settlement 240.

[81] Daniel Peat, "The Use of Court-Appointed Experts by The International Court of Justice" (2014) 84 British Yearbook of International Law 271, 289.

Whaling case, where the ICJ notably formed its own reading of the notion of "scientific research" without strictly following either parties' scientific expert position on the matter. As addressed above, the lengthy application of the reasonableness test touched upon several of the features that the *ex parte* scientific experts described as essential for identifying the "scientific" method. This illustrates that intrusive standards of review are conducive to a judicial appraisal that is closely informed by scientific arguments and expert assessments.

Moreover, intrusive standards of review do not yield epistemically arbitrary decisions, as employing each of them lies within the epistemic competence of legal adjudicators and respects the requirement of epistemic non-arbitrariness. Hence, they do not force judges to act as "super-experts," as they do not need to dwell on whether the scientific claim at hand is "the" single correct answer to the applicable scientific controversy. They only need to ascertain whether the respective claim can be regarded, for purposes of deciding the legal dispute, as "a" legitimate answer in light of the scientific evidence submitted.

Setting intrusive standards of review also promotes assuming an "informational catalyst"[82] role of courts. By reviewing whether the primary decision-makers have provided explanations that fully account for the complexities of scientific data and its plausible interpretation,[83] judges in fact seek to ensure that the competent authorities discharge their obligations to carefully examine complex scientific matters. In other words, adjudicators should touch upon the scientific aspects of disputes in order to "prompt responsible actors to engage in effective problem solving."[84] Such a judicial approach advances better scientific regulations without the need to act themselves as science courts.

Lastly, employing such science-intensive standards of review fits well with the epistemic competence of lawyer judges. As the *Whaling in the Antarctic* judgment so pertinently shows, hybrid scrutiny does not make it the task of a judicial panel to judge the correct (and hence, reasonable) nature of a sample size of an alleged research program for purposes of accepting it as part of the scientific discourse. Doing so requires high level of literacy in ecology, statistics, and other specialized fields of sciences. Yet, judges can very well conduct a reasonableness inquiry for purposes of evaluating the reasonableness of the sample size *from the law's perspective*. This appraisal requires expertise in abstract conceptual thinking, inferential reasoning and balancing, complemented by a basic understanding of the arguments provided by ecologists regarding their opinion on the scientific "reasonableness" of the sample size.

82 This term was coined by Ellen Vos: see Vos, "The European Court of Justice in the Face of Scientific Uncertainty and Complexity" (n 12) 152.

83 See in the WTO context, WTO Appellate Body Report, *US—Safeguard Measures on Imports of Fresh, Chilled or Frozen Lamb from New Zealand*, WT/DS177/AB/R (adopted 1 May 2001) [186].

84 Joanne Scott and Susan Sturm, "Courts as Catalysts: Re-Thinking the Judicial Role in New Governance" (2007) 13 Columbia Journal of European Law 565, 575.

In sum, the above features of an intrusive review ensure that judges meaningfully check the parties' scientific arguments while they act in a manner well within their epistemic and legal competence and mandate. Importantly, nothing in the above aims to suggest that granting deference to states can never be justified in respect of the internal decision-making authority of states. Deference can be justifiably granted to states in recognition of their source-based legitimacy[85] in questions of internal policy. The proposal set forth here only argues that a deferential review in such cases should not be based on scientific epistemic grounds, as international fora are emphatically capable of crafting tests for judicial review that can touch upon the scientific aspects of the measures under review and, at the same time, fall within their epistemic competence. Importantly, showing judicial respect for states' sovereign policy choices can only be justified to the extent appropriate under the applicable legal regime. Moreover, adjudicatory review should ensure that the cognitive power of scientific knowledge is not abused by litigants to constrain the extent and depth of the judicial review. It is equally necessary for a legitimate exercise of deference that international courts openly reveal the grounds of deference in their analysis.

5. Conclusion

The increasing intrusion of science into various spheres of human life transforms all major social institutions.[86] International adjudication can be no exception. The ever-increasing presence of scientific arguments in litigation shapes the ways in which adjudicators can craft persuasive and legitimate judgments. Since the second half of the twentieth century international law itself "[has] become a more and more complex and many-sided subject."[87] Against this background, setting more science-intensive standards of review appears to be inevitable, as it is the sole judicial approach that does justice to the complex factual aspects of science-based disputes and ensures that judges discharge their judicial function in a meaningful way in science-heavy litigation.

This analysis has posited that having a closer judicial look at the scientific dimensions of disputes entails epistemically more legitimate judgments compared to deferential judicial attitudes. Concern for epistemic legitimacy warns against affording total deference to litigants' technical claims. Hence automatic acceptance of sovereigns' scientific allegations ought to give way to more nuanced and epistemically intrusive standards of review. Legal tests interrogating the

[85] Shirlow, *Judging at the Interface* (n 6) 27.

[86] Sheila Jasanoff, "Ordering Knowledge, Ordering Society" in Sheila Jasanoff (ed), *States Of Knowledge: The Co-Production of Science and Social Order* (Routledge 2004) 13.

[87] Wolfgang Friedmann, *The Changing Structure of International Law* (Stevens & Sons 1964) 70.

reasonableness, consistency, or coherence of science-based reasoning were argued here to be epistemically legitimate techniques to assess the merits of such claims. Importantly, nothing of the present study suggests that the level of required intrusiveness should necessarily entail a *de novo* review.

This comparative overview also suggested that conducting an intrusive judicial review has wider implications for the judicial function. A more hands-on judicial approach towards reviewing science-based legal claims necessitates that judges "improve their overall level of understanding of the science at play in the given case."[88] In order to observe epistemic legitimacy, reasoners must be able to grasp the main scientific points of contention in a legal dispute.[89] Certainly, there are limits to lawyer adjudicators' capacity to engage with the scientific evidence even if they are vested with adequate procedural powers and institutional settings to benefit from expert assistance. Yet, as the above overview of the case law of international courts attests, conducting a science-intensive, intrusive scrutiny has already proved to be a feasible task for a number of jurisdictions.

Finally, this contribution stressed on the basis of epistemic legitimacy that judges cannot decide science-intensive legal questions persuasively without interacting and engaging to some extent with relevant scientific knowledge. If adjudicators marginalize the scientific profile of disputes or replace scientific authority in their assessments, science will haunt them by providing a persuasive tool to those critiquing their judgments and seeking to erode the legitimacy capital of respective judicial fora. If, however, scientific claims are adequately reviewed and scientific knowledge is properly accounted for in the judicial reasoning, international judges could harness the cognitive authority of science to buttress the persuasive and legitimate nature of their own findings. When legal disputes are increasingly becoming imbued with significant techno-scientific dimensions, judicial methods that facilitate reflecting on such aspects in their inquiry seem to be a necessary and legitimate response to the challenges of adjudication in the twenty-first century.

[88] *Pulp Mills on the River Uruguay (Argentina v Uruguay)* (Joint Dissenting Opinions of Judge Al-Khasawneh and Judge Simma) [2010] ICJ Rep 14 [16].

[89] For a similar argument, see Ballantyne, "Epistemic Trespassing" (n 80) 376.

PART II

CAUSATION IN INTERNATIONAL LAW

6

A "Missed" Secondary Rule?

Causation in the Breach of Preventive and Due Diligence Obligations

Alice Ollino

1. Introduction

This chapter addresses the role of causation in the establishment of wrongfulness. It critically revisits the International Law Commission (ILC) proposition in the Articles on the Responsibility of States for Internationally Wrongful Acts (ARSIWA)[1] that place causation at the level of primary rules. Specifically, the chapter questions the soundness of the ILC's final stand on rules about the breach of obligations to prevent and it queries whether the Commission should have paid more attention to the function served by causation vis-à-vis these obligations and, more broadly, vis-à-vis obligations of due diligence.

Scholarship's contribution to causation in the law of international responsibility is still scant but has received increasing attention over the past few years.[2] Most studies on the topic focus on the content of responsibility and the consequences of the injury, in line with the ARSIWA's approach that separates the concept of the breach from the question of damage, treating causation only as an element of the latter.[3] Few studies have discussed the function served by causation in establishing the international wrongful act (IWA). Furthermore, those that have addressed the question have done so in a sectoral fashion and not from a general perspective.[4]

[1] ILC, Articles on Responsibility of States for Internationally Wrongful Acts (ARSIWA), UN Doc A/56/83 (3 August 2001).

[2] See Ilias Plakokefalos, "Causation in the Law of State Responsibility and the Problem of Overdetermination: in Search of Clarity" (2015) 26 European Journal of International Law 471; Dàvid Pusztai, "Causation in the Law of State Responsibility" (PhD thesis, University of Cambridge 2017); Vladyslav Lanovoy, "Causation in the Law of State Responsibility" (2022) British Yearbook of International Law 1; Alice Ollino and Giuseppe Puma, "La causalità e il suo ruolo nella determinazione dell'illecito internazionale" (2022) 105 Rivista di diritto internazionale 313.

[3] See eg Brigitte Stern, *Le préjudice dans la théorie de la responsabilité internationale* (Pedone 1973).

[4] A notable exception is Andrea Gattini, "Breach of International Obligations" in André Nollkaemper and Ilias Plakokefalos (eds), *Principles of Shared Responsibility in International Law* (CUP 2014); sectorial studies include Vladislava Stoyanova, "Causation between State Omission and Harm within the Framework of Positive Obligations under the European Convention on Human Rights" (2018) 18 Human Rights Law Review 309; Patrick W Pearsall and Benton Heath, "Causation and Injury in Investor-State Arbitration" in Christina Beharry (ed), *Contemporary and Emerging Issues on the Law of Damages and Valuation in International Investment Arbitration* (Brill 2018).

Alice Ollino, *A "Missed" Secondary Rule?* In: *Secondary Rules of Primary Importance in International Law.*
Edited by: Gábor Kajtár, Başak Çalı, and Marko Milanovic, Oxford University Press.
DOI: 10.1093/oso/9780192869012.003.0006

By considering the role causation plays in the establishment of responsibility, this chapter seeks to address this gap.

The analysis of the function served by causation in the establishment of wrongfulness is part of the broader discussion on what type of rules qualify as secondary rules of responsibility and how they interact with primary norms. It is commonly acknowledged that the criterion on generality inspires secondary rules of the ARSIWA[5] and that the separation between primary and secondary rules builds on a functional rather than ontological distinction.[6] This is particularly true of Part I of the ARSIWA—devoted to identifying the elements for an IWA to accrue—which reveals the highest degree of continuity with the realm of primary rules and reflects substantive aspects of the latter. And yet, classifying a rule as of secondary character is not without consequences. Secondary rules of responsibility inevitably affect the scope and content of primary rules. Provisions of the ARSIWA have a bearing upon the nature of international obligations and contribute to defining their content.[7] Furthermore, if the criterion underlying secondary rules is that of generality, the assumption is that every standard or additional element arising at the responsibility level and labelled by the ILC as a question of primary rules must be subject to *in casu* judgments and cannot form the object of general propositions.

These two aspects emerge when one undertakes to analyze causation in relation to breaches of preventive and other due diligence obligations. First, the provision of article 14(3) of the ARSIWA laying down the temporal element of breaches of preventive obligations has impacted the interpretation of these obligations, somehow "obscuring" their due diligence character and downplaying the role that causation serves in their breaches. Second, the understanding of causation as an issue related to the content of specific primary rules obscures that causal queries are often "the heart of the matter" when assessing state responsibility for failure to act with due diligence.

With this in mind, this chapter begins by laying down some general observations on the meaning of causation in international responsibility and explores the ARSIWA's approach toward this concept (sections 2 and 3). The chapter proceeds with critically revisiting the ILC's choice to leave causation outside the secondary elements required for the breach of preventive obligations (section 4.1), and then discusses causality concerning these obligations and other due diligence duties. Finally, section 5 explores the normative function of causation and its "secondary" character in establishing state responsibility for failure to act diligently, followed by a brief conclusion.

[5] ARSIWA Commentary (n 1) art 31.

[6] James Crawford, "The ILC's Articles on Responsibility of States for International Wrongful Acts: A Retrospect" (2002) 96 American Journal of International Law 874, 879.

[7] Giorgio Gaja, "Primary and Secondary Rules in the International Law on State Responsibility" (2014) 97 Rivista di Diritto Internazionale 981.

2. General Issues

What is causation, and what does it mean to inquire about causality in the establishment of the IWA? This preliminary question is necessary given the complexity of the concept of causation in law. While every branch of the law is, at some point, concerned with causal problems and the extent to which the legal causation departs from causation in natural sciences,[8] the definition and relevance of cause in law vary significantly across legal systems and legal cultures.[9] For example, in criminal law, a causal link between the action of the accused and specific harm must often be demonstrated in order to establish the *existence* of liability. In tort law, however, causal queries between action and harm typically arise in order to establish not the existence of liability but its *extent*.[10] Similarly, some legal systems, and especially Anglo-American legal doctrine, distinguish between cause-in-fact and scope of liability and treat only the latter as a "true" causal inquiry. Specifically, these approaches regard the process of establishing cause-in-fact as a purely factual inquiry, based mostly on common sense and aimed at determining whether particular conduct physically caused an event. They regard as a "true" legal causal question only the determination of the scope of liability, that is, the process aimed at distinguishing whether the identified cause-in-fact is a simple condition of the event or the relevant (legal) cause of it.[11] On the contrary, European "continental" theories avoid the distinction between cause-in-fact and scope of liability and tend to treat the whole process of dealing with causes as a normative assessment.[12]

In this light, I adopt a broad definition of causation as the process connecting two occurrences, allowing one to affirm that one occurrence is the effect or consequence of the other.[13] Since, in legal theory, causality is usually invoked to connect the (in)action of an individual with a particular—harmful—outcome,[14] this chapter defines causation as the process of establishing a link between a *conduct* and a specific event. The chapter considers situations in which causal inquiries arise between *state* conduct and a harmful event. It does not consider causation as the process linking the state as a legal entity with a particular harmful outcome.

[8] Agamben defines causality as "the edifice of law", see Giorgio Agamben, *Karman: breve trattato sull'azione, la colpa e il gesto* (Bollati Boringhieri 2017); Kelsen's pure theory of law instead is concerned with distinguishing causality, which belongs to natural science, and imputation, seen as the functional connection between a fact and its normative consequences: see Hans Kelsen, "Causality and Imputation" (1950) 61 Ethics 1.

[9] For an overview of how causality in law is treated across systems and legal cultures, see Herbert LA Hart and Tony Honoré, *Causation in the Law* (OUP 1985).

[10] ibid 133.

[11] Jane Stapleton, "Legal Cause: Cause-in-Fact and the Scope of Liability for Consequences" (2001) 54 Vanderbilt Law Review 942.

[12] Hart and Honoré, *Causation in the Law* (n 9) 465–97; on how the distinction applies for instance to criminal law, see Paulo de Sousa Mendes, "A Semantic Model for Causation in Criminal Law and the Need of Logico-Legal Criteria for the Attribution of Causation" (2013) Law, Probability and Risk 207.

[13] Hart and Honoré, *Causation in the Law* (n 9) 10.

[14] ibid 87.

This is a necessary premise since there may be situations that seem at first sight to involve causal queries but that, in reality, deal with other issues, such as questions of attribution of conduct.[15]

From this perspective, in construing the function that causation plays in determining the *existence* of an IWA, this contribution takes the framework of the ARSIWA as a starting point. Before the ARSIWA, part of international scholarship did understand responsibility merely as a matter of direct or indirect factual causation between a harmful event and the state's international person.[16] However, with Special Rapporteur Ago introducing the notion of attribution of conduct, the ILC moved away from these theories. Ago created a conceptual separation between the *lien de rattachement* of a physical person's conduct with the state—grounded in the notion of attribution of conduct—and the *lien de rattachement* of the state with the harmful event—grounded in the concept of attribution of responsibility.[17] One may even argue that it is very much this understanding of attribution of conduct, coupled with the idea that damage is not a prerequisite for a breach to come to existence, which explains why causation is *prima facie* irrelevant in assessing international wrongfulness.

Finally, the following analysis is concerned primarily with causality in omissions. In international law, as will be shown, inquiries on how far causality between state conduct and a harmful event is necessary for wrongfulness to arise, mainly with state omissions. For this reason, I do not consider it necessary for the present purpose to make further consideration of the distinction between cause-in-fact and scope of liability, nor to demonstrate whether causation concerning wrongfulness belongs only to one or both processes. While international scholarship has somewhat relied on this separation,[18] there are good reasons to abandon the distinction in the analysis that follows. First, the separation between cause-in-fact and scope of liability has been subject to criticism because assessing whether conduct caused the harm is a factual exercise that often includes normative evaluations.[19] Second, and more importantly, the validity of this separation seems to collapse before omissions. Causality by omission is always a normative endeavor, as it is

[15] Yet, the approach reading attribution of conduct through a causal lens has been supported lately by some scholars: see Berenice Boutin, "Attribution of Conduct in International Military Operations: A Causal Analysis of Effective Control" (2017) 18 Melbourne Journal of International Law 154; Tom Dannenbaum, "Translating the Standard of Effective Control into a System of Effective Accountability: How Liability Should Be Apportioned for Violations of Human Rights by Member State Troop Contingents Serving as United Nations Peacekeepers" (2010) 51 Harvard International Law Journal 113, 157.

[16] See eg Rolando Quadri, "Cours général de droit international public" (1964) 113 Recueil de Cours de l'Académie de Droit International 245, 458–59.

[17] ARSIWA (n 1) arts 16, 17, 18.

[18] James Crawford, *The International Law Commission's Articles on State Responsibility: Introduction, Text and Commentary* (OUP 2002) 204; García Amador, "Sixth Report on State Responsibility" (1961) II(2) Yearbook of the International Law Commission 40–41.

[19] David Hamer, "'Factual Causation' and 'Scope of Liability': What's the Difference?" (2014) 77 Modern Law Review 155; Tony Honoré, *Responsibility and Fault* (Hart 1999) 94.

never built upon the effects of some active physical intervention over the course of events. Establishing causality by omission always requires first identifying an alleged omitted conduct and then embarking on an intellectual and counter-factual process, which is explicable as, "if the alleged omitted conduct had been performed, the course of the events would have changed, or the event would not have occurred." In law, these considerations are indeed normative[20] and depend on the type of causal test or approach that one adopts in the circumstances of the case. In this light, this contribution conceptualizes causality for establishing wrongfulness as the *entire* process aimed at connecting one's conduct with the occurrence of a (harmful) event.

3. The Approach of the ARSIWA Towards Causation

A cursory glance at the ARSIWA indicates that the articles do not consider causation a normative element of the international wrongful act. First, it is very much the definition of the IWA that excludes causation from the process of establishing wrongfulness. Article 2 of the ARSIWA affirms that responsibility arises from two necessary conditions: (1) conduct attributable to the state, which is (2) contrary to an international obligation to which the state is bound. This definition leaves out any causal nexus between internationally wrongful conduct and the occurrence of some damage, wrongful result, or injury and introduces an "objective control of legality" into the institution of responsibility.[21] What needs for wrongfulness to accrue is the state's failure to conform to the content of an international rule. This way, the ARSIWA creates an "objectivized" system in which responsibility exists independently of its effects.[22]

Indeed, the ARSIWA conceptually separates the notion of wrongfulness from that of reparation.[23] While wrongfulness rests merely on a state's failure to perform conduct in a way compatible with the content of an international obligation, reparation belongs to the *consequences* of international responsibility—that is, to any moral or material *effect* that the wrongful act (or omission) might have generated. Causal inquiries are inescapably attached to the content of responsibility and the *quantum* due in reparation. In this regard, article 31 of the ARSIWA provides that the responsible state is under the obligation to make full reparation for the injury

[20] On the normative character of omissions, see Sarah McGrath, "Causation by Omission: A Dilemma" (2005) 123 Philosophical Studies 125.

[21] Brigitte Stern, "The Elements of An Internationally Wrongful Act" in James Crawford, Alain Pellet, and Simon Olleson (eds), *The Law of International Responsibility* (CUP 2010) 194.

[22] Alain Pellet, "Remarques sur une révolution inachevée. Le projet d'Articles de la CDI sur la responsabilité des États" (1996) 42 Annuaire Française de Droit International 4.

[23] James Crawford, "First Report on State Responsibility" (1998) II(2) Yearbook of the International Law Commission 24.

caused by the IWA and that injury includes any moral or material damage brought about by the wrong.

During the ILC work on state responsibility, Special Rapporteur Arangio-Ruiz discussed the notion of cause concerning reparation and the types of causal tests used in practice to evaluate the links between a state's wrongful act and the damage produced.[24] However, in the final version of the ARSIWA, the articles are silent on how causation should operate with the content of responsibility. No reference is provided as to the standards of causation to be preferred when computing the extent of the injury. The articles only lay minimum basic principles. For example, article 39 establishes that the contribution to the injury by the willful or negligent action or omission of the injured state shall be taken into account in the determination of reparation. However, nothing is said about cases where the injury occurred due to the state's wrongful conduct combined with other circumstances, such as a fortuitous event or the action (or omission) of third parties, like states or individuals acting on their own. Nor is it explained why contributions to the injury in these last cases should raise no causal issues, whereas the contribution to the injury by the injured state implies an adaptation in the amount of reparation due.[25]

Despite the neat separation between wrongfulness and reparation, the ARSIWA does not entirely exclude that causality may also play a role in determining the IWA. The articles adopt a distinct approach that acknowledges the potential role of causation but steers clear of discussing its substance. Specifically, the commentary to article 2 notes that the breach of some rules may depend on assessing subjective elements (like fault) or objective standards, such as causation. These standards, however, pertain to the content of the primary rule and should not be treated as secondary issues of responsibility:

> [S]tandards vary from one context to another for reasons which essentially relate to the object and purpose of the treaty provision or other rules giving rise to the primary obligation. Nor do the articles lay down any presumption in this regard as between the different possible standards. Establishing this is a matter for the interpretation and application of the primary rules engaged in the given case.[26]

This approach gives rise to two considerations. First, the criterion that identifies secondary rules is essentially that of generality. The ARSIWA only provides general rules on international responsibility applicable across international law and regardless of the type of the international obligation and its application in a context.[27] Second, the relevance of causality for establishing the breach depends on *in*

[24] Gaetano Arangio-Ruiz, "Second Report on State Responsibility" (1989) II(2) Yearbook of the International Law Commission 12–16.

[25] See, however, James Crawford, *State Responsibility: The General Part* (CUP 2013) 500.

[26] ARSIWA (n 1) arts 34–35.

[27] But see ARSIWA (n 1) art 55.

casu judgments where interpreters consider the content and interpretation of the applicable primary norm.

4. Causation in the Establishment of the Breach

4.1 Prevention and Causation in the Work on the ARSIWA

A review of the work on the ARSIWA shows that the ILC did not always construe causation for the purpose of wrongfulness as an issue of primary rules. In 1963, the ILC Sub-Committee on State Responsibility had raised preliminary points on general aspects of the state responsibility to be submitted to the Commission for further consideration. These included the following:

> ...
> *First point: Origin of international responsibility.*
> (1) *International wrongful act:* ...
> (2) *Determination of the component parts of the international wrongful act* ...
> (3) *The various kind of violation of international obligations.* Questions relating to the practical scope of the distinctions which can be made.
> International wrongful acts arising from conduct alone and those arising from events. *The causal relationship between conduct and event.*[28]

The Sub-Committee had considered that questions on the existence of an IWA would depend on the type of international obligation violated. Specifically, concerning IWAs arising from events, issues of causality between state conduct, and the event would arise.

To understand the notion of international wrongful acts arising from events and why causation was initially considered relevant for their existence, one needs to reappraise the taxonomy of obligations made by Special Rapporteur Roberto Ago during his work in the ILC. Special Rapporteur Ago had introduced a tripartite classification that included obligations of conduct, obligations of result, and obligations to prevent [a given event]. Obligations of conduct were defined as obligations requiring the state to adopt a particular course of conduct, for they determine the means of attaining the result set by the obligation in question. Their breach would arise by virtue of a state adopting a course of conduct different from that required explicitly by the obligation.[29] Obligations of result, being "concerned with

[28] Roberto Ago, "First Report on State Responsibility" (1989) II(2) Yearbook of the International Law Commission 139 (last emphasis added).

[29] Roberto Ago, "Sixth Report on State Responsibility" (1977) II(2) Yearbook of the International Law Commission 5–6.

respect for the internal freedom of the State,"[30] merely required the state to ensure a particular result. A breach would arise if the state did not achieve the required result in exercising freedom of choice regarding the means to be adopted.[31] Hence, article 2(1) of the International Covenant of Economic, Social, and Cultural Rights (ICESCR)[32] requiring a state to "undertake to take steps ... with the view to achieving progressively the full realisation of the rights recognised in the present Covenant by all appropriate means" constituted for Ago a typical obligation of result. This is, in fact, an obligation imposing on a state to take measures to achieve the progressive realization of certain rights without specifying the course of conduct to be taken for this realization.[33]

As for preventive obligations, Special Rapporteur Ago linked them to the notion of the harmful event. Taking as illustrative examples states' obligation to protect the premises of a foreign embassy against injurious acts of third parties and, more generally, situations where the preventive action consists of state's surveillance and vigilance with a view to preventing a given event, Ago affirmed that breaches of preventive obligations required two conditions to be met. First, the event to be prevented had to occur. Second, a breach would only accrue if the harmful event was made possible by state's failure to act to prevent it. To stress the link between the event and the state's failure to prevent it, Ago noted that it was not sufficient for state conduct *per se* and the event to have occurred independently of each other,[34] state conduct had to be regarded "as the direct or indirect cause of the event."[35]

Ago considered obligations to prevent essentially as obligations of "negative result." On the one hand, these obligations allowed states to adopt any conduct provided that the event to be prevented did not occur. On the other hand, the event's occurrence would not engage *by itself* the responsibility of a state for failure to prevent it, since the event would have to be ascribed to negligence and a lack of vigilance on the part of the state.[36] In Ago's words: "it must be possible to establish the existence of a certain relationship of causality, at least indirect, between the conduct of state organs and the event; the conduct must have made possible the occurrence of the event which *otherwise* would not have occurred."[37]

Draft article 23—adopted by the ILC on the first reading—reflected Ago's understanding of obligations to prevent. It articulated the breach of these obligations in the following terms: "When the result required of a State by an international

[30] ibid.
[31] ibid 20.
[32] International Covenant of Economic, Social, and Cultural Rights (adopted 16 December 1966, entered into force 3 January 1976) 993 UNTS 3.
[33] ibid.
[34] Roberto Ago, "Second Report on State Responsibility" (1970) II(2) Yearbook of the International Law Commission 194.
[35] ibid.
[36] Roberto Ago, "Seventh Report on State Responsibility" (1978) II(2) Yearbook of the International Law Commission 32.
[37] ibid 35.

obligation is the prevention, by means of its own choice, of the occurrence of a given event, there is a breach of that obligation only if, *by the conduct adopted*, the State does not achieve that result."[38] This formulation confirmed that a breach would arise solely from the occurrence of the event coupled with state conduct causally linked to such event. To emphasize the need for a causal nexus, the commentary to this article also provided that "the said conduct may be regarded as a *sine qua non* of the event."[39]

In the current version of the ARSIWA, there is no provision corresponding to draft article 23. The only reference left is article 14(3), which deals with the temporal element of breaches of preventive obligations. Article 14(3) retains Ago's understanding that a breach of preventive obligations occurs when the event to be prevented occurs and extends over the entire period during which the event continues. However, the article is silent on a state's conduct vis-à-vis the event and fails to mention any causal link between the two. This change can be traced back to the revision by the last Special Rapporteur, Crawford, of the draft articles adopted on the first reading.

Crawford raised two major issues regarding the taxonomy of international obligations devised by Ago and initially supported by the ILC. First, for the Special Rapporteur, this taxonomy strayed too far in the field of primary obligations.[40] Its retention would have lessened the separation between primary and secondary rules and impinged on the domain of state responsibility, which was primarily devoted to consequences, effects, and results.[41] Any question related to the *type* of obligation had to be considered an issue of primary rules.[42] Furthermore, part of Crawford's criticism toward retaining Ago's taxonomy came from its substantive meaning, which the last Special Rapporteur labelled as "reversed" and "almost the opposite" of the domestic approach.[43] Indeed, in civil law systems, the distinguishing criterion between obligations of conduct and obligations of result builds on the notion of risk and not on determinacy of the means left to the state. Hence, obligations of result are obligations requiring the state to guarantee the attainment of a particular goal. Conversely, obligations of conduct are obligations to endeavor, only requiring the state to display best efforts towards achieving a particular result without the guarantee of success.

In relation to obligations to prevent, Crawford noted that, while their natural interpretation presupposes two conditions to be met—failure to take all available steps to prevent the event and occurrence of the event in question—this may not

[38] ILC, Report of the ILC on the Works of Its Forty-Eight Session, UN Doc A/51/10, 174 (1996) (emphasis added).

[39] ibid 176.

[40] James Crawford, "Second Report on State Responsibility" (1999) II(2) Yearbook of the International Law Commission 26.

[41] ibid 60–61.

[42] Crawford, "Second Report" (n 40) 26–27.

[43] ibid 21–22.

necessarily be the case.[44] First, there may be cases where the mere occurrence of the event triggers responsibility because the state has given the unconditional guarantee that the event will not occur.[45] These are, for example, obligations that make states liable for damages caused by activities undertaken in their territory or under their jurisdiction, like article 2 of the Convention on the International Liability for Damage Caused by Space Objects.[46] However, one must admit that, while clearly performing a preventive *function*, these obligations are hardly framed as obligations to prevent and usually takes the form of "direct" duties to pay compensation for damage caused.

Second, Crawford pointed to a further distinction between "pure" obligations to prevent and preventive obligations that are "true" obligations of conduct (in the civil law meaning). Pure obligations to prevent would effectively require the occurrence of the harmful event coupled with failure to prevent by state organs.[47] The second type of preventive obligations would instead comprise obligations of conduct imposing on the state a continuous effort to prevent harmful outcomes; their breach would accrue from the state's manifest failure to act, regardless of the occurrence of such event.[48] For example, article 22(2) of the Vienna Convention on Diplomatic Relations (VCDR) belonged for Crawford to this latter category, for it imposes a continuous effort on the host state to take appropriate measures to protect the mission.[49]

Against this backdrop, it strikes one that in the final version of the ARSIWA, the ILC opted for dropping any reference to the conduct adopted by the state (and causation) but did retain the event's occurrence as a secondary element of breaches of preventive obligations. If preventive obligations are indeed manifold, and primacy in their interpretation should always be given to the content of the primary rule, one would have expected that both conditions (conduct of the state causally linked to the event and occurrence of the event) would not have survived the final scrutiny of the ILC.

Instead, by maintaining the occurrence of the event as a secondary rule of responsibility and reducing causation to a question of primary rules, the articles inevitably affect the scope and understanding of *all* obligations to prevent. Indeed, article 14(3) precludes the interpretation of preventive obligations as pure obligations of conduct, whose focus is on the efforts to be made by the state toward the

44 ibid 29.

45 ibid.

46 Convention on the International Liability for Damage Caused by Space Object (adopted 29 March 1972, entered into force 1 September 1972) 961 UNTS 187.

47 Crawford labelled the obligation to prevent transboundary environmental harm as an obligation of this kind, see Crawford, "Second Report" (n 40) 28.

48 See Pierre-Marie Dupuy, "Reviewing the Difficulties of Codification: On Ago's Classification of Obligations of Means and Obligations of Result in Relation to State Responsibility" (1999) 10 European Journal of International Law 371.

49 Crawford, "Second Report" (n 40) 28.

achievement of specific results and not on the ultimate result achieved. To a certain extent, this "paradox" can be appreciated in the 2007 *Genocide* case. In the *Genocide* case, the International Court of Justice (ICJ) labelled the obligation to prevent genocide as one of due diligence arising "the instant that the State learns of, or should normally have learned of, the existence of a serious risk that genocide will be committed." Nevertheless, the ICJ noted that the breach of this obligation depends on the occurrence of genocide.[50] This understanding of prevention collapses even before one of the most classic preventive obligations, that is, the duty to prevent transboundary environmental harm. While the ICJ has so far construed the breach of such obligation in accordance with article 14(3), to identify the main focus of this obligation as non-occurrence of damage would overlook the international legal developments of the past fifty years as well as the ultimate aim of this rule, which is to anticipate the risk of harm through appropriate action.[51]

4.2 The Role of Causation in Due Diligence Obligations

There is also a second issue at stake in the final choice made by the ILC with article 14(3). If the event's occurrence is effectively a secondary element in assessing breaches of preventive obligations, this cannot be separated from the evaluation of conduct adopted by the state and its causal contribution to such an event. To clarify this point and why event and causation should be considered, if not as both secondary rules, at least in combination with each other, let us start by noting that the ARSIWA expressly identifies most preventive obligations as obligations of conduct.[52]

As obligations of conduct, preventive obligations only impose on the state the exercise of best efforts without asking for any warranty that the event will be prevented. These are obligations usually identified as due diligence obligations because of their strict connection with the notion of risk.[53] As a typology of international

[50] *Case Concerning Application of the Convention on the Prevention and Punishment of the Crime of Genocide (Bosnia Herzegovina v Serbia and Montenegro)* (Merits) [2007] ICJ Rep 430, 431.

[51] ILC Draft Articles on Prevention of Transboundary Harm from Hazardous Activities, with Commentaries (2001) II(2) Yearbook of the International Law Commission 153–55; *Certain Activities Carried Out by Nicaragua in the Border Area* (Costa Rica v Nicaragua) [2015] ICJ Rep 665; *Construction of a Road in Costa Rica along the San Juan River* (Nicaragua v Costa Rica) [2015] ICJ Rep 665 [192], [196], [207], [213], [216]–[217].

[52] ARSIWA Commentary (n 1) art 14(3).

[53] See Riccardo Pisillo-Mazzeschi, *Due diligence e responsabilitá internazionale degli Stati* (Giuffré 1989); Samantha Besson, "La due diligence en droit international" (2020) 409 Recueil de Cours de l'Académie de Droit International 22–57; on the link between risk and due diligence, see also Makane Moïse Mbengue, *Essai sur une theorie du risque en droit international public: l'anticipation du risque environnemental et sanitaire* (Pedone 2009) 75–95; on due diligence in general, see J Kulesza, *Due Diligence in international Law* (Brill 2016); ILA Study Group on Due Diligence in International Law, *Due Diligence in International Law: Second Report*, Johannesburg, 77th Session, 2016, available at <https://ila.vettoreweb.com/Storage/Download.aspx?DbStorageId=1427&StorageFileGuid=ed229726-4796-47f2-b891-8cafa221685f>.

obligations, primary rules of due diligence are postulated around the understanding that the object or purpose of the primary rule (ie prevention or protection of a harmful event; achievement of a specific goal) is outside the strict control of the state and cannot be guaranteed at any time and cost. A state under a due diligence obligation is a state expected to put in place measures to exercise its best effort (*due diligence*) toward attaining the object of the primary rule, but not to guarantee it. With obligations to prevent, states may not always be in a position to guarantee that prevention will be attained, for example, because the preventive action is designated against the activities of non-state actors or vis-à-vis lawful activities that are hazardous or carry some inherent risk. Hence, they are expected to act with due diligence *in order to* ensure prevention.

Regardless of their specific content and the areas of international law where they apply, primary rules of due diligence build around the concept of possibility.[54] Due diligence means requiring a state to exercise its best efforts toward a particular result, not to attain a result outside the state's ability to guarantee. Possibility thus shapes the *scope* of a state's duty to act with due diligence. If there is no possibility for a state to act in a particular circumstance, no duty to act arises in this case. Instead, the greater a state's ability is to act towards attaining the object of the primary rule of due diligence (eg prevention of a harmful act), the higher may be the level of effort and diligence required of a state to comply with its duty.

In the operation of due diligence obligations, the ability of a state to act (diligently) depends at least on two factual conditions. First, the state must be aware—or should be aware under normal circumstances—of the risk in relation to which it is expected to use due diligence. A state's duty to act with due diligence only arises if the state has knowledge or constructive knowledge of risks linked to the due diligence rule: a state cannot be expected to act upon risks unknown at the time the obligation of due diligence binds the state. One of the earliest and most authoritative accounts of this principle is the *Corfu Channel* case. The ICJ linked Albania's responsibility for having failed to avert damages to British vessels to Albania's knowledge of a minelaying in its territorial waters.[55] Yet, the notion that a duty to act arises should a state has knowledge or constructive knowledge of the risk linked to a due diligence rule is now recognized in the practice of due diligence obligations across international law.[56]

The second factual condition shaping the scope of a duty to act with due diligence is that the state has some power over the source of risk linked to the due

[54] On possibility as the basis of due diligence and specifically on the factual conditions that create possibility to act in due diligence obligations, see extensively Alice Ollino, *Due Diligence Obligations in International Law* (CUP 2022) 133–37.

[55] *Corfu Channel Case (UK v Albania)* (Merits) [1949] ICJ Rep 18–22.

[56] ILA, Second Report on Due Diligence (n 53) 12; Pasquale De Sena, "La 'due diligence' et le lien entre le sujet et le risqué qu'il faut prévenir: quelques observations" in Sarah Cassella (ed), *Le standard de due diligence et la responsabilité internationale* (Pedone 2018) 243.

diligence rule. If a state is bound to protect the premises of a diplomatic mission from external actions, for example, private individuals, a duty to act exists as long as the state holds some power over these individuals. Again, this has to do with possibility. If a state has no power over the source of risk, the state lacks the *capacity to affect* the situation that the primary rule of due diligence intends to change or manage. Hence, power over the source of risk determines a state's *capacity to affect* a specific outcome. This capacity creates the *possibility* for the state to act.

In assessing a state's capacity to affect a particular outcome, causation issues inevitably come to the fore. Appraising capacity to affect a situation toward which due diligence is required means that, should the risk linked to the primary rule of due diligence materialize, the question is whether and to what extent such materialization can be ascribed to the state. Specifically, suppose a state is under a due diligence obligation to prevent a harmful event, and this event occurs. In that case, failure to exercise due diligence only accrues if it is established that the state had the *power to* prevent, that is, the capacity to affect the situation toward which prevention was required. This clearly is a causal query.[57]

Practice on due diligence obligations confirms this finding. For due diligence obligations with a territorial dimension, causality between state conduct and the materialization of the risk is generally "embedded" in the state's control over its territory.[58] In other words, state's control over territory often operates as a presumption that the state has power over sources of risks emanating within it and thus the capacity to affect situations linked to the due diligence rule. However, even in these situations, should a state prove that it *effectively* lacked this power, causality between its conduct and the materialization of the risk will usually be excluded. Accordingly, the conclusion will be that it was not within the scope of a state's duty to act to exercise diligence toward the materialized risk. An example from human rights practice may clarify this point. In *Mastromatteo*, a man had been killed as a result of armed robbery by individuals granted temporary leave from Italian prisons. The European Court of Human Rights (ECtHR) had to assess whether it was within the scope of Italy's duty to protect life to afford protection to the victim. After finding that Italian legislation regarding alternative measures to imprisonment did not violate the general duty to protect the life of society at large, the Court evaluated whether Mastromatteo's death arose out of Italy's failure to protect him in the particular circumstances of the case. To this end, the ECtHR drew on causality and noted that "a mere condition *sine qua non* does not suffice to engage the state's responsibility under the Convention."[59] On the contrary, it was argued that although the decision of the Italian judge to grant the temporary leave had

[57] On responsibility for omission as derived by the agent's power to control, see Joseph Raz, "Responsibility and the Negligence Standard" (2010) 30 Oxford Journal of Legal Studies 1, 3–4.

[58] *Corfu Channel* (n 55) 18–22; *United States Diplomatic and Consular Staff in Teheran (United States of America v Iran)* (Merits) [1980] ICJ Rep 3 [63].

[59] *Mastromatteo v Italy* (Judgment) [24 October 2002] App no 37703/97, para 74.

sparked the chain of events leading to the killing, the authorities could have neither reasonably foreseen nor predicted the event.[60]

Mastromatteo is not the only case where the ECtHR has defined the scope of a state's duty to protect an individual's human rights as causality between the state's alleged failure to protect and the harmful event. The Court has in similar instances affirmed that a state's responsibility for failing to protect is engaged when there was a "sufficient nexus" between state omission and the harmful event;[61] when it was within the capacity of the state to "have a significant influence on the course of the events leading to the violation";[62] or when the state through its action "could have had a real prospect of altering the outcome or mitigating the harm."[63] Furthermore, the need to establish a causal dimension between an alleged failure to exercise due diligence and the materialization of risk linked to the due diligence rule is not an exclusive prerogative of human rights. Regarding the duty to protect foreign investments, arbitral tribunals have also argued that claimants need to prove a "causal connection" or a "clear link" between state's failure to act and damage to the investment.[64]

When due diligence obligations apply in extraterritorial contexts, the causal dimension between a state's failure to act and the materialization of the risk emerges even more forcefully. This is especially true when a state's capacity to affect the situation linked to a due diligence rule cannot be presumed in (extraterritorial) control over territory but derives from other forms of a state's power or control over the source of risk. For example, in the 2007 *Genocide* case, the ICJ grappled with Serbia's responsibility for the genocide in Srebrenica. Serbia did not exercise effective control over the territorial area where genocide occurred, nor was it the occupying power in Srebrenica. However, once the Court had excluded the acts of genocide committed by the Bosnian-Serbian militia as being attributable to Serbia under rules of attribution of conduct,[65] the question remained whether Serbia was still under an obligation to prevent genocide in the area. The Court famously concluded that a duty to act to prevent genocide on the part of Serbia had still arisen because of the political, military, and financial links between Serbia and the militia groups physically carrying out genocide.[66] In this regard, the Court affirmed that the strength of political, military, and other links between Serbia's authorities and

[60] ibid para 76.

[61] *Fadeyeva v Russia* (Judgment) [30 November 2005] App no 55723/00, para 92.

[62] *E and others v United Kingdom* (Judgment) [26 November 2002] App no 33218/96, para 100.

[63] *Opuz v Turkey* (Judgment) [9 June 2009] App no 33401/02, para 136. For a review of human rights practice and the use of causality to assess omissions for failure to prevent, see Stoyanova, "Causation between State Omission and Harm" (n 4) 309.

[64] *Marion Unglaube and Reinhard Unglaube v Costa Rica* ICSID Case Nos ARB/01/1 and ARB/09/20 (Award) (16 May 2012) [283]. For a review of practice in the context of the obligation to protect foreign investments, see Sebastián Mantilla Blanco, *Full Protection and Security in International Investment Law* (Springer 2018) 456–59.

[65] *Genocide* (n 50) [380]–[383], [395], [412]–[414].

[66] ibid [434].

the militia groups had informed Serbia's "capacity to influence effectively the action of persons likely to commit, or already committing, genocide."[67] Hence, the ICJ framed the scope of Serbia's duty to act to prevent genocide based on Serbia's power over the militia physically committing the genocidal acts.[68] The conceptualization of Serbia's conduct reminds one of the German *Tatherrschaft* causal theory, or domination over the act theory, by which a duty to act exists should it be established that the agent had a certain degree of influence and control over the execution of the criminal act.[69]

Another relevant example is provided by the 2016 *South China Sea Arbitration* case. This concerned, among other things, the responsibility of China for having failed to prevent illegal, unreported, and unregulated (IUU) fishing of commercial vessels flying its flag in the Exclusive Economic Zone (EEZ) of the Philippines.[70] In assessing the scope of a state's duty to act with due diligence to ensure that vessels flying its flag are not engaged in illegal fishing in the EZZ of other states, the Tribunal first admitted that this duty's precise scope of application is difficult to determine. It argued that "unlawful fishing will often be carried out covertly, far from official presence, *and will be far from obvious what the flag State could realistically have done to prevent it*."[71] However, in the present case, the Tribunal noted that, from the time Chinese commercial vessels had been engaged in fishing activities in the EZZ of the Philippines, they had been closely escorted by Chinese governmental vessels. According to the Arbitral Tribunal, not only had this "official" presence proved knowledge by China of illegal fishing activities; the presence of Chinese governmental vessels had also ensured China's effective power over the commercial vessels flying its flag and capacity to affect the outcome of their actions. This emerges from the Tribunal's finding, which concludes that Chinese government vessels could have had intervened and halted the IUU fishing had they chosen to do so.[72] Essentially, the potential for control over the merchant boats brought about causality between state conduct and the harmful event.

5. The "Secondary" Character of Causation in Establishing the Breach of Preventive and Other Due Diligence Obligations

These considerations call for some final reflections on the solution provided in the ARSIWA to the issue of causality and wrongfulness.

[67] ibid [430].
[68] ibid.
[69] Thomas Rotsch, *"Einheitstäterschaft" statt Tatherrschaft: Zur Abkehr von einem differenzierenden Beteiligungsformensystem in einer normativ-funktionalen Straftatlehre* (Mohr Slebeck 2009).
[70] *In the Matter of South China Sea Arbitration (Republic of the Philippines v People's Republic of China)* PCA Case No 2013-19 (Award) (12 July 2016) [754]–[755].
[71] ibid.
[72] ibid.

First, it has been shown that in obligations to prevent, the assessment of the "event" goes hand in hand with evaluating "conduct" adopted by the state to prevent.[73] In other words, when adjudicators assess a state's responsibility for failure to prevent harmful events, the evaluation of the "event" inevitably triggers questions of cause. If a judge is appointed to decide whether it was within the scope of a state's duty to prevent a harmful event, for a breach of this obligation to exist, it is not sufficient to verify that the event has indeed occurred; a judge will necessarily have to evaluate state conduct and (causally) link it to such event. The reason is that the scope of a duty to act with due diligence is limited by the possibility of action, and possibility exists as long as a state has the power to prevent. Power to prevent depends on knowledge or constructive knowledge of the risk linked to prevention and the state's power over the source of risk or capacity to affect. It is the assessment of a state's capacity to affect that is imbued with causality.

If appraising the scope of a state's duty to act to prevent violations triggers inevitably causal queries, the ILC's choice to leave causation—but not the event—outside article 14(3) remains at the least surprising. This is even more so if one concedes that causality ingrained in the fabric of preventive obligations only emerges when these obligations are assessed in the context of international responsibility. So long as the "event" has not yet occurred, a state is bound by the duty to prevent risks of which the state has (constructive) knowledge and a certain capacity to affect. Any causal query will surface only *ex post facto* once the event has materialized, and the scope of the state's obligations needs evaluation *in concreto* against the case's particular circumstances. From this perspective, causality related to preventive obligations becomes instrumental in the responsibility logic and fully integrates questions of "secondary" character. Hence, by retaining the "event" as the sole secondary element of breaches of preventive obligations, the ILC has not has only failed the opportunity to address the issue adequately but has also de facto eclipsed their due diligence nature and construed them as "negative" obligations of result.

Two further considerations arise from this argument. First, although this section has mainly focused on obligations to prevent, there is room to sustain the point that causality affects the *ex-post* assessment of other primary rules of due diligence, particularly those that incorporate duties to act vis-à-vis the activities of private individuals or third parties.[74] For instance, evaluating the extent to which a duty to exercise due diligence to "ensure" that non-state actors abide by specific international standards or that given results are attained usually requires assessing the state's causal contribution to these results.

[73] Clearly, we are still under the assumption stated at the outset, namely that the majority of preventive obligations are duties of conduct.

[74] See eg *Responsibility and Obligations of States Sponsoring Persons and Entities with Respect to Activities in the Area* (Request for an Advisory Opinion submitted to the Seabed Dispute Chamber) [2011] ITLOS Rep 109–10.

The second consideration regards the nature of due diligence obligations (including preventive ones) as obligations of conduct. Specifically, it may be queried whether construing causation as a "missed" secondary rule coexists with the idea that, as duties of a "best-effort" nature, for a breach of due diligence obligations to accrue the occurrence of the event (thus causality) should not be required. Admittedly, discussing this problem has more to do with the ILC's choice to keep the "event" as a required secondary element of article 14(3) rather than with "true" issues of causality.[75] However, it is worth briefly broaching the question to clarify the argument of the present analysis better. In this regard, indeed, a rigorous interpretation of preventive obligations as due diligence obligations should not treat the event to be prevented as a necessary element in their breach. As pointed out above, due diligence obligations are duties of a best-efforts nature, as they only expect states to adopt the necessary measures to attain a particular result, not to guarantee it. Logically, this means that a breach of a duty of due diligence should arise when the state has failed to adopt measures deemed necessary, regardless of the occurrence of any "event."

At the same time, it is also true that, unless the content of due diligence is "spelt out" in detail and measures deemed necessary to prevent are clearly set out,[76] it will be difficult for a judge to assess a state's failure to prevent harm in the absence of a harmful event indicating *prima facie* a potential lack of due diligence. What is more, when prevention is established concerning somebody else's injurious conduct (eg non-state actors), a duty to act with due diligence encompasses typically, along with the adoption of "preventive" measures, the exercise of some *vigilance* over the potentially harmful activity of third parties.[77] The occurrence of the event is often the only indicator to point to a state's lack of vigilance over risks generated by third parties. Put differently, the event is often a catalyst,[78] the necessary condition that *occasions* the breach of due diligence and triggers questions of responsibility. Despite not obliterating the paradox of treating "the event" as a secondary rule of responsibility entirely, this approach scales down the problem raised by the wording of article 14(3). In any event, reconciling due diligence obligations with article 14(3) does not invalidate the argument pursued in this chapter: "degrading" causality to the level of primary rules while maintaining the "event" as a secondary condition fails to capture the normative function served by causation in defining the scope of states' duties to prevent.

Finally, it is helpful to test causation as a "missed" secondary rule against the ILC's understanding of what integrates "a cause" in breaches of preventive obligations. In the Commentary to draft article 23, the ILC supported the idea that

75 Ollino, *Due Diligence Obligations in International Law* (n 54) 203–13.

76 See eg *Certain Activities* (n 51) [104]; *Construction of a Road* (n 51) [217].

77 *Case Concerning Pulp Mills on the River Uruguay (Argentina v Uruguay)* (Merits) [2010] ICJ Rep 14 [185], [188].

78 Ago, "Seventh Report" (n 36) 36.

breaches of preventive obligations would accrue if the state's failure to prevent were a *sine qua non* element of the event. In truth, the Commission's recourse to the but-for-test to explain causality in omissions is neither supported by international practice[79] nor should be considered desirable from a more theoretical perspective. From a theoretical standpoint, establishing causality in omissions by recourse to the but-for test is especially problematic. The "but for" test requires proving that but for the omission of the state, the harmful outcome would have been avoided. In practice, this is a challenging task since causality in omissions is always normative and hypothetical. One either restricts the existence of causality only to a very few situations in which the intervention of state's conduct would have avoided the harmful event with certainty; or one makes the scope of a state's duty to act potentially limitless in scope and acknowledges the link between the state's omission and the harmful event even when the latter is the result of an abnormal or irregular causal chain.

This is why in international practice, the connection between a state's failure to prevent and the harmful event will usually be explained by other causal tests. Since for many preventive obligations, the "direct" cause of the event is typically a third party's action, and the omission of the state is only a concurrent cause, efficient tests of causality are those establishing whether a state's action could have had, at least, a real prospect of altering the outcome.[80] In this regard, adjudicators often avoid inquiring whether a state's inaction was a *sine qua non* of the event. They only estimate whether the omission was sufficiently "immediate" or "proximate" to the event.[81] In many cases, the causal relationship between state omission and the harmful event is not even broached, and it is "absorbed" by the test of foreseeability.[82] As a "simplified" test conflating causal queries with issues related to knowledge and culpability, foreseeability facilitates adjudicators and only requires verifying if the harmful event was *within the risk* connected to the primary rule. Overall, international practice is far from homogeneous and may depend on context and the type of primary in question. However, one thing should appear clear: "failing" the "but for" test in causal inquiries related to wrongfulness

[79] Most notably, see *Genocide* (n 50) [430].

[80] The *Genocide* case is an illustrative example of the confusion between rejecting causation because the omission was not *a sine qua non condition* of the event, and recognizing that causality exists also if the omission was *only* a concurrent cause of the event, see *Genocide* (n 50) [462]; Andrea Gattini, "Breach of the Obligation to Prevent and Reparation Thereof in the ICJ's *Genocide* Judgment" (2007) 18 European Journal of International Law 695.

[81] *Biwater Gauff (Tanzania) Ltd v United Republic of Tanzani*a ICSID Case No ARB/05/22, 2008, [798]–[799]; *Wippermann case*, in Moore, *History and Digest of the International Arbitrations to which the United States Has Been a Party* (vol III) 3041; *Rantsev v Cyprus and Russia* (Judgment) [10 May 2010] App no 25965/04, para 286; on proximity of the risk, see eg *Öneryildiz v Turkey* (Judgment) [30 November 2004] App no 48939/99, para 73.

[82] UN Human Rights Committee (HRC), *Kindler v Canada*, UN Doc CCPR/C/48/D/470/1991 (1993) [13.2]; *El-Masri v The Former Yugoslav Republic of Macedonia* (Judgment) [13 December 2012] App no 39630/09, para 213.

by omissions does deny that a causal connection exists between state's failure to prevent and the harmful event. This link may be embedded in other causal tests, but it is always necessary to establish the IWA.

6. Conclusion

This chapter has critically revised the ILC's codification of breaches of preventive obligations. Article 14(3) of the ARSIWA construes preventive obligations as obligations of "negative result" and obscures the role of causality in their breach.

However, most obligations to prevent harmful events are obligations of due diligence that impose on states the exercise of best efforts without guaranteeing the result. To assess the scope of these obligations and the extent of a state's duty to act with due diligence, one needs to resort to causal queries. The causal dimension imbued in these obligations is "triggered" whenever adjudicators and interpreters are confronted with the extent of the state's responsibility for failure to act.

In light of the normative function served by causation concerning breaches of due diligence obligations, it is regrettable that the ILC eventually decided to exclude causality from the ARSIWA and systematize causal questions at the level of primary rules. By excluding this topic from the discussion, the Commission also ignored the different causal tests that may be at play when assessing breaches of due diligence obligations. The outcome of this operation is that causal issues related to wrongfulness are still very opaque in international practice, and a certain degree of confusion still exists between causality in wrongfulness and causality for reparation.

7

Depolluting the Doctrine on Causation in International Investment Law

The Case for Extracting "Legal Causation"

Martin Jarrett[*]

1. The Poverty of Causation in International Investment Law

Whenever the question of state responsibility arises in investor-state arbitration, the following causal question necessarily arises:[1] "Did the state conduct cause the investor's investment loss?" Its omnipresence might be surprising. None of the investment protection standards specify that the conduct, which they regulate, must be causative vis-à-vis some investment loss. But as investment protection standards implicitly contain a requirement for investors to prove some investment loss to establish state responsibility,[2] a further requirement necessarily arises for the consequence of the investor's investment loss to be caused by the state's conduct. This further requirement will be referred to as the "cause legal element" in this contribution. This conception of the doctrine will provoke an objection in some quarters. The objection will be that proof of an investment loss is not part of the equation for determining a state's international responsibility under an investment treaty.[3] Rather, proving the occurrence of this consequence is a task that is completed in the remedies phase or the quantum phase of an investment-treaty arbitration. Even if this objection is accepted, it does nothing to displace the central role of the causation question. In investment-treaty arbitrations, compensation is the

[*] This contribution is a revised version of a paper originally submitted for the ESIL-ELTE Joint Workshop "Attribution, Causality, and Evidentiary Rules." I thank all the attendees and the workshop organizers (Katalin Sulyok and Gabor Kajtar) for all of their comments on my paper and presentation. An ESIL Travel Grant supported my participation in this workshop and I very gratefully acknowledge this support. The usual caveat applies: any errors are mine alone.

[1] See Andrea Bjorklund, "Causation, Morality, and Quantum" (2009) 32 Suffolk Transnational Law Review 435, 436.

[2] Zachary Douglas, "International Responsibility for Domestic Adjudication: Denial of Justice Deconstructed" (2014) 63 International and Comparative Law Quarterly 867, 893.

[3] Pearsall and Heath, for example, view the causal question as a separate question from international responsibility, see Patrick W Pearsall and J Benton Heath, "Causation and Injury in Investor-State Arbitration" in Christina L Beharry (ed), *Contemporary and Emerging Issues on the Law of Damages and Valuation in International Investment Arbitration* (Brill 2018) 81.

Martin Jarrett, *Depolluting the Doctrine on Causation in International Investment Law* In: *Secondary Rules of Primary Importance in International Law.* Edited by: Gábor Kajtár, Başak Çalı, and Marko Milanovic, Oxford University Press.
 DOI: 10.1093/oso/9780192869012.003.0007

default response for remedying breaches.[4] As any award of compensation requires proof of a causal connection between the relevant loss and the unlawful conduct of the state,[5] the point remains that the causation question will always be one that arbitral tribunals have to grapple with.

Despite this omnipresence, developing the jurisprudence on causation in international investment law remains a neglected task.[6] Perhaps this dearth of theory tailored for use in this area of law is not surprising. Causation has a bad reputation among many legal scholars.[7] For some, its primitiveness means that it is impervious to meaningful analysis,[8] therefore making intuition the best guide for determining causal questions.[9] But adjudicators should aspire to rise above their intuitions on the causal question. The rule of law imposes few obligations on adjudicators, but one of them is rational legal reasoning[10]—an idea that is at odds with decision-making guided by intuition.

Accordingly, the task for academic jurists is to lay down theory on causation for application in legal disputes. But this is not an attractive endeavor for many of them. For one, the suspicion is that causation is viewed as a dull topic. For the reminder whose curiosity leads them to the philosophical scholarship on causation, what awaits them is a complex body of theory.[11] Moreover, this theory has been labelled as inapplicable in law,[12] as most famously recounted by Frederick Pollack:[13]

> [T]he lawyer cannot afford to adventure himself with philosophers in the logical and metaphysical controversies that beset the idea of cause.

[4] Borzu Sahabi, *Compensation and Restitution in Investor-State Arbitration: Principles and Practice* (OUP 2011) 91.

[5] Jonathan Law and Elizabeth A Martin (eds), *Oxford Dictionary of Law* (7th updated edn, OUP 2013) 114 (definition of "compensation").

[6] At the time of writing, only the following works specifically deal with the topic of causation in international investment law: see Martin Jarrett, *Contributory Fault and Investor Misconduct in Investment Arbitration* (CUP 2019) ch 3; George Somi, "*Bilcon v Canada*: A New Paradigm for Causation in Investor-State Arbitration?" in Julien Chaisse, Leïla Choukroune, and Sufian Jusoh (eds), *Handbook of International Investment Law and Policy* (Springer 2021) 1261. <https://papers.ssrn.com/sol3/papers.cfm?abstract_id=3448622&download=yes> accessed 21 April 2020; Pearsall and Heath, "Causation and Injury in Investor-State Arbitration" (n 3) 81; Stanimir Alexandrov and Joshua Robbins, "Proximate Causation in International Investment Disputes" (2009) 2008–2009 Yearbook on International Investment Law and Policy 318; and Bjorklund, "Causation, Morality, and Quantum" (n 1) 435.

[7] Jane Stapleton, "Law, Causation, and Common Sense" (1988) 8 Oxford Journal of Legal Studies 111.

[8] This is the view of the "causal singularists," of whom Michael Moore is the most prominent in the legal world. For his arguments on why singular theories of causation are most preferable, see Michael Moore, *Causation and Responsibility: An Essay in Law, Morals, and Metaphysics* (OUP 2009) 506–12.

[9] See eg the comments of Lord Justice Watkins in *Lamb v Camden LBC* where he notes that adjudicators will be guided by "instinctive feelings" on causal questions: see *Lamb v Camden LBC* [1981] EWCA Civ 7 per Watkins LJ.

[10] See International Commission of Jurists, *The Rule of Law in a Free Society* (A Report on the International Congress of Jurists, 5–10 January 1959) 279.

[11] Jane Stapleton, "Common Sense" (n 7) 111.

[12] Jane Stapleton, "Causation in the Law" in Helen Beebee, Christopher Hitchcock, and Peter Menzies (eds), *The Oxford Handbook of Causation* (OUP 2009) 744, 749.

[13] Frederick Pollack, *The Law of Torts* (6th edn, Stevens & Sons 1901) 36.

Starting from this premise, jurists have sought to carve out an autonomous meaning of cause for application in legal disputes.[14] Most of these efforts have been produced in respect of domestic criminal law and domestic tort law. Over the past century, these efforts have produced a voluminous amount of jurisprudence on causation in the law. Given the ready availability of this wealth of knowledge, the International Law Commission (ILC) had no hesitation in appropriating it for the purposes of the law on state responsibility,[15] and, via this appropriation, this jurisprudence has found its way into international investment law.[16] And this is the most probative explanation for the jurisprudential void on causation in international investment law: analyses of causal questions can borrow from the jurisprudence on causation from domestic law.

The thesis of this contribution is that this unchecked importation of domestic jurisprudence on causation into international investment law was wrong. It specifically argues that the second part of the dominant theory on causation developed for application in domestic law, what is called legal causation,[17] must be extracted from international investment law. In building to that conclusion, section 2 starts with an overview of the typical method for analyzing causal questions arising in investment-treaty arbitration. Section 3 puts forward the premises supporting the thesis, specifically that testing for legal causality in investor-state arbitration, one, is a potential delegitimizing factor in the international adjudication of investor-state disputes and, two, has no valid purpose bearing in mind the purpose of this process in domestic law. By extracting legal causation from international investment law, the fear will be that the arbitration floodgates will be opened to more investor claims. Section 4 demonstrates that this fear is unfounded. Finally, section 5 summarizes the findings of this contribution.

2. An Overview of Causation in International Investment Law

Although international investment law is notable for the fragmented nature of its substantive law, there is unity on the method for answering causal questions. It takes

[14] Michael Moore, "Causation in the Law" (*Stanford Encyclopaedia of Philosophy*, 3 October 2019) [4] <https://plato.stanford.edu/entries/causation-law/> accessed 12 July 2022.

[15] ILC, "Draft Articles on Responsibility of States for Internationally Wrongful Acts, with Commentaries" (2001) II(2) Yearbook of the International Law Commission 31, 92.

[16] See Alexandrov and Robbins, "Proximate Causation" (n 4) 322.

[17] Although it goes by any other number of descriptors, most particularly proximate causation. Whatever descriptor is used, it is unfortunate that it includes the word "causation" because the notions making up its content bear no relation to causation, see Jane Stapleton, "Factual Causation" (2010) 38 Federal Law Review 467, 469; Richard Wright, "Once More Into the Bramble Bush: Duty, Causal Contribution, and the Extent of Legal Responsibility" (2001) 54 Vanderbilt Law Review 1071, 1073. However, given the currency that this expression enjoys in international law, it will (reluctantly) be used.

its cue from the commentary attaching to the Articles on State Responsibility.[18] Following the lead of domestic tort law, this commentary specifies that the determination of causal questions consists of two phases,[19] what will be called "factual causation" and "legal causation." Beyond this specification, there is little detail on what the process of determining causal questions involves.[20] This omission was deliberate. As explained by Special Rapporteur James Crawford,[21] the nature of the causal inquiry varies according to the applicable primary rule, thereby making it inappropriate to issue commentary of general applicability on determining causal questions. Accordingly, the incumbent task is to examine what meanings "factual causation" and "legal causation" have acquired in respect of the primary rules of international investment law, namely the investment protection standards.

2.1 Factual Causation in International Investment Law

As explained in the commentary attaching to the Articles on State Responsibility,[22] the prong of factual causation tests whether the relevant state conduct was an actual cause of the consequence in question.[23] The nature of that causal link is not mentioned. Although the assumption is that the state conduct must be a necessary antecedent for the occurrence of the consequence,[24] the degree of necessity is not specified. Necessary connections come in different grades, specifically strict, strong, and weak.[25] With their frequent invocation of the but-for test,[26] arbitral tribunals for investment-treaty arbitration have opted for, whether knowingly or not, for strong necessity. The causal link of strong necessity arises if the antecedent was necessary for the occurrence of the consequence in the particular case,[27] which is

18 *The Islamic Republic of Iran v The United States of America*, Iran–United States Claims Tribunal Case No A15 (11 A) (Partial Award) (10 March 2020) [1792]; *Yukos Universal Limited (Isle of Man) v The Russian Federation* UNCITRAL PCA Case No 2005-04/AA227 (Final Award) (18 July 2014) [1598]; *Occidental Petroleum Corp and Occidental Exploration and Production Co v The Republic of Ecuador* ICSID Case No ARB/06/11 (Award) (5 October 2012) [668]; *El Paso Energy International Co v The Argentine Republic* ICSID Case No ARB/03/15 (Award) (31 October 2011) [682]; *Joseph Charles Lemire v Ukraine* ICSID Case No ARB/06/18 (Award) (28 March 2011) [155]; *Biwater Gauff (Tanzania) Ltd v United Republic of Tanzania* ICSID Case No ARB/05/22 (Award) (24 July 2008) [785]; and *CME Czech Republic BV v The Czech Republic, ad hoc* arbitration (UNCITRAL Arbitration Rules) (Partial Award) (13 September 2001) [580].

19 ILC, "Draft Articles" (n 15) 92–93.

20 Brigitte Stern, "The Obligation of Reparation" in James Crawford, Alain Pellet, and Simon Olleson (eds), *The Law of International Responsibility* (OUP 2010) 569.

21 James Crawford, *State Responsibility: The General Part* (CUP 2013) 493.

22 ILC, "Draft Articles" (n 15) 92.

23 Jane Stapleton, "Legal Cause: Cause-in-Fact and Scope of Liability for Consequences" (2001) 54 Vanderbilt Law Review 958.

24 ILC, "Draft Articles" (n 15) 92.

25 For an overview of the different gradients, see Richard W Wright, "Causation, Responsibility, Risk, Probability, Naked Statistics, and Proof: Pruning the Bramble Bush by Clarifying the Concepts" (1988) 73 Iowa Law Review 1001, 1020.

26 Pearsall and Heath, "Causation and Injury" (n 3) 93.

27 Wright, "Pruning the Bramble Bush" (n 25) 1020.

a matter that can be determined by the counterfactual question used in the but-for test.[28]

Yet the but-for test produces irrational results in cases of causal overdetermination.[29] Cases of causal overdetermination in the law of state responsibility arise when there are two or more independent groups of antecedents and each group could, having regard to the application of causal laws, produce the consequence in question, although only one group actually does produce this consequence.[30] An example would be where the state commits to enacting a new tax that completely devalues an investor's investment, but, before that tax takes effect, investor's investment suffers the same fate because a pandemic causes the same consequence. Both the tax and the pandemic could cause the consequence, but only one of them does, namely the pandemic. But because of the presence of the other antecedent (the enactment of the tax), the but-for test produces irrational results.[31] To illustrate this, consider how the but-for test should look in respect of this situation:

> If the state had not enacted the tax, would the investment have suffered a complete devaluation?

Obviously, the answer is "yes" because of the pandemic. But consider the question when pandemic replaces tax:

> If there was no pandemic, would the investment have suffered a complete devaluation?

Again, the answer must be "yes," meaning that neither the tax nor the pandemic is causal. On realizing the irrationality, most jurists flee strong necessity for another test, such as the "substantial factor" test,[32] or more specifically describe the antecedent in question to distinguish it from its competing antecedent.[33] Because there have been few cases in investment-treaty arbitration where questions of causal overdetermination have arisen, it is difficult to distill a general approach to navigating this problem among arbitral tribunals. Causal overdetermination was, however, in issue in the case of *Biwater v Tanzania*. There, the arbitral tribunal found that the investor's mismanagement would have eventually led to the

[28] Jane Stapleton, "An 'Extended But-For' Test for the Causal Relation in the Law of Obligations" (2015) 35 Oxford Journal of Legal Studies 697, 705.

[29] Richard W Wright and Ingeborg Puppe, "Causation: Linguistic, Philosophical, Legal and Economic" (2016) 91 Chicago-Kent Law Review 461, 474; Stapleton, "Legal Cause" (n 23) 958.

[30] Wright and Puppe, "Causation" (n 29) 471.

[31] For a more detailed discussion of this problem in the law on state responsibility, see generally Ilias Plakokefalos, "Causation in the Law of State Responsibility and the Problem of Overdetermination: In Search of Clarity" (2015) 26 European Journal of International Law 471.

[32] Richard W Wright, "Causation in Tort Law" (1985) 73 California Law Review 1735, 1739. See eg Michael Moore, *Causation and Responsibility: An Essay in Law, Morals, and Metaphysics* (OUP 2009) 88.

[33] Wright and Puppe, "Causation" (n 29) 474–75.

complete devaluation of its investment.[34] Shortly before that consequence was due to occur, Tanzania performed its wrongful conduct.[35] That state conduct had causative effect vis-à-vis the consequence before the investor's conduct could cause the same consequence. A majority of the arbitral tribunal found that the state conduct was not a factual cause,[36] meaning that Tanzania was not liable. The dissenting arbitrator came to the opposite conclusion.[37] In domestic tort law, causal overdetermination of the consequence does not usually save the respondent,[38] meaning that this jurisprudence favors the approach of the dissenting arbitrator.

A final point worth mentioning on factual causality is the standard of proof. In contrast to the usual rule requiring that evidence prove facts "on the balance of probabilities,"[39] a number of arbitral tribunals have indicated that factual causality must be proven to a higher standard,[40] such as "in all probability."[41]

2.2 Legal Causation in International Investment Law

Putting forth the meaning of legal causation in the international investment law is a task approached with some trepidation.[42] What explains this trepidation is the limited set of data from which there is to draw on. Arbitral tribunals infrequently engage in detailed analyses of causal questions. In fairness, however, it will be obvious in many cases that the state conduct is causal, thereby rendering the analysis superfluous. What is more problematic than the lack of data is what arbitral tribunals actually do when they engage with the causal question in a case. Unfortunately, there is a tendency to mention a few buzzwords and draw immediate conclusions from them, without detailing how the facts are, or are not, subsumed within the concepts that they invoke. Accordingly, what follows cannot be a definitive statement on legal causation in international investment law. It is rather an overview of the different approaches that arbitral tribunals have taken on legal causation. This overview provides the necessary context for section 3, which demonstrates why

34 *Biwater Gauff (Tanzania) Ltd v United Republic of Tanzania* ICSID Case No ARB/05/22 (Award) (24 July 2008) [798].

35 ibid [799].

36 ibid [798].

37 *Biwater Gauff (Tanzania) Ltd v United Republic of Tanzania* ICSID Case No ARB/05/22 (Concurring and Dissenting Opinion) (18 July 2008) [19].

38 Wright and Puppe, "Causation" (n 29) 479.

39 Frederic G Sourgens, Kabir Duggal, and Ian A Laird, *Evidence in International Investment Arbitration* (OUP 2018) para 5.09.

40 For a review of this jurisprudence, see *Bilcon of Delaware et al v Government of Canada* PCA Case No 2009-04 (Award on Damages) (10 January 2019) [110]–[113].

41 ibid [168].

42 The same comment might be applied to law more generally, see Moore, "Causation in the Law" (n 14) para 2.3.

legal causation is doctrinal pollution from domestic tort law in international investment law.

Getting to the meaning of legal causation begins with understanding the purpose of this doctrinal construct. Considering that a causal link between the state conduct and the investment loss will have already been established when testing for factual causality, it may not be apparent why legal causation needs to be tested for. But it has a purpose: to deal with the problem of infinite factual causes.[43] If the test for factual causality is applied literally, it theoretically[44] identifies all the antecedents necessary for the occurrence of the identified factual cause as additional factual causes.[45] For example, if the identified factual cause is the termination of an investment contract, the test for factual causality also identifies all the events which were necessary for that termination to be performed as factual causes because, without their occurrence, it could not have been performed. But common understanding does not view all of these factual causes as causes which should attract legal blame.[46] In the folk conception of causation, blame only attaches to the "difference-makers," that is, the factual causes which made the difference for the occurrence of the consequence.[47] And because legal causation is concerned with identifying factual causes worthy of blame, its content is made up of normative notions.[48] The question is: what notions are at play in international investment law?

These notions can be grouped under four headings:[49] policy-based notions, fault-based notions, autonomy-based notions, and potency-based notions. Policy-based notions seek to place causal responsibility, and hence liability for the relevant loss, where it should fall having regard to policy considerations, the foremost among which is social-wealth maximization.[50] Accordingly, an example of a policy-based notion in legal causation is the idea that causal responsibility should be placed on the person who is the best cost-avoider;[51] in other words, the person who can, with the least amount of money, avoid the incident giving rise to the loss.[52] There is little evidence that they have been influential on arbitrators in investment-treaty arbitrations.[53] And given that there is no mention of policy-based notions in

43 Stapleton, "Legal Cause" (n 23) 984.

44 In section 4, it is demonstrated how the problem of infinite causality is only a theoretical one.

45 Some authors, albeit sarcastically, say that a causal line can be drawn back to the actions of Adam and Eve: see eg Glanville Williams, "Causation in the Law" (1961) 19 Cambridge Law Journal 62, 64..

46 HLA Hart and Tony Honoré, *Causation in the Law* (2nd edn, OUP 1985) 70.

47 ibid 29.

48 *Iran v US* (n 18) [1793]; ILC, "Draft Articles" (n 15) 93.

49 Moore, "Causation in the Law" (n 14) para 5.5.

50 Wright, "Causation in Tort Law" (n 32) 1739.

51 Guido Calabresi, "Concerning Cause and the Law of Torts: An Essay for Harry Kalven, Jr" (1975) 43 University of Chicago Law Review 69, 100.

52 Stephen Gilles, "Negligence, Strict Liability, and the Cheapest Cost-Avoider" (1992) 78 Vanderbilt Law Review 1291, 1292.

53 In *Iran v US* (Case A15 (11:A)), the arbitral tribunal noted that "policy" could assist with testing for legal causality, but there is nothing in its reasoning that policy considerations guided its analysis, see *Iran v US* (n 18) [1793]. See also Alexandrov and Robbins, "Proximate Causation" (n 6) 345.

the commentary on the Articles on the State Responsibility, nor the scholarly commentary on these articles, this lack of traction should not be surprising.

By contrast, fault-based notions play a prominent role. These notions focus on the subjective or objective knowledge of the person performing the factual cause,[54] noting how law often imposes liability on those with knowledge of the relevant circumstances, and hence explaining the name "fault-based" notions.[55] The notion of foreseeability is the most well known.[56] This notion provides that if the relevant consequence was a foreseeable one, judged in light of common experience, at the time that the factual cause was performed, then that factual cause is a legal cause.[57] Given its explicit endorsement by the ILC,[58] it has been frequently invoked by arbitral tribunals in their analyses of the causal question.[59]

Next, there are the autonomy-based notions. These notions seek to place causal responsibility for a consequence on the person who directly caused it.[60] This rule derives from the broader principle that a person should be responsible for the consequences that he or she causes, without having the opportunity to point to the antecedents of his or her conduct to avoid causal responsibility, unless those antecedents impair his or her free will vis-à-vis his or her conduct that is the direct cause of the consequence.[61] Examples of these notions include directness, proximity,[62] and remoteness, all of which can be taken to refer to the idea that only direct causes qualify as legal causes. All of these notions are mentioned in the commentary attaching to the Articles on State Responsibility,[63] and, from there, have found their way into arbitral awards.[64] There are two potential meanings of "direct

[54] Benjamin C Zipursky, "Foreseeability in Breach, Duty and Proximate Cause" (2009) 44 Wake Forest Law Review 1247, 1267.

[55] In common parlance, fault is often used as a synonym for blame, see David G Owen, "Philosophical Foundations of Fault in Tort Law" in David G Owen (ed), *The Philosophical Foundations of Tort Law* (OUP 1997) 201.

[56] Moore, "Causation in the Law" (n 14) para 5.3.

[57] Leon Green, "The Wagon Mound No 2: Foreseeability Revisited" [1967] Utah Law Review 197, 206.

[58] ILC, "Draft Articles" (n 15) 93.

[59] *Iran v US* (n 18) [1793]; *Rompetrol Group NV v Romania* ICSID Case No ARB/06/3 (Award) (6 May 2013) [113]; *Joseph Charles Lemire v Ukraine* ICSID Case No ARB/06/18 (Award) (28 March 2011) [208]; *CME v Czechia* (n 18) [585]; *Ronald S Lauder v The Czech Republic, ad hoc* arbitration (UNCITRAL Arbitration Rules) (Final Award) (3 September 2001) [234].

[60] In the Anglo-American law, the most prominent author behind this theory is Richard Epstein, see Wright, "Causation in Tort Law" (n 32) 1750.

[61] For the various situations where free will is impaired, see Jarrett, *Contributory Fault* (n 6) 71–78.

[62] In this context, "proximate" is used in its common way to signify a cause "immediately next to" the consequence, see eg Joseph H Beale, "The Proximate Consequences of an Act" (1920) 33 Harvard Law Review 633, 644.

[63] ILC, "Draft Articles" (n 15) 93.

[64] *Unión Fenosa Gas SA v Arab Republic of Egypt* ICSID Case No ARB/14/4 (Award) (31 August 2018) [8.45] ("proximate cause"); *Blusun SA, Jean-Pierre Lecorcier, and Michael Stein v Italian Republic* ICSID Case No ARB/14/3 (Award) (27 December 2016) [387] ("proximate cause," although this proximate cause was not used to signify the legal cause in this case, but rather used to as a synonym for "direct cause"); *LG&E Energy Corp, LG&E Capital Corp, and LG&E International Inc v Argentine Republic* ICSID Case No ARB/02/1 (Award) (25 July 2007) [50] ("proximate cause"); *Link-Trading Joint*

cause."[65] One definition holds that a direct cause is the last cause immediately preceding the consequence.[66] The other definition is broader. It identifies direct causes as those antecedents forming part of the group of antecedents which, when they spatiotemporally convened, produced the consequence.[67] Deductively, for the factual causes in the group of antecedents which produced any direct cause, these indirect courses are not legal causes. The case of *CME v Czechia* can be used to exemplify this idea.[68] There, the direct cause of the investment loss was the termination of the contract, while all the other causes motivating that conduct and creating the environment for its performance were indirect causes, including Czechia's denial of the legal validity of a crucial clause of this contract and other Czech conduct coercing the investor to change its joint venture arrangement with the person who executed the contract termination.[69] In any case, arbitral tribunals have rarely invoked the notion that causal responsibility falls on that person who directly caused it.[70]

Potency-based notions sit on another theoretical foundation compared to autonomy-based notions. Rather than being based on the idea that causal responsibility of a cause should stop in respect of its direct consequence, potency-based notions have been developed on the idea that some causes are so causally potent that they discount the causal potency of other causes. As regards how to determine the causal potency of one factual cause compared to another factual cause, various theories have been proposed,[71] including examining the amount of energy that a factual cause exerts on a consequence[72] or looking at whether a factual cause changed the usual course of events.[73] Notions that seemingly encapsulate the idea

Stock Co v Department for Customs Control of the Republic of Moldova, *ad hoc* arbitration (UNCITRAL Arbitration Rules) (Final Award) (18 April 2002) [91] ("direct cause").

[65] Hart and Honoré, *Causation in the Law* (n 46) 179–80.
[66] Sometimes known as the last wrongdoer rule, see Charles E Carpenter, "Workable Rules for Determining Proximate Cause" (1932) 20 California Law Review 229, 236–37.
[67] The definition that William Prosser promoted, see ibid 180.
[68] The facts of this case are recounted in further detail in section 3.1.
[69] *CME v Czechia* (n 18) [585]. Although, in an award arising out of the same dispute, the arbitral tribunal in *Lauder v Czechia* found that Czechia's denial of the legal validity of the crucial was not causal and the investor agreed to make changes to its joint venture arrangement, rather than being coerced into doing so, see *Lauder v Czechia* (n 59) [274] and [302], respectively.
[70] *Link-Trading v Moldova* is one rare case, see *Link-Trading v Moldova* (n 64) [91]. Another instance was in *CME v Czechia*, although this conclusion was only expressed in a dissenting opinion and the analysis of the causal question is later muddied by a finding that the indirect cause, which the investor asserted was legally causal, was not legally causal because the investment loss was not a foreseeable consequence of indirect cause, see *CME Czech Republic BV v The Czech Republic*, ad hoc arbitration (UNCITRAL Arbitration Rules) (Dissenting Opinion of the Arbitrator Jaroslav Hándl against the Partial Arbitration Award) (11 September 2001) [18].
[71] For an overview, see Hart and Honoré, *Causation in the Law* (n 46) 438–42.
[72] ibid 438. For example, imagine a situation where one person is beaten up (the consequence) and there are two factual causes: (1) the victim was restrained by one person and (2) another person inflicts the various bodily blows. Out of these two factual causes, the act of inflicting the bodily blows on the victim would be seen as the most causally potent and the act of restraining would have less causal potency.
[73] ibid 440.

of causal potency include dominant cause,[74] efficient cause,[75] operative cause,[76] and substantial factor.[77] In investment-treaty arbitration, the idea of causal potency was apparently in use in *Blusun v Italy*. There, the causal question was:[78] what motivated potential financiers of the investor's investment project not to commit their capital? Two explanations were possible: (1) the investor's design of its project or (2) Italy's allegedly wrongful conduct.[79] In ruling that the former was causative, the arbitral tribunal held that it was "of far greater weight" than Italy's conduct.[80] Tying this result back into the theory on causal potency, it should be seen that, in the usual course of events, if the investment project did not receive finance, then it would fail, meaning that the causal inquiry had to seek out the most powerful explanation of this usual course of events.

3. The Case for Dispensing with Legal Causation in International Investment Law

As regards the content of legal causation in international investment law, not much can be said with conviction.[81] Arbitral tribunals have treated the different normative notions used to test for legal causality as a smorgasbord of options to choose from, as opposed to selecting one notion and justifying why it is particularly applicable for use in a particular case. But there is conviction on this point: legal causation should be dispensed with in international investment law. Two premises entail this conclusion, namely the delegitimizing potential of legal causation on the international adjudication of investor-state disputes and the tension between the purpose of testing for legal causality and the purpose of investment protection standards. The explanations underlying these premises are provided in sections 3.1 and 3.2.

3.1 The Delegitimizing Potential of Legal Causation

With one exception, the application of the normative notions for testing legal causality has the potential to delegitimize the international adjudication of

[74] *Iran v US* (n 18) [1793].
[75] Hart and Honoré, *Causation in the Law* (n 46) 438–39.
[76] *Blusun v Italy* (n 64) [394].
[77] First articulated in the English language by Jeremiah Smith: see Jeremiah Smith, "Legal Cause in Actions of Tort [Concluded]" (1912) 25 Harvard Law Review 303, 309–11. See also Moore, "Causation and Responsibility" (n 32) 105.
[78] *Blusun v Italy* (n 64) [387].
[79] ibid [394].
[80] ibid.
[81] The same comment was also made in respect of Anglo-American tort law in its formative decades, see John Salmond, *The Law of Torts* (6th edn, Sweet & Maxwell 1924) 142.

investor-state disputes. The exception is the autonomy-based notion that only factual causes directly related to the consequence in question are legally significant. As detailed elsewhere,[82] the notion of direct cause can be defined with some precision, particularly in comparison to other notions used for testing factual causality. Additionally, a notion grounded in individual responsibility fits well within international investment law because the nature of the disputes falling within its realm. These disputes arise out of state conduct. Because of the power of the state, it enjoys a degree of control over its behavior that humans lack, thereby justifying a stricter application of the principle of individual responsibility.

For these reasons, this notion that only direct causes qualify as legal causes is the one that should be retained. All the other normative notions should be jettisoned. Starting with the idea of causal potency, the basic problem here is that it is completely artificial. The idea that adjudicators can examine causes and attach degrees of potency to them according to, for example, the amount of energy they exhibit, is scientifically naïve.[83] Because this process has no grounding in science, what adjudicators presumably do when determining causal potency is revert to their intuitions,[84] which is what the original proponent of causal potency in German law confessed to,[85] or the inquiry dovetails off into an examination of the probity of the evidence on factual causality, which is seemingly what happened in *Blusun v Italy*. As explained in more detail in section 4, although the arbitral tribunal in *Blusun v Italy* ultimately found that Italy's conduct was not the operative cause of the investment loss, it repeatedly indicated that Italy's conduct might not be causal at all.[86]

Moving to the fault-based notions, there is no objection that foreseeability is a concept that some meaning can be given to. But it must be recognized what the process of its deployment by adjudicators actually involves. Contrary to what is hoped, adjudicators cannot drink from the fountain of common sense to decide what is an objectively foreseeable consequence according to the folk conception of causality.[87] In actuality, the deployment of this concept involves recourse to adjudicators' personal experiences. But this is not necessarily objectionable. When answering questions of fact, particularly when assessing the credibility of evidence, adjudicators inevitably refer to their own experiences of what is probable and what is not. This practice is well accepted. And it is similar to testing legal causality with

[82] For a full explanation on the meaning of directness in respect of causation in international investment law, see Jarrett, *Contributory Fault* (n 6) 53–78.

[83] Richard W Wright, "Causation: Metaphysics or Intuition?" in Kimberly Kessler Ferzan and Stephen J Morse (eds), *Legal, Moral, and Metaphysical Truths: The Philosophy of Michael S Moore* (OUP 2016) 184.

[84] Although some scholars of causation in the law have endorsed the use of intuition, see generally Henry Edgerton, "Legal Cause" (1924) 72 University of Pennsylvania Law Review 211

[85] Karl von Birkmeyer, *Über Ursachenbegriff und Kausalzusammenhang im Strafrecht* (Wentworth PR 1885) 18.

[86] See (n 118).

[87] Remembering that the objective is to align adjudicative determinations on causality in legal disputes with common conceptions of causal responsibility, see Stapleton, "Common Sense" (n 7) 112.

the foreseeability notion because adjudicators will refer to their personal experiences and, if they indicate that the relevant consequence often follows the factual cause in question, the result is that this factual cause is a legal cause.

While this practice might be adequate for cases involving the legal causality of direct causes,[88] it has difficulties navigating cases involving indirect causes; in other words, in situations where other conduct lies between the factual cause in question and the consequence. This in-between conduct is usually known as a new intervening act.[89] When the question arises whether the consequence was foreseeable from the perspective of the indirect cause, inconsistent decision-making on the causal question is the likely outcome. The theory supporting this hypothesis is that as causal chains grow longer with intervening acts, there are more causal link points at which adjudicators can find: here, the chain has been broken. And given that the presiding adjudicators will be referring to their own differing personal experiences when answering the question on continuity of the causal chain, there is real potential for inconsistent decision-making. A case where this potential became the reality was *CME v Czechia*. There, the investor's local partner terminated a contract,[90] a contract which provided the main source of income for the investment,[91] thereby completely devaluing the investment.[92] The termination was made possible because the investor agreed to change its joint venture arrangement with the local partner, although Czechia initiated this change.[93] Additionally, Czechia denied the legal validity of a crucial clause of the terminated contract.[94] The majority reasoned that both these actions were causal because it was foreseeable that they would lead to the investment loss.[95] The dissenting arbitrator came to the opposite conclusion.[96]

The limits of foreseeability in cases involving indirect causes are well known.[97] To avoid them, the solution is to further clarify the content of foreseeability, particularly with other fault-based notions. An example of such clarification is the rule that a new intervening act performed with intent to take advantage of the environment created by the conduct of another person breaks the chain of causation.[98] This rule could have been applied in *CME v Czechia*: through its weakening of the investor's legal position, a situation was created where the investor's local

[88] Beale, "Proximate Consequences" (n 62) 644.
[89] Although it goes by a number of other names, including "isolating cause," "superseding cause," "extraneous causes," "*novus causa interveniens*," or "*novus actus interveniens*": see Michael Moore, "The Metaphysics of Causal Intervention" (2000) 88 California Law Review 827.
[90] *CME v Czechia* (n 18) [18].
[91] ibid [574].
[92] ibid [18].
[93] ibid [11].
[94] ibid [243].
[95] ibid [585].
[96] *CME v Czechia* (Dissenting Opinion) (n 70) 18.
[97] Zipursky, "Foreseeability" (n 54) 1249.
[98] Hart and Honoré, *Causation in the Law* (n 46) 136.

partner could terminate the contract, with the result that the local partner should have been viewed as the causal agent. On the flip side, an indirect cause performed with the intention to cause the relevant consequence will be causal, even if a more direct cause of the consequence is in some way faultworthy because, for example, it was negligent.[99] The basic rule from domestic law is that the more faultworthy the relevant conduct is, the more likely it is that causal responsibility will stick to it. And given the overriding concern with fault,[100] it makes sense that domestic tort law would adopt this approach. But it would not be appropriate in international investment law. The fault of states is not the foundation of any finding of liability against them.[101] Their poor governance is the basis for any such findings.[102] Accordingly, the logic that justifies the use of fault-based notions when testing for legal causality in domestic law is not applicable in international investment law.

Finally, there are the policy-based notions. As previously noted, using these notions when testing for legal causality in international investment law has yet to gain a foothold. And it is hope that it stays that way. For when adjudicators resort to using policy-based notions, they go beyond adjudication and enter into the domain of policy implementation. This is not to imply that adjudicative-policy implementation is necessarily objectionable. In some instances, it is inevitable and necessary. But testing for legal causality in the context of investor-state arbitration is not one of those instances. The reason for this inadmissibility is that, as detailed in section 3.2, the concept of legal causation has no place in international investment law. And because legal causation lacks a place in international investment law, engaging in adjudicative-policy implementation when testing for legal causality looks like the arbitrary imposition of the adjudicators' preferred policies. This practice can only delegitimize the international adjudication of investor-state disputes. And the same observation can be made in respect of other defects resulting from the use the other normative notions, with the exception of "direct cause."

3.2 No Purpose for Legal Causation in International Investment Law

But it is understood that the potential delegitimizing effect of testing for legal causality will not alone be accepted as entailing the extraction of legal causation

[99] ibid 152. See eg the rule in *R v Cheshire* stipulating that negligent medical care, which was the direct cause of the victim's death, did not break the chain of causation, which started with the intentional act of shooting the victim: see *R v Cheshire* [1991] 3 All ER 670.

[100] Owen, "Philosophical Foundations" (n 55) 201–02.

[101] In the law on state responsibility, the starting point is that fault is not a necessary component of liability, unless the relevant primary rules provide otherwise, see Crawford, *State Responsibility: The General Part* (n 21) 219.

[102] Charles N Brower and Stephan W Schill, "Is Arbitration a Threat or a Boon to the Legitimacy of International Investment Law?" (2009) 9 Chicago Journal of International Law 471, 476.

from international investment law. This non-acceptance should not arise on account of doubts regarding its truthfulness. The quality of legal reasoning when testing for legal causality has always been suspect.[103] It is rather suspected that there is an ambivalent attitude towards this problem. The most probable reason for this ambivalence is the low probative value attributed to it. For although the quality of legal reasoning on causal questions might be low, difficult causal questions rarely arise in investment-treaty arbitrations. Additionally, intuitive determinations on causal questions are generally accepted, while different decisions on the same causal question can be tolerated because the ill-effects of the inconsistency are limited to one case. Moreover, testing for legal causality is viewed as a legal and practical necessity. And because of this necessity, a "bad test is better than no test at all."[104] A knockout blow must be delivered to this belief, starting with the idea that legal causation is a legal necessity. As argued below, the opposite is true.

The oft-stated purpose of testing for legal causality is to limit the scope of liability.[105] But that is only half the story. For when adjudicative bodies limit the scope of liability, the loss from which the claim originates does not go away. It rather stays where it landed, on the claimant. Accordingly, in practical terms, limiting the scope of liability means choosing to place the burden of a loss on one person rather than another. And this feeds into a fundamental purpose of domestic tort law: to decide where the burdens for the losses arising in modern societies should fall.[106] Two points should be noted about these losses. First they are inevitable and unavoidable in the sense that human error is a part of the human condition. Second, they arise in the throes of complex modern societies. To cope with the challenge of deciding where these losses should fall, a vast body of tort law jurisprudence has been built. That jurisprudence should usually provide the necessary guidance. But as these losses will arise in a multiple of different ways and considering the complexity of modern society, a flexible doctrinal tool is sometimes needed to complete the task of deciding who should carry the burden. Metaphorically speaking, this is a doctrinal last chance saloon where adjudicators have a final opportunity to check whether they want to impose liability on the respondent or leave the loss with the claimant. Because of this role, the various theories of tort liability have all concentrated their efforts on defining its content,[107] hence explaining the variety of different normative notions at play when testing for legal causality.

[103] See Richard W Wright, "The Nightmare and the Noble Dream: Hart and Honoré on Causation and Responsibility" in Matthew H Kramer and others (eds), *The Legacy of HLA Hart: Legal, Political, and Moral Philosophy* (OUP 2008) 169.

[104] Jeremiah Smith, "Legal Cause in Actions of Tort" (1911) 25 Harvard Law Review 103, 105.

[105] See eg *Methanex Corp v United States of America*, ad hoc arbitration (UNCITRAL Arbitration Rules) (Partial Award) (Preliminary Award on Jurisdiction and Admissibility) (7 August 2008) [138].

[106] The philosophy of tort law debates what principles should guide this function, but there is no debate that deciding where losses fall is the ultimate purpose, see Jules Coleman, Scott Hershovitz, and Gabriel Mendlow, "Theories of the Common Law of Torts" (*Stanford Encyclopaedia of Philosophy*, 17 December 2015) para 1.3.2 <https://plato.stanford.edu/entries/tort-theories/> accessed 12 July 2022.

[107] Calabresi, "Concerning Cause" (n 51) 90.

On one level, international investment law is also interested in deciding where investment losses should fall. But these losses are of a different nature compared to those losses occurring in domestic tort law. Unlike human conduct, the quality of governments' conduct need not be unavoidably bad on occasions. Governance consists of considered measures, not careless moments; in other words, investor-state disputes arise out of state conduct that is deliberated over, such as the enactment on the laws, not momentary losses of concentration while driving, for example.[108] Put simply, bad governance is a choice. And when it is not the product of choice, there are specific defenses that states can plead to stave off findings of liability against them.[109] But the running assumption must be that bad governance is a choice, thereby meaning that the investment losses that they cause are avoidable. So while domestic tort law needs a flexible doctrinal tool to spread around unavoidable losses, there is no apparent reason why international investment law needs the same tool. In fact, there are reasons why it does not. First, if the decision on liability in investment-treaty arbitration is ultimately grounded in the idea that the state engaged in bad governance, then the normative notions of legal causation look decidedly out of place considering that they have no relation to the idea of governance. Second, as investment losses are avoidable, arbitral tribunals are justified in adopting a stricter approach to the question of state responsibility, compared to their counterparts applying domestic tort law. Again, speaking metaphorically, arbitral tribunals should bypass the last chance saloon of legal causation and head directly for the destination of state responsibility.

4. Quelling the Protests on Excessive State Responsibility

As it is considered that the notion that 'legal causes' should be limited to direct causes (of the consequence in question) should be retained,[110] this is not a complete extraction of legal causation from international investment law, but it is nonetheless a dramatic conclusion in light of the general endorsement of legal causation in the law on state responsibility by the ILC.[111] With this conclusion, there might be some silent protest to the Cardozo-inspired tune of "state responsibility in an indeterminate amount for an indeterminate time to an indeterminate class."[112] Such protests are without merit. For the idea that, without legal causation, there will be an infinite chain of causes is an old wives' tale.

[108] Jeremy Waldron, "Moments of Carelessness and Massive Loss" in David G Owen (ed), *The Philosophical Foundations of Tort Law* (OUP 1995) 389.

[109] Force majeure, distress, and necessity, all of which are codified in the Articles on State Responsibility in arts 23, 24, and 25, respectively: see ILC, "Draft Articles" (n 15) 76, 78, 80.

[110] See section 3.1.

[111] ILC, "Draft Articles" (n 15) 92–93.

[112] See *Ultramares Corp v George A Touche* (1931) 255 NY 170, 179 per Cardozo J.

The first reason for this conclusion is a basic one: the requirement of proof.[113] In other words, proving to the applicable standard of proof that a particular antecedent was a factual cause of a consequence. This is particularly difficult when the antecedent is an indirect cause because it allegedly motivates the performance of conduct directly necessary for the occurrence of the consequence. An example of this difficulty was evident in *CME v Czechia*. As detailed above,[114] a direct cause of the investment loss was the termination of a contract. As this conduct was not attributable to Czechia, the investor had to prove that other Czech conduct motivated the termination, thereby indirectly causing the consequence. The investor succeeded in proving this causal link.[115] But, in *Lauder v Czechia*, an investment-treaty arbitration based on the same investment dispute, the arbitral tribunal concluded that this same causal link was lacking.[116] Similarly, in *Blusun v Italy*, the investor could have stumbled on this same hurdle. As detailed in section 2.2, for the indirect cause of the investment loss, there were two potential causes: the conduct of the investor (the design of its business plan) or Italy (changes to the regulatory regime applicable to the investor's investment). Although the arbitral tribunal ultimately decided that the investor's conduct was the legal cause of its investment loss,[117] it repeatedly cast doubt on whether Italy's conduct was factually causal at all.[118]

Another tool for dealing with the problem of infinite causality, which is sporadically used in domestic tort law,[119] is testing for the factual causality of the tortious or wrongful aspect of the relevant conduct. The practice of arbitral tribunals for investment-treaty arbitrations is to only test whether the relevant state conduct alone was factually causal.[120] When testing whether the tortious aspect of certain conduct was actually causal, the focus is not on whether the conduct alone was causal, but whether the wrongful aspect of that conduct was causal.[121] A typical tort case can help illuminate the distinction.[122] If the respondent was driving a car at 50 kilometers per hour in a 30 kilometers per hour zone, testing for the factual causality of the tortious aspect of the respondent's conduct involves examining whether driving 20 kilometers per hour over the speed limit was causal, not the conduct of driving itself. To determine what the wrongful aspect is, the applicable liability-creating rule, which is the rule that the respondent has allegedly breached,

[113] Tony Honoré, "Causation in the Law" (*Stanford Encyclopaedia of Philosophy*, 17 November 2010) para 3.2 <https://plato.stanford.edu/archives/fall2019/entries/causation-law/> accessed 12 July 2022.

[114] See section 3.2.

[115] *CME v Czechia* (n 18) [575].

[116] *Lauder v Czechia* (n 59) [274].

[117] *Blusun v Italy* (n 64) [394].

[118] ibid [388]–[392].

[119] Wright, "Causation in Tort Law" (n 32) 1766–67.

[120] One exception is the arbitral tribunal for *Lemire v Ukraine*, see further (n 124).

[121] Wright, "Into the Bramble Bush" (n 17) 1082.

[122] This example is inspired by a similar example in Sandy Steel, "Defining Causal Counterfactuals in Negligence" (2014) 130 Law Quarterly Review 564, 565.

must be examined to identify its conduct-evaluating legal element. A legal element is a fact in the predicate section of a liability-creating rule,[123] while a conduct-evaluating legal element is one looking at the quality of the respondent's conduct. Take, for example, the standard on fair and equitable treatment. To prove a breach of this rule, the state conduct must be unfair and inequitable, which is the conduct-evaluating part of this rule. Accordingly, when testing for factual causality in respect of the standard on fair and equitable treatment, it is the unfair and inequitable aspect of the state contact which, according to this method, should be tested for factual causality in respect of the consequence.[124] Given the limits on the scope of this contribution, this tool can only be briefly introduced, meaning that the questions whether international investment law should adopt this approach and how the test for this purpose should be formulated are questions that cannot be addressed here.

5. Conclusion

If the practice of testing for the factual causality of the wrongful aspect of state conduct is adopted, and if it works in tandem with the notion that only direct causes are legal causes, any protest of indeterminate state responsibility on account of the extraction of legal causation from international investment law should ring hollow. Hence, there is no practical necessity for retaining legal causation in its current form in international investment law. The last hurdle standing in the way of final extraction is a psychological one: the reverence shown by arbitral tribunals to the commentary of the ILC on legal causation. It is a mistake for arbitral tribunals to blindly adopt the jurisprudence of the ILC into international investment law.[125] A manifestation of this erroneous approach has become apparent with respect to the testing for legal causality investment-treaty arbitrations. As argued in section 3.2, the doctrinal function that the process of testing for legal causality serves in domestic law is not applicable in international investment law. Further, as argued in section 3.1, any attempt to test for legal causality with notions imported from domestic law has the potential to delegitimize the international adjudication of investor-state disputes. What has to be emphasized in this conclusion is that this potential is significant. In any investment-treaty arbitration that reaches the merits phase, the arbitral tribunal invariably has to analyze the causal question, regardless

[123] Frederick Schauer, *Playing by the Rules: A Philosophical Examination of Rule-Based Decision-Making in Law and in Life* (OUP 1993) 23.

[124] See eg *Lemire v Urkaine* (n 59) [171].

[125] See James Crawford, "Investment Arbitration and the ILC Articles on State Responsibility" (2010) 25 ICSID Review: Foreign Investment Law Journal 127, 130.

of which investment protection standard the state has allegedly breached. Because of this omnipresence, causation goes to the heart of state responsibility in international investment law. Recognizing this, it is time to get the process for testing for causation right, which can begin with extracting legal causation from international investment law.

8

A Priori Causal Inferences in the Law of the World Trade Organization

Catherine E Gascoigne

1. Introduction

> The mind can never possibly find the effect in the supposed cause [. . .] For the effect is totally different from the cause, and consequently can never be discovered in it. Motion in the second Billiard-ball is a quite distinct event from motion in the first; nor is there anything in the one to suggest the smallest hint of the other. [. . .] In a word, then, every effect is a distinct event from its cause. It could not, therefore, be discovered in the cause, and the first invention or conception of it, *a priori*, must be entirely arbitrary.[1]

David Hume's insight into the impossibility of inferring an effect simply by examining the nature of its cause forms the central critique of the World Trade Organization (WTO) jurisprudence that will be examined in this chapter. Specifically, this chapter will discuss three areas of WTO jurisprudence that require the Appellate Body (AB) to make determinations about causation. For the purposes of this chapter, the terms, "causation" or "causal link" might be understood in the context of the need to establish that an injury, effect or outcome was brought about by a government policy and was not caused by any other independent phenomenon that may have occurred at the same time.[2] This chapter will argue that there is a tendency in the jurisprudence to make conclusions about the effects of a supposed cause simply by making an *a priori* judgment about the nature of that cause. To put it another way, instead of interrogating the empirical effects

[1] David Hume, *An Enquiry Concerning Human Understanding*, LA Selby-Bigge (ed), (1st ed, OUP 1975) Section IV, Pt I, 25. This quotation was taken from a larger passage in which David Hume was observing the importance of experience in helping observers to make causal links between factors.

[2] This definition draws, to some extent, on the definition of "causation" in Marion Jansen, Joost Pauwelyn, and Theresa Carpenter, " The Use of Economics in International Trade and Investment Disputes: Complex, Contentious but Oh-So-Important for the Sustainability of Trade and Investment" in Marion Jansen, Joost Pauwelyn, and Theresa Carpenter (eds), *The Use of Economics in International Trade and Investment Disputes* (CUP 2017) 5.

Catherine E Gascoigne, A Priori *Causal Inferences in the Law of the World Trade Organization* In: *Secondary Rules of Primary Importance in International Law*. Edited by: Gábor Kajtár, Başak Çalı, and Marko Milanovic, Oxford University Press.
 DOI: 10.1093/oso/9780192869012.003.0008

of a cause, there is a propensity in the jurisprudence to predict what the effects are likely to be simply by looking at what is presumed to have caused them. The three areas of law that this chapter will examine are: (1) Serious Prejudice (articles 5(c) and 6.3 of the Agreement on Subsidies and Countervailing Measures (SCM Agreement));[3] (2) the General Exceptions (article XX of the General Agreement on Tariffs and Trade[4] (GATT 1994) and article XIV of the General Agreement on Trade in Services[5] (GATS)); and (3) the calculation of nullification and impairment for the purposes of retaliatory measures (article 22.6 of the Understanding on Rules and Procedures Governing the Settlement of Disputes (DSU)[6] and article 4.10 of the SCM Agreement).

After completing an analysis of the jurisprudence in question, this chapter will propose an alternative approach to determining causation in these three areas of WTO law by putting forward a three-step approach to determining causation based on guidance given by the AB in *US—Wheat Gluten*[7]—that is, in the context of determining causation under the Agreement on Safeguards.[8] It will be suggested that the AB's approach to determining causation in that case may be adapted to the three areas of jurisprudence examined in this chapter. This three-step approach will be referred to as the Tripartite Non-Attribution/Causation Analysis throughout this chapter.

Far from being a mere technicality, this chapter suggests that the way in which causation is interrogated forms one of the most difficult and important parts of litigating the three areas of WTO law under examination. It will be seen that the interpretive choices that are made in respect of the causal analysis go on to have profound policy implications. For instance, use of the Tripartite Non-Attribution/Causation Analysis makes it harder to make out causation than when a causal test based on *a priori* inferences is used. Moreover, it will also be demonstrated in section 5.2.2 below that the way in which the causal threshold is set also directly impacts the ease with which causation is made out. Finally, the Tripartite Non-Attribution/Causation Analysis, with its emphasis on the interrogation of real-world effects, allows for a more analytically rigorous and accurate assessment of causation than the use of *a priori* inferences. In these ways it is suggested that

[3] Agreement on Subsidies and Countervailing Measures (adopted 15 April 1994, entered into force 1 January 1995) LT/UR/A-1A/9 (SCM Agreement).

[4] General Agreement on Tariffs and Trade 1994 (adopted 15 April 1994, entered into force 1 January 1995) LT/UR/A-1A/1/GATT/1 (GATT 1994).

[5] General Agreement on Trade in Services (adopted 15 April 1994, entered into force 1 January 1995) LT/UR/A-1B/S/1 (GATS).

[6] Understanding on Rules and Procedures Governing the Settlement of Disputes (adopted 15 April 1994, entered into force 1 January 1995) LT/UR/A-2/DS/U/1 (DSU).

[7] WTO Appellate Body Report, *United States—Definitive Safeguard Measures on Imports of Wheat Gluten from the European Communities*, WT/DS166/AB/R (adopted 22 December 2000) (AB, *US—Wheat Gluten*) [69].

[8] Agreement on Safeguards (adopted 15 April 1994, entered into force 1 January 1995) LT/UR/A-1A/8 (Safeguards Agreement).

causation is far from a secondary rule of minimal importance, but rather, an intellectually demanding question from which many profound policy implications follow. With this in mind, the chapter will now consider the first area of WTO law in which causation is sometimes determined using *a priori* causal inferences—namely, serious prejudice.

2. Serious Prejudice

Article 5 of the SCM Agreement provides for three forms of "adverse effects" that are potentially the result of subsidies and, if demonstrated, are actionable. The overwhelming majority of claims alleging "adverse effects" as a result of a subsidy have been brought in relation to the third of the listed potential adverse effects—namely, serious prejudice, set out in article 5(c) of the SCM Agreement.[9] Accordingly, the focus of this chapter is confined to a consideration of the causal requirements involved in a determination of serious prejudice under the SCM Agreement. The term "serious prejudice" is not defined in article 5; but article 6.3 sets out the circumstances in which serious prejudice "may" be held to apply. Serious prejudice is not so much concerned with the condition of a Member's particular domestic injury as with the "negative effects on a Member's trade interests in respect of a product caused by another Member's subsidization."[10]

In order to decide whether subsides are responsible for the adverse effect on a market, a fact-finder must determine whether the market phenomenon is actually caused by subsidies. To that end, a fact-finder must be careful not to attribute blame to subsidies for those things that were, in fact, caused by some other source. This chapter will use the term, "other known factors"[11] to mean all those factors that could potentially adversely affect a Member's trade interests, other than subsidies. In other words, the fact-finder must engage in a causation analysis that

[9] In WTO Panel Report, *European Communities and certain member States—Measures Affecting Trade in Large Civil Aircraft*, WT/DS316/R (adopted 30 June 2010), the US claimed that the subsidies at issue caused injury to its domestic industry within the meaning of art 5(a). In that case, the Panel concluded that the US failed to establish such injury within the meaning of art 5(a). This finding was not appealed. Moreover, in WTO Panel Report, *Korea—Measures Affecting Trade in Commercial Vessels*, WT/DS273/R (adopted 7 March 2005) (Panel, *Korea—Commercial Vessels*), the EC also argued a claim for injury to its domestic industry under art 5(a) before the EC's Request for Establishment of the Panel; but this claim was later discontinued. With respect to art 5(c), Mexico argued in WTO Panel Report, *United States—Continued Dumping and Subsidy Offset Act of 2000*, WT/DS217/R, WT/DS234/R (adopted 16 September 2002) that both the granting and maintaining of subsidies by the Continued Dumping and Subsidy Offset Act of 2000 (CDSOA) caused "non-violation" nullification or impairment. The Panel found against Mexico, saying that Mexico had failed to demonstrate that the CDSOA had caused "adverse effects" within the meaning of art 5(b) of the SCM Agreement.

[10] Panel, *Korea—Commercial Vessels* (n 9) [7.578].

[11] This term is used by the AB in WTO Appellate Body Report, *United States—Anti-Dumping Measures on Certain Hot-Rolled Steel Products from Japan*, WT/DS184/AB/R (adopted 24 July 2001) [226] in the context of anti-dumping measures, where discussion is being had as to the non-attribution analysis.

contains both positive and negative features—namely, a positive determination of a causal link between subsidies and injury (a causation analysis), as well as a negative determination that the adverse effect was not instead brought about by other known factors (a non-attribution analysis). There is a cleavage in the jurisprudence as to whether to examine the causal relationship between a subsidy or subsidies and the adverse effect on the market in one step (the unitary approach) or two steps (the bifurcated approach).

Whilst the unitary and bifurcated approach represent diametrically opposite approaches to determining causation, both have the same objectives in view—namely, to interrogate: (1) whether a particular market phenomenon exists (eg a decline in market share or the impedance of a Member's exports of a competitive product into the market); and (2) whether the market phenomenon was the effect of a subsidy or subsidies, or was instead brought about by other known factors. Under the "unitary approach," the particular market phenomenon identified in the subparagraphs of article 6.3 and the causal relationship between the market phenomenon and the challenged subsidies are both analyzed together.[12] For example, an analysis of whether "price suppression" has taken place is conducted at the same time as an analysis of what caused the price suppression.

In contrast, the bifurcated approach involves, first, an analysis of the market phenomenon, and then, as a secondary step, an examination of whether a causal link exists between the potential causes and the market phenomenon.[13] The bifurcated approach was used by the Panel in *US—Upland Cotton*,[14] where the Panel considered: (1) whether there was price suppression in the world market for upland cotton and whether this price suppression was significant; and (2) whether a causal relationship existed between the significant price suppression and certain price-contingent subsidies.[15]

The AB has indicated that the unitary approach is the preferred approach. For instance, the AB, in *US—Upland Cotton (Article 21.5—Brazil)* held that "at least in respect of identifying price suppression and its causes [the unitary approach] has a sound conceptual foundation."[16] The AB does not further elaborate on its basis for finding that the unitary approach has a "sound conceptual foundation." In a

[12] WTO Appellate Body Report, *European Communities and certain member States—Measures Affecting Trade in Large Civil Aircraft*, WT/DS316/AB/R (adopted 18 May 2011) [1107] (AB, *EC and certain member States—Large Civil Aircraft*).

[13] AB, *EC and certain member States—Large Civil Aircraft* (n 13) [1107]. The AB in WTO Appellate Body Report, *United States—Subsides on Upland Cotton*, WT/DS/267/AB/R (adopted 3 March 2005) (AB, *US—Upland Cotton*) said that they saw "no legal error in this approach": AB, *US—Upland Cotton* ibid [431].

[14] WTO Panel Report, *United States—Subsidies on Upland Cotton*, WT/DS267/R (adopted 8 September 2004) [7.1275]–[7.1363].

[15] ibid.

[16] WTO Appellate Body Report, *United States—Subsidies on Upland Cotton (Recourse to Article 21.5 of the DSU by Brazil)*, WT/DS267/AB/RW (adopted 2 June 2008) [354] (AB, *US—Upland Cotton (Article 21.5—Brazil)*).

similar vein, the AB in *EC and certain member States—Large Civil Aircraft* said that "a unitary approach that uses a counterfactual will generally be the more appropriate approach."[17]

It is suggested that the unitary approach is fundamentally flawed as a methodology for interrogating the link between subsidies and a market phenomenon for two reasons. First, the unitary approach involves identifying the effect of the subsidy (ie the market phenomenon, such as price suppression) at the same time that it seeks to establish its cause (ie the subsidies). In this sense, under the unitary approach, the nature of the effect of the subsidy is not fully established at the time that the fact-finder is seeking to understand its cause. To put this in symbolic terms, whilst causal tests generally ask, "Did C cause E?", the unitary approach asks, "What is E? And is it the effect of C?" This form of questioning represents a logical error in two respects. First, the unitary approach falsely assumes that an effect may be knowable *a priori* simply through analyzing its cause. Second and relatedly, it is premised on the false assumption that cause and effect are not entirely distinct concepts, since the one cause may produce a plurality of possible effects; and the effect is not knowable until it has fully been manifested. Indeed, to this end, it is instructive at this point to reconsider the quotation from Hume with which this chapter opened—namely, "every effect is a distinct event from its cause."[18] It follows from Hume's point that the effect-based phenomenon (ie the effect) must be identified *prior* to any analysis of its cause (ie the subsidy/subsidies or the other known factors).

It also follows from the basic conceptual misunderstanding of causation that the unitary approach to causation results in circular reasoning. That is, the unitary approach requires a fact-finder to address the question of whether a market phenomenon is in existence before addressing "the effect of the subsidy." Essentially, then, this requires contending that a market phenomenon was brought about as a result of subsidies, and then using this conclusion to support a finding of causation between a subsidy and its effect. In this sense, the conclusion is embedded in the premise, which makes the inquiry determinative. The US made this point in its appellant's submissions in *US—Upland Cotton*.[19] It is suggested, therefore, that the unitary approach does not have the "sound conceptual foundation" asserted by the AB in *US—Upland Cotton (Article 21.5—Brazil)*.[20]

The second reason that the unitary approach is flawed is that it does not allow for a genuine non-attribution analysis to be undertaken. That is, it was seen above that the jurisprudence in respect of cases concerning serious prejudice requires that a non-attribution analysis be performed in order to ensure that any factors

17 AB, *EC and certain member States—Large Civil Aircraft* (n 13) [1109].
18 Hume (n 1) Section IV, Pt I, 25.
19 United States' appellant's submission at [230] (quoted in AB, *US—Upland Cotton* (n 14) [430]).
20 AB, *US—Upland Cotton (Article 21.5—Brazil)* (n 17) [354].

that played no causative role in bringing about a market phenomenon do not confound the causation analysis.[21] The unitary approach, however, leaves no scope for conducting a rigorous non-attribution analysis. This is because the very method of defining the market phenomenon is dependent upon subsidies being the sole cause. To put it another way, the nature of the market phenomenon is defined in terms of the effect of subsidies. Accordingly, it becomes impossible to then decide in light of a non-attribution analysis that the subsidies actually played no or minimal causative role and that the market phenomenon was caused by other known factors. It follows that it is difficult, in turn, to reconcile the unitary approach with statements made in the jurisprudence about the importance of conducting a non-attribution analysis.

In sum, the unitary approach is inappropriate for determining the cause and effect of a market phenomenon for the purposes of article 6.3 of the SCM Agreement and should arguably be abandoned. It is suggested that the bifurcated approach is superior, as it is the only approach that reflects a coherent vision of causation. Section 3 considers the way in which determining causation based on *a priori* causal inferences is also present in the jurisprudence relating to the General Exceptions.

3. The General Exceptions

Both article XX of the GATT 1994 and article XIV of the GATS (collectively, "the General Exceptions") set out conditional exceptions to the disciplines of the GATT 1994 and the GATS. To avail itself of an exception, a Member must satisfy two analytical limbs: (1) its measure may be prima facie exempted under one or more of the subparagraphs of the General Exceptions; and (2) the measure must also fulfill the requirements of the introductory clause or "chapeau" of the General Exceptions.[22] This second analytical limb is beyond the scope of this chapter. In relation to the first analytical limb, the AB must consider a number of factors when determining whether a measure satisfies the first analytical limb. One of the most critical of these is the level of contribution that a measure must make to the realization of its intended policy objective.[23] It is this question that forms the central preoccupation

21 AB, *US—Upland Cotton* (n 13) [438]; Panel, *US—Upland Cotton* (n 14) [7.1344].

22 The idea of approaching the analysis of the General Exceptions in this two-tiered manner has been called into question: see Lorand Bartels, "The Chapeau of the General Exceptions in the WTO GATT and GATS Agreements: A Reconstruction" (2015) 109(1) American Journal of International Law 105. A discussion of this approach is beyond the scope of this chapter.

23 The level of contribution that a measure makes to the realization of its intended policy objective is an important factor to consider in relation to seeking exemption under each of the subparagraphs of the General Exceptions. The AB in *Korea—Various Measures on Beef* held that a determination of whether a measure is "necessary" for the purposes of the General Exceptions involves "weighing and balancing" a series of factors, including: (1) the contribution of a measure to a policy objective; (2) the relative importance of the policy objective; and (3) the trade-restrictiveness of the challenged measure (WAB test): see WTO Appellate Body Report, *Korea—Measures Affecting Imports of Fresh,*

of this section. In particular, this section is principally concerned with the way in which a fact-finder can demonstrate that a measure made a causal contribution to a policy objective.

It will be argued in this section that the relationship between a measure and its intended policy objective is impliedly a causal relationship. Indeed, this idea has been argued by a number of Members in the jurisprudence;[24] and even the Panel in *Dominican Republic—Import and Sale of Cigarettes* referred to the link between a measure and its policy objective as a "causal link."[25] Nonetheless, despite the Panel's acknowledgement of the role of causation in this relationship, the Panel and the AB have so far refused to follow-up this insight with the use of causal tests that interrogate causation. Instead of using traditional causal tests, the panels and the AB have expressly resisted laying down a methodology to assess the contribution of a measure to its policy objective.[26] The AB has held on several occasions that a determination as to the effectiveness of a measure may be made using both qualitative and quantitative evidence.[27] To date, all of the relevant panels and the AB have relied on so-called "qualitative" evidence in making the determination. Several cases have assessed the contribution of a measure to the policy objective by examining

Chilled and Frozen Beef, WT/DS161/R, WT/DS169/R (adopted 11 December 2000) [162]–[164] (AB, *Korea—Various Measures on Beef*); and WTO Appellate Body Report, *Colombia—Measures Relating to the Importation of Textiles, Apparel and Footwear*, WT/DS461/AB/R (adopted 7 June 2016) [5.71]–[5.73], [5.77]. Moreover, the contribution of a measure towards realizing a policy objective is also important in relation to art XX(g), where measures must be "primarily aimed at" or have a "direct connection" with the policy objective: see WTO Panel Report, *United States—Standards for Reformulated and Conventional Gasoline*, WT/DS2/R (adopted 29 January 1996) [6.40] (Panel, *US—Gasoline*); WTO Appellate Body Report, *United States—Standards for Reformulated and Conventional Gasoline*, WT/DS2/AB/R (adopted 29 April 1996) [19] (AB, *US—Gasoline*). Finally, in relation to art XX(j), the same "WAB test" required in relation to those subparagraphs containing the word "necessary" must also be undertaken in relation to measures seeking exemption under art XX(j): WTO Appellate Body Report, *India—Certain Measures Relating to Solar Cells and Solar Modules*, WT/DS456/R (adopted 24 February 2016) [5.63] (AB, *India—Solar Cells*). It seems that the threshold for contribution must be higher under art XX(j) than that which is expected under subparagraphs containing the word "necessary": AB, *India—Solar Cells* [5.62].

24 WTO Panel Report, *Korea—Measures Affecting Imports of Fresh, Chilled and Frozen Beef*, WT/DS161/R, WT/DS169/R (adopted 31 July 2000) [254]; Venezuela's Appellee's Submission (18 March 1996); Venezuela's Statement at the Oral Hearing (27 March 1996); China's appellant's submission, para 208 cited at WTO Appellate Body Report, *China—Measures Related to the Exportation of Rare Earths, Tungsten, and Molybdenum*, WT/DS/AB431/AB/R, WT/DS/432/AB/R, WT/DS433/AB/R (adopted 7 August 2014) [5.102].

25 WTO Panel Report, *Dominican Republic—Measures Affecting the Importation and Internal Sale of Cigarettes*, WT/DS302/R (adopted 26 November 2004) [7.226].

26 WTO Appellate Body Report, *Brazil—Measures Affecting Imports of Retreaded Tyres*, WT/DS332/AB/R (adopted 3 December 2007) [145] (AB, *Brazil—Retreaded Tyres*). This was recalled with approval by the AB in WTO Appellate Body Report, *European Communities—Measures Prohibiting the Importation and Marketing of Seal Products*, WT/DS400/AB/R and WT/DS401/AB/R (adopted 22 May 2014) [5.210] (AB, *EC—Seal Products*).

27 AB, *Brazil—Retreaded Tyres* (n 26) [146]; AB, *EC—Seal Products* (n 26) [5.215].

the "design and structure" of the measure[28] or the "design, structure and operation" of the measure.[29]

It is by no means clear what the design, structure and operation of a measure means, nor how they assist in determining the contribution of a measure to achieving a policy objective. For example, to take the analogy of subsidies or trade remedies, it would be nonsensical to attempt to interrogate the causal contribution of a subsidy or import to injuring another Member simply by looking at the "design and structure" of that particular subsidy or import with no regard to its effects. This is not to say that qualitative or non-quantitative features cannot be used effectively to interrogate causation; but rather, that those features would need to relate to the qualities of necessity or sufficiency. Instead, the "design, structure and operation" test requires that a fact-finder interrogate causation by looking at the features of the alleged *cause*, instead of looking at the features of the *causal link*.

The "design and structure" approach involves the same logical fallacy that was discussed in relation to serious prejudice—namely, assuming that an effect may be knowable *a priori* simply by examining the nature of the cause. Again, Hume's critique of deriving an effect simply by examining the cause is apposite here.[30] In sum, a panel or the AB is no more capable of deriving a causal link between a measure and its policy objective through the process of examining the "design and structure" of a measure than Hume was of predicting the motion of the second Billiard-Ball simply from examining the movement of the first. Moreover, as with the unitary test in the serious prejudice context, the "design and structure" test also fails to leave any scope for a non-attribution analysis. It surely follows from this that the "design and structure" test cannot be relied upon accurately to interrogate causation and should be abandoned. Section 4 of this chapter will demonstrate how this same logical fallacy is embedded into the analysis of causation in the determination of retaliatory measures under article 22.6 of the DSU and article 4.10 of the SCM Agreement.

4. Retaliatory Measures

The concept of reparation is an important principle in general international law,[31] and the concept of causation is fundamental to the way in which reparation is

[28] WTO Appellate Body Report, *United States—Import Prohibition of Certain Shrimp and Shrimp Products*, WT/DS58/AB/R (adopted 12 October 1998) [138] (AB, *US—Shrimp*); WTO Panel Report, *Argentina—Measures Affecting the Export of Bovine Hides and the Import of Finished Leather*, WT/DS155/R (adopted 19 December 2000) [11.303].

[29] See eg WTO Panel Report, *Brazil—Certain Measures Concerning Taxation and Charges*, WT/DS472/R, WT/DS497/R (adopted 30 August 2017) [7.920].

[30] Hume (n 1) Section IV, 25.

[31] *Case Concerning the Factory at Chorzów* (Jurisdiction) PCIJ Rep Series A No 9 p 21; art 31 of the Draft Articles on the Responsibility of States for Internationally Wrongful Acts, Report of the ILC on the Work of its 53rd Session, UN GAOR, 56th Sess, Supp No 10, p 43, UN Doc A/56/10 (2001).

calculated.[32] Reparation as such, however, does not exist in WTO law because remedies are prospective—that is, the objective of the dispute settlement mechanism is to bring about a mutually acceptable solution to the parties going forward,[33] and in the absence of that, to secure the withdrawal of the measures that are inconsistent with the covered agreements.[34] If both these primary aims fail, a Member may seek compensation from the other;[35] and, even then, compensation is only a voluntary remedy.[36] The last resort for Members of the WTO to resolve their dispute involves the possibility of retaliation. This may be used where a Member fails to bring its measure into compliance with the covered agreement(s) and the other Member "suspend[s] the application of concessions or other obligations under the covered agreements on a discriminatory basis vis-à-vis the other Member, subject to authorization by the DSB of such measures"[37] ("retaliatory measures").[38]

The value of the retaliatory measures suspended must be "equivalent" to the nullification or impairment of benefits that the measure has caused,[39] except in the context of the SCM Agreement, where the retaliatory measures must be "appropriate."[40] Arbitrators, in the context of article 22.6 of the DSU and article 4.10 of the SCM Agreement are required to quantify the complainant Member's level of nullification and impairment. Article XXIII:1 of the GATT 1994 provides that the nullification or impairment must arise "as a result of [...] the failure of another contracting party to carry out its obligations under this Agreement." In other words, article XXIII:1 of the GATT 1994 would seem to require arbitrators to quantify the level of nullification and impairment that was actually "a result of [...]" or *caused by* the failure of a responding Member to bring its measure into conformity with the DSB ruling.

As a logical matter, therefore, it follows that the first consideration for arbitrators must be whether there was a causal link between a responding Member's failure to bring its measure into conformity with a DSB ruling and the complainant Member's nullification and impairment. Only then, as a secondary step, would it be appropriate for arbitrators to attempt to estimate the level of nullification and impairment caused to a complainant Member's industry. The current jurisprudence

32 Article 31(2) of the Draft Articles on the Responsibility of States for Internationally Wrongful Acts (n 46); Para 9 of the ILC's Commentary to art 31 ARSIWA, Report of the International Law Commission on the Work of its 53rd session, 2001, UN Doc A/56/10, para 77, at 92.

33 DSU (n 6) art 3.7.

34 ibid.

35 ibid.

36 DSU (n 6) art 22.1.

37 ibid art 3.7.

38 The suspension of concessions occurs when Member A denies a benefit to Member B that Member A is otherwise legally required to grant. For example, the DSB might authorize Member A to suspend its tariff concessions on products imported from Member B because of Member B's failure to implement its DSB ruling. The words "retaliation" or "retaliatory measures" are not used in the DSU, though they will be used throughout this chapter.

39 DSU (n 6) art 22.4.

40 SCM Agreement (n 3) art 4.10.

demonstrates, however, that arbitrators have not set out any clear, rigorous method for interrogating the causal link between a Member's failure to conform with a DSB ruling and a complainant Member's nullification and impairment. Indeed, the jurisprudence reflects a general paucity of discussion regarding the way in which the causal link should be drawn; and causation appears only to be discussed in those cases in which the causal link is *not* made out.[41] Accordingly, it is difficult to discern the basis on which a positive causal link is found.

This omission would seem to lead to the conclusion that there is some kind of presumption in place in this context that a causal link exists, unless found otherwise—that is, the presumption is rebutted. Just as arbitrators have failed to elucidate the basis on which causation may be made out, so, too, have they failed to engage in any formal non-attribution analysis. To put this in symbolic language, arbitrators skip to quantify the effect of C, without first making a determination that C actually caused E, or that E was not partially caused by X, Y and/or Z. Accordingly, by skipping over any true non-attribution and causation analysis, arbitrators are just as guilty as ordinary Panels of presuming the causal link between a responding Member's failure to comply with its DSB ruling and the nullification and impairment to a complaining Member's industry. Here again, then, Hume's observation about the dangers of presuming an effect based on the nature of the cause[42] is relevant.

That is, by making this presumption of nullification and impairment as a result of a Member's failure to comply with its DSB ruling, the arbitrators are making the same logical fallacy as the AB was observed to have made in relation to serious prejudice and the General Exceptions. That is, such a presumption is essentially a way of leaping from the existence of a supposed cause to an effect without demonstrating the causal link between the two. Nullification and impairment to a complaining Member's industry, however, cannot be presumed simply from the responding Member's failure to comply with a DSB ruling. Section 5 of this chapter will discuss an alternative approach to determining causation in WTO law.

5. An Alternative Approach

Having seen that the current approach in the jurisprudence to determining causation based on *a priori* inferences is flawed, this chapter now turns to consider

[41] See Decision by the Arbitrators, *Canada—Export Credits and Loan Guarantees for Regional Aircraft—Recourse to Arbitration by Canada under Article 22.6 of the DSU and Article 4.11 of the SCM* Agreement, WT/DS222/ARB (adopted 17 February 2003) (*Canada—Aircraft Credits and Guarantees (Recourse to Arbitration—Article 22.6 and Article 4.11)*); and Decision by the Arbitrators, *European Communities—Measures Concerning Meat and Meat Products (Hormones)—Recourse to Arbitration by the European Communities under Article 22.6*, WT/DS26/ARB (adopted 12 July 1999) (*EC—Hormones (US (Recourse to Arbitration—Article 22.6))*.

[42] Hume (n 1) Section IV, 25.

an alternative approach, which incorporates both a positive causation analysis together with a non-attribution analysis. This alternative approach draws on the guidance given by the AB, in *US—Wheat Gluten*, in the safeguards context. In that case, the AB provided a three-step process for conducting a non-attribution/causation analysis as follows: (1) separate the injurious effects of increased imports from the injurious effects produced by other known factors; (2) attribute to imports the harm they alone have produced before attributing to other known factors the harm that they have occasioned in turn; and (3) in the final step, determine whether there is a causal link between imports and "serious injury or threat thereof"; and, if so, whether such a causal link involves a "genuine and substantial relationship of cause and effect" between these two elements.[43] A diagrammatic overview of these three steps can be seen in Figures 8.1, 8.2, and 8.3. The first two of these three steps relate to the non-attribution limb, while the third step pertains to the causation analysis. Although the Tripartite Non-Attribution/Causation Analysis was proposed in the context of the Safeguards Agreement, it is suggested that this three-step approach could be adapted to the three areas of WTO law discussed above in this chapter.

5.1 First Step of the Tripartite Non-Attribution/ Causation Analysis

The first step of the Tripartite Non-Attribution/Causation Analysis involves dividing the injuries or effects into smaller, more specific injuries or effects. For example, in relation to the law of serious prejudice, a fact-finder might divide the effect of subsidies on the affected industry into "sub-effects." By "sub-effects," it is meant the specific effect on a feature of the industry (as opposed to the overall effect on the industry as a whole). For instance, to take the example of the effect of subsidies on a cotton industry, sub-effects in relation to the law of serious prejudice might include: (1) displacement of imports of cotton within the meaning of article 6.3(a); (2) displacement of exports of cotton within the meaning of article 6.3(b); and (3) significant lost cotton sales within the meaning of article 6.3(c) of the SCM Agreement. There may well be more sub-effects than those which have been identified here and in Figure 8.1. A representation of the separation of the sub-effects of subsidies can be seen in Step 1 of Figure 8.1. It is important to clarify that, whilst Figure 8.1 depicts each of the sub-effects of the subsidies as being of equal size spatially, in reality, each sub-effect might well be of greater or lesser significance to the ultimate finding of serious prejudice.

Next, this chapter turns to consider the application of the first step of the Tripartite Non-Attribution/Causation Analysis to the law of the General Exceptions. It will be recalled that the focus of the inquiry is to consider the effect

[43] AB, *US—Wheat Gluten* (n 7) [69].

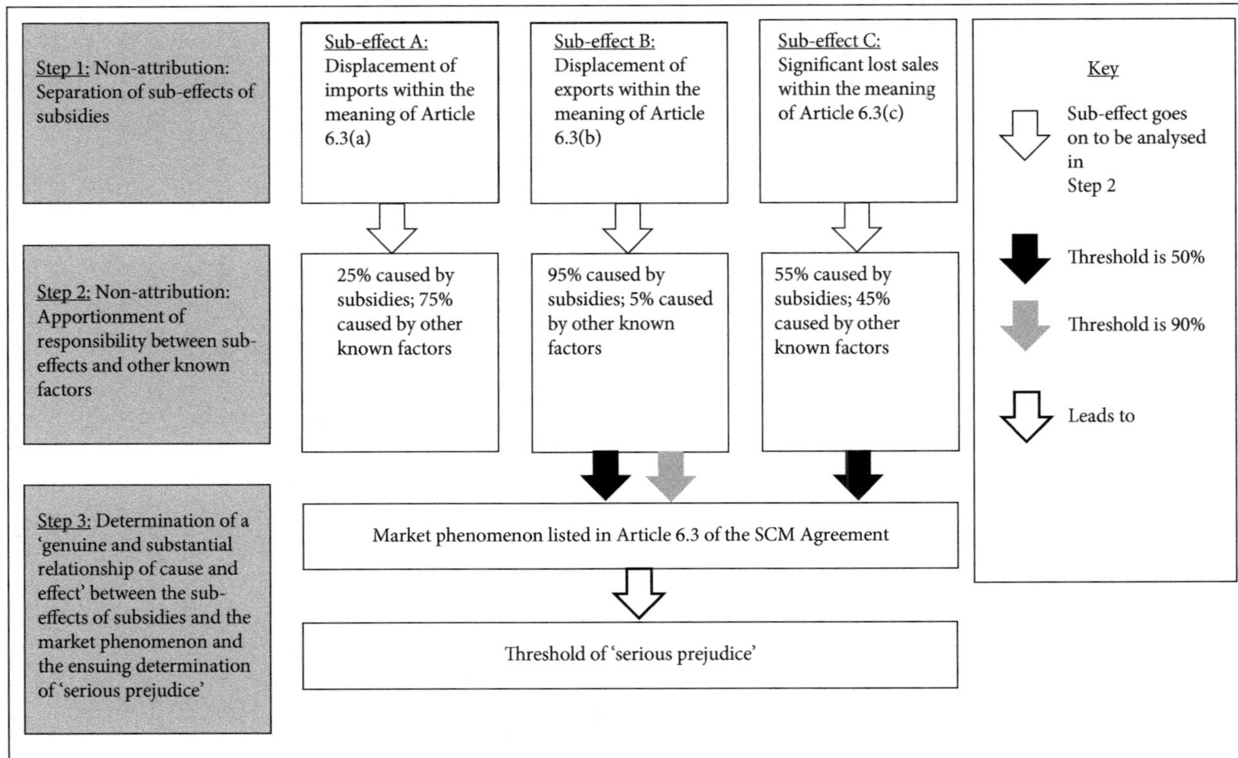

Figure 8.1 Overview of Steps 1, 2 and 3 of the Tripartite Non-Attribution/Causation Analysis with respect to Article 6.3 of the SCM Agreement

of the measure on the policy objective. As in relation to the law of serious prejudice, the types of effects must be separated and distinguished. Again, the term "sub-effects" is a convenient way of distinguishing the specific effects that the measure had on the policy objective from the overall effect of the measure on the policy objective. For instance, to take the example of the EU Seal Measure from the *EC—Seal Products* case, the sub-effects of the measure on the policy objective are: (1) a reduction in the number of seal deaths; (2) a reduction in the number of commercial sealers; (3) a reduction in the corporate profits accruing to the sealing industry; and (4) a reduction in the amount of consumer demand for seal fur skins. A representation of the separation of the sub-effects of a measure can be seen in Step 1 of Figure 8.2. Once again, the size of the sub-effects in Figure 8.2 is not indicative of their importance to the overall effect of the measure.

Finally, the non-attribution analysis might be adapted to the law relating to retaliatory measures. In this context, the aim of the first step of the non-attribution process is to separate the injuries caused by a Member's failure to comply with a DSB ruling vis-à-vis the injuries caused by other known factors. The arbitrators would be required to separate all of the injurious effects to the complainant member's industry into smaller injuries, which this chapter will call "sub-injuries." Taking up the example of an injured cotton industry again, inflicted sub-injuries might include: (1) loss of productivity; (2) suppressed utilization of capacity; (3) injury to corporate profits; (4) negative effects on cash flow, etc. Figure 8.3 below sets out a representation of the separation of the sub-injuries. Whilst Figure 8.3 represents each sub-injury to the cotton industry as being of equal size, in reality, the impact on each sub-injury may vary significantly.

5.2 Second Step of the Tripartite Non-Attribution/ Causation Analysis

The second step of the non-attribution process aims to determine the source of the effect on the industry/policy. That is, non-attribution is used to interrogate whether the sub-effects/sub-injuries (depending on the legal agreement in question) are the product of other known factors or the potential source of sub-effects/sub-injuries that is regulated by the WTO agreement, or some combination of the two. For the rest of this chapter, the short form, "regulated source" will be used to mean the source of sub-effects/sub-injuries regulated by the WTO agreement—namely, subsidies (in the case of serious prejudice), the measure (in the case of the General Exceptions) or the failure to comply with a DSU ruling (in the case of retaliatory measures). It is possible that the sub-effects/sub-injuries are a result of: (1) exclusively the regulated source; (2) exclusively the other known factors; or (3) a combination of the regulated source and other known factors.

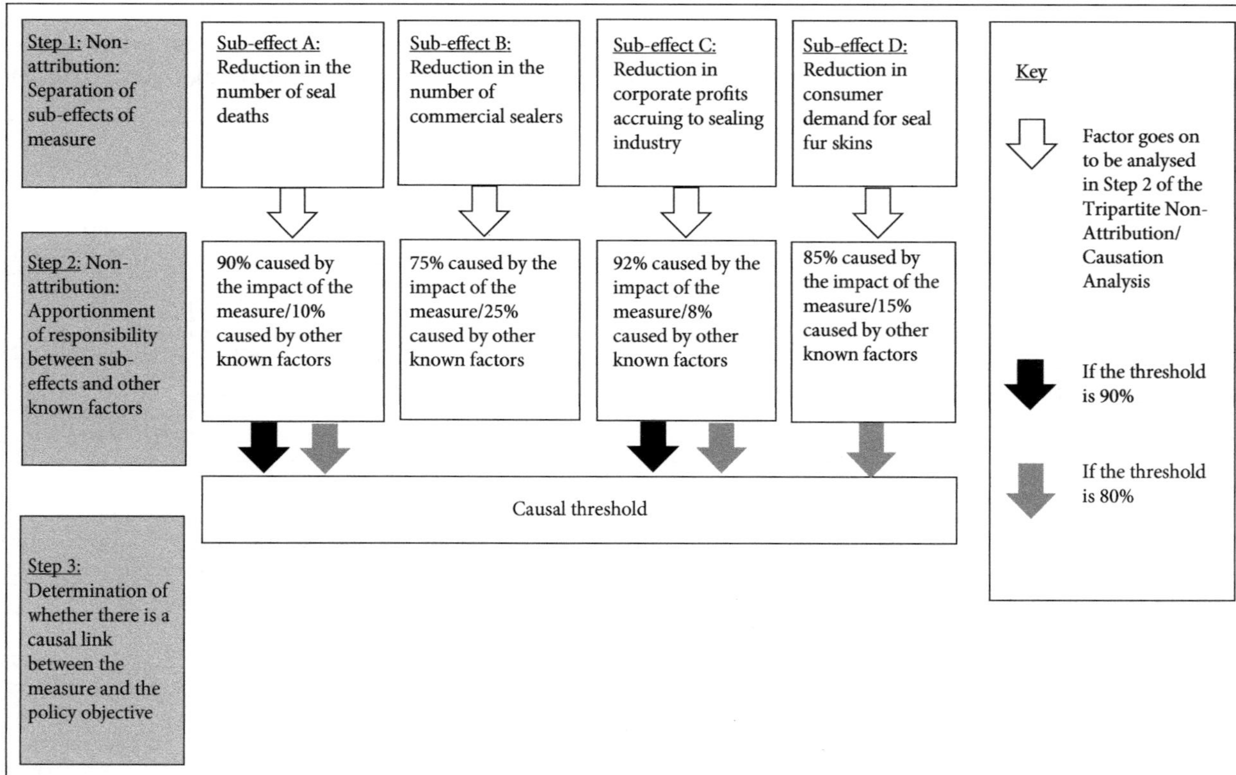

Figure 8.2 Overview of Steps 1, 2 and 3 of the Tripartite Non-Attribution/ Causation Analysis with respect to Article XX GATT and Article XIV GATS

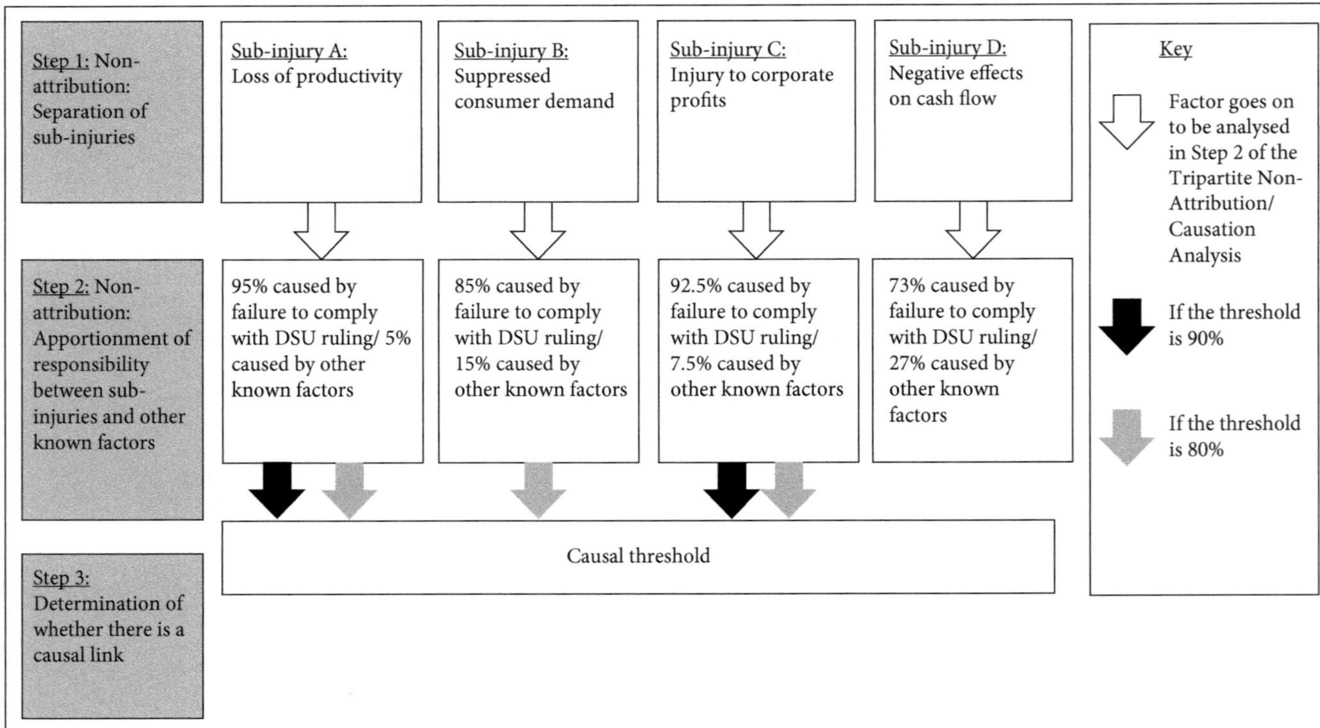

Figure 8.3 Overview of Steps 1, 2 and 3 of the Tripartite Non-Attribution/ Causation Analysis with respect to Article 22.6 DSU and 4.10 SCM Agreement

Step 2 of the Tripartite Non-Attribution/Causation Analysis involves two main kinds of analysis: (1) an apportionment analysis, which involves apportioning causal responsibility for the sub-effects/sub-injuries between the regulated source vis-à-vis other known factors; and (2) a qualification analysis, which involves determining which sub-effects/sub-injuries would qualify for inclusion in the final causation analysis. A representation of the ultimate aim of the second step of the non-attribution process can be seen in Step 2 of Figures 8.1, 8.2, and 8.3.

5.2.1 Apportionment analysis

The apportionment analysis involves: (1) identifying other known factors that may have contributed to the sub-injury/sub-effect; and (2) disentangling other known factors from the regulated source. This chapter now turns to examine what is involved in each of these phases.

5.2.1.1 Identification of other known factors stage

The complainant Member would be required to raise any other known factors that may also have contributed to the sub-injury/sub-effect. Given that the complainant Member may not necessarily be aware of all possible other known factors (particularly as they may pertain to some domestic matters of which a complainant Member may not have knowledge), it may be that Panels have a duty to investigate other known factors, as do the domestic competent authorities in the safeguards context.[44]

5.2.1.2 Disentanglement stage

This chapter has discussed the way in which the jurisprudence has tended to infer the effects of a regulated source simply from the qualitative features of that source. It was further seen how this approach meant that there was little need to separate the effects of the regulated source from other known factors because the non-attribution analysis was frequently not performed or was only performed in a tokenistic fashion. As it was seen that there are many fundamental drawbacks in attempting to derive causation from the qualitative nature of a regulated source, it is suggested that a quantitative approach based on econometric models can offer an alternative way forward.[45] It is important to note, however, that such a quantitative approach has its own drawbacks—namely that: (1) methodologically unsound econometric models can suggest correlations between two variables that are statistically related but not, in fact, causally linked;[46] (2) there may not be sufficient

[44] ibid [52]–[56].

[45] Pablo Bentes reaches similar conclusions in relation to drawing a causal link in the law of serious prejudice: see Pablo Bentes, "In Search of a "Genuine and Substantial" Cause: The Analysis of Causation in Serious Prejudice Claims" in Jansen, Pauwelyn and Carpenter (eds), *The Use of Economics in International Trade and Investment Disputes* (n 2) 260.

[46] See, eg, Ted Goertzel, "Myths of Murder and Multiple Regression" (2002) 26(1) *The Skeptical Inquirer* 19, 20.

real-world data available; [47] and (3) the mathematics underlying econometric models can make it difficult for lawyers to understand and apply.[48] Where these challenges can be adequately managed, however, a quantitative methodology can offer a robust alternative to causal analysis based on inference.

Once the effects of other known factors vis-à-vis the regulated source have been quantified, econometric analysis might then be used to separate those effects. The United States International Trade Commission has used a number of econometric analyses designed to separate the effects of imports vis-à-vis other known factors on the domestic industry in the context of safeguards and antidumping measures.[49] Additionally, some econometricians have put forward ways of separating the effects of trade remedies vis-à-vis other known factors.[50] It is suggested that these approaches could be drawn upon and adapted to separate the regulated source from other known factors. Moreover, panels have the ability, pursuant to article 13.2 of the DSU, to establish "expert review groups" for the purpose of adapting the econometric approaches used in the trade remedies context to the current analysis.

5.2.2 Qualification analysis

Once the effects of the regulated source have been separated from other known factors, the final element of Step 2 of the Tripartite Non-Attribution/Causation Analysis involves analyzing which sub/injuries or sub-effects qualify for inclusion in the causation analysis that makes up Step 3 of the Tripartite Non-Attribution/Causation Analysis. To that end, in order to determine which sub-injuries or sub-effects qualify for the causation analysis, it must be determined whether sub-injuries or sub-effects can only be included in the causation analysis if they were 100% caused by the regulated source. Alternatively, it may be possible to include those sub-injuries/sub-effects that were the product of some kind of *combination* of the regulated source and other known factors. On this point, in the serious prejudice context, the AB, in *US—Large Civil Aircraft (Second Complaint)*, found that

[47] James Flett, "The Client's Perspective" in Jansen, Pauwelyn, and Carpenter (eds), *The Use of Economics in International Trade and Investment Disputes* (n 2) 90–91.

[48] See generally, Marios C Iacovides and Marion Jansen, "Lost in Translation: Communication and Interpretation Challenges Related to Economic Evidence in Trade Disputes," in Jansen, Pauwelyn, and Carpenter (eds) *The Use of Economics in International Trade and Investment Disputes* (n 2) 191.

[49] For an overview of the five most common approaches used by the USITC in reaching material injury determinations in antidumping investigations, see Seth Kapla, "Injury and Causation in USITC Antidumping Determinations: Five Recent Approaches" in PKM Tharakan (ed), *Policy Implications of Antidumping Measures* (Elsevier Science 1991). For an overview of approaches taken in relation to separating imports from other known factors in antidumping and safeguards investigations, see JP Durling and MP McCullough, "Teaching Old Laws New Tricks: The Legal Obligation of Non-Attribution and the Need for Economic Rigour in Injury Analyses Under US Trade Law" in EK Choi and J Hartigan (eds), *Handbook of International Trade* (OUP 2005) vol II.

[50] See Kenneth Kelly, "The Analysis of Causality in Escape Clause Cases" (1988) 37(2) Journal of Industrial Economics 187; Douglas A Irwin, "Causing Problems? The WTO Review of Causation and Injury Attribution in US Section 201 Cases" (2003) 2(3) World Trade Review 297; Dukgeun Ahn and William J Moon, "Alternative Approach to Causation Analysis in Trade Remedy Investigations: 'Cost of Production' Test" (2010) 44(5) Journal of World Trade 1023, 1041–47.

subsidies need not be the sole cause of adverse effects on an industry.[51] In other words, there is some tolerance for sub-effects that are the result of *both* subsidies and other causal factors. Whilst the issue has not been raised in the context of the General Exceptions or retaliatory measures, it seems logical to allow some tolerance of sub-injuries or sub-effects that were partially the product of other known factors. This is because, with something as complex as a financial market, it is rarely the case that a sub-injury or sub-effect would be the result of one casual factor alone. Indeed, the idea that a sub-injury or sub-effect was caused by only one causal factor would seem to be unrealistic. Accordingly, it would surely be overly rigid to discount a sub-injury or sub-effect from inclusion in the causation analysis because of a small causal contribution from other known factors. This being the case, the better approach appears to be to set some kind of threshold that would allow a degree of tolerance for other known factors in the causation analysis.

Policy implications follow from allowing sub-injuries or sub-effects that are partially the result of other known factors to be included in the causal analysis. That is, it is arguably harder to make out causation using the Tripartite Non-Attribution/Causation Analysis than when the *a priori* approach to determining causation is used. This is because the Tripartite Non-Attribution/Causation Analysis requires a fact-finder to separate the regulated source form other known factors by way of a non-attribution analysis, whereas the *a priori* test tends to presume that the regulated source is 100% responsible for the injury or effect.

The question is begged, however, where this threshold should be set. That is, should a 10% tolerance be given to other known factors, a 25% tolerance, or more? It is difficult to predict how a panel or the AB would approach this question. Self-evidently, the more tolerance that is extended to other known factors, the more sub-injuries/sub-effects qualify for inclusion in the causation analysis at the third stage of the Tripartite Non-Attribution/Causation Analysis. This can be seen in Figure 8.4.

It can be seen from Figure 8.4 that the higher the tolerance threshold, the less sub-injuries or sub-effects qualify for inclusion. For example, in Figure 8.4, all four sub-injuries or sub-effects surpass the threshold level of 30% tolerance of other known factors; whereas, when the tolerance threshold is set at 10%, only sub-injury or sub-effect A reaches the causal threshold (and therefore qualifies for inclusion Step 3 of the Tripartite Non-Attribution/Causation Analysis).

From a policy perspective, a number of implications follow from the interpretative choices associated with setting the causal threshold in a manner that allows some tolerance for other known factors. First, in the context of serious prejudice law, the lower the causal threshold is set, the easier it is to make out causation, and

[51] WTO Appellate Body Report, *United States—Measures Affecting Trade in Large Civil Aircraft (Second Complaint)*, WT/DS353/AB/R (adopted 12 March 2012) [914] (AB, *US—Large Civil Aircraft (Second Complaint)*).

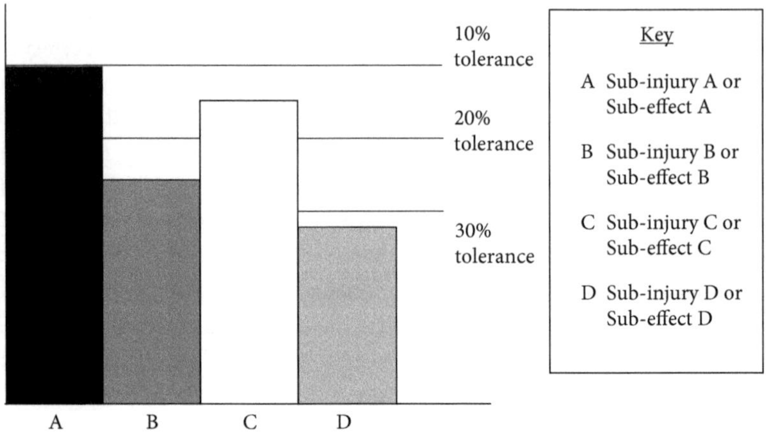

Figure 8.4 The impact of different tolerance thresholds on whether sub-injuries/sub-effects would pass the causal threshold

therefore, the more likely it is that a complainant Member will find that a responding Member caused serious prejudice as a result of its subsidies. The easier it is to make out a serious prejudice claim, the easier it is for a complainant Member to bring countervailing duties against another Member. From an economic perspective, some have argued that countervailing duties do "more harm than good" and that global welfare would be improved if countervailing duties were reduced in number or even eliminated.[52] Following this logic, the lower the tolerance for other causal factors, the less likely a causal link will be found between subsidies and effects, making it more difficult to justify the introduction of countervailing duties.

Second, in terms of the General Exceptions, the more easily that causation is made out, the greater the likelihood, in turn, that a responding Member's measure will be found to have been effective in producing the intended policy objective. That said, this is only one of a number of considerations that a Panel or the AB must have regard to in determining whether a measure ought to be exempted under the General Exceptions. Accordingly, even if it is easier for a measure to be found to have caused a policy objective, it does not automatically follow from this that the measure will be exempted under the General Exceptions. That is, the first tier of analysis includes other considerations that require weighing and balancing, such as the relative importance of the policy objective and the trade-restrictiveness of the challenged measure. Moreover, the second tier of analysis involving the chapeau also requires separate treatment. In this sense, the analytical choices made here are

[52] Alan O Sykes, "The Economics of WTO Rules on Subsidies and Countervailing Measures" (University of Chicago John M Olin Law and Economics Working Paper 186, 2003) 1.

important to one component of the decision about whether a measure ought to be exempted, but they are by no means determinative of the outcome.

Finally, in relation to retaliatory measures, the lower the threshold is set, the more sub-injuries would qualify for the causation analysis and the likelihood that the causal link is made is increased. The more likely that causation is made out, the greater the probability, in turn, that a responding Member will be required to provide compensation to the complainant Member for its failure to comply with the DSB ruling. In this sense, a lower threshold favors complainant Members. Having now set out the process of engaging in a non-attribution analysis, this chapter now turns to consider how causation might be made out.

5.3 Causation: The Third Step of the Tripartite Process

Once it has been determined which sub-injuries/sub-effects qualify for the causation stage, it then remains to decide whether the sub-injuries/sub-effects are sufficiently significant to be said to have caused the overall injury/effect on the industry. In the context of serious prejudice, the only guidance is that, as in relation to trade remedies, the causal link must involve a "genuine and substantial relationship of cause and effect."[53] No such causal standard has been given in relation to the law of the General Exceptions or retaliatory measures, which follows from the fact that the jurisprudence has never explicitly required that a formal causation test be undertaken in relation to these areas of WTO law.

Nonetheless, the third step of the Tripartite Non-Attribution/Causation Analysis must surely involve examining those sub-injuries/sub-effects that have passed the threshold and determining whether they are sufficient in number and extent to be deemed to have caused the injury or effect. To this end, the most appropriate causal tests are those that measure necessity as well as sufficiency. There are three kinds of causal tests that analyze both necessity and sufficiency: (1) the "causally relevant factor" account, developed by Hart and Honoré;[54] (2) the Necessary Element of a Sufficient Set (NESS) test, put forward by Richard Wright;[55] and (3) John Mackie's "INUS" test, based on the idea that any one factor may be "an *insufficient* but *non-redundant* part of an *unnecessary* but *sufficient* condition" or "INUS" condition.[56] These tests might collectively be known as "weak necessity/strong sufficiency" tests. Whilst a detailed explanation of each of these tests is beyond the scope of this chapter, the key quality that each of these weak necessity/strong sufficiency tests share is that they analyze causation in terms of a *set* of factors, rather than as a

[53] AB, *US—Upland Cotton* (n 14) [438] (quoting AB, *US—Wheat Gluten* (n 7) [69]).

[54] HLA Hart and Tony Honoré, *Causation in the Law* (2nd edn, OUP 1985) 113.

[55] See generally Richard W Wright, "Causation in Tort Law" (1985) 73(6) California Law Review 1735.

[56] John L Mackie, *The Cement of the Universe* (OUP 1974) 62.

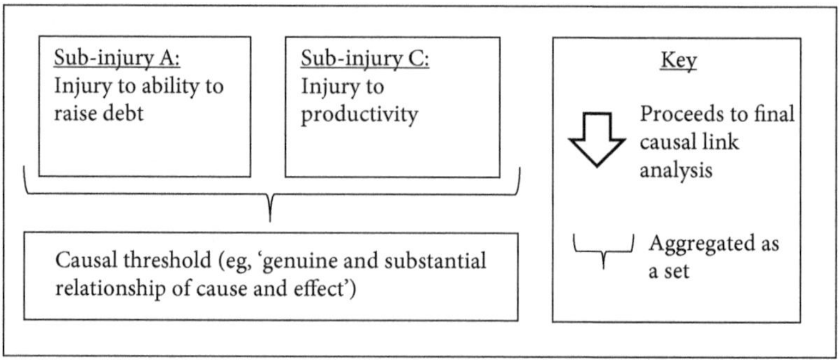

Figure 8.5 Step 3 of the Tripartite Non-Attribution/Causation Analysis

single factor.[57] That is, the sub-injuries or sub-effects must be necessary to a set of factors, and it is that *set* which must be sufficient to have caused the overall effect or injury. This is illustrated in Figure 8.5.

6. Conclusion

Determining causation is a notoriously difficult exercise.[58] Indeed, David Hume himself said:

> There is no question, which on account of its importance, as well as difficulty, has caus'd more disputes both among antient and modern philosophers, than this concerning the efficacy of causes, or that quality which makes them be follow'd by their effects.[59]

This chapter has highlighted that determining causation is a complex and intellectually demanding exercise that can be performed in a number of different ways. This chapter has analyzed the approach to determining causation in three different parts of WTO jurisprudence: (1) Serious Prejudice; (2) the General Exceptions; and (3) retaliatory measures. Common to each of these parts of WTO law is a tendency in the jurisprudence to make conclusions about causation by inferring the

[57] The weak necessity/strong sufficiency test owes a debt to the causal account of JS Mill, particularly Mill's insight that "[t]he cause [. . .] philosophically speaking, is the sum total of the conditions, positive and negative taken together": see JS Mill, *A System of Logic Ratiocinative and Inductive* (JM Robson ed) (Routledge 1973) Bk III, ch V, § 3.

[58] See James Flett, "The Client's Perspective" in Jansen, Pauwelyn, and Carpenter (eds), *The Use of Economics in International Trade and Investment Disputes* (n 2) 87–88.

[59] David Hume, *A Treatise of Human Nature*, LA Selby-Bigge (ed), (OUP 1978) Bk I, Pt III, Section xiv, 200.

effects from the nature of the supposed cause. This recurring logical fallacy results in specious causal conclusions.

A second problem with making *a priori* conclusions about effects based on their supposed cause is the fact that this approach leaves no scope for conducting a rigorous non-attribution analysis. This is because such an approach is premised on the presumption that the phenomenon identified as the cause did not have contributions from other known factors. This presumption, however, should not be made because other known factors must always be a consideration in making determinations about causation.

Accordingly, this chapter has put forward an alternative approach to determining causation in these three areas of WTO law—namely, the application of a three-step model set out by the AB in *US—Wheat Gluten* (which this chapter has called the Tripartite Non-Attribution/Causation Analysis) to determine causation in relation to Serious Prejudice, the General Exceptions and retaliatory measures. This chapter has suggested that this approach represents an alternative approach to performing both a non-attribution and causation analysis than the current approach in the jurisprudence based on *a priori* inferences. Specifically, it allows for a genuine non-attribution analysis to be undertaken and its causal conclusions are more likely to be analytically sound because they are based on real-world data. Use of this model is considerably more involved and complex than the current approach in the jurisprudence and also requires several difficulties associated with the use of econometric models to be managed, but such complexity reflects the nature of causation itself.

This chapter has highlighted that analyzing causation involves making interpretative choices that can dramatically affect the ease with which a causal link is drawn. Specifically, it was seen that the Tripartite Causation/Non-Attribution Analysis makes it harder to draw a causal link than when *a priori* causal inferences are used. This is because the Tripartite Non-Attribution/Causation Analysis separates the causal contributions of other known factors, so as to ensure that the causal contributions of the regulated source and other known factors are not confused. This chapter has also shown that it is possible to set the causal threshold of the Tripartite Non-Attribution/Causation Analysis at the second stage in different ways, which also affects the ease with which the causal link is drawn. In short, this chapter has illustrated that, far from causation being a technical question of secondary importance, the way in which causation is analyzed is complex and has important policy implications.

PART III

EVIDENTIARY RULES IN INTERNATIONAL LAW

9

Presumptions as Secondary Rules in the Judicial Interpretation of International Human Rights

Tilmann Altwicker and Alexandra Ellen Hansen

1. Management of Uncertainty

1.1 Concept and Operation of Presumptions

Presumptions are both a phenomenon of ordinary and of legal reasoning. Douglas Walton draws a distinction between ordinary presumptions and legal presumptions.[1] In one case, he describes a man in a cave who has to pass some unidentified object to exit the cave. The object may be a piece of rope, or, it may also be a deadly snake. The man must now decide whether he will take the risk of just walking over it, assuming that it is a piece of rope, or whether he will jump over it, under the presumption that it is a snake. The decision of jumping versus walking is the person's individual choice; in whichever way he decides, in both cases his decision is based on a presumption in a situation of uncertainty. Walton contrasts this case to one from the legal sphere: the legal presumption of death if someone has disappeared for a number of years. The number of years may vary from one legal system to another, however, it is a widely accepted and standardized rule that courts apply in a general manner. In both cases, a presumption is used to construct a reason for action in a situation of factual uncertainty. Action can be taken, despite the fact that there is insufficient evidence.

By relating to uncertainty, both ordinary and legal presumptions concern, broadly speaking, aspects of knowledge. As the philosopher Leibniz states: "To *presume* is to hold for certain until the opposite is proved … *For certain* is what we follow in action as if it were certain."[2] Leibniz refers to the idea of cognitive

[1] Douglas Walton, *Burden of Proof, Presumption and Argumentation* (CUP 2014) 90–91.

[2] Gottfried Wilhelm Leibniz, *Elementa Juris Naturalis*, Variants, A VI, 2, No 12 (quote taken from Andreas Blank, "Presumptions and Cognitive Simplicity in Leibniz and Early Modern Legal Theory" in

Tilmann Altwicker and Alexandra Ellen Hansen, *Presumptions as Secondary Rules in the Judicial Interpretation of International Human Rights* In: *Secondary Rules of Primary Importance in International Law.* Edited by: Gábor Kajtár, Başak Çalı, and Marko Milanovic, Oxford University Press.
DOI: 10.1093/oso/9780192869012.003.0009

simplicity: In the absence of knowledge, it is more rational to follow the presumption with the smaller amount of ontological and cognitive requisites. This procedure will lead to a qualified manner of pursuing the truth. Until more information becomes available, or until the contrary is proven, the assumption can be justified, albeit in a provisional manner.[3] Similarly, the philosopher Nicholas Rescher argues that presumptions are a procedural tool, one that allows the development of a cogent case.[4] The important question to Rescher is: how can we reach our cognitive goals without spending more effort than necessary? This suggests that presumptions can be useful from the viewpoint of cognitive economy. This idea is relevant to legal proceedings operating under certain constraints of, for example, time and resources, strategic behavior of the parties and (imperfect) laws or lack of information. Applying Rescher's idea to the legal context, one could say that presumptions are needed in situations of uncertainty to "fill the gap," to make a coherent argument in order to find a solution to a legal case.

How do presumptions operate? Presumptions build on a specific, accepted course of reasoning or *ratiocinatio*.[5] In each case, the cognitive boundaries are transcended by an operation of inference. The process of inference, here, involves the conclusion from a "known" to a "known-unknown." Inference as the *modus operandi* of presumptions is emphasized in Merriam Webster's definition: Here, the concept of presumption is understood as "a legal inference as to the existence or truth of a fact not certainly known that is drawn from the known or proved existence of some other fact."[6] In other words, presumptions embody or substantiate legal knowledge which can be relied upon for inferring new legal knowledge (usually for the purpose of allowing for the case to reach the level of *res judicata*). They are used as a procedural tool in the deliberation process, providing a rational way out of situations of uncertainty. The deliberation process is accelerated and simplified with the help of presumptions in order to surpass cognitive boundaries, thus serving the principle of procedural economy.

Tilmann Altwicker, Francis Cheneval, and Matthias Mahlmann (eds), *Rechts- und Staatsphilosophie bei GW Leibniz* (Mohr Siebeck 2020) 40).

[3] ibid.

[4] Nicholas Rescher, *Presumption and the Practices of Tentative Cognition* (CUP 2006) 3.

[5] For a philosophical analysis of decision making in situations of ignorance or uncertainty, with references to Rawls' veil of ignorance and Plato's cave, see Daniel R DeNicola, *Understanding Ignorance: The Surprising Impact of What We Don't Know* (MIT Press 2017) ch 4. For more on this, see Adolfo Giuliani, "Civilian Treatises on Presumptions, 1580–1620" in Richard H Helmholz and WDH Sellar (eds), *The Law of Presumptions: Essays in Comparative Legal History* No 27 (Duncker & Humboldt 2009) 22–24.

[6] See <www.merriam-webster.com/dictionary/presumption> accessed 9 March 2019.

1.2 Presumptions in the Context of International Human Rights Law

From the above, two (abstract, non-legal) conditions of application for presumptions can be derived. The first application condition for presumptions is the existence of a "gap" in the fact-finding or the (legal) reasoning, preventing the court from making a cogent case. Courts, thus, resort to the use of presumptions in situations of "cognitive insufficiency." As will be developed below, the latter can be informational uncertainty resulting from unclear, insufficiently established, or missing facts; practical uncertainty resulting from the need to rely on factual generalizations; or legal uncertainty resulting from, for example, the absence of sufficient legal rules. The second application condition is "necessity." Presumptions are used by courts to enable "the system to reach a *res judicata* level even without being able to ascertain the whole truth."[7] In the context of legal proceedings, presumptions serve a practical purpose, their use enables the court to go forward, to reach a decision under non-ideal circumstances. The use of presumptions is a deviation from the ordinary fact-finding process or from full legal argument. Thus, the necessity condition states that presumptions are only applicable if the *res judicata* stage cannot be reached by "ordinary" means of fact-finding or legal reasoning. In sum, then, presumptions can be understood as a procedural tool used by courts to manage situations of factual or legal uncertainty in order to reach the *res judicata* stage in legal proceedings.

Presumptions play an important role in international human rights proceedings. Take, for example, the most famous and widely codified presumption in international human rights law (IHRL), the presumption of innocence.[8] The European Court of Human Rights (ECtHR) has held that this presumption "requires, *inter alia*, that when carrying out their duties, the members of a court should not start with the preconceived idea that the accused has committed the offence charged; the burden of proof is on the prosecution, and any doubt should benefit the accused."[9] It is the state that carries the burden of proof "beyond reasonable doubt." Hence, in cases where it is not clear whether the accused really did commit an offence, that is, where there is insufficient evidence, the presumption of innocence provides the way out: the lack of information benefits the accused. However, this

[7] *Saadi v Italy* App no 37201/06 (Concurring Opinion of Judge Zupancic) (ECtHR, 28 February 2008).

[8] See eg Convention for the Protection of Human Rights and Fundamental Freedoms (European Convention on Human Rights (ECHR), as amended), art 6, para 2; Universal Declaration of Human Rights (adopted 10 December 1948 UNGA Res 217 A(III) (UDHR), art 11; International Covenant on Civil and Political Rights (adopted 16 December 1966, entered into force 23 March 1976) 999 UNTS 171 (ICCPR), art 14; American Convention on Human Rights, "Pact of San Jose" (Costa Rica, 22 November 1969) (ACHR), art 8, para 2; UN Human Rights Committee (HRC), CCPR General Comment No 13, art 14 (Administration of Justice), Equality before the Courts and the Right to a Fair and Public Hearing by an Independent Court Established by Law (13 April 1984).

[9] *Barberà, Messegué and Jabardo v Spain* App no 10590/83 (ECtHR, 6 December 1988), para 77.

right to be presumed innocent is not absolute. For instance, it is permissible to push the burden of proof onto the registered owner of a car if that person denies to have been the actual driver at the time of a given incident.[10] It was also deemed permissible to presume liability for the smuggling of narcotics of a person who was in possession of said narcotics.[11] Thus, under the case law of the ECtHR, it is permissible for member states to penalize the existence of certain objective facts.[12] However, this must be done in a manner that takes into account the circumstances of the case and the importance of what is at stake.[13] For example, in the case of human trafficking, there is growing acceptance among human rights bodies of a presumption of age in cases where children are involved. Under this practice, if there is a possibility that a person may be a child, the court proceeds on the presumption that the victim is underage unless there is evidence to the contrary. The reason for this presumption is that the identification of child victims should not be further complicated.[14] Another example concerns the presumed existence of mental and moral harm of family members in cases where serious human rights violations have occurred, for example forced disappearances or massacres. This practice relates to the factual foundation of the "victim" status.[15] These examples show that presumptions constitute a repository of knowledge, knowledge which has proven to be correct in several previous cases (eg presuming the existence of mental and moral harm of family members in cases where serious human rights violations have occurred), knowledge which is of evident practical use (eg the presumption in relation to the age of victims of human trafficking) or certain ethical knowledge (eg the presumption of innocence).

[10] See eg *O'Halloran and Francis v United Kingdom* App nos 15809/02 and 25624/02 (ECtHR, 29 June 2007), para 29; *Falk v Netherlands* App no 66273/01 (ECtHR, 19 October 2004).

[11] See *Salabiaku v France* App no 10519/83 (ECtHR, 7 October 1988), para 27.

[12] See also *Janosevic v Sweden* App no 34619/97 (ECtHR, 21 May 2003), para 100.

[13] See European Court of Human Rights, "Guide on Article 6 of the European Convention on Human Rights: Right to a Fair Trial (Criminal Limb)" (*Council of Europe*, 30 April 2022), para 338 <https://www.echr.coe.int/Documents/Guide_Art_6_criminal_ENG.pdf> accessed 26 April 2019, with references to *Salabiaku v France* App no 10519/83 (ECtHR, 7 October 1988), para 28; *Radio France v France* App no 53984/00 (ECtHR, 30 March 2004), para 24; *Västberga Taxi Aktiebolag and Vulic v Sweden* App no 36985/97 (ECtHR, 21 May 2003), para 113; *Klouvi v France* App no 30754/03 (ECtHR, 30 September 2011), para 41; *Iasir v Belgium* App no 21614/12 (ECtHR, 26 April 2016), para 30.

[14] OHCHR, "Human Rights and Human Trafficking: Fact Sheet No 36" (UN, 2014) <https://www.ohchr.org/Documents/Publications/FS36_en.pdf> accessed 18 February 2019.

[15] Juan-Pablo Perez-Leon-Acevedo, "International Human Rights Law in the Reparation Practice of the Extraordinary Chambers in the Courts of Cambodia" in Giuliana Z Capaldo (ed), *The Global Community Yearbook of International Law and Jurisprudence 2017* (OUP 2018) 225; with references to the Inter-American Court of Human Rights (IACtHR) case law: *Goiburú v Paraguay* (Merits, Reparations, and Costs) IACtHR Series C no 153 (22 September 2006) [96]–[97]; *La Cantuta v Peru* (Merits, Reparations, and Costs) IACtHR Series C no 162 (29 November 2006) [218].

1.3 Main Argument and Structure

Our main argument is that presumptions, in the context of IHRL, are a complex legal phenomenon because they constitute secondary rules (in a Hartian sense) on both primary and other secondary rules. The structure of this chapter is as follows: section 2 establishes the law governing the use of presumptions in IHRL. Section 3 distinguishes three functions of presumptions in international human rights proceedings. These functions are, in section 4, related to the primary/secondary rules-distinction. Section 5 reflects on the problem of legitimacy of the use of presumptions in human rights proceedings. Finally, section 6 concludes by summarizing the most important findings and drawing some implications for judges.

2. Codified Rules on Presumptions in International Human Rights Law

Codified rules on presumptions are rare in IHRL. However, the case law of the ECtHR and the Inter-American Court of Human Rights (IACtHR) provides some guidance regarding the use of presumptions *domestically* (which is not the focus of the present contribution). The European Convention on Human Rights (ECHR), for instance, is interpreted as not prohibiting the use of legal presumptions in principle. However, the ECtHR requires domestic presumptions to reflect what is at stake[16] and to take into account the context.[17] Similarly, the IACtHR has held that "circumstantial evidence, indicia, and presumptions may be considered, so long as they lead to conclusions consistent with the facts."[18] It can be argued that similar considerations apply in the case of presumptions under IHRL.

As a rare example, a secondary rule on the use of presumptions can be found in the Rules of Procedure of the Inter-American Commission on Human Rights (IACmHR):

> The facts alleged in the petition, the pertinent parts of which have been transmitted to the State in question, shall be presumed to be true if the State has not provided responsive information during the period set by the Commission under the provisions of Article 37 of these Rules of Procedure, as long as other evidence does not lead to a different conclusion.[19]

[16] *Salabiaku v France* App no 10519/83 (ECtHR, 7 October 1988), para 28; *Radio France v France* App no 53984/00 (ECtHR, 30 March 2004), para 24.

[17] *Daktaras v Lithuania* App no 42095/98 (ECtHR, 17 January 2001), para 43; *AL v Germany* App no 72758/01 (ECtHR, 28 July 2005), para 31.

[18] *Velásquez-Rodríguez v Honduras* (Merits) IACtHR Series C no 4 (29 July 1988) [130].

[19] Article 38 of the Rules of Procedure of the Inter-American Commission on Human Rights (entry into force 1 August 2013) <http://www.oas.org/en/iachr/mandate/basics/rulesiachr.asp> accessed 26 April 2019.

A functionally equivalent provision can be found in the Rules of Court of the ECtHR:

> (1) Where a party fails to adduce evidence or provide information requested by the Court or to divulge relevant information of its own motion or otherwise fails to participate effectively in the proceedings, the Court may draw such inferences as it deems appropriate.
> (2) Failure or refusal by a respondent Contracting Party to participate effectively in the proceedings shall not, in itself, be a reason for the Chamber to discontinue the examination of the application.[20]

Both norms address the procedural consequences of noncooperation by respondent states regarding fact-finding.[21] They serve the interests of procedural efficiency: when there is insufficient access to the factual information necessary in order to resolve the issue, and the respondent state is not cooperating, there is either the presumption of truth of the allegations made in the petition (in the Inter-American context) or the court is entitled to draw inferences as it sees fit (in the European case). The procedural efficiency aspect can be illuminated by considering the legislative history of the Inter-American provision: The rule has its origins in the 1970s and 1980s, when states used human rights violations for intimidation purposes and did not cooperate with the Commission.[22]

Procedurally, both norms seek to prevent that a respondent state benefits from its own non-cooperation (by making the passing of a judgment impossible). Though not explicitly speaking of presumptions, the relevant provision in the Rules of Court of the ECtHR establishes a procedural rule as to the circumstances under which the Court may draw factual inferences. Rule 44C of the ECtHR's Rules of the Court is closely linked to article 38 of the ECHR. Article 38 contains an obligation of the respondent state to cooperate with the ECtHR.[23] Non-cooperation would lead to an ineffective adjudication process. Initially, there had been no such concrete obligation to cooperate in the Convention because the drafters had assumed that the states would comply in good faith.[24] However, in 2004, a concretization of article 38 of the ECHR was introduced by rules 44A to 44C of the ECtHR's Rules of Court, where rule 44A explicitly confirmed the rule to cooperate.[25] Although

[20] Rule 44C of the ECtHR Rules of the Court (1 August 2018) <https://www.echr.coe.int/documents/rules_court_eng.pdf> accessed 17 March 2022.

[21] This relates closely to the discussion below on the function of presumptions as "Overcoming Information Asymmetry and Information Inaccessibility," see section 3.1.

[22] Jo M Pasqualucci, *The Practice and Procedure of the Inter-American Court of Human Rights* (2nd edn, CUP 2013) 105–06. See also *Villagrán-Morales et al ("Street Children") v Guatemala* (Merits) IACtHR Series C no 63 (19 November 1999) [67]–[68] for this presumption of truth.

[23] See *Petrov and X v Russia* App no 23608/16 (ECtHR, 23 October 2018), para 78.

[24] Helena de Vylder and Yves Haeck, "The Duty of Cooperation of the Respondent State During the Proceedings Before the European Court of Human Rights" in Yves Haeck and Eva Brems (eds), *Human Rights and Civil Liberties in the 21st Century* (Springer 2014) 64–65.

[25] ibid.

the rules do not delineate the type of inferences the ECtHR may draw, the need to introduce these rules shows that the initial assumption of cooperation in good faith was not adequately met. This diagnosis is confirmed by quantitative research: Since 1999, the number of violations of article 38 of the ECHR have increased and the contexts in which they occur have been deemed "grave."[26]

The fact that presumptions under IHRL are largely unchartered territory means that international courts usually grant themselves great discretion as to how and when they may rely on presumptions.

3. The Functions of Presumptions in Human Rights Proceedings

3.1 Overcoming Information Asymmetry and Information Inaccessibility

A first function of presumptions relates to situations of unavailable or insufficient factual information: presumptions may serve to overcome situations of information asymmetry or information inaccessibility. Information asymmetries arise when the potential victim of a human rights violation is not in the possession of the necessary documentation and the holder of the information, usually the state, is unwilling to cooperate. As the examples below show, human rights courts and other adjudicating bodies must sometimes resort to presumptions in order to make IHRL practical and effective. Situations of information inaccessibility occur, for example, when the facts cannot be established because of the passing of time since the event or if the information is unavailable for legal reasons.

One group of human rights cases in which presumptions are employed to overcome information asymmetry concerns missing persons. Typically, human rights courts have resorted to presumptions in cases of missing persons in which states withhold information on the whereabouts of these persons.[27] For instance, by employing the presumption of death of a victim of enforced disappearance, the IACtHR reallocates the burden of proof, shifting it to the state that was in control of the detained persons.[28] Furthermore, the IACtHR also applies a presumption of torture of a disappeared person in cases where a systematic practice could be detected, and where there was a failure to investigate by the relevant authorities. In these cases, the IACtHR allows the inference to be drawn that the victims suffered, at a minimum, some form of cruel, inhuman, or degrading treatment.[29] Similarly,

[26] ibid.
[27] *Godínez-Cruz v Honduras* (Merits) IACtHR Series C no 5 (20 January 1989) [137].
[28] *Radilla Pacheco v Mexico* (Merits) IACtHR Series C no 209 (23 November 2009) [47], [48].
[29] *Velásquez-Rodríguez v Honduras* (Merits) IACtHR Series C no 4 (29 July 1988) [156].

the ECtHR has, in various cases, found violations of the right to life (article 2 of the ECHR) on account of the presumed death of the missing person(s) and on account of inadequate or ineffective investigations into the detention or disappearance of missing persons.[30] The right to life (article 2 of the ECHR) is also presumed to be violated when the missing person was last seen alive in life-threatening circumstances and if the respondent state is not able to provide an explanation that convincingly shows the whereabouts or the fate of the victim.[31] In *Cyprus v Turkey*, the ECtHR found the Turkish authorities in violation of the right to life (article 2 of the ECHR) for not having conducted an effective investigation into the whereabouts of the persons who had disappeared in circumstances that were deemed life-threatening. In addition, the lack of information provided to the families of the victims due to the silence of the authorities was considered an ongoing violation of the right to personal liberty (article 5 of the ECHR) and the prohibition of torture (article 3 of the ECHR). The Court held that the withholding of information in circumstances where the relatives were facing real concerns over the victims had reached a level of severity that amounted to inhumane treatment.[32]

Another group of cases relates to persons (allegedly) mistreated while in state detention or police custody. Human rights adjudication bodies have often ruled that if a person is detained and suffers injuries or even death during detention, there is a strong presumption that the state authorities are responsible.[33] It is up to them to prove wrong the application of the presumption and to provide a convincing alternative explanation. If no such explanation is given, the court can make inferences that can be unfavorable against the state concerned.[34]

Presumptions have also played a role in cases in which information about the facts of the case are, for various reasons, inaccessible. One reason for the inaccessibility of facts could be the "passage of a substantial period of time," as was the case in *Keser v Turkey*, concerning the expulsion of inhabitants from Turkish villages by the state security forces.[35] In this case, the ECtHR was confronted with a dispute that evolved around events that had occurred eleven years ago. Due to this passage of time, the Court held that it would be unable to conduct fact-finding because it would be difficult to summon witnesses and for them to recall

[30] See eg *Orhan v Turkey* App no 25656/94 (ECtHR, 18 June 2002); *Er v Turkey* App no 23016/04 (ECtHR, 31 July 2012); *Meryem Celik v Turkey* App no 3598/03 (ECtHR, 16 April 2013); *Pitsayeva v Russia* App nos 53036/08 et al (ECtHR, 9 January 2014).

[31] *Bazorkina v Russia* App no 69481/01 (ECtHR, 27 July 2006), paras 110–12.

[32] *Cyprus v Turkey* App no 25781/94 (ECtHR, 10 May 2001).

[33] *Çakıcı v Turkey* App no 23657/94 (ECtHR, 8 July 1999), para 85; *Salman v Turkey* App no 21986/93 (ECtHR, 27 June 2000), para 100; *Rupa v Romania (No 1)* App no 58478/00 (ECtHR, 16 December 2008), para 97. See also *Orhan v Turkey* App no 25656/94 (ECtHR, 18 June 2002), para 274. In the context of the IACtHR, see *Neira-Alegria et al v Peru* (Reparations) IACtHR Series C no 29 (19 September 1996) [65].

[34] *El Masri v the Former Yugoslav Republic of Macedonia* App no 39630/09 (ECtHR, 13 December 2012), paras 151–52.

[35] *Keser v Turkey* App nos 33238/96 and 32965/96 (ECtHR, 2 February 2006), para 75.

the events in detail and sufficient accuracy.[36] The applicants were not able to corroborate their allegations and the Court held that the evidence presented had been insufficient to prove a violation of articles 3 and 8 of the ECHR, as well as of article 1 of Protocol 1.[37] Furthermore, in the *Keser* case, the Court held that there was a rebuttable presumption that authorities, if they were presented with a complaint, would have acted upon it.[38] In the case at hand, it was up to the applicant family to show that they had indeed filed a complaint to the relevant authorities. However, because the applicants were unable to provide a copy of the alleged letter, the Court found the applicant family to have failed at rebutting the presumption.[39] In sum, in cases involving information asymmetry or information inaccessibility, presumptions are used to infer facts from other (established) facts.

3.2 Bridging General Facts and Legal Assessment in Individual Cases

A second function of presumptions is to reduce the complexity of legal argumentation about international human rights. As will be shown below, presumptions sometimes serve as a substitute for (further) legal argument, in particular, by bridging general facts and the legal assessment of the individual case. Under the ECHR, this function of presumptions has played a role in the context of the prohibition of torture, freedom from inhuman or degrading treatment (article 3 of the ECHR), non-discrimination (article 14 of the ECHR), and in the context of non-pecuniary damages (article 41 of the ECHR).

In an article 3 of the ECHR case concerning the conditions of detention, *Khlaifia v Italy*, the personal space of detainees and the issue of overcrowding were at issue. The ECtHR employed "a weighty but not irrebuttable presumption of a violation of Article 3" if the personal floor space of a detainee falls under three square meters.[40] A rebuttal of the presumption is possible if it can be demonstrated that other cumulative effects compensate for this limited space.[41] In this case, the legal argument is simplified: Without providing any scientific evidence (eg reference to psychological studies) and without reference to other legal authorities, the ECtHR presumed a violation, that is, it drew a legal conclusion from the presence of certain facts, leaving open, however, the possibility of rebuttal. In the case of *Muršić v Croatia*, the ECtHR Grand Chamber unanimously ruled that Croatia had violated a prisoner's rights under article 3 of the ECHR when holding him in a cell of less

[36] See also *İpek v Turkey* App no 25760/94 (ECtHR, 10 November 2015), para 116.
[37] *Keser* (n 35) para 87.
[38] ibid para 81.
[39] ibid.
[40] *Khlaifia v Italy* App no 16483/12 (ECtHR, 15 December 2016), para 166.
[41] ibid.

than three square meters for twenty-seven consecutive days.[42] However, it did not find such a violation with regard to other instances where the applicant was held in a cell of less than three square meters. This was due to the fact that the periods of confinement had been shorter and mitigating factors compensated for the small personal space, such as freedom of movement and activities outside of the cell.[43] Whether or not the small cell space does amount to inhumane and degrading treatment is determined by the Court on a case by case basis and depending on the abovementioned factors.[44] Thus, interestingly, in the case of *Vladimir Belyayev v Russia*, the ECtHR had held that holding a person for twenty-six consecutive days in a cell that was under three square meters did not amount to a violation because of the presence of compensating factors.[45]

Furthermore, presumptions have played a role as a substitute for legal argument in cases of indirect discrimination, that is, when a seemingly neutral norm has disproportionate adverse effects on a protected group.[46] The ECtHR famously held in *DH v Czech Republic* that a disproportionate effect of a measure on a protected group, which could be established on the basis of statistical evidence, lead to a presumption of discrimination.[47] Without such a presumption and the resulting shift of the burden of proof to the respondent state, indirect discrimination would be difficult to prove. Here, the presumption provides the missing link between the generalized statistical evidence and the individual case. It thereby reduces the complexity of the legal argumentation.

Finally, presumptions are employed as a substitute for legal argument in the context of non-pecuniary damages (article 41 of the ECHR). In *Scordino v Italy (No 1)*, the ECtHR held "that there is a strong but rebuttable presumption that excessively long proceedings will occasion non-pecuniary damage."[48] Non-pecuniary damages are not automatically awarded in length of proceedings cases. The ECtHR states that, although lengthy proceedings may sometimes result in non-pecuniary damage, in other cases, the awarded damages might only be minimal. There is even the possibility that no non-pecuniary damages are awarded at all, despite the length of proceedings.[49] The domestic remedy of a member state must fulfill certain criteria for it to be able to rebut the presumption of the existence of a claim

[42] *Muršić v Croatia* App no 7334/13 (ECtHR, 20 October 2016), para 171.

[43] ibid.

[44] A rebuttal is only possible if the factors are cumulatively met. The factors relate to the timeframe, outside-of-cell activities as compensation and appropriateness. For a full list of the three factors, see *Muršić v Croatia* App no 7334/13 (ECtHR, 20 October 2016), para 138.

[45] *Vladimir Belyayev v Russia* App no 9967/06 (ECtHR, 17 January 2014), paras 33–36.

[46] On the concept of indirect discrimination, see Tilmann Altwicker, *Menschenrechtlicher Gleichheitsschutz: Beiträge zum ausländischen öffentlichen Recht und Völkerrecht* (Springer 2011) 266–303.

[47] *DH v Czech Republic*, App no 57325/00 (ECtHR, 13 November 2007), paras 188–89.

[48] *Scordino v Italy (No 1)* App no 36813/97 (ECtHR, 29 March 2006), para 204 (referring to *Nardone v Italy* App no 34368/02 (ECtHR, 25 November 2004)).

[49] *Scordino v Italy (No 1)* (n 48) para 204.

to non-pecuniary damages in lengthy proceedings.[50] Resorting to the strong presumption that non-pecuniary damages are to be awarded if the proceedings are lengthy avoids the complexity of the calculations.

3.3 Avoiding Normative Conflict

A third function of presumptions is to avoid normative conflicts between legal regimes. This function is evidenced in the statement in the fragmentation report by the International Law Commission holding that "[i]n international law, there is a strong presumption against normative conflict."[51] Apart from presumptions, there are several other, more prominent argumentative tools by which courts seek to avoid situations of normative conflict: the idea of litispendence (as a procedural device), the margin of appreciation doctrine by the ECtHR (grounded upon the idea of subsidiarity), and the method of harmonious interpretation to name a few.[52] Resorting to presumptions can be viewed as a strategic choice by courts in order to avoid findings on normative conflicts involving IHRL.

For example, a scenario in which the ECtHR relied on a presumption in order to avoid findings on a normative conflict between legal regimes concerns the relationship between human rights obligations and obligations of states under the Charter of the United Nations (UNCh). Famously, the ECtHR coined a presumption in *Al-Jedda* holding that the UN Security Council (UNSC) is presumed not to intend to impose "any obligation on member States to breach fundamental principles of human rights." The *Al-Jedda* presumption is further fleshed out by the court as follows: if there is "any ambiguity in the terms of a United Nations Security Council resolution, the Court must [. . .] choose the interpretation which is most in harmony with the requirements of the Convention and which avoids any conflict of obligations." A rebuttal of the presumption is only possible if "clear and explicit language" is used in the resolution (reflecting the intention by the UNSC to require states "to take particular measures which would conflict with their obligations under international human rights law").[53] In the *Al-Jedda* case, in the absence of "clear and explicit language" in the UNSC resolution, the ECtHR concluded that the presumption was not rebutted. The *Al-Jedda* presumption was put to a test in

[50] ibid.

[51] ILC Study, Fragmentation of International Law: Difficulties Arising from the Diversification and Expansion of International Law, UN Doc A/CN.4/L.682 (13 April 2006) (finalized by Martti Koskenniemi) (ILC Study).

[52] On the margin of appreciation and subsidiarity, see Eyal Benvenisti, "The Margin of Appreciation, Subsidiarity and Global Challenges to Democracy" (2018) 9 Journal of International Dispute Settlement 240–53. See also Björnstjern Baade, *Der Europäische Gerichtshof für Menschenrechte als Diskurswächter: Zur Methodik, Legitimität und Rolle des Gerichtshofs im demokratisch-rechtsstaatlichen Entscheidungsprozess—Beiträge zum ausländischen öffentlichen Recht und Völkerrecht* (Springer 2017).

[53] *Al-Jedda v United Kingdom* App no 27021/08 (ECtHR, 7 July 2011), para 102.

the *Nada* case. In that case, the ECtHR faced a situation which arguably involved "clear and explicit language" in a resolution conflicting with the states' human rights obligations under the ECHR.[54] In other words, *Nada* provided the ECtHR with the situation in which the *Al-Jedda* presumption could have been rebutted. However, instead of finding the *Al-Jedda* presumption rebutted, the ECtHR re-stated the presumption and adapted it to the context of the case at hand.[55]

Another scenario in which the ECtHR employs a presumption in order to avoid (potential) normative conflict concerns the relationship between EU law and the ECHR. This relationship has caused some headache over the past decades.[56] Because the EU as a whole is not a signatory state to the ECHR, the ECtHR has no jurisdiction over the EU *ratione personae*.[57] Thus, there can be tensions as to which court is competent in a given human rights case and issues as to when the ECtHR can determine a case that the CJEU has already decided; and what happens when the ECtHR contradicts the CJEU. The delimitation of competences in human rights cases between the ECtHR and the Court of Justice of the European Union (CJEU) was somewhat clarified in the famous *Bosphorus v Ireland* case of 2005.[58] The ECtHR spelled out in this case that it presumed that the protection provided by EU law is equivalent to that of the ECHR.[59] Furthermore, because member states of the EU are presumed to comply with their obligations, a state's conduct can be justified by the fact that it is a member of the EU. This presumption can be rebutted if the protection of the Convention rights is considered to have been manifestly

[54] The conflict was between UNSC Resolution 1267 and arts 8 and 13 of the ECHR, see *Nada v Switzerland* App no 10593/08 (ECtHR, 12 September 2012), para 172. For a detailed analysis of the judgment, see Frank Meyer, "Der Fall Nada vor dem EGMR: Nichts Neues zur Normhierarchie zwischen UN-Recht und EMRK?, Besprechung zu EGMR HRRS 2013 Nr. 224 (Nada v Schweiz)" (2013) Onlinezeitschrift für Höchstrichterliche Rechtsprechung zum Strafrecht, <https://www.zora.uzh.ch/id/eprint/85270/1/Meyer_HRRS_2013.pdf>.

[55] The CJEU decided this question in its *Kadi* judgment, see Joined Cases C-402/05 P and C-415/05 P *Yassin Abdullah Kadi and Al Barakaat International Foundation v Council of the European Union and Commission of the European Communities* [2008] ECR I–6351 (Judgment of the Grand Chamber of 3 September 2008).

[56] For a useful analysis and discussion of the EU's accession to the ECHR, see eg Fisnik Korenica, *The EU Accession to the ECHR: Between Luxembourg's Search for Autonomy and Strasbourg's Credibility on Human Rights Protection* (Springer 2015).

[57] On the presumption of territorial jurisdiction under art 1 of the ECHR, see eg *Assanidze v Georgia* App no 71503/01 (ECtHR, 8 April 2004), para 139; and the Council of Europe's "Guide on Article 1 of the European Convention on Human Rights: Obligation to Respect Human Rights—Concepts of 'Jurisdiction' and Imputability" (30 April 2022) <https://www.echr.coe.int/Documents/Guide_Art_1_ENG.pdf> accessed 09 August 2022.

[58] *Bosphorus Hava Yollari Turizm Ve Ticaret Anonim Sireketi v Ireland* App no 45036/98 (ECtHR, 30 June 2005).

[59] The principle of equivalent protection first surfaced in the European Commission's decision *M & Co v Federal Republic of Germany* in 1990, see *M & Co v Federal Republic of Germany* App no 13258/87 (ECommHR, 9 February 1990) DR 64, 138. Relevant decisions with regard to this principle are also *Cantoni v France* App no 17862/91 (ECtHR, 15 November 1996); *Matthews v United Kingdom* App no 24833/94 (ECtHR, 18 February 1999).

deficient.[60] In the *Avotins* case, the Court in Strasbourg chose to maintain the presumption of equivalent protection. However, the ECtHR came close to a rebuttal.[61] This shows that the relationship between the ECHR and EU law is not set in stone and the presumption that is in place now, might change over time.[62]

In sum, presumptions function as argumentative tools to avoid having to pronounce on normative conflicts in the interpretation of international legal obligations. Thus, courts appear to ascribe a mediating effect to presumptions.

4. Presumptions as Rules on Primary and Secondary Rules

In their normative use, presumptions can be classified as "secondary rules" in the meaning coined by HLA Hart.[63] In the Hartian understanding, primary rules regulate conduct (eg by establishing obligations), whereas secondary rules of adjudication set the normative scene for the primary rules, pertaining to their identification, enforcement (interpretation), and change. The Hartian notion of secondary rules seems wider than that in the ILC's "Second Report on State Responsibility."[64] The report defines primary norms as norms that impose a particular obligation, whereas secondary norms are those that determine the consequences of non-fulfilment of primary obligations (state responsibility).[65] We cannot use the narrower, ILC definition here because presumptions do not, as such, stipulate consequences in the sense of state responsibility. Rather, presumptions are employed by courts as procedural tools of judicial decision-making under specific conditions of uncertainty. In this sense, all presumptions are *secondary* rules in the Hartian sense. Yet, presumptions do not fully fit the Hartian distinction either: presumptions are secondary rules in the sense that they are "rules on rules" (not establishing obligations or duties themselves). However, as we will demonstrate here, some

[60] *Bosphorus Hava Yollari Turizm Ve Ticaret Anonim Sireketi v Ireland* App no 45036/98 (ECtHR, 30 June 2005), paras 150–56; this decision was confirmed in *Avotins v Latvia* App no 17502/07 (ECtHR, 23 May 2016).

[61] *Avotins v Latvia* App no 17502/07 (ECtHR, 23 May 2016); For a full analysis, see Paul Gragl, "An Olive Branch from Strasbourg? Interpreting the European Court of Human Rights' Resurrection of Bosphorus and Reaction to Opinion 2/13 in the Avotiņs Case" (2017) 13 European Constitutional Law Review 551–67.

[62] Another tension in the European context can be found in asylum cases where the presumption of "safe countries" was developed in light of the non-refoulement principle under art 3 of the ECHR. With regard to art 3 of the ECHR in asylum contexts, see eg the above mentioned case of *Khlaifia v Italy* App no 16483/12 (ECtHR, 15 December 2016) and the case of *MSS v Belgium and Greece* App no 30696/09 (ECtHR, 21 January 2011).

[63] For the primary/secondary rules distinction, see HLA Hart, *The Concept of Law* (3rd edn, OUP 2012) 91–97.

[64] R Ago, "Second Report on State Responsibility: The Origin International Responsibility" (1970) II Yearbook of the International Law Commission 179.

[65] Anastasios Gourgourinis, "General/Particular International Law and Primary/Secondary Rules: Unitary Terminology of a Fragmented System" (2011) 22(4) European Journal of International Law 1017 (referring to Ago, "Second Report" ibid).

presumptions constitute secondary rules about primary rules of conduct, others are secondary rules about other secondary rules. The reason is that the uncertainty-management potential of presumptions (outlined above) is needed in respect of both types of rules—primary and secondary—in the Hartian distinction.

Presumptions constitute secondary rules on *primary* rules of conduct when they are used to bridge general facts and the assessment of the individual case. In these cases, presumptions guide the interpretation of a primary rule of conduct. For example, in the prison cell cases outlined above, the primary rule of article 3 of the ECHR (prohibition of torture/freedom from inhuman or degrading treatment) was interpreted by the ECtHR with the help of a presumption: namely, the rebuttable presumption that article 3 of the ECHR is violated if the floor space of a detainee falls under a particular minimum level.

Presumptions function as secondary rules on *secondary* rules of adjudication when they are applied in the context of uncertainties in fact-finding. That is, presumptions guide the application of, for example, the evidentiary standard of "proof beyond reasonable doubt," a secondary rule of adjudication. This is the case, for example, in situations of factual uncertainty whether or not a victim was indeed subjected to torture while in prison. The consequence of application of a presumption here is the shifting of the burden of proof. Arguably, presumptions also function as secondary rules on secondary rules in the above-mentioned cases of avoiding normative conflict as, ultimately, the rules that are interpreted with the help of presumptions are secondary rules on competences.

5. Legitimacy of Employing Presumptions

What makes the use of presumptions in human rights proceedings legitimate? There are basically two lines of argument to defend the use of presumptions: a first legitimacy argument relates to the general conditions of inference in human rights proceedings, a second reason revolves around considerations of "the lesser evil."

The first legitimacy argument pertains to the conditions under which presumptions are "made" by human rights courts. Stated simply, if the conditions under which human rights courts make inferences are considered as legitimate, so are the resulting presumptions. This is, of course, not the place to look at the legitimacy conditions of international human rights adjudication in any detail.[66] However, the notion of procedural justice (or fairness) will evidently be relevant here. The notion of procedural justice concerns the questions of *how* a court reaches its decision. Tom Tyler identifies four criteria of procedural justice: voice ("the opportunity to tell their side of the story in their own words before decisions are made"),

[66] See Armin von Bogdandy and Ingo Venzke, *In Whose Name?: A Public Law Theory of International Adjudication* (OUP 2016).

neutrality (perception of "judges as neutral, principled decision makers who make decisions based upon rules and not personal opinions, and who apply legal rules consistently across people and over cases"), respect (people "are viewed as important and valuable"), and trust ("sincerity and caring" of the judges).[67] Putting this into our present context: Presumptions curtail the argumentative process before the court (eg when facts are not established by evidence but inferred from the presence of other facts). As such, their use may impact the value of participation. Thus, considerations of procedural justice require human rights courts to make only sparse use of presumptions, to employ them only as a tool of "last resort" (the above-mentioned application condition of "necessity" should, thus, be interpreted narrowly). Also, for reasons of "voice," a presumption should generally be rebuttable. Equally, however, considerations of procedural justice may sometimes even command the use of presumptions. The human rights principle of "equality of arms" in legal proceedings may be understood as a legal manifestation of the idea of respect. As already outlined above, this idea may in certain cases involving information asymmetries require a human rights court to rely on presumptions: for example, it would be considered a lack of respect if a detainee were to be required to provide evidence as to who is responsible for injuries inflicted whilst being in detention. Furthermore, the value of neutrality is put to test by presumptions which are not applied consistently over time.[68] The aspect of neutrality can be enhanced by establishing secondary rules on presumptions.[69] Finally, considerations of trust play a role here: the court is required to base its presumptions on accepted sources of knowledge (common sense, influential authorities). As Adolfo Giuliani writes: "The leap of imagination which connects known to unknown fact, however, is not a leap in the dark, for there are a number of caveats and limitations that guide the inferential path, the first of which is a belief in the regularity of the course of nature."[70] The presumptions' factual or legal basis from which new knowledge is inferred should constantly be monitored and, if there are significant changes, the presumption should either be discarded or adapted.

A second (consequentialist) legitimacy argument makes use of the ethical notion of the "lesser evil."[71] Put simply, the argument runs as follows: The use of presumptions in legal proceedings is a departure from the procedural ideal of a fully reasoned decision based on fully established facts. The procedural ideal assumes (1) sufficient information of the court (eg that the decision-makers have full access

[67] Tom R Tyler, "Procedural Justice and the Courts," 44(1/2) (2007) Court Review: Journal of the American Judges Association 30–31. See also Eva Brems and Laurens Lavrysen, "Procedural Justice in Human Rights Adjudication: The European Court of Human Rights" (2013) 35 Human Rights Quarterly 176–200; Filippo Fontanelli and Paolo Busco, "The Function of Procedural Justice in International Adjudication" (2016) 15 Law and Practice of International Courts and Tribunals 1–23.

[68] See, above, the problem of the *Al Jedda*-presumption, 12–13.

[69] ibid.

[70] Giuliani, "Civilian Treatises" (n 5) 25.

[71] See Thomas E Hill, "Moral Purity and the Lesser Evil" (1983) 66 The Monist 213–32.

to domestic files, that the respondent states fully honor their obligations to cooperate with the court, etc); and (2) the existence of a coherent and comprehensive international legal order. Both conditions are not fulfilled in practice. Under non-ideal conditions, resorting to presumptions may sometimes be considered legitimate as the "lesser evil." Without the instrument of presumptions, international human rights adjudication would in some cases be impossible, some particularly grave violations could not be successfully adjudicated in court.[72] For instance, if perfect information were to be required in cases where a prisoner claims to have been tortured during his or her time in prison, he or she would never be able to make a case. Full information about what happened behind prison walls will often not be available. Thus, it is important to resort to presumptions in order for the court to proceed with the adjudication of the complaint and to make human rights practical and effective.

6. Conclusion

Presumptions are tools to manage situations of uncertainty. Their complexity derives from the fact that presumptions are *secondary rules* on both primary rules of conduct and secondary rules of adjudication. In the context of IHRL, presumptions are mostly judicially created. Problematically, their creation and application are largely ungoverned by legal rules. The main functions that presumptions assume in the context of human rights proceedings are (1) overcoming information asymmetries or the inaccessibility of information, (2) helping to bridge general facts and the legal assessment in individual cases, and (3) helping to avoid normative conflicts between legal regimes. Presumptions are necessary tools in the judicial decision-making process. However, judges must take utmost care when resorting to presumptions: presumptions are a judicial tool of last resort as their use tends to abridge the ordinary legal process of fact-finding or legal reasoning. Presumptions should not be used lightly, their application is only legitimate if other means are unavailable and the factual or legal basis upon which new legal knowledge is inferred from is made explicit in the courts' reasoning. Thus, judges must be transparent when and why they employ presumptions to guide their interpretation in a given case, and they must state the source or basis from which new legal knowledge is inferred.

[72] Karen Petroski, "The Public Face of Presumptions" (2009) 5 Episteme 388–401, 388.

10

Proving Bad Faith in International Law

Lessons from the Article 18 Case Law of the European Court of Human Rights

Başak Çalı

1. Introduction

In the last decade and a half, the European Court of Human Rights (ECtHR) has started to entertain the idea that a Convention provision may have been restricted for a purpose that is not prescribed by the Convention. In so doing, it has breathed doctrinal life into article 18 of the European Convention on Human Rights (ECHR) entitled "Limitation on use of restriction on rights." Article 18 proscribes a prohibition stating that: "[R]estrictions permitted under [the] Convention to the said rights and freedoms shall not be applied for any purpose other than those for which they have been prescribed."[1] Starting in 2004, there has been a surge in findings of violations of article 18 by the Court,[2] leading to the emergence of what we may now term as the "bad faith case law" of the ECtHR.[3]

[1] Convention for the Protection of Human Rights and Fundamental Freedoms (adopted 4 November 1950, entered into force 3 September 1953) 213 UNTS 221, art 18. No other regional or international human rights treaty has a provision equivalent to art 18 save for art 30 of the American Convention on Human Rights (adopted 22 November 1969, entered into force 18 July 1978) 1144 UNTS 123.

[2] *Gusinskiy v Russia* App no 70276/01 (ECtHR, 19 May 2004); *Cebotari v Moldava* App no 35615/05 (ECtHR, 30 November 2007); *Lutsenko v Ukraine* App no 6492/11 (ECtHR, 3 July 2012); *Tymoshenko v Ukraine* App no 49872/11 (ECtHR, 30 April 2013); *Mammadov v Azerbaijan* App no 15172/13 (ECtHR, 22 May 2014); *Jafarov v Azerbaijan* App no 69981/14 (ECtHR, 17 March 2016); *Merabishivili v Georgia* App no 72508/13 (ECtHR, 14 June 2016); *Merabishvili v Georgia* [GC] App no 72508/13 (ECtHR, 28 November 2017); *Mammadli v Azerbaijan* App no 47145/14 (ECtHR, 19 April 2018); *Hasanov v Azerbaijan* App nos 48653/13, 52464/13, 65597/13, and 70019/13 (ECtHR, 7 June 2018); *Aliyev v Azerbaijan* App nos 68762/14 and 71200/14 (ECtHR, 20 September 2018); *Navalnyy v Russia* [GC] App nos 29580/12, 36847/12, 11252/13, 12317/13, and 43746/14 (ECtHR, 15 November 2018); *Navalnyy v Russia (No 2)* App no 43734/14 (ECtHR, 9 April 2019); *Natig Jafarov v Azerbaijan* App no 64581/16 (ECtHR, 7 November 2019); *Ibrahimov and Mammadov v Azerbaijan* App no 63571/16 et al (ECtHR, 13 February 2020); *Khadija Ismayilova v Azerbaijan (No 2)* App no 30778/15 (ECtHR, 27 February 2020); *Kavala v Turkey* App no 28749/18 (ECtHR, 10 December 2019); *Selahattin Demirtaş v Turkey (No 2)* [GC] App no 14305/17 (ECtHR, 22 December 2020).

[3] Başak Çalı, "Coping with Crisis: Whither the Variable Geometry in the Jurisprudence of the European Court of Human Rights" (2018) 35(2) Wisconsin International Law Journal 237.

Başak Çalı, *Proving Bad Faith in International Law* In: *Secondary Rules of Primary Importance in International Law.* Edited by: Gábor Kajtár, Başak Çalı, and Marko Milanovic, Oxford University Press.
DOI: 10.1093/oso/9780192869012.003.0010

The idea that the abusive or bad faith exercise of a right/power must be sanctioned is a long-standing idea in domestic law[4] and has also seen debates in international law.[5] The more specific prohibition on the use of a power for purposes other than what is legally proscribed ("*détournement de pouvoir*") is found in the administrative law of many domestic systems[6] and is treated by some authors as a sub category of the more broadly conceived abuse of rights doctrine in international law.[7] Yet, the use of the concept of a bad faith violation has been traditionally underdeveloped both in international law[8] and in domestic constitutional or public law[9] both as a matter of primary rules prohibiting it and as a matter of evidentiary rules to prove its violation.

In this context, the emergence of the bad faith case law of the ECtHR since 2004 raises a range of novel and important questions concerning the development of primary rules as well as secondary rules of evidence in international human rights law, and public international law more generally. At the level of primary rules, one may ask whether findings of bad faith violations of substantive articles of the ECHR is at all necessary, given that general international law does not ultimately distinguish between the finding of a violation in good faith and a violation in bad faith as a matter of consequences. In fact, the principle of good faith is a systemic presumption of international law and international lawyers, by default, assume that states discharge their obligations in good faith.[10] Furthermore,

[4] HC Gutteridge, "Abuse of Rights" (1933) 5(1) Cambridge Law Journal 22, 30ff; BO Iluyomade, "Scope and Content of Abuse of Right" (1975) 16 Harvard International Law Journal 47, 55–61; Michael Byers, "Abuse of Rights: An Old Principle, A New Age" (2002) 47 McGill Law Journal 389, 391–97.

[5] Alexandre Kiss, *Abus de droit en droit international* (Librairie générale de droit et de jurisprudence 1952); Hersch Lauterpacht, *The Function of Law in the International Community* (OUP 2011) 294ff; Ian Brownlie, *Principles of Public International Law* (7th edn, OUP 2008) 443–45; Nicolas Politis, "Le Problème des limitations de la souveraineté et la théorie de l'abus des droits dans les rapports internationaux" (1925) 6 Collected Courses of the Hague Academy of International Law 1.

[6] Iluyomade, "Scope and Content" (n 4) 51–52; Gutteridge, "Abuse of Rights" (n 4) 35; *Merabishvili* [GC] (n 2) para 166; *Collected Edition of the* "Travaux Préparatoires" *of the European Convention on Human Rights*, vol V (Martinus Nijhoff 1979) 293.

[7] Kiss categorizes abuses of rights into three types: (1) the exercise of a right which interferes with another state's due exercise of its own right; (2) where the power is used for a purpose other than specifically proscribed when the right is conferred; and (3) unjustifiable and arbitrary use of power. See Alexandre Kiss, "Abuse of Rights" (*The Max Planck Encyclopedia of Public International Law*, December 2006) paras 4–6 <https://opil.ouplaw.com/view/10.1093/law:epil/9780199231690/law-9780199231690-e1371?rskey=tAL8TN&result=1&prd=MPIL> accessed 15 July August 2022.

[8] Steven Reinhold, "Good Faith in Public International Law" (2013) 2 UCL Journal of Law and Jurisprudence 40, 49.

[9] András Sajó, "Abuse of Fundamental Rights or the Difficulties of Purposiveness" in András Sajó (ed), *Abuse: The Dark Side of Fundamental Rights* (Eleven International 2006) 29, 33–34; David E Pozen, "Constitutional Bad Faith" (2016) 129(4) Harvard Law Review 885.

[10] The ICJ's *obiter dicta* in the *Nuclear Tests* case, exemplifies this presumption: "One of the basic principles governing the creation and performance of legal obligations whatever their source is good faith. Trust and confidence are inherent in international cooperation, in particular in an age when this cooperation in many fields is becoming increasingly essential. Just as the very rule of *pacta sunt servanda* in the law of treaties is based on good faith, so also is the binding character of an international obligation. Thus interested states may take cognizance of unilateral declarations and place confidence in them, and are entitled to require that the obligation thus created be respected": see *Nuclear Tests Case (Australia v France)* (Merits) [1974] ICJ Rep 253 [46].

in public international law, the abuse of power has primarily been seen as a vehicle for the development of vague primary rules of international law.[11] If an international legal right or a duty is not well defined, it is often thought that findings of an abuse of that right or duty may help develop the primary law on the matter.[12] Primary rules of European human rights law, however, do not suffer from a general state of under-development. It is regarded as one of the most sophisticated and well-developed bodies of international law, thanks to its full time and compulsory court. Given that the Court does not need bad faith to develop its existing primary rules,[13] what purpose then does the finding of bad faith violations serve with regard to the primary rules of European human rights law?

As a matter of development of secondary rules of evidence, asking whether a state violated its obligations through abuse of its powers, and, therefore, in bad faith raises important questions about what counts as evidence of bad faith violations of the Convention. This assessment, for example, may require an inquiry into the actual motives of states or the actual results of their acts or omissions.[14] Whilst motivational analysis is a common trait in international criminal law exemplified in the *mens rea* element of international crimes,[15] it is less familiar in areas of international law that focus on state responsibility as a matter of secondary rules of adjudication.[16] In public international law, general wisdom also indicates that proving that a state, as an abstract entity, acted in bad faith would face serious evidentiary challenges.[17] First, there is the issue of whether proving bad faith requires proving subjective intention to act maliciously on the part of individuals whose actions are attributable to the state or whether a more objective evidentiary standard can be set

[11] Byers, "An Old Principle, A New Age" (n 4) 429–30.

[12] Lauterpacht, *The Function of Law in the International Community* (n 5) 294ff.

[13] The Court has a wide range of doctrines to develop the interpretation of the primary rules of the Convention. For a recent reinstatement of these, see Janneke Gerards, *General Principles of the European Convention on Human Rights* (CUP 2019) 46–77.

[14] Iluyomade, "Scope and Content" (n 4) 77–79. Indeed, Lauterpacht, for example, argued that: "[T]he problem of abuse of rights is only to a limited extent identical with the question of malicious exercise of rights" and "for the determination of such abuse of rights the question of subjective fault and intention may, but need not always, be material." See Lauterpacht, *The Function of Law in the International Community* (n 5) 302ff and 294ff, respectively.

[15] Convention on the Prevention and Punishment of the Crime of Genocide (adopted 9 December 1948, entered into force 12 January 1951) 78 UNTS 277, art II; Rome Statute of the International Criminal Court (adopted 17 July 1998, entered into force 1 July 2002) 2187 UNTS 3, art 30; International Criminal Court, *Elements of Crimes* (ICC 2011) 1; Robert Cryer, *An Introduction to International Criminal Law and Procedure* (CUP 2007) 318–20; Roger S Clark, "The Mental Element in International Criminal Law: The Rome Statute of the International Criminal Court and the Elements of Offences" (2002) 12 Criminal Law Forum 291.

[16] Vladimir Paul, "The Abuse of Rights and Bona Fides in International Law" (1977) 28 Österreichische Zeitschrift für Öffentliches Recht und Völkerrecht 107, 121.

[17] GDS Taylor, "Content and Rule against Abuse of Rights in International Law" (1972) 46 British Yearbook of International Law 323; Georg Schwarzenberger, "Uses and Abuses of the 'Abuse of Rights' in International Law" (1956) 42 Transactions of the Grotius Society 147, 153, 159; Steven Reinhold, "Good Faith in Public International Law" (2013) 2 UCL Journal of Law and Jurisprudence 40, 50; Gutteridge, "Abuse of Rights" (n 4) 26.

to demonstrate bad faith.[18] Second is the issue of what counts as evidence of bad faith and whether one is required to have direct evidence to proof bad faith. Third is the challenge of distinguishing good faith from bad faith. As Schwarzenberger and Brown point out in the context of proving abuse of rights, "it is difficult to establish what is supposed to amount to an abuse, as distinct from a harsh but justified use, of a right under international law."[19] In the case of human rights law, too, it may be difficult to distinguish an act or omission that is manifestly arbitrary from one that pursues a malicious agenda beyond arbitrariness. Lastly, searching for bad faith evidence blurs the line between judicial and political decision-making as to what is admissible as evidence. In the words of Gutteridge, commenting in the context of the utility of the abuse of rights doctrine in international law, it "may get out of hand and result in serious inroads on individual rights, thus becoming an instrument of dangerous potency in the hands of the demagogue and the revolutionary."[20] In the context of pronouncements of bad faith violations of human rights law, such findings may also have a negative influence on compliance with human rights as states found to be in bad faith may believe themselves to be unfairly targeted.

The aim of this chapter is to analyze the ECtHR's evolving bad faith jurisprudence against this backdrop of the difficulties associated with proving bad faith violations in international law. By way of a close reading of the case law of the Court between 2004, when it found its first violation of article 18, until 2020, the chapter investigates how the Court has come to treat good faith as a rebuttable presumption, how the secondary rules of evidence concerning bad faith violations have developed in the case law of the Court over time, and the consequences of these developments on the primary rule provided in article 18 of the Convention. The chapter argues that the development of secondary rules of evidence to prove bad faith violations of the Convention are closely interrelated with the recent developments in the interpretation of primary rules of the Convention under article 18. The ECtHR's bad faith case law has, over time, evolved away from a direct and subjective evidence paradigm to a circumstantial and indirect evidence paradigm. At the same time, the substantive interpretation of article 18 of the Convention, too evolved, to signal that the use of domestic laws and judicial proceedings in the service of anti rule of law and antidemocratic agendas constitutes a violation of the Convention.[21] These developments make the ECtHR an *avant-garde* adjudicatory

[18] Taylor, "Content and Rule" (n 17) 331ff.

[19] Georg Schwarzenberger and Edward Brown, *A Manual of International Law* (6th edn, Milton Professional Books 1976) 84.

[20] Gutteridge, "Abuse of Rights" (n 4) 43–44.

[21] *Collected Edition of the* "Travaux Préparatoires" *of the European Convention on Human Rights*, vol IV (Martinus Nijhoff 1977) 130 See also Helen Keller and Corina Heri, "Selective Criminal Proceedings and Article 18 ECHR: The European Court of Human Rights Untapped Potential to Protect Democracy" (2016) 37 Human Rights Law Journal 1.

body in developing secondary rules of evidence for deciding whether states violate their international law obligations in bad faith.

In what follows, Section 2 offers an account of the emergence of the ECtHR's bad faith case law and the underlying reasons for article 18 to be the least developed primary norm under the Convention prior to 2004. Section 3 analyzes the shifts in the secondary rules, that is, evidentiary standards employed by the Court in proving bad faith between 2004 and 2020. Section 4 lays out the normative consequences of the turn to circumstantial and indirect evidence and the interplay between secondary and primary rules in this domain. Section 5 concludes by discussing whether Strasbourg's approach to proving bad faith could be transferable to other international judicial contexts either as a matter of secondary rules of evidence.

2. From the Periphery to the Center: Development of the Article 18 Case Law of the European Court of Human Rights

Article 18 of the ECHR was there right from the start. It was not until 2004, however, that it received any real attention in the Court's case law.[22] The *Travaux Préparatoires* of the Convention show that the insertion of article 18 into the Convention was a late but conscious choice. This was due to the concerns of the drafters that pre-World War II (WWII) practices of using state power in subtle ways to purposively undermine rights may be a possibility in post-WWII Europe.[23] There was, therefore, a need to distinguish legitimate and illegitimate restrictions of the ECHR. In the preparatory work, the reason for including article 18 was justified and it is worth quoting in full:

> [T]he international collective guarantee will have, as its purpose, to ensure that no State shall in fact aim at suppressing the guaranteed freedom, by means of minor measures which, while made with the pretext of organizing the exercise of these freedoms on its territory, or of safeguarding the letter of the law, have the opposite effect. […] It is legitimate and necessary to limit, sometimes even to restrain, individual freedoms, to allow everyone the peaceful exercise of their freedom and to ensure the maintenance of morality, of the general well-being, of the common good and of public need. When the State defines, organises, regulates

[22] Başak Çalı and Kristina Hatas "History as an Afterthought: The (Re)discovery of Article 18 in the Case Law of the European Court of Human Rights" in Helmut Aust and Esra Demir-Gürsel (eds), *The European Court of Human Rights: Current Challenges in Historical and Comparative Perspective* (Edward Elgar 2021) 158–76.

[23] *Collected Edition of the* "Travaux Préparatoires" *of the European Convention on Human Rights*, vol I (Martinus Nijhoff 1975) 136; *Collected Edition of the* "Travaux Préparatoires" *of the European Convention on Human Rights*, vol V (Martinus Nijhoff 1979) 294

> and limits freedoms for such reasons, in the interest of, and for the better insurance of, the general well-being, it is only fulfilling its duty. That is permissible; that is legitimate.
>
> But when it intervenes to suppress, to restrain and to limit these freedoms for, this time, reasons of state; to protect itself according to the political tendency it represents, against an opposition which it considers dangerous; to destroy fundamental freedoms which it ought to make itself responsible for coordinating and guaranteeing, then it is against public interest if it intervenes. Then the laws which it passes are contrary to the principle of international guarantee.[24]

Yet, the former European Commission on Human Rights and the ECtHR treated "article 18 risks" as not prominent in their pre-2004 jurisprudence. Instead, the ECtHR, operating under a strong and systemic presumption of the good faith of the state parties,[25] developed its jurisprudence focusing on violations of the Convention though acts of omission or commission. The Court told its state parties that they incorrectly applied the Convention standards by way of defect laws, judicial or executive practices[26] or that they lacked an adequate legal, regulatory or institutional framework to give full effect to the Convention standards.[27] The closest that case law has come to hinting at the abuse of powers is, perhaps, when the Court finds the conduct of the state arbitrary.[28] Arbitrariness, however, is not a standard that explicitly points to the presence of illegitimate motives in the course of rights restrictions. It merely points to the lack of rights-respecting attitudes in law, or practice, without delving into the underlying reasons for any lack of such respect.[29]

The first ever case that discussed article 18 in substance was *Kamma v Netherlands* in 1974.[30] Kamma had been arrested and held in detention while an investigation was conducted against him on charges of extortion and robbery. His detention was repeatedly extended by the district court, which stated that detention was permissible in any lawful place of detention in the Netherlands. While in

[24] *Collected Edition of the* "Travaux Préparatoires" *of the European Convention on Human Rights*, vol IV (Martinus Nijhoff 1977) 130

[25] A review of the database of the case law of the ECtHR, HUDOC, shows that neither the Commission nor the Court found any violations of art 18, together with any of the rights protected under the Convention, until 2004. On the Court's recognition of a strong presumption of good faith, see also *Khodorkovskiy v Russia* App no 5829/04 (ECtHR, 31 May 2011), para 255.

[26] See *Opuz v Turkey* App no 33401/02 (ECtHR, 9 June 2009); *Khamila Isayeva v Russia* App no 6846/02 (ECtHR, 15 November 2007).

[27] See *Siliadin v France* App no 73316/01 (ECtHR, 26 July 2005); *Dink v Turkey* App nos 2668/07, 6102/08, 30079/08, 7072/09, and 7124/09 (ECtHR, 14 September 2010).

[28] See, representatively, *Assanidze v Georgia* App no 71503/01 (ECtHR, 8 April 2004); *Ilaşcu v Moldova and Russia* App no 48787/99 (ECtHR, 8 July 2004).

[29] It must be noted that some analytical work on abuse of rights consider manifest arbitrariness as one type of abuse of rights alongside the infringement of another state's right and the exercise of a power for a wrongful purpose. On this, see Kiss, "Abuse of Rights" (n 7) paras 4–6.

[30] *Kamma v Netherlands* (dec) App no 4771/71 (Commission, 14 July 1974).

detention on this charge, the applicant was also questioned about his possible involvement in a murder, without having been detained in connection to that charge. During this time, the applicant was transferred and detained in a different location in the Netherlands at police headquarters.

The former European Commission of Human Rights found the claim of a breach of article 18 in conjunction with article 5 of the ECHR admissible in this case. It stated that the detention was in itself lawful and the restriction of the applicant's liberty in conformity with article 5(1)(c), and examined whether a breach of article 18 arose because the detention of the applicant in the police headquarters was for any other purpose than that provided for in article 5(1)(c). The Commission did not find an ulterior purpose because nothing in the Convention or Dutch law prohibited the police from questioning a person about a number of criminal investigations. It found that the police had not taken advantage of the applicant's situation, as the period during which he was questioned at the police headquarters was "only" two days longer than the period for which he could legally be remanded had he previously been at liberty, and because the court order expressly allowed the applicant to be remanded anywhere in the Netherlands. Also, the detention had not put the applicant at a disadvantage as related to the murder investigation, which was later closed due to insufficient evidence.

Against this factual background, the Commission approached article 18 narrowly. It held that article 18 is not an autonomous article and, therefore, can only be raised in conjunction with other articles of the Convention that allow for restrictions to be placed on rights.[31] The Commission further held that the mere suspicion by applicants that their rights were restricted for illegitimate purposes cannot be enough, and that the applicants must bear the burden to convincingly establish illegitimate purposes underpinning the restrictions.[32] The Commission, therefore, made the trigger of article 18 an onerous task, and required applicants to bear the responsibility to furnish proof that state authorities had acted in bad faith.

Looking back at the facts of *Kamma*, it may be suggested that the Commission may have made the trigger of article 18 onerous because it did not want it to be raised every time an article 5(1)(c) complaint concerning unlawful detention is raised. In the cases that came after *Kamma*, the Court has followed the Commission's interpretive lead. Not only did it not find any violations of article 18, it did not even consider the examination of article 18 claims necessary when raised by applicants[33] and instead focused on developing standards of interpretation of the substantive articles protecting the rights of the applicant.

[31] ibid para 9.

[32] ibid para 10.

[33] See *Engel v Netherlands* App nos 5100/71, 5101/71, 5102/71, 5354/72, and 5370/72 (ECtHR, 8 June 1976); *Sunday Times v United Kingdom* App no 6538/74 (ECtHR, 26 April 1979); *Sporrong and Lönnroth v Sweden* App no 7151/75 (ECtHR, 23 September 1982); *Bozano v France* App no 9990/82 (EctHR, 18 December 1986); *United Communist Party of Turkey v Turkey* App no 19392/92 (EctHR, 30 January 1998); *Ipek v Turkey* App no 25760/94 (ECtHR, 17 February 2004).

It was thirty years later, in 2004, that a Chamber of the Court found the first violation of article 18 in *Gusinskiy v Russia*.[34] Similar to *Kamma*, *Gusinskiy* claimed this violation in conjunction with article 5(1)(c). The case concerned the detention of the Chairman of the Board of, and majority shareholder in, ZAO Media Most, a private Russian media holding company, which also owned NTV, a popular television channel.[35] The detention of the applicant ended when he agreed to sell his company to Gazprom, a Russian state-controlled energy company, under conditions favorable to Gazprom.[36] Gusinskiy argued that his detention amounted to an abuse of power by the authorities and that he was detained in order to force him to sell his company.[37] Gusinskiy further argued that the authorities intended to silence his media outlets (which had been critical of the government) through this forced sale.[38]

The Court's initial approach when finding its first violation under article 18, in conjunction with article 5, in *Gusinskiy* was surprisingly brief. The Court, following *Kamma*, emphasized that article 18 of the Convention did not have an autonomous role and that it could only be applied in conjunction with other articles of the Convention.[39] The Court, however, found that the direct evidence provided by the applicant was sufficiently compelling to prove an illegitimate purpose on the part of the state authorities' decision to detain him. The fact that Gazprom asked the applicant to sign an agreement when he was in prison, and that a state minister endorsed such an agreement was the direct evidence.[40] All charges against the applicant were dropped as soon as he signed the agreement.[41] Perhaps more significantly, Russian authorities did not contest this direct evidence presented to the Court.[42] All of these facts, the Court held, suggested that the applicant's prosecution had an illegitimate motive. It was used to "intimidate him."[43]

This, perhaps accidental, discovery of article 18 in 2004 led to a rise in article 18 claims by other applicants before the Court. In cases that followed *Gusinskiy*, the Court found violations of article 18, in conjunction with article 5(1)(c) with respect to unlawful grounds of detentions of applicants in Moldova, Ukraine, Azerbaijan, Georgia, Russia, and Turkey.[44] By 2019, the Court's interest in the interpretation of article 18 expanded beyond decisions to detain in bad faith. In *Aliyev v Azerbaijan* the Court found an article 18 violation in conjunction with article 8 (right to private and family life),[45] in *Navalny v Russia* in conjunction with article 11 (freedom

[34] *Gusinskiy* (n 2).
[35] ibid para 136.
[36] ibid paras 136, 138–40.
[37] ibid para 150.
[38] ibid paras 150–51.
[39] ibid para 151.
[40] ibid para 150.
[41] ibid paras 138–40.
[42] ibid para 151.
[43] ibid.
[44] For the list of cases up until December 2020, see (n 2).
[45] *Aliyev* (n 2).

of assembly),[46] and in *Demirtaş v Turkey* Chamber judgment in conjunction with article 5(3) (prolonged detention).[47]

Since 2004, there have also been cases where the Court did not see the need to examine article 18 claims,[48] or examined the claim, but did not find a violation.[49] What is more, the Grand Chamber of the Court addressed article 18 referrals three times, first in *Merabishvili v Georgia*,[50] then in *Navalny v Russia*[51] and in *Demirtaş v Turkey*.[52] In the case of *Mammadov v Azerbaijan* the lack of compliance with a judgment that found a violation of article 5(1)(c) in conjunction with article 18 has also been subject to infringement proceedings before the ECtHR under article 46 of the Convention.[53]

A common thread that connects the applicants of article 18 cases between 2004 and 2020 provides an opportunity to assess the broader political context in which article 18 has been developed. Article 18 applicants are critical of their governments as businessmen, human rights defenders, journalists, or as politicians. They invariably assert that their treatment by judicial authorities falls well outside the rule of law safeguards.[54] Cebotari, like Gusinksy was a businessman, the then-head of Moldtranselectro, a Moldovan state-owned power distribution company. Lutsenko was a former Minister of the Interior and the leader of the opposition party Narodna Samooborona in Ukraine.[55] Tymoshenko was a former Ukrainian

[46] *Navalny* [GC] (n 2).

[47] *Demirtaş* (n 2).

[48] *Hasan İlhan v Turkey* App no 22494/93 (ECtHR, 9 November 2004); *Issa v Turkey* App no 31821/96 (ECtHR, 16 November 2004); *Toğcu v Turkey* App no 27601/95 (ECtHR, 31 May 2005); *Houbal v Czech Republic* App no 75375/01 (ECtHR, 14 June 2005); *Dağ and Yaşar v Turkey* App no 4080/02 (ECtHR, 8 November 2005); *Kaya v Turkey* App nos 33420/96 and 36206/97 (ECtHR, 22 November 2005); *Josephides v Turkey* App no 21887/93 (ECtHR, 22 September 2009); *Navalnyy and Yashin v Russia* App no 76204/11 (ECtHR, 4 December 2014); *Navalnyy v Russia* App no 29580/12 (ECtHR, 2 February 2017); *Mehmet Altan v Turkey* App no 13237/17 (ECtHR, 20 March 2018); *Şahin Alpay v Turkey* App no 16538/17 (ECtHR, 20 March 2018); *Sabuncu v Turkey* App no 23199/17 (ECtHR, 10 November 2020); and *Şık v Turkey (No 2)* App no 36493/17 (ECtHR, 24 November 2020).

[49] *Altun v Turkey* App no 24561/94 (ECtHR, 1 June 2004); *Şirin Yılmaz v Turkey* App no 35875/97 (ECtHR, 29 July 2004); *Abdülsamet Yaman v Turkey* App no 32446/96 (ECtHR, 2 November 2004); *Dicle v Turkey* App no 34685/97 (ECtHR, 10 November 2004); *Menteşe v Turkey* App no 36217/97 (ECtHR, 18 January 2005); *Nesibe Haran v Turkey* App no 28299/95 (ECtHR, 6 October 2005); *Kumru Yılmaz and others v Turkey* App no 36211/97 (ECtHR, 2 February 2006); *Öztoprak v Turkey* App no 33247/96 (ECtHR, 2 February 2006); *Şayli v Turkey* App no 33243/96 (ECtHR, 2 February 2006); *Ağtaş v Turkey* App no 33240/96 (ECtHR, 2 February 2006); *Artun v Turkey* App no 33239/96 (ECtHR, 2 February 2006); *Keser v Turkey* App nos 33238/96 and 32965/96 (ECtHR, 2 February 2006); *Aksakal v Turkey* App no 37850/97 (ECtHR, 15 February 2007); *Khodorovskiy* (n 25); *OAO Neftyanaya Kompaniya Yukos v Russia* App no 14902/04 (ECtHR, 20 September 2011); *Khodorkovskiy and Lebedev v Russia* App nos 11082/06 and 13772/05 (ECtHR, 25 July 2013); *Korban v Ukraine* App no 26744/16 (ECtHR, 4 July 2019).

[50] *Merabishvili* [GC] (n 2).

[51] *Navalny* [GC] (n 2).

[52] *Demirtaş* [GC] (n 2).

[53] *Ilgar Mammadov v Azerbaijan (Infringement Proceedings)* [GC] App no 15172/13 (ECtHR, 29 May 2019); Başak Çalı, "No Going Nuclear in Strasbourg" (*Verfassungsblog*, 30 May 2019) <https://verfassungsblog.de/no-going-nuclear-in-strasbourg/> accessed 27 August 2019.

[54] Kim Lane Scheppele, "The Rule of Law and the Frankenstate: Why Governance Checklists Do Not Work" (2013) 26 Governance 559.

[55] *Lutsenko* (n 2) para 7.

Prime Minister and one of the leaders of the Orange Revolution.[56] Merabishvili was a former Prime Minister and Minister of the Interior in Georgia.[57] In cases that followed, opposition politicians who spoke out against the long-standing regimes of Aliyev in Azerbaijan (Mammadov), Putin in Russia (Navalny), and Erdoğan in Turkey (Demirtaş) brought article 18 cases concerning the detentions and judicial proceedings against them by domestic authorities. The rest of the cases concern civil society activists, journalists, lawyers, and human rights defenders who were subject to restrictions such as pre-trial detentions and travel bans and who allege that these measures were used to intimate or silence them.[58]

3. Proving Bad Faith: From Direct to Circumstantial Evidence

The former Commission in *Kamma* held that the evidence to prove bad faith on the part of the authorities had to be direct evidence furnished by the applicant herself. This approach, requiring an exacting standard of direct proof falling on the applicant, was also followed in the earlier article 18 violations found by the Court.

In *Gusinsky v Russia*, the Court emphasized that the applicant was forced to sign an agreement as a condition of his release whilst in detention and that the government did not dispute this direct evidence. This was proof of the existence of an illegitimate purpose or hidden agenda for his detention. In *Cebotari v Moldova*, the applicant argued that his charge and detention was directly connected to the application that his company, Oferta Plus RL, made before the ECtHR. Having found a violation of article 34 in the *Oferta Plus RL* case with respect to the obstacles placed on Cebotari's right to individual petition before the Court,[59] the Court held that no objective person could identify the commission of an offence by Cebotari and the applicant convincingly showed the existence of a hidden agenda for his detention.[60] *Cebotari* is thus the first case where a previous judgment of the Court with respect to the same facts was decisive evidence for finding an article 18 violation in relation to a detention.

In the two Ukrainian cases that followed, *Lutsenko* and *Tymoshenko*, both applicants claimed that their detentions had the ulterior motive of excluding them from political life and preventing them standing in the parliamentary elections of 28 October 2012. The Court focused on the reasons provided by domestic prosecutors and judicial authorities for the arrest and detention of the former leaders as direct evidence. In both cases, the Court found that what the judicial authorities said went beyond arbitrary restrictions and openly acknowledged an illegitimate

56 *Tymoshenko* (n 2) paras 8–12.
57 *Merabishvili* (n 2) para 6.
58 *Jafarov* (n 2) para 6.
59 *Oferta Plus RL v Moldova* App no 14385/04 (ECtHR, 19 December 2006).
60 *Cebotari* (n 2) paras 52–53.

agenda of aiming to curb their political activities.[61] These cases, therefore, allowed the Court to distinguish an arbitrary detention from a detention that served an illegitimate purpose. The evidence for such an illegitimate purpose was provided by direct evidence immediately surrounding the facts of the cases.

It was in 2011, in *Khodorkovskiy v Russia*, that the applicants before the Court sought to challenge both the high burden placed on the applicants to provide direct evidence and the lack of adequate regard by the Court of circumstantial evidence.[62] In this case the applicant maintained that whilst he did not have immediate direct proof surrounding the facts of the case that his criminal prosecution had been politically motivated, he nevertheless maintained that he, at the very least, adduced "*prima facie* evidence."[63] He maintained that:

> his arrest and consequent detention on 25 October 2003, just a few weeks before the Duma elections on 7 December 2003 and shortly before the completion of the Sibneft/Yukos merger, had been orchestrated by the State to take action against an opposition which it considered "dangerous," contrary to Article 18.[64]

In addition, *Khodorkovskiy* provided the Court with reports from international and Russian media, various governmental and non-governmental organizations, a PACE report, US Senate resolutions, European Parliament reports, documents of the UK House of Commons, decisions by the UK courts in cases of extradition of several former Yukos managers to Russia, and decisions by the Cypriot, Dutch, and Swiss courts.[65] In response, the Court held that "there is nothing in the Court's case law to support the applicant's suggestion that, where a *prima facie* case of improper motive is established, the burden of proof shifts to the respondent Government. The Court considers that the burden of proof in such a context should rest with the applicant."[66]

What is more, and in line with the concerns of the skeptics of the use of bad faith reasoning in international law, the Court also recognized that an article 18 claim holding that a states' procedures with respect to a person *ab initio* served a hidden agenda was a very serious allegation.[67] In 2013, in *Khodorkovskiy and Lebedev v Russia*,[68] the Court reiterated this position once again, holding that the finding of an article 18 violation happened rarely and required direct and exacting proof.

In 2014, in *Mammadov v Azerbaijan*, the Court continued to defend its exacting standard that the applicant "must convincingly show that the real aim of

[61] *Lutsenko* (n 2) and *Tymoshenko* (n 2).
[62] *Khodorkovskiy* (n 24).
[63] ibid para 251.
[64] ibid.
[65] ibid para 253.
[66] ibid para 256.
[67] ibid para 260.
[68] *Khodorkovskiy and Lebedev* (n 49).

the authorities was not the same as that proclaimed"[69] but at the same time relaxed its requirement of direct proof by holding that the real aim can also be reasonably inferred from the context. In this case and, similar to *Khodorkovskiy*, there was no evidence of verbal or written pronouncements or acts of state officials immediately surrounding the detention of Mr Mammadov. Yet, the Court was willing to focus on the temporal links between when the applicant made critical remarks of the government and when he was arrested and detained and found that there was no available explanation other than illegitimate purposes as to the timing of the applicant's detention. In this case, the Court also relied strongly on the fact that it had already found the applicant's detention arbitrary, but that the facts of the case went beyond arbitrariness and revealed that the detention served a purpose not provided by the Convention.[70] *Mammadov*, therefore, has overturned much of what was held in *Khodorkovskiy*.

3.1 A Principled Embrace of Broader Context and Associated Circumstantial Evidence

It was in 2016 in the cases of *Jafarov v Azerbaijan* and *Merabishvili v Georgia* that the Court's strong position on direct and exacting proof as well as the laying of the burden of proof on the applicant for article 18 violations saw a significant shift. In this context, and following Mammadov two questions emerged in the case law: (1) whether circumstantial evidence alone, without the presence of direct evidence can prove an article 18 violation; and (2) whether the exacting standard requiring the applicant to prove bad faith can be relaxed in favor of a "beyond reasonable doubt standard."[71]

It was in the case of *Jafarov v Azerbaijan* in 2016, which concerns the continuing detention of human rights defenders in the country, that the Court, for the first time, embraced a principled approach to the importance of broader context as relevant evidence and held that circumstantial evidence can have a wider scope than what can be derived from the immediate context. The Court then turned its attention beyond the immediate facts surrounding the applicant's arrest and prosecution, to the broader facts concerning the general state of human rights defenders and government critics in Azerbaijan. It placed a significant emphasis on the "heavy international criticism" concerning the general conditions of how human rights defenders are treated in the country and the domestic and hostile characterization of human rights defenders by pro-government outlets.[72] The Court finally

[69] *Mammadov* (n 2) para 137.
[70] ibid paras 141–44.
[71] See *Jafarov* (n 2) paras 153–63. See also *Merabishvili* (n 2) paras 102–07.
[72] ibid paras 159–61.

insisted that the immediate facts of the arrest and detention of Mr Jafarov cannot be isolated from the similar treatments of others who are in a similar situation.[73] It was these three arguments "taken as a whole" that led the Court to hold that Jafarov's arrest and detention went beyond a mere finding of arbitrariness and crossed into the domain of bad faith restrictions of rights. In *Jafarov*, the Court also abandoned its *Khodorkovskiy* line that the *ab initio* abuse of power by authorities was a very serious allegation. Instead, it underlined that good faith was a rebuttable presumption and that this rebuttal may be discharged by inferences that can reasonably be drawn from the context of the application.[74]

In *Merabishvili v Georgia*, in the same year, the Court started to debate whether the exacting burden of proof falling on the applicants is the adequate standard of proof. The Chamber judgment in this case held that the burden of proof does not necessarily have to rest solely on the applicant to show the pursuance of illegitimate purposes by state authorities.[75] Some of the burden for disproving a hidden agenda may also fall on the government authorities, if the facts of the case so require.[76] In this case the Court also, for the first time, abandoned its view that a bad faith violation was an aggravated form of arbitrariness on the part of the state. It found that even if the Court finds no violation of a substantive article by itself (in this case article 5), that does not mean that there may not be a violation of that article in conjunction with article 18.[77]

Both of these points have been challenged by the Georgian government before the Grand Chamber, which, expectedly, demanded a clarification for why the Chamber abandoned the *Khodorkovskiy* standards.

The Grand Chamber judgment of the ECtHR in 2017 in *Merabishvili v Georgia* marked a significant consolidation of the ongoing shifts in the article 18 case law of the Court in three significant ways. First, the Grand Chamber abandoned the *Kamma* legacy in its entirety and decided that the burden to prove bad faith should be identical to proving violations of any other provision of the Convention.[78] It should, therefore, not be exclusively "borne by one or the other party"[79] and governed by the standard of "beyond reasonable doubt."[80] This decisive lowering of the standard of proof for bad faith violations has provided a new flexibility to the Court to investigate bad faith violations.[81] Second, the Grand Chamber fully embraced the circumstantial evidence paradigm that began to govern the reasoning of the

[73] *Jafarov* (n 2).
[74] ibid.
[75] *Merabishvili* (n 2) para 83.
[76] ibid paras 311–12.
[77] ibid para 102.
[78] *Merabishvili* [GC] (n 2) paras 310, 316.
[79] ibid para 311.
[80] ibid para 314.
[81] In the Court's own words, however, circumstantial evidence "means information about the primary facts, or contextual facts or sequences of events which can form the basis for inferences about the primary facts": ibid para 317.

first section of the Court in *Mammadov* and *Jafarov* and therefore, abandoned the requirement of direct and exacting evidence to prove ulterior purposes on the part of the authorities. In other words, the Grand Chamber has favored *Jafarov* at the expense of *Khodorkovskiy*. The *Kamma* legacy was no longer.

What is more significant, however, was the Grand Chamber's proposition that a bad faith violation can be found even when the Court does not find a violation of a substantive right under the Convention. In so doing the Grand Chamber has introduced two tracks for finding bad faith violations. In the first track, a bad faith violation of the Convention can be found if it can be proven that the illegitimate motivations are part of the decision making of the authorities right from the start. This was in fact what the case law said up until 2017. In the second track are those bad faith violations where bad faith is not present right from the start, but that it becomes a "predominant purpose" at other time alongside a legitimate purpose to restrict rights.[82] That is, the Court recognized that state authorities may have a singular, or a plurality, of purposes when restricting a Convention right, some legitimate and other ulterior and illegitimate. If there is a plurality of purposes what matters is whether, at any given time, the predominant purpose, based on the entirety of evidence, can be construed as a predominantly illegitimate purpose.[83] This has allowed the Court to adopt a "time slicing" approach in assessing evidence for bad faith violations. Even when the Court does not see itself having evidence of bad faith *ab initio*, it has, therefore held, that it will assess whether the evidence amounts to an article 18 violation in the course of the proceedings and events presented before it.

3.2 Article 18 Cases Under the New Standard of an Ongoing Assessment of Circumstantial Evidence Over Time

The circumstantial evidence paradigm, beyond reasonable doubt standard and the consideration of whether evidence reaches a threshold of proving ulterior illegitimate purposes over time have diversified the Court's case law on its assessment of evidence.

In *Navalny*, in 2018, the Grand Chamber followed the new *Merabishvili* standard in asking whether the suppression of dissent could be construed as a predominant ulterior motive of the authorities in the seven episodes of interference to right to assembly and in turn arrests that *Navalny* was subjected to. In this case, the Court closely associated itself with the time slicing approach, arguing that whilst in the earlier arrests of the applicant, there may have not been enough evidence of ulterior purpose, in the latter arrests, the evidence of bad faith became more plausible.[84] In

82 *Merabishvili* [GC] (n 2).
83 ibid.
84 *Navalny* [GC] (n 2).

this reasoning, the Court also pointed out that in the latter arrests of the applicant, the government did know that their actions were against the freedom of assembly standards of the Convention, as the Court delivered similar violation judgments only a short period before the arrests had taken place with respect to the same applicant in *Navalny and Yashin* and therefore, treated its case law as part of evidentiary assessments.[85] The Court also went beyond the repetitive nature of the arrests and highlighted that it was convinced by the corroborating contextual evidence that the case of the applicant was not an isolated incident and that public assemblies of a political nature and those of the political opposition leaders, in particular, were subject to increased restrictions in the Russian context.[86] It is in the light of this sequential pattern of evidence that the Court found an article 18 violation in the fifth and the sixth arrests of the applicant together with article 5, but not in the earlier arrests.

In *Demirtaş v Turkey* in December 2020, however, the Grand Chamber of the Court overturned the time slicing approach adopted by the Chamber. In this case, the Chamber agreed with the domestic courts that there was a reasonable suspicion to detain the applicant under article 5(1)(c) on his first day of detention, but it then held that the prolonged detention of the applicant under article 5(3) of the Convention had the ulterior purpose because this prevented him from taking part in Presidential elections. In so doing, the Chamber made use of speeches made by the President of Turkey and other government officials concerning the applicant and reports that in the aftermath of the declaration of the state of emergency in Turkey in June 2016, the political influence on the judiciary has significantly increased.[87] Relying on this general, broader finding, it held that an objective observer may reasonably doubt that Demirtaş, a presidential candidate in the 2017 elections, was kept in pretrial detention solely for legitimate reasons.[88] In contrast, the Grand Chamber, reassessed the totality of evidence at the beginning and during the course of the detention of Mr Demirtaş and held that the evidence taken as a whole was capable of proving predominant ulterior both on his first day of detention and at any time after that. In making this determination, the Grand Chamber relied on (a) the timing of the initial detention of the applicant, (b) the temporal links between the speeches of the President against the applicant and legal measures taken against him, and (c) return of the applicant to pretrial detention under a different charge, but based on the same facts.[89] In addition, the Grand Chamber also took into account evidence deduced from the general context. It found that

[85] *Navalny and Yashin v Russia* App no 76204/11 (ECtHR, 4 December 2014).

[86] ibid para 172.

[87] For a systematic exposure of the good faith doctrines of the ECtHR, see Gerards, *General Principles of the European Convention on Human Rights* (n 13).

[88] *Demirtaş* (n 2) para 273. But note that this case is pending before the Grand Chamber (GC) of the ECtHR.

[89] *Demirtaş* (n 2) paras 429–31, 432–33.

(1) the detention of the applicant was not an isolated case and was part of a broader pattern of legal measures taken against members of opposition, and (2) the well-documented concerns about the independence of judiciary, in particular as laid out by the Venice Commission.[90]

4. Proving Bad Faith: The Interplay Between Secondary and Primary Rules

Since its first violation judgment in 2004, the ECtHR has significantly transformed its case law under article 18 as a matter of secondary rules of evidence. The Court moved from direct and exacting standards of proof to circumstantial evidence and the beyond reasonable doubt standard. The Court's handling of circumstantial evidence has also seen significant changes over time. Whilst the Court first started to admit circumstantial evidence immediately surrounding facts such as the close temporal links between political speeches and judicial measures, it has since expanded its understanding of circumstantial evidence to cover evidence that can be deduced from long term and broader contexts predating or corresponding with the individual restriction itself. Over time, therefore, the outlook of circumstantial evidence has expanded. On what can be admitted as circumstantial evidence of the broader context, the Court has also shown increased openness to evidence that seeks to establish that a restriction of the Convention rights is not an isolated instance, but flows from motives that can be deduced from the health of human rights protections, rule of law and democracy in a particular country. For the Court, such motivational context can be adduced from multiple sources. These include international human rights reports of intergovernmental organizations and NGOs as well as domestic media reports concerning the treatment of the larger group that the individual belongs to. The Court, for example, has pointed to the treatment of opposition politicians,[91] and the treatment of NGOs and human rights defenders more generally[92] in its case law as evidenced by international reports, reports by Council of Europe organs, domestic media outlets and statements made by government figures.

In addition, the Court has also started to rely on its own case law and substantive standards developed therein as evidence. In *Navalny*, for example, the Court used its previous case law on findings of freedom of assembly violations in Russia to argue that a lack of knowledge of Convention standards cannot have a probative value.[93] Similarly in *Aliyev v Azerbaijan*, the Court referred to its previous findings

[90] ibid paras 426–28, 434.
[91] *Navalny* [GC] (n 2) para 172; *Demirtaş* (n 2) paras 426–28.
[92] *Jafarov* (n 2) paras 81–84.
[93] *Navalny* [GC] (n 2) para 149.

of article 18 violations against Azerbaijan as evidence.[94] This trend of the Court using its case law as part of the totality of evidence, however, is not consistent. As seen in the multiple dissenting opinions of Judge Kuris in a series of Turkish cases which did not find a violation of article 18 in conjunction with article 5 after the Grand Chamber judgment in *Demirtaş*, judges of the Court are in disagreement as to how much the broader context of rights restrictions count in making assessments in individual cases.[95]

These significant innovations in the reformulation of the secondary rules of evidentiary standards cannot be treated in isolation from the development of the primary rules of the Convention as well as the good faith presumption. A key development, in this respect, is the Court's gradual embracing of the notion that, in the context of the decay of rule of law and democratic societies that has gained pace in the past decades in Europe, the Convention may be violated in good faith as well as in bad faith in some of its member states. In this respect, the Court is sensitive to the broader political developments in Europe and in response to such developments, it has chosen to move away from its exacting direct evidence requirements. A central innovation in terms of the primary rules of the case law is the spelling out of the ulterior motives of states. The Court has identified that ulterior motives can be both political and economic.[96] In both cases, the Court is now accepting that rights restrictions may serve the calculated political or economic goals of ruling regimes and that state authorities use domestic laws and domestic judicial procedures for their own gain. The Court now also openly acknowledges that the use of domestic law and judicial actions can serve the aim of intimidating applicants,[97] to secure a certain economic benefit,[98] or to silence or punish individuals who are seen as threats against by the ruling regimes.[99]

The shifts in the secondary rules thus capture fundamental changes that have taken place in the political regimes of the court's member states, which include embracing forms of authoritarian legalism, rule by men and women as opposed to rule of law. It is, therefore, no coincidence that the article 18 case law of the Court thus far is primarily focused on the treatment of dissent and judicial harassment.

[94] *Aliyev* (n 2) paras 212–15.

[95] See the dissenting opinion of Judge Kūris protesting that the majority did not find an art 18 violation in the cases of *Sabuncu v Turkey* App no 23199/17 (ECtHR, 10 November 2020); *Şık v Turkey (No 2)* App no 36493/17 (ECtHR, 24 November 2020); and *Ahmet Hüsrev Altan v Turkey* App no 13252/17 (ECtHR, 13 April 2021).

[96] *Khodorkovskiy* (n 25) para 254; *OAO Neftyanaya Kompaniya Yukos* (n 49) para 665; *Khodorkovskiy and Lebedev* (n 49) para 889; *Nastase v Romania (dec)* App no 80563/12 (ECtHR, 18 November 2014), para 109; *Tchankotadze v Georgia* App no 15256/05 (ECtHR, 21 June 2016), para 114; *Merabishvili* (n 2) para 332.

[97] *Gusinskiy* (n 2) para 76; *Cebotari* (n 2) para 53; *Merabishvili* [GC] (n 2) para 353; *Dochnal v Poland* App no 31622/07 (ECtHR, 18 September 2012), para 116.

[98] *Khodorkovskiy* (n 25) para 254; *OAO Neftyanaya Kompaniya Yukos* (n 49) para 665.

[99] *Ramishvili and Kokhreidze v Georgia (dec)* App no 1704/06 (ECtHR, 27 June 2007); *Lutsenko* (n 2) para 109; *Tymoshenko* (n 2) para 299; *Mammadov* (n 2) para 143; *Jafarov* (n 2) para 162; *Mammadli* (n 2) para 104; *Hasanov* (n 2) para 125.

In the first ever infringement judgment that the Court has delivered, the reinstatement of the Court's zero tolerance approach to the prohibition of ulterior motives has also seen important developments in the remedial case law of the Court. In this case, the Court has held that domestic decisions made in violation of article 18 of the Convention should be "vitiated" as a matter of the Convention.[100] Furthermore, states cannot enjoy a margin of appreciation when it comes to remedial action to remove the consequences of Convention violations if their motives in bringing about such violations were ulterior ones.

5. Conclusion

The recent case law of the ECtHR no longer coheres with the view that it is notoriously difficult to prove bad faith when adjudicating international treaties.[101] This is a significant development not only for European human rights law but also for international law more generally.

The ECtHR has had a bumpy ride in recalibrating its secondary rules of evidence for proving bad faith against the backdrop of significant decay in rule of law guarantees in the Council of Europe member states. The Court's innovations in its evidentiary rules could not have been possible without the existence of the primary rule concerning the prohibition of abuse of power in article 18 of the Convention. Yet, it was the rise in the legal-policy significance of this primary norm in Europe that has led to further developments in the secondary rules of evidence, leading to adoption of less demanding standards of evidence.

This chapter has shown the development of secondary rules of adjudication with respect to article 18 of the ECHR cannot be seen in isolation from the interpretive context of the primary rules at stake. What is more, these developments cannot be qualified as mere technicalities and they go into the heart of how violations of the ECHR are established. The normative implications of the new secondary rules of evidence are broad. They enable the Court to openly identify and criticize the motives of state authorities when restricting rights. Yet, this development is not immune from the standard criticisms regarding the difficulty of proving bad faith under international law. The embrace of broader contexts as part of circumstantial evidence in particular inevitably blurs the boundary between political criticism and legal reasoning and between adjudication and naming and shaming. Whilst the new secondary rules of the Court, which allow it to delve into a review of motives allows it to speak truth to power, the risk of politicization of what seemed to be less politically contentious forms of judicial decision making under good faith review cannot be underestimated. One may argue that the strength of the

[100] *Mammadov (Infringement proceedings)* (n 52) paras (i)(a), (ii)(a).
[101] Pozen (n 9) 910. See also references cited at (n 17).

European Convention system can withhold the pressure from states whose political and economic motives are now subject to stronger forms of the review by the Court, thanks to its new standards of evidence. The new bad faith review standard of the ECtHR may also inspire other human rights courts and quasi-judicial bodies to not only review actions or omissions, but also motivations of states when restricting rights. Whether a review of states' motives through this new paradigm of secondary rules can get a foot in the door in international law adjudication more generally, remains to be seen.

11

The Evidentiary Implications of a Party's Non-Participation in the Proceedings

*Christopher Lentz**

Notwithstanding the proliferation of international courts and tribunals, it remains unexceptional for a party to decline to participate in proceedings before them. This poses a challenge to international adjudicators who, once satisfied that they are appropriately exercising jurisdiction, must determine how to resolve the merits of the case, despite being deprived of arguments and evidence from the non-participant.

Like other secondary rules, those concerning non-participation can have substantial implications for how individual cases are resolved, despite there being no inherent relationship between non-participation and the underlying merits. If the applicable secondary rules called for a stay of proceedings, a default judgment, or a shifting of the burden of proof, then they would be tantamount to a dispositive determination of the case, regardless of whether they were dressed up as technical procedural rules. Conversely, if the approach taken is less absolute in terms of outcome, the international body must then resolve further secondary rule issues of potentially similar magnitude: whether to consider only the material placed before it by the litigating party or whether instead to look outside the evidentiary record and, if the latter, how far to go in seeking out external material.

As non-participation in international fora has become more frequent in recent decades, it has also become ever more important to understand the secondary rules applicable to these cases when they arise. A comprehensive search was therefore performed of every international court, body, and panel that hears cases arising from inter-state disputes, international human rights law, international administrative law, international trade law, and international criminal law.[1]

* This chapter was prepared in my personal capacity, and the views reflected herein do not necessarily represent those of any organization with which I am or have been affiliated.

[1] Others may wish to build upon this chapter by examining bodies that are more regional, supranational, or national in nature. An even-handed assessment of these other bodies, however, is not within the scope of this chapter, nor could one be accommodated in light of limitations on length. With respect to the field of international environmental law, it does not have a dedicated dispute resolution mechanism, and cases are instead brought before other international fora that have been canvassed here. The sole exception to this chapter's comprehensive assessment of international bodies is the Human Rights Committee, for which a non-exhaustive search of hundreds of cases identified sixty examples of non-participation since 2000.

Christopher Lentz, *The Evidentiary Implications of a Party's Non-Participation in the Proceedings* In: *Secondary Rules of Primary Importance in International Law.* Edited by: Gábor Kajtár, Başak Çalı, and Marko Milanovic, Oxford University Press.
 DOI: 10.1093/oso/9780192869012.003.0011

Notably, not one of these fields has been immune from having to face a party's non-participation. Although there is one case from international trade law and two from international criminal law that fall within the scope of this chapter, they are not given detailed consideration here because of the limited guidance they offer as to how international adjudicators address non-participation.[2] Instead, this chapter focuses on those fields where non-participation has been most extensive and where the secondary rules surrounding non-participation are most developed.

Section 1 addresses inter-state disputes and the international bodies to have faced non-participation to date (the ICJ, PCA, and ITLOS),[3] section 2 likewise examines international human rights law (CCPR, CAT, and CEDAW Committee),[4] and section 3 discusses international administrative law and its experiences with non-participation (UNAT).[5] Section 4 then identifies uniform features in how secondary rules concerning non-participation are employed by international decision-makers, before focusing on the divergence seen among the approaches. The principal difference concerns the willingness of the international body to go beyond the strict confines of the record to identify and assess both legal arguments and evidentiary material as it reaches a conclusion about the merits of the case. Section 4 also offers some reasons that might account for this divergence before proposing that the best explanation is grounded in the language used in the constitutive documents of each international body. In light of the role being played by these foundational texts, this chapter suggests that, in the future, those creating international dispute resolution mechanisms or modifying how they function should pay attention to how the legal framework addresses non-participation. This is discussed, with concluding remarks, in section 5.

[2] For international trade law, see World Trade Organization (WTO) *EC—Bananas III (Article 21.5—EC)* (Panel Report) WT/DS27/RW/EEC (12 April 1999) (this case has a unique procedural history before the WTO, and the Panel Report has no legal status because it is unadopted) (WTO *EC—Bananas III (Article 21.5—EC)* Panel Report). With respect to international criminal law, see *Prosecutor v Ayyash et al* (Redacted Version of the Amended Consolidated Indictment) STL-11-01/T/TC/F2640/A03 (12 July 2016) (the Special Tribunal for Lebanon was proceeding *in absentia* against four persons and had yet to reach the judgment stage at the time of writing, making it difficult to glean anything conclusive about its evidentiary approach to non-participation); *Trial of the Major War Criminals before the International Military Tribunal* (Judgment) (30 September–1 October 1946) vol XXII Blue Series 411 [585]–[587] (the International Military Tribunal proceeded *in absentia* against Martin Bormann, but the judgment is from a different era and touches only briefly on the non-participation aspect) (IMT *Major War Criminals* Judgment).

[3] These are the International Court of Justice (ICJ), the Permanent Court of Arbitration (PCA), and the International Tribunal for the Law of the Sea (ITLOS).

[4] These refer to the Human Rights Committee (CCPR), the Committee against Torture (CAT), and the Committee on the Elimination of Discrimination Against Women (CEDAW Committee).

[5] This is the United Nations Appeals Tribunal (UNAT).

1. Non-Participation in Inter-State Disputes: ICJ, PCA, and ITLOS

The most high-profile instances of non-participation before international courts and tribunals have arisen in inter-state dispute resolution. Some decades ago, the ICJ was in the vanguard in formulating how to approach a party's non-participation in the proceedings, but in recent years this issue has flourished before the PCA and ITLOS. Each institution, however, has addressed non-participation in different ways, as set out below.

1.1 Non-Participation Before the ICJ

The ICJ has rendered eleven judgments in which one of the parties did not participate,[6] the most recent being the 1986 merits judgment in *Military and Paramilitary Activities in and against Nicaragua* (*Nicaragua*). As this judgment is the one in which the ICJ most thoroughly elaborates its approach to non-participation, it will be the focus here.

After the United States (US) stopped participating following the ICJ's judgment on jurisdiction,[7] the ICJ promptly dismissed the notion of entering a default judgment on the merits, for its Statute required the Court to "satisfy itself" that the claim of the participating party was "well founded in fact and law."[8] This "implie[d] that the Court must attain the same degree of certainty as in any other case that the

[6] *Military and Paramilitary Activities in and against Nicaragua (Nicaragua v United States)* (Merits Judgment of 27 June 1986) [1986] ICJ Rep 14 (ICJ *Nicaragua* Judgment on Merits); *United States Diplomatic and Consular Staff in Tehran (United States v Iran)* (Judgment of 24 May 1980) [1980] ICJ Rep 3; *Aegean Sea Continental Shelf (Greece v Turkey)* (Judgment of 19 December 1978) [1978] ICJ Rep 3; *Nuclear Tests (New Zealand v France)* (Judgment of 20 December 1974) [1974] ICJ Rep 457 (ICJ *Nuclear Tests (New Zealand v France)* Judgment); *Nuclear Tests (Australia v France)* (Judgment of 20 December 1974) [1974] ICJ Rep 253 (ICJ *Nuclear Tests (Australia v France)* Judgment); *Fisheries Jurisdiction (Germany v Iceland)* (Merits Judgment of 25 July 1974) [1974] ICJ Rep 175; *Fisheries Jurisdiction (United Kingdom v Iceland)* (Merits Judgment of 25 July 1974) [1974] ICJ Rep 3; *Fisheries Jurisdiction (Germany v Iceland)* (Jurisdiction Judgment of 2 February 1973) [1973] ICJ Rep 49; *Fisheries Jurisdiction (United Kingdom v Iceland)* (Jurisdiction Judgment of 2 February 1973) [1973] ICJ Rep 3; *Nottebohm (Liechtenstein v Guatemala)* (Preliminary Objection Judgment of 18 November 1953) [1953] ICJ Rep 111; *Corfu Channel (United Kingdom v Albania)* (Compensation Judgment of 15 December 1949) [1949] ICJ Rep 244. For the *Nicaragua*, *Nottebohm*, and *Corfu Channel* judgments cited here, both parties had participated in an earlier or later aspect of the proceedings. This list does not include instances where a party did not participate in discrete portions of the ICJ proceedings but was identified in the judgment as having been represented, as well as any instances of non-participation in an advisory opinion.

[7] See ICJ *Nicaragua* Judgment on Merits (n 6) [8]–[10], [17].

[8] ibid [28]; ICJ Statute, art 53 (providing that "[w]henever one of the parties does not appear before the Court, or fails to defend its case, the other party may call upon the Court to decide in favour of its claim," but that before doing so "[t]he Court must […] satisfy itself, not only that it has jurisdiction […] but also that the claim is well founded in fact and law").

claim of the party appearing is sound in law, and, so far as the nature of the case permits, that the facts on which it is based are supported by convincing evidence."[9]

With regard to factual issues that need to be resolved based on an incomplete record, the ICJ considered that it is "not bound to confine its consideration to the material formally submitted to it by the parties."[10] In this respect, the ICJ had previously affirmed that when one side does not appear, it is particularly important for the Court to satisfy itself that it has all the available facts at its disposal.[11] Yet the ICJ recognized that its own efforts to obtain information were an imperfect substitute, and that its mastery of the factual matters would necessarily be limited.[12] The Court therefore noted that the non-participating party not only surrenders the ability to present evidence in its favor, but also "forfeits the opportunity to counter the factual allegations of its opponent."[13]

The ICJ astutely observed a phenomenon that describes not only its own experience but also inter-state disputes in other fora: that "[t]hough formally absent from the proceedings, the party in question frequently submits to the Court letters and documents, in ways and by means not contemplated by the Rules."[14] In *Nicaragua* at the merits stage, the ICJ noted that it had the benefit of the parties' earlier pleadings,[15] which had been rather extensive.[16] Moreover, the US had circulated to the ICJ a document concerning its policy towards Nicaragua, which the Court was willing to take into account.[17] In light of these communications, the ICJ sought to strike a balance between taking into account the views expressed by the non-participant, while ensuring that the Court did not approach this information in a way that rewarded non-appearance and unduly disadvantaged the appearing party.[18]

Indeed, the ICJ not only referred to external material to ascertain the position of the US, but also went to great lengths to adjudicate the counter-arguments contained therein, even if they had not been expressly put before the Court for its consideration on the merits.[19] It was no empty exercise either, for the ICJ ruled

[9] ICJ *Nicaragua* Judgment on Merits (n 6) [29].
[10] ibid [30].
[11] ICJ *Nuclear Tests (New Zealand v France)* Judgment (n 6) [32]; ICJ *Nuclear Tests (Australia v France)* Judgment (n 6) [31].
[12] ICJ *Nicaragua* Judgment on Merits (n 6) [30], [57].
[13] ibid [30].
[14] ibid [31].
[15] ibid [28].
[16] See eg *Military and Paramilitary Activities in and against Nicaragua (Nicaragua v United States)* ICJ Pleadings vol II (Counter-Memorial of the United States), <https://www.icj-cij.org/public/files/case-related/70/9627.pdf>.
[17] ICJ *Nicaragua* Judgment on Merits (n 6) [73]; Document Informally Made Available to Members of the Court by the United States Information Office in The Hague <https://www.icj-cij.org/public/files/case-related/70/9633.pdf>.
[18] ICJ *Nicaragua* Judgment on Merits (n 6) [31], [59].
[19] ibid [126], [128]–[131], [140]–[142], [146], [161]–[163], [173]–[174], [180], [187], [190], [201], [224], [229], [248], [280].

in favor of the US on a possible key issue.[20] Non-participation did not necessarily entail non-success, even on factual matters. Moreover, the ICJ expressly referred to the non-participation of the US before engaging, *proprio motu*, in an enquiry into other legal positions that might have justified certain activities by the US,[21] even if this ultimately proved fruitless in that case.[22]

The *Nicaragua* Merits Judgment, at one time, looked as if it represented the culmination of non-participation before the ICJ. But after more than thirty years, the ICJ is facing this issue once more,[23] providing the Court with another opportunity to contribute to the development of the secondary rules governing a party's non-participation.

1.2 Non-Participation Before the PCA

By contrast, arbitral tribunals undertaken before the PCA have only experienced a state's non-participation in recent times. Despite there being no such cases for its first 100 years, the PCA has seen eight instances of non-participation in the past decade. Three of these occurrences were in investor-state arbitration cases that ended in non-public awards, and as a result they are not considered here. The other five instances arose in two cases of inter-state arbitration—*Arctic Sunrise* and *South China Sea*—initiated under the United Nations Convention on the Law of the Sea (UNCLOS). In both those cases, the Arbitral Tribunal identified, solicited, and obtained extensive evidentiary material and arguments to assist its decision-making process.

In *Arctic Sunrise*, and in parallel to litigation before ITLOS that is addressed below, the Netherlands initiated arbitration in 2013 over the detention of a ship and its crew.[24] But after the Arbitral Tribunal invited the parties to comment on the procedure, Russia informed the PCA that it would not be taking part in the arbitration.[25] Uniquely for inter-state dispute resolution, no further information was received from the non-participating state, at least not in a way that could be taken into account in detail by the decision-makers.[26]

[20] ibid [163]–[164].

[21] ibid [201].

[22] ibid [209], [211], [268]–[270], [292].

[23] See *Relocation of the United States Embassy to Jerusalem (Palestine v United States)* (Order of 15 November 2018) [2018] ICJ Rep 708 [709]; *Arbitral Award of 3 October 1899 (Guyana v Venezuela)* (Order of 19 June 2018) [2018] ICJ Rep 402 [403].

[24] *Arctic Sunrise Arbitration (Netherlands v Russia)* PCA Case No 2014-02 (Award on Jurisdiction) (26 November 2014) [3], [7]–[8] (PCA *Arctic Sunrise* Award on Jurisdiction).

[25] ibid [17], [19].

[26] See *Arctic Sunrise Arbitration (Netherlands v Russia)* PCA Case No 2014-02 (Award on Compensation) (10 July 2017) [5], [8]; *Arctic Sunrise Arbitration (Netherlands v Russia)* PCA Case No 2014-02 (Award on the Merits) (14 August 2015) [6]–[7], [18] (PCA *Arctic Sunrise* Award on Merits); PCA *Arctic Sunrise* Award on Jurisdiction (n 24) [48]. One week before the Award on the Merits, Russia delivered a position paper to the Arbitral Tribunal, which decided to take no formal action on the

This left the Arbitral Tribunal in a difficult position, as it was deprived of Russia's views on the underlying factual and legal issues, including any response to the arguments proffered by the Netherlands.[27] Recalling the UNCLOS provision that in the event of a party's absence, "the arbitral tribunal must satisfy itself not only that it has jurisdiction over the dispute but also that the claim is well founded in fact and law,"[28] the arbitrators took various measures to obtain the information that they considered necessary to perform their functions.[29]

The Tribunal considered that it was "required" by the UNCLOS provision to rely not only on evidence received from the participating state, but also to "ma[k]e use of the primary sources available to it."[30] This included dozens of video recordings, more than 1000 photographs, the vessel's logbook, and a range of documents from Russian proceedings.[31] Moreover, the Tribunal obtained and relied upon a number of Russian laws and regulations,[32] while also referring to various websites that were publicly accessible.[33] Finally, the Tribunal directed multiple questions both to the Netherlands and to testifying witnesses.[34] Notably, even though the Arbitral Tribunal recognized that the evidence was not comprehensive,[35] it was not dissuaded from making exceptionally detailed factual findings on what had taken place in the matter before it.[36]

Likewise in *South China Sea*, the Arbitral Tribunal started its assessment of China's non-participation by quoting the text of UNCLOS on the effect of a party's absence.[37] In light of this text, the arbitrators expressly affirmed that they would not be discontinuing the proceedings, rendering a default judgment, or simply adopting as accurate the uncontested claims from the appearing party, the Philippines.[38]

paper for a few reasons, including that it was "satisfied that the relevant issues are fully addressed in this Award": see PCA *Arctic Sunrise* Award on Merits (n 26) [68].

27 PCA *Arctic Sunrise* Award on Merits (n 26) [19].
28 ibid [11] (quoting UNCLOS, Annex VII, art 9).
29 ibid [19].
30 ibid [71].
31 ibid.
32 ibid [66], [71], [218].
33 ibid, fns 25, 28, 76, 81, 93, 102, 121, 125, 200, 223, 227–228, 265, 282, 284, 296, 299, 301, 330, 332.
34 ibid [58], [60], [62], [72].
35 ibid [73].
36 ibid [70], [74]–[139], [250], [256]–[257], [263]–[266], [270]–[275], [314]–[322].
37 *South China Sea Arbitration (Philippines v China)* PCA Case No 2013-19 (Award) (12 July 2016) [12], [117] (quoting UNCLOS, Annex VII, art 9) (PCA *South China Sea* Award on Merits); *South China Sea Arbitration (Philippines v China)* PCA Case No 20213-19 (Award on Jurisdiction and Admissibility) (29 October 2015) [11]–[12], [113] (quoting UNCLOS, Annex VII, art 9) (PCA *South China Sea* Award on Jurisdiction).
38 PCA *South China Sea* Award on Merits (n 37) [12], [129]; PCA *South China Sea* Award on Jurisdiction (n 37) [11]–[12].

Instead, the Arbitral Tribunal "actively sought to satisfy itself" and remained "particularly vigilant" in discharging its duties.[39] The Tribunal's task was facilitated by China's ongoing provision of material relating to the arbitration proceedings,[40] allowing the arbitrators to use that material to discern China's position on various claims advanced by the Philippines.[41]

Even with the benefit of these views, the Arbitral Tribunal still sought out further arguments and evidence. At the jurisdiction phase, the arbitrators not only asked the Philippines for additional submissions and documentation, but also considered *proprio motu* possible barriers to jurisdiction that had not been raised by China.[42]

Similarly at the merits stage, the Tribunal acknowledged that although the UNCLOS provision on non-participation does not shift the burden or standard of proof, China's absence nevertheless prompted further steps in order to "test the evidence provided by the Philippines and to augment the record."[43] The Arbitral Tribunal therefore questioned the counsel and experts for the Philippines multiple times, retained its own independent experts for technical matters, and solicited additional evidence to complement the record, on which it invited comments from both parties.[44] While the arbitrators ruled in favor of the Philippines on most every point, it was not a complete victory for the participating state, as the PCA-administered panel considered there was insufficient evidence to enter a factual finding on one of the claims made by the Philippines.[45]

1.3 Non-Participation Before ITLOS

ITLOS's experience with non-participation has also come recently, first in the 2013 *Arctic Sunrise* case and, again, six years later in *Three Ukrainian Naval Vessels*, both of which concerned provisional measures. This subsection will focus largely on the former case, as it more clearly demonstrates the Tribunal's approach to non-participation.

In *Arctic Sunrise*, the Netherlands sought an order for Russia to release a detained vessel and its crew.[46] Given Russia's absence from the proceedings, ITLOS

[39] PCA *South China Sea* Award on Merits (n 37) [15]; PCA *South China Sea* Award on Jurisdiction (n 37) [13].

[40] PCA *South China Sea* Award on Merits (n 37) [13], [37], [42], [51], [53], [61], [82], [96]–[97], [100], [102]–[103].

[41] ibid [18]; PCA *South China Sea* Award on Jurisdiction (n 37) [14], [19].

[42] PCA *South China Sea* Award on Merits (n 37) [15]; PCA *South China Sea* Award on Jurisdiction (n 37) [13]–[15], [179], [190], [256]–[258], [274]–[276], [292]–[293], [303]–[304], [311]–[313], [357]–[360], [367]–[373], [392].

[43] PCA *South China Sea* Award on Merits (n 37) [131].

[44] ibid [15], [131]–[141].

[45] ibid [975], [1203].

[46] *Arctic Sunrise (Netherlands v Russia)* ITLOS Case No 22 (Provisional Measures Order) (22 November 2013) [1], [33]–[35], [86] (ITLOS *Arctic Sunrise* Order).

observed that it needed to guarantee the procedural rights of both sides, including that they be treated equally and that the appearing side was not put at a disadvantage by the other party's absence.[47] This proved to be a challenge,[48] prompting the Tribunal to consider that it must assess the matter on "the best available evidence."[49] Just where this standard came from, and just what it means, were not elucidated. Although ITLOS repeated this principle in *Three Ukrainian Naval Vessels*, it offered no elaboration of its contours there either.[50]

In *Arctic Sunrise*, at least, "the best available evidence" meant only information of which the Tribunal was made aware by the parties. For instance, in order to determine that there was a dispute under its jurisdiction, ITLOS identified Russia's position from a *note verbale* received by the Tribunal.[51] Likewise, when granting provisional measures, the Tribunal relied not only on uncontested statements from the Netherlands, but also on a Russian judicial order and official report on the seizure of the vessel, both of which had been annexed by the Netherlands to its initial request to ITLOS.[52]

In contrast to *Arctic Sunrise*, Russia's non-participation in *Three Ukrainian Naval Vessels* was more measured. While Russia did not participate in the hearing on provisional measures, it still communicated ahead of time both written observations and translations of relevant material for ITLOS's benefit.[53] Despite these overtures, ITLOS still considered that Russia had absented itself from the proceedings.[54] Nevertheless, the Tribunal benefitted from having the non-participant's views and referred to them regularly in deciding the matter before it,[55] a situation that has recurred throughout inter-state disputes.

2. Non-Participation in International Human Rights Law: CCPR, CAT, and CEDAW Committee

Human rights cases heard by international bodies feature a less expansive process to non-participation by a respondent state. Lacking a response on the merits, international committee members declare that they will give "due weight" to the allegations "to the extent that they have been properly substantiated." Such language has been applied by multiple United Nations (UN) treaty bodies, and it evinces an

[47] ibid [53], [56].
[48] ibid [55].
[49] ibid [57].
[50] *Detention of Three Ukrainian Naval Vessels (Ukraine v Russia)* ITLOS Case No 26 (Provisional Measures Order) (25 May 2019) [29] (ITLOS *Three Ukrainian Naval Vessels* Order).
[51] ITLOS *Arctic Sunrise* Order (n 46) [65], [68].
[52] ibid [87]–[92]; *Arctic Sunrise (Netherlands v Russia)* ITLOS Case No 22 (Request for the Prescription of Provisional Measures) (21 October 2013) [10]–[11].
[53] ITLOS *Three Ukrainian Naval Vessels* Order (n 50) [8], [12]–[13], [21].
[54] ibid [29].
[55] ibid [50]–[54], [68], [73], [84]–[85], [107]–[108], [117].

approach to deciding claims based solely on the information that has been placed before them by the parties.

At the time of writing, all complaints adjudicated by UN treaty bodies have been initiated through individual complaints against a state party to the relevant convention or protocol. A non-exhaustive search identified more than sixty examples since 2000 where one party—inherently the respondent state—did not participate in any aspect of the proceedings.[56] Almost all of these cases concerned complaints before the CCPR that alleged non-compliance with the International Covenant on Civil and Political Rights (ICCPR). Three examples were also identified from the CAT,[57] and one case of non-participation has arisen before the CEDAW Committee.[58]

For the most part, the CCPR cases follow a consistent pattern. After summarizing the allegations of the complaining author, the CCPR comments on the state's lack of cooperation. This is mostly formulaic, with the CCPR affirming some variation of the standard that absent a reply from the state, "due weight must be given to the author's allegations, to the extent that they have been properly substantiated,"[59] before turning to admissibility and merits.

Although this "due weight" standard does not reflect a high hurdle for the claimant, it also does not translate into an automatic victory for the aggrieved author. Particularly with regard to the threshold issue of admissibility, the CCPR has exhibited a willingness to find specific claims inadmissible—notwithstanding silence from the respondent state—be it on legal or jurisdictional grounds,[60] for being insufficiently substantiated,[61] or for a mixture of the two.[62] Indeed, in three cases where the state remained absent from the proceedings, the CCPR deemed

[56] Citations for thirty-one of these cases are provided below, the remainder being omitted from this chapter due to limitations on length.

[57] *Guerrero Larez v Venezuela* (Decision) CAT/C/54/D/456/2011 (15 May 2015) (CAT *Guerrero Larez* Decision); *Ntikarahera v Burundi* (Decision) CAT/C/52/D/503/2012 (12 May 2014) (CAT *Ntikarahera* Decision); *Bendib v Algeria* (Decision) CAT/C/51/D/376/2009 (8 November 2013) (CAT *Bendib* Decision).

[58] *X v Timor-Leste* (Views) CEDAW/C/69/D/88/2015 (26 February 2018) (CEDAW *X* Views).

[59] *Barkovsky v Belarus* (Views) CCPR/C/123/D/2247/2013 (13 July 2018) [4] (CCPR *Barkovsky* Views). See also *Belamrania v Algeria* (Views) CCPR/C/118/D/2157/2012 (27 October 2016) [6.1]; *Bee and Obiang v Equatorial Guinea* (Views) CCPR/C/85/D/1152&1190/2003 (31 October 2005) [4]; *Rolando v Philippines* (Views) CCPR/C/82/D/1110/2002 (3 November 2004) [4.1] (CCPR *Rolando* Views).

[60] See *Khelifati v Algeria* (Views) CCPR/C/120/D/2267/2013 (28 July 2017) [5.4] (CCPR *Khelifati* Views); *Saidova v Tajikistan* (Views) CCPR/C/81/D/964/2001 (8 July 2004) [5.3] (CCPR *Saidova* Views).

[61] See eg *Sannikov v Belarus* (Views) CCPR/C/122/D/2212/2012 (6 April 2018) [5.4] (CCPR *Sannikov* Views); *El Hojouj Jum'a et al v Libya* (Views) CCPR/C/111/D/1958/2010 (21 July 2014) [5.3]–[5.4] (CCPR *El Hojouj Jum'a et al* Views); *Torobekov v Kyrgyzstan* (Views) CCPR/C/103/D/1547/2007 (27 October 2011) [5.3]–[5.7] (CCPR *Torobekov* Views); *Kurbonov v Tajikistan* (Views) CCPR/C/86/D/1208/2003 (16 March 2006) [5.3] (CCPR *Kurbonov* Views); *Mulezi v Democratic Republic of the Congo* (Views) CCPR/C/81/D/962/2001 (8 July 2004) [4.4] (CCPR *Mulezi* Views).

[62] See *Lumbala Tshidika v Democratic Republic of the Congo* (Views) CCPR/C/115/D/2214/2012 (5 November 2015) [5.4]–[5.5]; *Gorji-Dinka v Cameroon* (Views) CCPR/C/83/D/1134/2002 (17 March 2005) [4.4]–[4.8], [4.10]; CCPR *Rolando* Views (n 59) [4.4]–[4.5].

all the claims to be inadmissible and consequently took no further action on the allegations.[63]

But claims that do get considered on their merits are generally sustained "[i]n the absence of any information from the State party."[64] While the CCPR might appreciate receiving corroborative evidence such as contemporaneous press clippings and a documented medical history,[65] such detail is hardly necessary to substantiate a claim. In one perfunctory example, the CCPR merely "note[d] the author's allegation" about what happened to his father, before concluding that "[i]n the absence of any relevant information from the State party which might contradict the author's allegations, the Committee considers that the facts laid before it reveal a violation."[66] In another case, the CCPR noted that the state did not contest allegations of torture, arbitrary arrest, and inhumane conditions of imprisonment, and for each of these allegations "due weight must be given to them and it must be assumed that the events occurred as described by the author."[67]

The CCPR bases this approach on the constitutive document giving it jurisdiction over such complaints, the ICCPR Optional Protocol, which informs the Committee that the complaints must be considered "in the light of all written information made available to it by the individual and by the State Party concerned."[68] Reflecting this mandate, the CCPR frequently couches its conclusions in light of the information before it,[69] and largely limits its consideration to material provided by the parties. The same practice is also seen in both the CAT and the CEDAW Committee,[70] whose individual complaint mechanisms were established by agreements that similarly require them to consider the complaints "in the light of all information made available to it by or on behalf of" the complainant(s) and the state concerned.[71]

[63] See *NDM v Democratic Republic of the Congo* (Decision) CCPR/C/113/D/1971/2010 (30 March 2015) [5.4]–[6] (CCPR *NDM* Decision); *Tiyagarajah v Sri Lanka* (Decision) CCPR/C/98/D/1523/2006 (19 March 2010) [5.2]–[5.4] (CCPR *Tiyagarajah* Decision); *NT v Kyrgyzstan* (Decision) CCPR/C/98/D/1522/2006 [5.2]–[6] (19 March 2010) (CCPR *NT* Decision).

[64] CCPR *Barkovsky* Views (n 59) [6.5]. See also *Al-Rabassi v Libya* (Views) CCPR/C/111/D/1860/2009 (18 July 2014) [7.4], [7.7] (CCPR *Al-Rabassi* Views); *Gunan v Kyrgyzstan* (Views) CCPR/C/102/D/1545/2007 (25 July 2011) [6.3].

[65] See *McCallum v South Africa* (Views) CCPR/C/100/D/1818/2008 (25 October 2010) [6.2]–[6.4], [6.7]–[6.8].

[66] *Basongo Bondonga v Democratic Republic of the Congo* (Views) CCPR/C/96/D/1483/2006 (30 July 2009) [6.2].

[67] *Vargas Más v Peru* (Views) CCPR/C/85/D/1058/2002 (26 October 2005) [6.1]–[6.3].

[68] Optional Protocol to the ICCPR, art 5(1) (ICCPR Optional Protocol).

[69] See eg CCPR *Barkovsky* Views (n 59) [6.1], [6.5]; CCPR *Sannikov* Views (n 61) [6.1], [6.4]; *Kitenge Baruani v Democratic Republic of the Congo* (Views) CCPR/C/110/D/1890/2009 (27 March 2014) [6.1], [6.4].

[70] See CEDAW *X* Views (n 58) [4], [5.2]–[5.4], [5.6], [6.1]; CAT *Guerrero Larez* Decision (n 57) [4], [5.2], [6.1], [6.6]–[6.8], [6.10]; CAT *Ntikarahera* Decision (n 57) [4], [5.2]–[6.2], [6.6]; CAT *Bendib* Decision (n 57) [4], [5.2]–[6.2], [6.5]–[6.6].

[71] Convention Against Torture and Other Cruel, Inhuman or Degrading Treatment or Punishment, art 22(4) (Convention against Torture); Optional Protocol to the Convention on the Elimination of All Forms of Discrimination against Women, art 7(1) (CEDAW Optional Protocol).

Yet, in three instances, the CCPR has gone beyond the information made available to it by the parties and expressly incorporated insight gleaned through other aspects of the Committee's work.[72] Those references were brief, unnecessary in the context of the cases, and have not been repeated in more recent determinations even when they involved the same state as a non-participant.[73] But they nevertheless suggest that another factor might have been at issue. In all three cases, the CCPR observed that the respondent state is often the sole party with access to necessary information, raising the possibility that the CCPR's decision-making function might be especially impacted by non-participation.[74] Similar language in other non-participation cases, however, did not entail recourse to additional material.[75] Whatever the reason, these three instances appear to be outliers to the otherwise consistent manner in which UN treaty bodies apply secondary rules when faced with a party's non-participation.

3. Non-Participation in International Administrative Law: UNAT

A wider range of approaches can be identified in the field of administrative law, when staff members initiate an employment-related claim against their employing organization. In this litigation, the employee is always the applicant and the employer typically responds in an effort to justify its decision-making process. No cases were identified where one party did not participate in first-instance proceedings, and the judgments of most administrative tribunals are not subject to appeal.[76]

The UN, however, provides its staff members with a two-tier system, in which either the Secretary-General or the staff member may appeal the first-instance judgment rendered by the United Nations Dispute Tribunal (UNDT) before the UNAT.[77] Consequently, even if both parties have participated in the initial proceedings, occasionally one side appeals and the other party opts out of further

[72] See CCPR *Al-Rabassi* Views (n 64) [7.3] (noting that the state produced no evidence, and adding that the CCPR was aware of similar factual circumstances in previous cases as well); *Benali v Libya* (Views) CCPR/C/106/D/1805/2008 (1 November 2012) [6.4] (same) (CCPR *Benali* Views); *Il Khwildy v Libya* (Views) CCPR/C/106/D/1804/2008 (1 November 2012) [7.12] (same) (CCPR *Il Khwildy* Views).

[73] See *Mohamed v Libya* (Views) CCPR/C/112/D/2046/2011 (17 October 2014); *Al Daquel v Libya* (Views) CCPR/C/111/D/1882/2009 (21 July 2014); CCPR *El Hojouj Jum'a et al* Views (n 61).

[74] See CCPR *Al-Rabassi* Views (n 64) [7.2]; CCPR *Benali* Views (n 72) [6.2]; CCPR *Il Khwildy* Views (n 72) [7.2].

[75] See eg CCPR *Khelifati* Views (n 60) [6.4]; *Shikhmuradova v Turkmenistan* (Views) CCPR/C/112/D/2069/2011 (17 October 2014) [6.2]; CCPR *El Hojouj Jum'a et al* Views (n 61) [6.2].

[76] See International Labour Organization Administrative Tribunal Statute, art VI(1); Administrative Tribunal of the International Monetary Fund Statute, art XIII(2); World Bank Administrative Tribunal Statute, art XI(1).

[77] See UNAT Statute, art 2(2).

participation. Sixteen such cases were identified from the ten-year history of the UNAT.[78] Yet despite the relative frequency of non-participation, these cases do not reveal any convergence towards a uniform judicial practice when the appellate bench is faced with this issue. The three cases that are most helpful in understanding the secondary rules concerning non-participation are set out here, and they reveal three different approaches that can be taken by an administrative tribunal when faced with non-engagement.

In *Scheepers et al*, after the UNDT ruled in favor of one staff member and awarded him monetary compensation, the Secretary-General appealed and asked that the UNDT's findings be vacated along with the entire award.[79] Despite having an award to defend, the staff member did not respond to the appeal, thereby depriving the UNAT of any counter-arguments on the merits.[80] Instead, the UNAT considered the relevant submissions proffered by the staff member before the UNDT, which were evidently located from the UNDT judgment rather than resorting to the earlier submissions that may not have formed part of the record on appeal.[81] In the end, the UNAT found errors of both fact and law and consequently vacated the award, ruling against the non-participating staff member.[82]

An initially similar situation arose in *Oummih*, where the UNDT ruled in favor of a staff member and granted her a financial award, which the Secretary-General appealed.[83] The staff member, however, "purported to file an answer and cross-appeal, which did not conform to the format and content requirements," so the Tribunal granted additional time to correct the filing.[84] But as an updated version was never filed, the Tribunal indicated that it would not take into account the staff member's views, even though it had access to them from her non-conforming submission.[85] This resonates as a counter-example to the common practice seen

[78] *Ozturk v Secretary-General* (Judgment) 2018-UNAT-892 (26 October 2018) (UNAT *Ozturk* Judgment); *Rehman v Secretary-General* (Judgment) 2018-UNAT-882 (26 October 2018) (UNAT *Rehman* Judgment); *Wright v Secretary-General* (Judgment) 2017-UNAT-767 (14 July 2017); *Alsado v Secretary-General* (Judgment) 2017-UNAT-766 (14 July 2017); *Crotty v Secretary-General* (Judgment) 2017-UNAT-763 (14 July 2017); *Nyasulu v Secretary-General* (Judgment) 2016-UNAT-698 (28 October 2016) (UNAT *Nyasulu* Judgment); *Gehr v Secretary-General* (Judgment) 2016-UNAT-613 (24 March 2016); *Saffir v Secretary-General* (Judgment) 2015-UNAT-565 (2 July 2015); *Scheepers et al v Secretary-General* (Judgment) 2015-UNAT-556 (2 July 2015) (UNAT *Scheepers et al* Judgment); *Gehr v Secretary-General* (Judgment) 2014-UNAT-475 (17 October 2014); *Saffir and Ginivan v Secretary-General* (Judgment) 2014-UNAT-466 (17 October 2014); *Khisa v Secretary-General* (Judgment) 2014-UNAT-422 (2 April 2014); *Oummih v Secretary-General* (Judgment) 2014-UNAT-420 (2 April 2014) (UNAT *Oummih* Judgment); *Cooke v Secretary-General* (Judgment) 2013-UNAT-380 (17 October 2013); *Beaudry v Secretary-General* (Judgment) 2011-UNAT-125 (11 March 2011); *Sefraoui v Secretary-General* (Judgment) 2010-UNAT-048 (1 July 2010).

[79] UNAT *Scheepers et al* Judgment (n 78) [1], [15], [21].

[80] ibid [1].

[81] Compare ibid [22] (reproducing almost verbatim the description provided by the UNDT) with *Scheepers et al v Secretary-General* (Judgment) UNDT/2014/089 (26 June 2014) [112].

[82] UNAT *Scheepers et al* Judgment (n 78) [56], [58].

[83] UNAT *Oummih* Judgment (n 78) [1], [5]–[6].

[84] ibid [1].

[85] ibid [1], [13].

elsewhere, in which an international tribunal generally tries to mitigate non-participation by considering that party's views as expressed outside the formal record. Although not elaborated in the case, the UNAT may have reasoned that it had no choice but to disregard this imperfect filing, for its Rules of Procedure provide that when corrections to an answer are sought but never made, "the Appeals Tribunal will adjudicate the matter on the basis of the appeal lodged by the appellant,"[86] suggesting that no reference could be made to the rejected filing.

A third approach to non-participation was hinted at in *Nyasulu*, where the UNDT ordered the Secretary-General to either reinstate a staff member to his former position or pay him a specific amount based on expected earnings.[87] The Secretary-General appealed the method of calculating this amount, submitting that the UNDT must have used the wrong exchange rate, resulting in an inflated award.[88] The staff member did not answer.[89] Intriguingly, the UNAT stated that the staff member "does not rebut this appeal, so presumably he has no objection to the compensation being re-calculated in the manner suggested by the Secretary-General."[90] The basis of such an evidentiary presumption against the non-participant is unclear and was not identified by the UNAT. This presumption, however, does appear to have been accurate in these proceedings: after the case was remanded, both parties agreed on the method that the Secretary-General had proposed in his appeal.[91]

These three cases do not reveal an evolution towards a common means of addressing non-participation. The UNAT rendered those judgments in less than three years: refusing to look at imperfect submissions filed before it in 2014 (*Oummih*), considering previous submissions as described by the UNDT in 2015 (*Scheepers et al*), and suggesting an adverse inference in 2016 (*Nyasulu*). This might well be a situation where the approach is dictated by the circumstances of each individual case. But to the extent that a uniform procedure is intended when a party is absent, this is not readily discernible to an external observer. What may be discerned, however, is that the non-participating party will not face a default judgment. To the contrary, the non-participant occasionally wins, as seen in two other cases before the UNAT.[92] Even if it is difficult to predict how international administrative

[86] UNAT Rules of Procedure, art 9(5).

[87] UNAT *Nyasulu* Judgment (n 78) [2], [6].

[88] ibid [8]–[16].

[89] ibid [1].

[90] ibid [19].

[91] Compare *Nyasulu v Secretary-General* (Judgment on Relief) UNDT/2017/017 (10 March 2017) [7]–[9] with UNAT *Nyasulu* Judgment (n 78) [14]–[16].

[92] UNAT *Ozturk* Judgment (n 78) [1], [4]–[6], [13]–[47] (without commenting on the staff member's non-participation in the appeal and after detailed reasoning focused mainly on legal issues, the UNAT affirmed the judgment in favor of the staff member); UNAT *Rehman* Judgment (n 78) [1], [10], [14]–[16], [20], [22]–[25] (dismissing the staff member's appeal even though the Secretary-General did not participate in it, after finding that the staff member did not establish any error in the remedy awarded by the UNDT).

judges might address non-participation, the possibilities do not include automatic defeat.

4. Understanding the Approaches to Non-Participation

Having described the ways in which international bodies apply secondary rules concerning a party's non-participation in the proceedings, this chapter now turns to a comparative assessment of these practices. After discussing commonalities in the approaches, this section will address the principal difference and what may be determining the varying practice among international adjudicators. While some explanations are advanced as meriting consideration, this chapter proposes that the most convincing one pertains to the language used by the foundational text establishing or conferring jurisdiction on each institution.

Perhaps it is helpful to first make clear what does *not* occur in any international case. No decision-maker discontinues the proceedings because one party is absent from them. No court or panel enters a default judgment against the non-participant. No one shifts the burden of proof to the absent party.

Quite to the contrary, international adjudicators regularly go to great lengths to ensure that the proceedings are beyond reproach. Indeed, while not common, it is possible for a party that does not participate to nevertheless emerge victorious in the proceedings.[93] Even if the non-participant cannot claim total victory, it might still win on discrete jurisdictional or legal issues,[94] not least because these grounds are closely examined by the adjudicating body.[95] On case-specific factual matters, too, the decision-makers sometimes rule in favor of the absent party based on the evidentiary record before them.[96] While the secondary rules concerning non-participation do not qualify as mere technicalities, their application also does not dictate the outcome of international litigation.

Yet variances emerge from the application of these secondary rules, particularly with respect to whether an international body will seek out and consider additional information as well as the extent of its analysis before making findings. As seen above, inter-state dispute panels go beyond the strict confines of the record to identify and assess arguments that might benefit the absent party, thereby providing

[93] See UNAT *Ozturk* Judgment (n 78) [47]; UNAT *Rehman* Judgment (n 78) [25]; CCPR *NDM* Decision (n 63) [6]; CCPR *Tiyagarajah* Decision (n 63) [5.4]; CCPR *NT* Decision (n 63) [6]; WTO *EC—Bananas III (Article 21.5—EC)* Panel Report (n 2) [5.1] (declining to make any findings requested by the participating party).

[94] See eg CEDAW *X* Views (n 58) [5.4]; CCPR *Khelifati* Views (n 60) [5.4]; CCPR *Kurbonov* Views (n 61) [5.3]; CCPR *Saidova* Views (n 60) [5.3].

[95] See eg ICJ *Nicaragua* Judgment on Merits (n 6) [29].

[96] See PCA *South China Sea* Award on Merits (n 37) [975]; CCPR *Torobekov* Views (n 61) [6.3]; CCPR *Rolando* Views (n 59) [5.4]; CCPR *Mulezi* Views (n 61) [5.2]; ICJ *Nicaragua* Judgment on Merits (n 6) [163]–[164]; IMT *Major War Criminals* Judgment (n 2) [585], [587] (finding Martin Bormann not guilty on one of the three charges against him due to insufficient evidence of his knowledge).

a more exhaustive determination of the underlying dispute. Conversely, international human rights committees remain focused on the material brought to their attention in relation to a given complaint and examine the allegations accordingly. While those bodies largely address non-participation in a consistent manner, the same cannot be said for international administrative law, which features treatment that is case-specific and difficult to generalize. These differences may be observed in recent cases in all three fields of international law discussed in this chapter, belying the notion that there may be evolution towards a common practice concerning non-participation.

What might explain the differences among the various international bodies? One possibility is that finite time and resources force the busiest decision-makers to abbreviate any efforts to fill the gap from a party's absence. At first blush, this appears to be an attractive explanation: the CCPR is now concluding over 100 cases each year,[97] more than any other body addressed here,[98] and this pace might be hampered were the CCPR to invest more time into its non-participation cases. This explanation, however, fails to account for why the CEDAW Committee would take a similar approach to the CCPR even though it has a smaller caseload.[99] Moreover, while the inter-state disputes might be less numerous than international human rights cases, they also tend to be more voluminous, so that a numerical comparison of the dockets is unhelpful in determining whether one set of adjudicators is busier than its counterparts.

Another possibility might be that non-participation manifests in different ways, thereby prompting decision-makers to react differently. In disputes between states, the non-participant regularly communicates its views to those seised of the case in one way or another.[100] If inter-state dispute mechanisms have access to this information through "off-the-record" communications known to both parties, it seems sensible to take them into account so long as this is done transparently and is otherwise permissible. Conversely, respondent states appear less motivated to ensure that international human rights committees know their views on every individual complaint. For such cases, limiting analysis to the information already received avoids the pitfalls of speculation and self-research, even if there

[97] UNGA "Report of the Human Rights Committee" (2019) UN Doc A/74/40 [28].

[98] The PCA administered 148 cases the year of the *South China Sea* Award on the merits, seven of which were inter-state arbitrations. See PCA, Annual Report 2016 [18]. But there is no basis to suspect that the individual arbitrators were engaged in nearly that quantity of cases. While many of the PCA-administered cases remain confidential, of the forty-two additional cases identified in 2016, only three of them involved any of the five arbitrators who rendered the *South China Sea* Award that year. See ibid [19]–[27].

[99] See UNGA, Report of the Committee on the Elimination of Discrimination against Women (2018) UN Doc A/73/38 (Part 1, 24), (Part 2, 22), (Part 3, 21) (in the annual period when it adopted its views concerning *X*, the CEDAW Committee resolved eleven other cases).

[100] See eg ITLOS *Three Ukrainian Naval Vessels* Order (n 50) [8], [12]–[13]; PCA *South China Sea* Award on Merits (n 37) [13], [37], [42], [51], [53], [61], [82], [96]–[97], [100], [102]–[103]; ICJ *Nicaragua* Judgment on Merits (n 6) [31], [73].

might remain temptations to consider external material, which perhaps accounts for the three instances when the CCPR contemplated information not provided by the parties.[101] While feasible, this explanation does not account for international bodies' fidelity to their constitutive framework, which is evident even in the outlier cases in the CCPR.[102]

A further explanation, and the one advanced by this chapter as the most convincing, is that the variations arise out of each international body's foundational texts, which themselves identify or suggest divergent practices for how to approach non-participation. An analysis of each institution's practice reveals that the panels are taking their cue from the language used in their respective legal framework. In this way, what appears to be variance among specific international bodies is actually reflective of similarity at a more general level.

It is evident that the ICJ's approach comes from its Statute,[103] while the PCA arbitral tribunals relied on UNCLOS given that it served as the basis for the arbitrators' jurisdiction over those cases.[104] One may surmise that if the PCA were to oversee an arbitration grounded in a different agreement than UNCLOS, the arbitrators would approach non-participation in line with the standards enunciated in the relevant, foundational text. While ITLOS contemplated "the best available evidence" rather than adhering to its statutory provisions on non-participation,[105] this appears to have resulted from concerns that the text might apply only for a merits determination, but not for the provisional measures matters of which it was seised.[106]

In the human rights field, UN treaty bodies also follow the dictates of the underlying conventions or protocols mandating that they consider complaints in light of the information received by the complainant and the state party, which suggests that they are not meant to seek or consider information from elsewhere.[107] As noted above, even for the three outlier cases, the CCPR still referred expressly

[101] See CCPR *Al-Rabassi* Views (n 64) [7.3]; CCPR *Benali* Views (n 72) [6.4]; CCPR *Il Khwildy* Views (n 72) [7.12].

[102] See CCPR *Al-Rabassi* Views (n 64) [7.1]; CCPR *Benali* Views (n 72) [6.1]; CCPR *Il Khwildy* Views (n 72) [7.1].

[103] See eg ICJ *Nicaragua* Judgment on Merits (n 6) [28] (quoting ICJ Statute, art 53).

[104] See eg PCA *South China Sea* Award on Merits (n 37) [12], [117] (quoting UNCLOS, Annex VII, art 9); PCA *Arctic Sunrise* Award on Merits (n 26) [11] (same).

[105] See ITLOS Statute, art 28.

[106] See ITLOS *Arctic Sunrise* Order (n 46), Joint Separate Opinion of Judge Wolfrum and Judge Kelly [3]–[4] (indicating a preference to also apply the statutory text to provisional measures proceedings), Separate Opinion of Judge Paik [1]–[7] (same).

[107] See CEDAW Optional Protocol, art 7(1); Convention against Torture, art 22(4); ICCPR Optional Protocol, art 5(1). See eg CEDAW *X* Views (n 58) [6.1] ("The Committee has considered the present communication in the light of all the information placed at its disposal by the author, without the benefit of the State party's observations, in accordance with the provisions of article [7(1)] of the Optional Protocol."); CAT *Guerrero Larez* Decision (n 57) [6.1] ("as required under article 22, paragraph 4, of the Convention"); CCPR *El Hojouj Jum'a et al* Views (n 61) [6.1] ("as provided for under article 5, paragraph 1, of the Optional Protocol").

to the relevant provision of the ICCPR Optional Protocol in setting out how it intended to resolve the complaints.

This explanation further accounts for the case-specific practice seen in the UNAT. Its legal framework does not foresee non-participation or suggest how its occurrence might be handled. Instead, as a matter that is not expressly provided for, the UNAT's Rules of Procedure indicate that the absence of a party should be "dealt with by decision of the Appeals Tribunal on the particular case."[108] With this in mind, it should not come as a surprise that the UNAT has acted in various ways when addressing non-participation.

Not only does this explanation best describe the divergence among international bodies, it also makes sense intuitively. It is easy to understand how a panel's decision-makers would be guided by the foundational texts underlying the existence and procedures of their institution. Moreover, given that bodies in the same field of international law frequently share similar statutory language on non-participation, this explains why there is often a coherent approach among international adjudicators within specific fields.

5. Conclusion

The secondary rules applied by international adjudicators to a party's non-participation in the proceedings can have substantial, if not necessarily determinative, effects in a given case. While a comparative analysis reveals some uniformity in the approaches taken, differences throughout international law can be observed as well. After exploring possible explanations for the variance, this chapter proposes that the most convincing one lies in the precise language used in the constitutive legal document of each institution.

This provides further confirmation of the crucial role played by statutory drafters in setting a new institution upon its eventual path, including with respect to the implications for non-participation. Should any international dispute resolution bodies be created or modified in the future, the drafters would be well advised to include specific provisions addressing non-participation and to ensure that this text is calibrated towards the desired approach.

In the meantime, it appears likely that international adjudicators will see further instances of non-participation in the coming years. This will offer additional opportunities to refine how they apply the secondary rules concerning a party's absence in international proceedings.

[108] UNAT Rules of Procedure, art 31(1) (concerning "Procedural matters not covered in the rules of procedure").

PART IV

ATTRIBUTION IN INTERNATIONAL LAW

12

State Acquiescence or Connivance in the Wrongful Conduct of Third Parties in the Jurisprudence of the European Court of Human Rights

Marko Milanovic[*]

1. Introduction

This chapter examines the jurisprudence of the European Court of Human Rights (ECtHR) with regard to the acquiescence or connivance of states parties to the European Convention on Human Rights (ECHR) in the wrongful conduct of third states (which themselves may or may not be parties to the ECHR) or non-state actors. It discusses the origins of the acquiescence or connivance test in the Court's case law, which is idiosyncratic and does not stem from general international law. The chapter also discusses the test's legal nature, arguing that its conceptual basis remains unclear, and that the current state of the case law could support two theories.

First, that acquiescence or connivance, as applied in the Court's most recent cases, is an ECHR-specific rule of attribution of conduct, which deviates from the general rules of attribution in international law, as codified by the International Law Commission (ILC) in its Articles on Responsibility of States for Internationally Wrongful Acts (ARSIWA).[1] The ARSIWA themselves do allow for the possibility of sector-specific rules of state responsibility—article 55 of the ARSIWA, entitled *lex specialis*, thus provides that the ARSIWA "do not apply where and to the extent that the conditions for the existence of an internationally wrongful act or the content or implementation of the international responsibility of a State are governed by special rules of international law." One view of the Court's acquiescence or connivance

[*] I am very grateful to Miles Jackson and Harriet Moynihan for their comments on a draft of this chapter.

[1] Report of the International Law Commission on the work of its 53rd session, Official Records of the General Assembly, 56th session, Supplement No 10 (A/56/10), chp.IV.E.2) (ARSIWA).

Marko Milanovic, *State Acquiescence or Connivance in the Wrongful Conduct of Third Parties in the Jurisprudence of the European Court of Human Rights* In: *Secondary Rules of Primary Importance in International Law.*
Edited by: Gábor Kajtár, Başak Çalı, and Marko Milanovic, Oxford University Press.
DOI: 10.1093/oso/9780192869012.003.0012

test is thus that it provides us with an example of a *lex specialis* rule of attribution of conduct in the sense of article 55 of the ARSIWA.

The alternative view, however, is that the Court's acquiescence or connivance jurisprudence would best be conceptually framed as an ECHR-specific theory of state complicity. Under such a framing, the state acquiescing or conniving in the wrongful conduct of a third party is being held responsible for the assistance it provides to that third party, rather than for the third party's own conduct—in other words, the complicity rule is not necessarily an attributive one. While such a rule would arguably differ from the ILC's general approach to wrongful state aiding and assisting in article 16 of the ARSIWA, it would not be an ECHR-specific rule of attribution, or at least it would not always operate with an attributive effect. I argue that such a conceptual framing would best accommodate human rights-specific needs while maintaining coherence with general international law. Even under such a framing, however, there are many aspects of the acquiescence or connivance test that require further clarification by the Court.

The basic issue that this chapter will examine, therefore, is whether the Court is fragmenting the general attribution framework articulated in the ARSIWA, and if so whether such a deviation is justified or could be avoided. The analysis below will show how a proto-attributive rule emerges solely from the Court's interpretative activity, without reference to sources external to the ECHR. It will also show how this rule is not a mere technicality, but serves the fundamental purpose of fair labelling of wrongdoing. It emerges, primarily, because the Court had to find an intermediate label of state culpability between, on the one hand, the state *committing* a human rights violation, and, on the other, *failing to prevent* such a violation by a third party.

2. Origins of the Acquiescence or Connivance Test

The Court first explicitly articulated a state acquiescence or connivance test in the 2001 inter-state case of *Cyprus v Turkey*, which dealt with Turkey's responsibility with regard to human rights violations committed by the separatist authorities of the Turkish Republic of Northern Cyprus (TRNC).[2] As we will soon see, however, the acquiescence or connivance language can be traced to earlier cases against Turkey before the Convention institutions. *Cyprus v Turkey* primarily concerned violations committed by TRNC officials and the relationship between the TRNC and Turkey. As in the prior *Loizidou* case,[3] there was a substantial lack of clarity in that regard as to whether the Court considered the conduct of TRNC authorities to be directly attributable to Turkey, whether therefore Turkey was being found liable

[2] *Cyprus v Turkey* [GC] App no 25781/94 (ECtHR, 10 May 2001).
[3] *Loizidou v Turkey* App no 15318/89 (Preliminary Objections) (ECtHR, 23 February 1995).

for violating *negative* obligations or for failing to fulfill the *positive* obligation to secure human rights, and a remarkable degree of confusion between state responsibility and the concept of state jurisdiction in article 1 of the ECHR.[4] One aspect of the inter-state case, however, concerned Turkey's responsibility for human rights violations committed by purely private parties, that is, individuals who were not officials of the separatist TRNC, and here the Court held as follows:

> The Court concludes, accordingly, and subject to its subsequent considerations on the issue of private parties ... that the matters complained of in the instant application fall within the "jurisdiction" of Turkey within the meaning of Article 1 of the Convention and therefore entail the respondent State's responsibility under the Convention ... As to the applicant Government's further claim that this "jurisdiction" must also be taken to extend to the acts of private parties in northern Cyprus who violate the rights of Greek Cypriots or Turkish Cypriots living there, the Court considers it appropriate to revert to this matter when examining the merits of the specific complaints raised by the applicant Government in this context. It confines itself to noting at this stage that *the acquiescence or connivance of the authorities of a Contracting State in the acts of private individuals which violate the Convention rights of other individuals within its jurisdiction may engage that State's responsibility under the Convention*. Any different conclusion would be *at variance with the obligation contained in Article 1 of the Convention*.[5]

Note, again, the unfortunate conflation between article 1 jurisdiction and state responsibility, and the use of ambiguous formulations such as that state responsibility may be engaged. On the assumption that the Court had to have some kind of coherent theory of the case in mind, two readings of this holding are possible: either the conduct of private individuals in which Turkey had "acquiesced or connived" was being attributed to Turkey, or Turkey was being held responsible for failing to secure Convention rights per its article 1.

The Court's first articulation of the acquiescence or connivance test was thus shrouded in uncertainty, but, as we shall see, it was later used with much more prominence and impact in several quite important cases. First, however, we should explore the origins of this formula, which the Court did not actually invent out of whole cloth in *Cyprus v Turkey*. In fact, that language appears a few years before—but not as any kind of formalized test—in several individual cases brought against

[4] In particular, the Court in *Loizidou* defined article 1 jurisdiction in spatial terms, as effective overall control of an area by a state, which has frequently been misconstrued as an attribution test. See M Milanovic, *Extraterritorial Application of Human Rights Treaties: Law, Principles, and Policy* (OUP, 2011) 41–53; M Milanovic, "Jurisdiction and Responsibility: Trends in the Jurisprudence of the Strasbourg Court," in A van Aaken and I Motoc (eds), *The ECHR and General International Law* (OUP 2018) 97; J Crawford and A Keene, "The Structure of State Responsibility under the European Convention on Human Rights" ibid 178.

[5] *Cyprus v Turkey* (n 2) paras 80–81 (emphasis added).

Turkey, all of which regarded allegations of violence against persons of Kurdish origin at the hands of private individuals, rather than the Turkish state. The cases were initially dealt with by the now defunct European Commission on Human Rights, and then by the Court; most were litigated on behalf of the applicants by Kevin Boyle and Françoise Hampson as counsel.

The first was *Yaşa v Turkey*. The applicant was subjected to violence and intimidation because he was selling a pro-Kurdish newspaper, the *Özgür Gündem*. He was shot at, and his uncle was killed, by unknown persons. Before the Commission, the applicant alleged that "he and his uncle were shot due to their involvement in the distribution of the newspaper *Özgür Gündem* as part of a campaign of attacks against that and other newspapers and *that this campaign was with the connivance or acquiescence, if not involving the direct participation, of agents of the State*. The Government deny that there has been any such campaign."[6] Note how the "connivance or acquiescence" language first appears in the *arguments of the applicant*.[7] The Commission then concluded that the evidence before it did not permit a finding that the violations were perpetrated by state agents for whose actions the state would bear "direct responsibility"[8] and, similarly, that it could not "find it established that the Turkish Government have failed in their obligation to protect the lives of the applicant and his uncle through preventive or protective measures."[9] However, the Commission did find that Turkey failed to *properly investigate* the applicant's claims regarding a concerted campaign of violence:

> The Commission recognises the seriousness of the allegations being made against the authorities in the South-East [of Turkey] with respect to *acquiescence or connivance* in a campaign of targeted attacks and can understand a certain reluctance or disbelief in the Government to accept that these might be well-founded. It nonetheless behoves a Contracting State, respecting the rule of law and having regard to its obligation under Article 1 […] of the Convention to secure to everyone within its jurisdiction the enjoyment of the rights and freedoms guaranteed therein, to verify whether allegations, based on actual facts and events, of serious wrongdoing, whether committed by State officials or other persons, are in any respect well-founded. […] The Commission is of the opinion that the failure to make any further or more detailed investigation into the attacks on the applicant and his uncle amounts to a failure to protect the right to life.[10]

[6] *Yaşa v Turkey* App no 22495/93 (Commission Report) (ECtHR, 8 April 1997), para 81 (emphasis added).

[7] See also ibid para 90.

[8] ibid para 94.

[9] ibid para 100.

[10] ibid paras 106–07 (emphasis added).

Here, in finding the violation of the procedural obligation to investigate, the Commission again uses the acquiescence or connivance language by referring to the applicant's *allegations*, without endorsing that language explicitly, but nonetheless as part of its chain of reasoning. When the case then came to the Court, it only used the word "connivance" (and not acquiescence) when summarizing the applicant's arguments[11] and affirmed all of the findings of the Commission.[12]

A month after the Court's judgment in *Yaşa* the Commission published its report in the *Kılıç* case.[13] The applicant's brother, a journalist working for the *Özgür Gündem* newspaper, was assassinated by unknown assailants. As in *Yaşa*, the applicant claimed that the killing was done with the involvement or connivance of state agents,[14] while the Commission found that it could not be proved that state agents committed the killing.[15] But it also went further, by itself adopting the applicant's language of acquiescence or connivance in finding that Turkey failed to fulfill its positive obligation to protect the right to life. The Commission was explicit that it was using the framework of positive obligations because it could not conclusively establish who killed the applicant's brother.[16] However, on the basis of a government report which was made publicly available, the Commission did establish that "the authorities were aware of and *connived at* unlawful acts, including murder,"[17] and that, based on a pattern of violence and lack of effective investigation, "the legal structures in the south-east of Turkey during the relevant period in this case, namely, in or about 1993, operated in such a manner that security force personnel and others acting under their control *or with their acquiescence* were often unaccountable for their actions."[18] The Commission thus found that "there is strong suspicion, supported by some evidence, to substantiate the allegations that risk derived from targeting by State officials or those acting on their behalf or *with their connivance or acquiescence*"[19] and that "the applicant's brother fell into a category of people who were at risk from unlawful violence from targeting by State officials or those acting on their behalf or *with their connivance or acquiescence*."[20]

On the same day the Commission also rendered its report in the related *Mahmut Kaya* case, in which the applicant's brother was similarly unlawfully killed.[21] Here,

[11] *Yaşa v Turkey* App no 22495/93 (ECtHR, 2 September 1998), paras 7, 83.

[12] The same pattern of use of the term "connivance" by the Commission and the Court can be observed in another contemporary case: see *Tanrıkulu v Turkey* App no 23763/94 (Commission Report) (ECtHR, 15 April 1998), paras 223, 241, 245, 261; and the Court's judgment in the case, 8 July 1999, paras 7, 45, 62, 85, 90, 96, 99.

[13] *Kılıç v Turkey* App no 22492/93 (Commission Report) (ECtHR, 23 October 1998). Note that the version of the report available in HUDOC consistently misspells the Turkish *ı* as a *k*, so that the applicant's name is incorrectly rendered as Kklkç.

[14] ibid paras 4, 48, 171.

[15] ibid paras 188, 189.

[16] ibid paras 209–17.

[17] ibid para 222 (emphasis added).

[18] ibid para 227 (emphasis added).

[19] ibid para 229 (emphasis added).

[20] ibid para 230 (emphasis added).

[21] *Mahmut Kaya v Turkey* App no 22535/93 (Commission Report) (ECtHR, 23 October 1998).

too, the Commission made repeated references to connivance or acquiescence, and again did so in its own reasoning, rather than solely when summarizing the arguments of the applicant, using the same formulations as in *Kılıç*.[22] A few days later the Commission published its report in a case brought by the editors of the *Özgür Gündem* newspaper, which, unlike the previous cases, it examined primarily from the standpoint of the freedom of expression.[23] Again we can observe references to acquiescence or connivance in the Commission's own reasoning,[24] and again we can see that the Commission clearly did not consider that the threats against the applicants' freedom of expression could be attributed to Turkey, which was instead being held responsible for failing to fulfill its positive obligation to protect the applicants' rights.[25]

In short, it is crystal clear that the Commission did *not* think that acquiescence or connivance was some kind of attribution test, that is, that if such acquiescence or connivance on behalf of the state in the conduct of third parties was proved, this would suffice to attribute the third party's conduct to the state. Rather, references to acquiescence or connivance appear in the context of the Commission's analysis of Turkey's compliance with its positive protective obligations under the Convention, which the Commission explicitly distinguished from Turkey's negative obligations.

The three cases then went to the Court, which decided them all in March 2000, a bit more than a year before its judgment in *Cyprus v Turkey*. In all three cases, the Court affirmed the Commission's approach: (1) the direct violation of human rights (eg the killing) could not be attributed to the state; (2) however, Turkey was held liable for failing to fulfill its positive obligation of protection; and (3) passing references were made to the Turkish authorities' knowledge of, or acquiescence or connivance in the violation, either when summarizing the applicants' arguments or in the context of the analysis of Turkey's positive obligations.[26] It is again quite

[22] ibid paras 4, 271, 336, 360, 362, 363.

[23] *Ersöz v Turkey* App no 23144/93 (Commission Report) (ECtHR, 29 October 1998). Because the first applicant had died and the application on their behalf was not maintained, the case was in subsequent proceedings referred to not as *Ersöz* but as *Özgür Gündem*.

[24] ibid paras 40, 90, 115, 142, 149, 203.

[25] See ibid paras 143, 145.

[26] See *Özgür Gündem v Turkey* App no 23144/93 (ECtHR, 16 March 2000), paras 38, 40–46, 67; *Kılıç v Turkey* App no 22492/93 (ECtHR, 28 March 2000), paras 1, 57, 68, esp para 64: "In the present case, it has not been established beyond reasonable doubt that any State agent or person acting on behalf of the State authorities was involved in the killing of Kemal Kılıç (see ibid paras 48, 50). The question to be determined is whether the authorities failed to comply with their positive obligation to protect him from a known risk to his life." See also *Mahmut Kaya v Turkey* App no 22535/93 (ECtHR, 16 March 2000), paras 1, 74, 80, 91, esp para 87: "[T]he Court recalls that it has not been established beyond reasonable doubt that any State agent was involved in the killing of Hasan Kaya. There are, however, strong inferences that can be drawn on the facts of this case that the perpetrators of the murder were known to the authorities [...] The question to be determined by the Court is whether in the circumstances the authorities failed in a positive obligation to protect Hasan Kaya from a risk to his life." See also ibid para 91: "[T]he authorities were aware, or ought to have been aware, of the possibility that this risk derived from the activities of persons or groups acting with the knowledge or acquiescence of elements in the security forces." See also another Kurdish case with a similar fact pattern, *Akkoç v Turkey* App nos 22947/93 and 22948/93 (ECtHR, 10 October 2000), paras 74, 79, 83.

clear that, like the Commission before it, prior to *Cyprus v Turkey* the Court did not consider acquiescence or connivance as a test of attribution, but looked at situations in which the state acquiesced or connived in human rights violations by third parties through the prism of positive obligations.

But then, as we have seen, in *Cyprus v Turkey* the Court was not as careful in distinguishing between negative and positive obligations, holding rather ambiguously that "the acquiescence or connivance of the authorities of a Contracting State in the acts of private individuals which violate the Convention rights of other individuals within its jurisdiction may engage that State's responsibility under the Convention."[27] However, the Court actually did nothing with this language on the facts of the case. Acquiescence or connivance was raised by the applicant Cypriot government with regard to violence committed by Turkish settlers in Northern Cyprus against Greek Cypriots, but the Court ultimately ruled that this conduct was outside the scope of the case.[28] In short, the reference to the engagement of state responsibility on the basis of acquiescence or connivance was both clearly inspired by prior Kurdish cases against Turkey and entirely *obiter* in *Cyprus v Turkey* itself.

3. Subsequent Case Law on the Acquiescence or Connivance Test

After *Cyprus v Turkey*, the Court has used the acquiescence or connivance formula in four types of cases.

First, in two leftover Kurdish cases against Turkey, which are in material respects identical to the cases examined above.[29]

Second, in numerous judgments in which either the Grand Chamber or a Chamber used the acquiescence or connivance language when recapitulating earlier case law, normally by referring expressly to *Cyprus v Turkey*, but without

[27] *Cyprus v Turkey* [GC] (n 2) para 81.

[28] ibid para 73. See also paras 130–31: "The Court notes that the evidence given of killings carried out directly by Turkish soldiers or with their connivance relates to a period which is outside the scope of the present application. Indeed, it is to be noted that the Commission was unable to establish on the facts whether any of the missing persons were killed in circumstances for which the respondent State can be held responsible under the substantive limb of Article 2 of the Convention. The Court concludes, therefore, that it cannot accept the applicant Government's allegations that the facts disclose a substantive violation of Article 2 of the Convention in respect of any of the missing persons. [. . .] For the Court, the applicant Government's allegations must, however, be examined in the context of a Contracting State's procedural obligation under Article 2 to protect the right to life." Note how the Court, as in the Kurdish cases, pivoted to positive obligations in the absence of conclusive proof of killing by state agents.

[29] See *Avşar v Turkey* App no 25657/94 (ECtHR, 10 July 2001), paras 404, 406, 415 (mentioning acquiescence or connivance in the context of a failure to properly investigate), as well as paras 411–13 (connivance or acquiescence in the killing itself; however, the Court ultimately attributes the killing to state agents (village guards acting in official capacity and "acting on authority")); *Uçar v Turkey* App no 52392/99 (ECtHR, 11 April 2006), paras 3, 98, 99, 102, 107 (abduction not attributable to the state).

applying the formula in any meaningful way on the facts of the case, for instance because the conduct at issue in the case was committed by *de jure* state organs.[30] A paradigmatic example would be *Ilascu*, in which the Court also added to the formula by underscoring its relevance with regard to separatist entities operating in areas under a state's control: "the acquiescence or connivance of the authorities of a Contracting State in the acts of private individuals which violate the Convention rights of other individuals within its jurisdiction may engage the State's responsibility under the Convention [. . .] That is particularly true in the case of recognition by the State in question of the acts of self-proclaimed authorities which are not recognised by the international community."[31] Another useful example would be the Grand Chamber judgment in *Sindicatul*, in which one of the applicant's complaints was that the respondent state hindered the right to individual petition.[32] The Court referred to the acquiescence or connivance formula,[33] and then seemed to distinguish between the conduct of state officials and their tolerance of private conduct, that is, between negative and positive obligations, finding no violation on the facts of the case.[34]

Third, the Court used the formula in a cluster of four cases dealing with hate-motivated crimes, two of which dealt with Jehovah's Witnesses in Georgia, and two with members of the LGBT community in Georgia and Romania. In *Begheluri*, the first such case, the applicants were a group of ninety-nine Jehovah's Witnesses who claimed that numerous Convention rights had been breached "on account of the large-scale religiously motivated violence to which they had been subjected [in Georgia] and the relevant authorities' total failure to prevent, stop or redress the alleged violations."[35] The Court referred to acquiescence or connivance several times in the judgment, all but once in the context of the state failing to fulfill either substantive or procedural positive obligations, that is, the conduct being attributed was the omissions of state organs.[36] In one instance, however, the Court appeared to be attributing the conduct of private parties to the state, but did not do so unambiguously, since the relevant incident involved the active participation of state organs as well.[37] The subsequent Jehovah's Witnesses case contained only fleeting

[30] See *Solomou v Turkey* App no 36832/97 (ECtHR, 24 June 2008), para 46; *Moldovan v Romania* App nos 41138/98 and 64320/01 (ECtHR, 12 July 2005), para 94; *Lăcătuş v Romania* App no 12694/04 (ECtHR, 13 November 2012), para 83; *Khalikova v Azerbaijan* App no 42883/11 (ECtHR, 22 October 2015), para 140; *Burlya v Ukraine* App no 3289/10 (ECtHR, 6 November 2018), paras 119, 129–37.

[31] *Ilascu v Moldova and Russia* [GC] App no 48787/99 (ECtHR, 8 July 2004), para 318.

[32] *Sindicatul "Păstorul cel Bun" v Romania* [GC] App no 2330/09 (ECtHR, 9 July 2013).

[33] ibid para 76.

[34] ibid paras 77–80, esp para 79.

[35] *Begheluri v Georgia* App no 28490/02 (ECtHR, 7 October 2014), para 3.

[36] ibid paras 98, 118–21, 145, 163–65, 174.

[37] ibid paras 111–12: "Even if the Court accepts in part the Government's claim that the Orthodox extremist group that led the attack of 8 September 2000 *was made up of private individuals*, it is still of the opinion, in view of the evidence in the file, that the attack concerned *would have been impossible without the involvement, connivance, or at least acquiescence of the competent authorities*. The fact that the Zugdidi police were present throughout that time in and around the village of Rokhi but did nothing to put an end to the violence, only underlines their responsibility. [. . .] As the Government submitted

reference to acquiescence or connivance, again in the context of positive obligations,[38] as did the two LGBT cases.[39]

Finally, and most importantly, the Court used the acquiescence or connivance formula in a series of cases dealing with extraordinary rendition in the "war on terror."[40] The Court set the foundations of its approach to such cases in its 2012 Grand Chamber judgment in *El-Masri v Macedonia* (which actually preceded the four cases on hate-motivated crimes above),[41] and then followed up in four very significant Chamber judgments brought by the same two applicants against Poland, Lithuania, and Romania, three European countries which hosted so-called Central Intelligence Agency (CIA) "black sites" in which high-value detainees were coercively interrogated. As we shall see, it is in these rendition cases that acquiescence or connivance really got to shine.

4. *El-Masri* and Other Rendition Cases

Let us start with *El-Masri*. The applicant was arrested in Macedonia, detained by Macedonian agents in a hotel in Skopje for several weeks, then transferred to a CIA rendition team at Skopje airport where he was severely mistreated, from there he was then taken to a US detention facility in Afghanistan. With regard to the mistreatment in particular, the Court noted that it:

> [M]ust firstly assess whether the treatment suffered by the applicant at Skopje Airport at the hands of the special CIA rendition team *is imputable to the respondent State*. In this connection it emphasises that the acts complained of were carried out in the presence of officials of the respondent State and within its jurisdiction. Consequently, the respondent State *must be regarded as responsible* under the Convention for acts performed by *foreign officials on its territory with the acquiescence or connivance of its authorities* (see *Ilaşcu and Others v Moldova and Russia* [GC], no 48787/99, §318, ECHR 2004-VII).[42]

no evidence capable of refuting the applicants' allegations, *it must be found to be established that the Zugdidi police officers directly participated in the attack of 8 September 2000. Consequently, the responsibility for the matters complained of lays with the authorities in question*" (emphasis added). The point that the "attack would have been impossible" without the connivance or acquiescence of the authorities appears to be an implied assessment of "but for" causality.

[38] *Tsartsidze v Georgia* App no 18766/04 (ECtHR, 17 January 2017), paras 78, 86–87.

[39] *Identoba v Georgia* App no 73235/12 (ECtHR, 12 May 2015), para 77; *MC and AC v Romania* App no 12060/12 (ECtHR, 12 April 2016), para 124.

[40] See generally N Jørgensen, "Complicity in Torture in a Time of Terror: Interpreting the European Court of Human Rights Extraordinary Rendition Cases" (2017) 16 Chinese Journal of International Law 11.

[41] *El-Masri v the Former Yugoslav Republic of Macedonia* [GC] App no 39630/09 (ECtHR, 13 December 2012).

[42] ibid para 206 (emphasis added).

This paragraph has many moving parts. Note, first, how the Court framed its inquiry as being about the *imputation*, that is, attribution, of the mistreatment of the applicant to Macedonia, even though the mistreatment was actually done by CIA agents. In the next sentence it talks about these acts being done "in the presence" of Macedonian officials and within its jurisdiction. And from there it draws the conclusion that Macedonia "must be regarded" as responsible for acts of foreign officials committed with its acquiescence or connivance. Note also that the citation to *Ilascu* is a slight sleight of the judicial hand—the cited paragraph of *Ilascu* talks about acquiescence or connivance in the acts of *private individuals*,[43] not those of foreign officials, as do all other cases referring to acquiescence or connivance prior to *El-Masri*.

The *El-Masri* Court very much seems to be using the acquiescence or connivance formula as an attribution test, whereas virtually all prior cases employing this terminology and actually applying it to the facts, used it in the analysis of a state failure to fulfill positive substantive or procedural obligations. In *El-Masri*, by contrast, the Court is not holding Macedonia responsible for *failing to protect* the applicant from mistreatment by US agents, but is attributing that conduct to Macedonia itself.[44] The Court thus concluded that "such treatment amounted to torture in breach of article 3 of the Convention. The respondent State must be considered *directly responsible* for the violation of the applicant's rights under this head, since its agents *actively facilitated the treatment* and then *failed to take any measures* that might have been necessary in the circumstances of the case to prevent it from occurring."[45] Again the Court's analysis mixes in several different concepts—it talks about Macedonia's *direct responsibility*, which implies that the torture was attributable to it, then refers to Macedonia *facilitating* the torture, which looks like a complicity rule of some kind, and then moves to its *failure to take preventive measures*, which is the language of a positive obligation.

The conceptual basis of the Court's approach in *El-Masri* is thus a constantly shifting one. Arguably, the Court regarded Macedonia's behavior towards the applicant as so egregious that it was not content to treat it solely from the standpoint of a failure to fulfill positive obligations, and therefore reached for the acquiescence or connivance formula to fashion a more direct attribution test. But the Court did not stop there. Moving to the issue of the arbitrary deprivation of the applicant's liberty, the Court found Macedonia responsible not only for the period of detention in Macedonia itself, but *also* for his subsequent detention at the hands of US

[43] See n 31 and accompanying text.

[44] See also A Nollkaemper, "The ECtHR Finds Macedonia Responsible in Connection with Torture by the CIA, but on What Basis?" (*EJIL: Talk!*, 24 December 2012) <https://www.ejiltalk.org/the-ecthr-finds-macedonia-responsible-in-connection-with-torture-by-the-cia-but-on-what-basis/> accessed 6 June 2022.

[45] *El-Masri* (n 41) para 211 (emphasis added).

authorities. To reach this outcome, however, the Court did *not* resort to the acquiescence or connivance formula:

> In such circumstances, the Court considers that it should have been clear to the Macedonian authorities that, having been handed over into the custody of the US authorities, the applicant faced a real risk of a flagrant violation of his rights under Article 5. In this connection the Court reiterates that Article 5 of the Convention lays down an obligation on the State not only to refrain from active infringements of the rights in question, but also to take appropriate steps to provide protection against an unlawful interference with those rights to everyone within its jurisdiction (see *Storck v Germany*, No 61603/00, §§100–01, ECHR 2005-V, and *Medova v Russia*, No 25385/04, §123, 15 January 2009). The Macedonian authorities *not only failed to comply with their positive obligation to protect the applicant* from being detained in contravention of Article 5 of the Convention, *but they actively facilitated* his subsequent detention in Afghanistan by handing him over to the CIA, despite the fact that they were aware or ought to have been aware of the risk of that transfer. The Court considers therefore that *the responsibility of the respondent State is also engaged* in respect of the applicant's detention between 23 January and 28 May 2004 (see, mutatis mutandis, *Rantsev v Cyprus and Russia*, No 25965/04, §207, ECHR 2010).[46]

Again, the Court does not want to frame the issue as one of compliance with positive obligations, but effectively creates a complicity rule—if an ECHR state party *actively facilitates* arbitrary detention by another state, which itself need not be an ECHR state party, the entire continuing act of arbitrary detention will be attributed to the assisting state. In fact, the only authority that the Court cites in support of its analysis—a paragraph in the *Rantsev* case—is entirely immaterial, since it is firmly framed in the context of violations of positive obligations, and never refers to "active facilitation" or any similar concept.[47] And thus the Court held that "in

[46] ibid para 239 (emphasis added).

[47] See *Rantsev v Cyprus and Russia* App no 25965/04 (ECtHR, 7 January 2010), para 207: "The applicant's complaints against Russia in the present case concern the latter's alleged failure to take the necessary measures to protect Ms Rantseva from the risk of trafficking and exploitation and to conduct an investigation into the circumstances of her arrival in Cyprus, her employment there and her subsequent death. The Court observes that such complaints *are not predicated on the assertion that Russia was responsible for acts committed in Cyprus or by the Cypriot authorities*. In light of the fact that the alleged trafficking commenced in Russia and in view of the obligations undertaken by Russia to combat trafficking, it is not outside the Court's competence to examine whether Russia complied with *any obligation it may have had to take measures within the limits of its own jurisdiction and powers to protect* Ms Rantseva from trafficking and to investigate the possibility that she had been trafficked. Similarly, the applicant's Article 2 complaint against the Russian authorities concerns their failure to take investigative measures, including securing evidence from witnesses resident in Russia. It is for the Court to assess in its examination of the merits of the applicant's Article 2 complaint the extent *of any procedural obligation incumbent on the Russian authorities and whether any such obligation was discharged in the circumstances of the present case*" (emphasis added).

the case of a series of wrongful acts or omissions, the breach extends *over the entire period* starting with the first of the acts and continuing for as long as the acts or omissions are repeated and remain at variance with the international obligation concerned ... the Court concludes that the Government is to be held responsible for violating the applicant's rights under Article 5 of the Convention *during the entire period of his captivity*."[48]

In short, the *El-Masri* Grand Chamber clearly and unambiguously held Macedonia responsible for the torture inflicted on the applicant by CIA agents and for his subsequent detention in Afghanistan at the hands of US authorities. It did so unanimously, despite the fact that the attribution of the relevant conduct does not align clearly with any of the rules in the ARSIWA, which are mentioned in the judgment only in a section setting out relevant international legal documents and are never referred to in the Court's reasoning.[49] Apparently, such was the unanimity in the Court that neither of the separate opinions in the case addressed any of these issues, and in particular the consistency of the Court's approach with general international law.

As noted above, the Court followed up on *El-Masri* in two pairs of Chamber cases dealing with the deprivation of liberty and and ill treatment of Al-Qaeda high value detainees in CIA black sites in Eastern Europe, and their subsequent rendition. Each pair of cases was decided by the same Chamber on the same day—unanimously and without separate opinions. In the first pair, *Al Nashiri v Poland*[50] and *Husayn (Abu Zubaydah) v Poland*,[51] the Court at first glance faithfully followed *El-Masri*, reaffirming that "in accordance with its settled case-law, the respondent State must be regarded as responsible under the Convention for acts performed by foreign officials on its territory with the acquiescence or connivance of its authorities,"[52] and concluding that:

> The Court has already found that Poland knew of the nature and purposes of the CIA's activities on its territory at the material time and cooperated in the preparation and execution of the CIA rendition, secret detention and interrogation operations on its territory. [...] It is true that, in the assessment of the experts—which the Court has accepted—the interrogations and, therefore, the torture inflicted on the applicant at the Stare Kiejkuty black site were the exclusive responsibility of the CIA and that it is unlikely that the Polish officials witnessed or knew exactly what happened inside the facility [...]
>
> However, under Article 1 of the Convention, taken together with Article 3, Poland was *required to take measures* designed to ensure that individuals within

48 *El-Masri* (n 41) paras 240–41 (emphasis added).
49 ibid para 97.
50 *Al Nashiri v Poland* App no 28761/11 (ECtHR, 24 July 2014).
51 *Husayn (Abu Zubaydah) v Poland* App no 7511/13 (ECtHR, 24 July 2014).
52 *Al Nashiri v Poland* (n 50) para 452. See also *Husayn (Abu Zubaydah) v Poland* (n 50) para 449.

its jurisdiction were not subjected to torture or inhuman or degrading treatment or punishment, including ill-treatment administered by private individuals [...]

Notwithstanding the above Convention obligation, Poland, for all practical purposes, *facilitated the whole process, created the conditions for it to happen and made no attempt to prevent it from occurring.* As the Court has already held above, on the basis of their own knowledge of the CIA activities *deriving from Poland's complicity in the HVD Programme* and from publicly accessible information on treatment applied in the context of the "war on terror" to terrorist suspects in US custody the authorities—even if they did not witness or participate in the specific acts of ill-treatment and abuse endured by the applicant—must have been aware of the serious risk of treatment contrary to Article 3 occurring on Polish territory.

Accordingly, the Polish State, on account of its "acquiescence and connivance" in the HVD Programme *must be regarded as responsible* for the violation of the applicant's rights under Article 3 of the Convention committed on its territory [...][53]

There is, however, a greater degree of ambiguity here than in *El-Masri* about whether the conduct of US agents is being directly attributed to Poland. Much of the paragraph quoted above would be consistent with a theory of positive obligations (eg the reference to measures that Poland was required to take and the fact that it made no attempt to prevent violations from occurring). The Court avoids the terminology of attribution, imputation or direct responsibility, while the ARSIWA are again simply cited *en passant*.[54] Moving in a different conceptual direction, the Court refers to Polish facilitation of the violations, expressly uses the term "complicity," and makes an implicit reference to some kind of consideration of causality when it says that Poland "created the conditions" for the violations to happen.

When we compare the operative paragraphs of each judgment it becomes even clearer that the *Al Nashiri/Abu Zubaydah* Chamber had a somewhat different legal theory of state responsibility than the *El-Masri* Grand Chamber (see Table 12.1).

The references in *Al Nashiri/Abu Zubaydah* to Poland's *complicity* and it *enabling* the misconduct of US authorities are revealing—the Chamber's theory of the case was more one of wrongful assistance or complicity than of direct responsibility, in addition to violations of positive obligations.[55] And we can observe the exact same terminology and outcome in the two subsequent rendition cases against Lithuania

[53] *Al Nashiri v Poland* (n 50) para 517 (emphasis added). See also *Husayn (Abu Zubaydah) v Poland* (n 50) para 512.

[54] *Al Nashiri v Poland* (n 50) para 207. See also *Husayn (Abu Zubaydah) v Poland* (n 50) para 201.

[55] This is also evident from the Court's analysis of the art 5 detention issue, with regard to which it noted that: "The rendition operations had therefore largely depended on *cooperation, assistance an active involvement of the countries* which put at the USA's disposal their airspace, airports for the landing of aircraft transporting CIA prisoners and, last but not least, premises on which the prisoners could be securely detained and interrogated. While, as noted above, the interrogations of captured terrorist suspects was the CIA's exclusive responsibility and the local authorities were not to be involved, *the cooperation and various forms of assistance of those authorities*, such as for instance customising the premises for the CIA's needs, ensuring security and providing the logistics *were the necessary condition* for the

Table 12.1 Comparison of the operative paragraphs of the *El-Masri* and *Al Nashiri/Abu Zubaydah* judgments

El-Masri, **op. paras 5, 8**	***Al Nashiri/Abu Zubaydah*, op. paras 5, 6**
Holds that the respondent state is responsible for the ill-treatment to which the applicant was subjected at Skopje Airport and that this treatment must be classified as torture within the meaning of art 3 of the Convention.	*Holds* that there has been a violation of art 3 of the Convention in its substantive aspect, on account of the respondent state's complicity in the CIA High-Value Detainees Program in that it enabled the US authorities to subject the applicant to torture and ill treatment on its territory and to transfer the applicant from its territory despite the existence of a real risk that he would be subjected to treatment contrary to art 3.
Holds that the respondent state is responsible under art 5 of the Convention for the applicant's subsequent captivity in Afghanistan.	*Holds* that there has been a violation of art 5 of the Convention on account of the applicant's undisclosed detention on the respondent state's territory and the fact that the respondent state enabled the US authorities to transfer the applicant from its territory, despite the existence of a real risk that he would be subjected to further undisclosed detention.

and Romania, decided fours years later by a different Chamber of the Court, which reproduced verbatim the reasoning of the *Al Nashiri/Abu Zubaydah* Chamber, rather than attempting to follow the *El-Masri* Grand Chamber more closely.[56] A fifth rendition case, *Nasr*, decided by yet another Chamber in between the two *Al Nashiri/Abu Zubaydah* pairs of cases and dealing with the rendition by the CIA of an individual in Italy, is so totally unclear with regard to the conceptual basis of its reasoning that its precedential value can I think safely be discounted.[57]

effective operation of the CIA secret detention facilities": *Al Nashiri v Poland* (n 50) para 530 (emphasis added). See also *Husayn (Abu Zubaydah) v Poland* (n 50) para 524.

[56] See *Al Nashiri v Romania* App no 33234/12 (ECtHR, 31 May 2018), paras 594, 676–77, 690, op. paras 5 and 6; *Abu Zubaydah v Lithuania* App no 46454/11 (ECtHR, 31 May 2018), paras 581, 641–42, 656, op. paras 6 and 7.

[57] *Nasr and Ghali v Italy* App no 44883/09 (ECtHR, 23 February 2016). At para 262, the Chamber reaffirms the acquiescence or connivance formula, but does not do anything with it later in the case. At para 282, it frames the inquiry into the violation of art 3, on account of the ill-treatment administered to the applicant by CIA agents, as one of imputability to Italy. At para 288, the Chamber finds Italy responsible for exposing the applicant to risk of ill-treatment at the hands of the CIA, while at para 289 it finds Italy "directly responsible" for the violation of the applicant's rights, since Italy had failed to take appropriate measures to protect him. Relying on *El-Masri*, the Chamber at para 302 then finds Italy responsible not only for the applicant's abduction but also for his subsequent detention at the hands of

5. Evaluation

The analysis above allows us to have a clearer picture of the evolution of the acquiescence or connivance formula in Strasbourg case law. First, in the Kurdish cases before the European Commission, and then the Court, the language is used solely in the analysis of the respondent state's compliance with its substantive and procedural positive obligations. The language initially appeared in the applicants' pleadings and was then taken aboard by the ECHR institutions. It is clear that at the time the formula was not used as an attribution test. Second, the first time that language was framed as a proto-attribution test was in the Grand Chamber judgment in *Cyprus v Turkey*, in which it was actually not applied to the facts. Third, the acquiescence or connivance reference in *Cyprus v Turkey* then gets repeatedly reaffirmed in subsequent cases. Again, however, that language is never applied as anything resembling an attribution test. With one possible exception,[58] it is, as in prior cases, always used in the context of positive obligations. Fourth, *El-Masri* is a genuine turning point. The Grand Chamber arguably attributed the torture and subsequent detention of the applicant at the hands of US agents to Macedonia, using the language of acquiescence or connivance for the former, and of active facilitation for the latter. Moreover, the Grand Chamber for the first time used the language of acquiescence or connivance with regard to the conduct of third state officials, rather than that of private individuals. Finally, the four rendition cases after *El-Masri* appeared to give that judgment a subtly different conceptual reading, as laying down rules of state responsibility for *complicity* in the wrongful conduct of a third state, rather than directly attributing that conduct to the assisting state. That said, the absence of a full and clear explanation of what the Court is exactly doing and why is pervasive throughout this jurisprudence.

When the Court fails to properly explain itself, any outside inquiry can necessarily only be tentative and contingent on further developments in the case law. But such an inquiry into the legal nature of the acquiescence or connivance test can nonetheless usefully be attempted. First, in that regard, if the formula was seen as an aspect of a positive obligations analysis, as the Court clearly regarded it in the vast majority of cases in which it was actually applied, then there would be no inconsistency with the responsibility framework of general international law as set out by the ILC and the ICJ. But while *Cyprus v Turkey* could possibly accommodate such an interpretation, if not without effort, this is not the case with *El-Masri* and its progeny, where the Court was quite clearly doing something else.

US authorities. The Court thus constantly vacillates between different negative and positive obligations and, therefore, between different theories of Italy's responsibility.

[58] See note 37 and accompanying text.

If, therefore, acquiescence or connivance in the conduct of a third party was seen as rule of attribution, the problem is that neither of these concepts is recognized as such in general international law.[59] The ARSIWA require more than acquiescence for the conduct of a third party to be attributed to the state—it either has to instruct, direct or control such a party to commit the act in question,[60] or acknowledge and adopt the conduct as its own.[61] On the other hand, acquiescence/consent *can* be a definitional element of a primary rule by which it is characterized as wrongful. For example, the definition of torture in article 1 of the United Nations Convention Against Torture (CAT) requires pain and suffering to be "inflicted by or at the instigation of *or with the consent or acquiescence of a public official* or other person acting in an official capacity."

Connivance similarly does not figure as such in the ARSIWA. But it is worth unpacking that idea a bit. Even at a purely textual level, connivance implies active assistance to a third party committing a wrongful act that goes beyond the mere acquiescence in such an act, that is, some kind of theory of complicity. Recall that this is exactly how the Court used it in the four post-*El-Masri* rendition cases, in which it also employs the language of facilitation. And there is a (much discussed) analogue to such a concept in article 16 of the ARSIWA, which prohibits aid and assistance by one state to another which is committing an internationally wrongful act. The precise contours of article 16 are controversial, particularly with regard to the mental element of the rule.[62] But they are also to some extent beside the point for the present discussion. What matters here is that complicity issues in international law have progressively become more acute over the years, across different subfields, have inspired some rigorous scholarship, and have arisen or are likely to arise in a variety of different scenarios.[63]

[59] See Crawford and Keene, "The Structure of State Responsibility" (n 4) 189.

[60] ARSIWA, art 8.

[61] ARSIWA, art 11. Acquiescence in the conduct of a third party, that is, a state's express or tacit consent in it, could also serve a completely different purpose under art 20 of the ARSIWA, as a circumstance precluding wrongfulness. Conduct by state A that would otherwise be adversely affecting the rights of state B, and would thus be wrongful, would not be regarded as such if B consented to it, for example with regard to a use of force on its territory. This is, in fact, precisely how the consent of the territorial state operates in rendition cases. If the territorial state *consents* to a rendition operation, it cannot then claim that the operation breached its sovereignty, which it otherwise would have. But the territorial state has no capacity to consent to the violation of human rights which accrue to the relevant individual directly—such a rendition would be a violation of human rights law even if it was not a violation of the territorial state's sovereignty, because of its consent.

[62] While the text of art 16(a) provides that the assisting state will be responsible if it assists the wrongdoing state "with knowledge of the circumstances of the internationally wrongful act," the commentary to the provision says (at para 3) that "aid or assistance must be given with a view to facilitating the commission of that act," that is, it *prima facie* sets out some kind of intent or purpose requirement.

[63] See generally H Aust, *Complicity and the Law of State Responsibility* (CUP 2011); M Jackson, *Complicity in International Law* (OUP 2015); V Lanovoy, *Complicity and Its Limits in the Law of International Responsibility* (Hart 2016); H Moynihan, "Aiding and Assisting: Challenges in Armed Conflict and Counterterrorism" *International Law Programme: Chatham House*, November 2016) <https://www.chathamhouse.org/sites/default/files/publications/research/2016-11-11-aiding-assisting-challenges-armed-conflict-moynihan.pdf> accessed 6 June 2022.

For our purposes, the key point is that nothing prevents the European Court and other human rights bodies from developing their own complicity doctrines.[64] Such doctrines can better take into account the specificities of the human rights context than the rule in article 16 of the ARSIWA. They can, for example, quite sensibly cover complicity in the wrongful conduct of non-state actors, unlike the purely inter-state rule in article 16.[65] Indeed, until *El-Masri*, the Court applied the acquiescence or connivance formula *only* in the context of relationships between states and non-state actors. They can use different mental elements. They can cover complicity in the wrongful conduct of third states, regardless of whether they were parties to the ECHR or not, as was in fact the case in the Strasbourg rendition judgments we looked at above. In some circumstances such complicity doctrines could be *imputational*, in the sense that the accomplice is regarded as equally legally and morally liable as the principal,[66] in others that need not be the case, as with the rule in article 16 of the ARSIWA.[67]

In short, *El-Masri* and its progeny could be seen as the point of emergence of a new state complicity doctrine in human rights law, rather than as an example of the use of a special rule of attribution of conduct in the sense of article 55 of the ARSIWA. This is an outcome to be preferred both as a matter of common sense and in order to preserve coherence in the rules of attribution.[68] What Macedonia, Poland, Lithuania, and Romania *actually did* was *not* the mistreatment or subsequent deprivation of liberty of the applicants; what they *did* was to *assist* the United States in such misconduct, through their consent to the US presence on their territories, the provision of facilities for their use, permitting the passage of rendition

[64] For reasons of space I cannot engage here in extensive comparisons between ECHR jurisprudence and that of other human rights bodies in this regard. See, however, *Mohammed Alzery v Sweden* (Views of the UN Human Rights Committee) CCPR/C/88/D/1416/2005 (10 November 2006) [11.6] (using acquiescence as an attribution rule); *Velásquez-Rodríguez v Honduras* (Merits) IACtHR Series C no 4 (29 July 1988) [173] (referring to state support and acquiescence in the context of a positive obligations analysis); *Mapiripán Massacre v Colombia* (Judgment) IACtHR Series C no 134 (15 September 2005) [120]–[123] (vacillating between several different conceptual bases of state responsibility, including arguably attribution on account of the state's collaboration, acquiescence, and tolerance in the conduct of non-state actors). See also Jackson, *Complicity in International Law* (n 63) 190–99.

[65] While the text of art 16 is expressly confined to inter-state aid and assistance, in the *Bosnian Genocide* case the ICJ used it by analogy to interpret the meaning of prohibited complicity in genocide under the terms of the Genocide Convention, which does extend to complicity in the conduct of non-state actors. See *Application of the Convention on the Prevention and Punishment of the Crime of Genocide (Bosnia and Herzegovina v Serbia and Montenegro)* (Judgment) [2007] ICJ Rep 43 [420].

[66] See eg Jackson, *Complicity in International Law* (n 63) 10–47, 86–88.

[67] See ILC Commentary to art 16, para 10: "[I]n accordance with article 16, the assisting State is responsible for its own act in deliberately assisting another State to breach an international obligation by which they are both bound. It is not responsible, as such, for the act of the assisted State."

[68] Coherence is of course not some kind of absolute goal in itself. The basic problem of special attribution tests is that it is difficult to justify why the particular attributive approach in question is only warranted in one specific context, that is, why it should not seep into others, where it might have undesirable consequences. See eg M Milanovic, "Self-Defense and Non-State Actors: Indeterminacy and the *jus ad bellum*" (*EJIL:Talk!*, 21 February 2010) <http://www.ejiltalk.org/self-defense-and-non-state-actors-indeterminacy-and-the-jus-ad-bellum/> accessed 6 June 2022; Jackson, *Complicity in International Law* (n 63) 197.

flights, and the like. The complicity frame provides a better fit for assessing the wrongfulness of the conduct of the assisting states, and the acquiescence or connivance formula should best be seen in that light.

6. Conclusion

The Court's innovations with respect to the acquiescence or connivance test stem from the need to find a middle ground between two different forms of state responsibility for human rights violations—those of negative or positive obligations, depending on whether the wrongful conduct being attributed to the state was one of action or of omission. The Court needed something in between for those situations in which the principal wrong was not committed by the state's own organs or agents, but in which it would also be unsatisfactory to find the state liable for the "mere" failure to protect an individual for someone else's misconduct.[69] A doctrine of complicity—fully theorized or not—naturally occupied this middle ground.[70]

Two other considerations drive complicity cases such as *El-Masri*. First, the Court's assessment that the state officials making the relevant decisions in such cases acted with a higher degree of culpability than the mere awareness of a (substantial) risk that human rights violations could be committed by a third party, which would normally suffice for the triggering of a due diligence positive obligation. Second, the Court's assessment that the conduct of the complicit state causally significantly contributed to the human rights violation, again to an extent that goes beyond a mere failure to exercise due diligence.

These two concerns are evident in the language that the Court uses, even if that language is imprecise and ambiguous. Acquiescence and connivance sound like *mens rea* standards. The former implies a higher degree of knowledge or certainty than that required for a mere failure to exercise due diligence, as well as a conscious decision to accept the consequences of someone else's wrongful actions.[71] The latter implies some degree of inferred intent to assist the principal in their wrongful conduct. With regard to causality, as we have seen the Court makes frequent references to the territorial state actively facilitating or enabling the misconduct of the third party, or the assistance provided being "a necessary condition" or "creating the conditions" for the human rights violation to happen. Thus, in the rendition cases the territorial state did not just tolerate the egregious activities of US agents, but provided them with facilities, landing permits, logistical assistance,

[69] See also Nollkaemper, "ECtHR Finds Macedonia Responsible" (n 44) (discussing the heightened "normative power" of the Court's approach compared to the general law of state responsibility).

[70] See Jørgensen, "Complicity in Torture" (n 40) 33.

[71] See ibid (arguing that actual knowledge is logically a prerequisite for acquiescence—although one could also acquiesce with the knowledge of a risk of a violation occurring, rather than with certainty in that regard).

and so forth. In due diligence, positive obligation cases there is no need to prove that, had the state acted in a particular way, it likely would have managed to prevent the human rights violation from occurring. On the other hand, in cases such as *El-Masri* it is, in fact, evident that without the territorial state's toleration and assistance provided to the third party the latter would most likely not have been able to engage in its misconduct.

There is nothing surprising in the Court's reliance on considerations of culpability and causality. Even if its approach is manifestly undertheorized, it is broadly in line with common moral intuitions and various approaches to degrees of blameworthiness in comparative law, especially criminal law. We would generally regard conduct which a person engages in knowingly or purposely to be more blameworthy than the same conduct committed negligently. And we would generally regard wrongful actions to be more blameworthy than wrongful omissions (eg the distinction between killing someone and standing by while someone is killed).[72]

If the Court's acquiescence or connivance test ultimately develops into a fully fledged complicity doctrine, this could serve several different purposes. First, it could lead to greater descriptive and conceptual accuracy, and hence greater certainty and predictability. Second, it could enhance the Court's ability to apportion blameworthiness, allowing it room to express variability in the stigma attached to human rights violations, as a mid-way point on a spectrum which ranges from the "mere" failure to diligently protect an individual to the actual attribution of the violation to the state. Finally, it could feed more rigorously into the Court's decision-making on the apportionment of damages and other forms of reparation. These are, of course, matters on which the Court has been notoriously flexible and not particularly rule-bound, and may not want to become more rule-bound in the future for the sake of more coherence and clarity. That said, it is reasonably clear that a complicity doctrine, even a non-imputational one, can always take into account the consequences of the wrongful provision of assistance further down in the causal chain, such as the subsequent mistreatment or prolonged detention of the applicants at the hands of third parties, as in *El-Masri* and the other rendition cases. In other words, one need not attribute the entirety of a person's detention or mistreatment to an assisting state, which the Court did in *El-Masri* but arguably did not do in the four *Al Nashiri/Abu Zubaydah* judgments, in order to require the state to fully compensate a person so detained or mistreated due to the wrongful assistance that the state had provided.

Obviously there is no way of knowing in which direction precisely will the Court take its acquiescence or connivance formula. It remains to been seen how rigorous and how careful the Court will be in setting out and applying the elements of its

[72] For an extensive examination, see M Moore, *Causation and Responsibility: An Essay in Law, Morals, and Metaphysics* (OUP 2009). See also C Sartorio, "Moore on Doing versus Allowing Harm" (2011) 42 Rutgers Law Journal 435.

complicity doctrine, and delineating it from alternatives, be they human rights-specific (eg positive obligations to ensure or protect human rights) or based in general international law (eg tests of attribution and the aid and assisting rule in article 16 of the ARSIWA). The key doctrinal issue is whether the Court will be developing a single or variegated theory of complicity, with associated variable degrees of attached stigma and reparations, on the basis of different levels of the complicit state's culpability/*mens rea* and causal contribution to the principal's violation of the applicant's rights.[73] Similarly, the Court will need to decide whether its complicity theory or theories will cover only *some* or *all* human rights in the Convention, for example whether state complicity in violations of the freedom of expression or the right to private life should be treated essentially in the same way as complicity in torture or deprivations of life or liberty.[74]

More fundamentally, it remains to be seen just how far the Court will be prepared to go in proscribing complicit state conduct, at the cost of potentially inhibiting cooperation between states (and non-state actors) serving other purposes which potentially advance general welfare. One specific item of uncertainty is that *El-Masri* and its progeny have dealt with complicit behavior on the state's own territory, in which the individual concerned was located. A more fraught question regards complicity in extraterritorial situations—think only of the provision of weapons or intelligence by European states to third parties engaged in serious violations of human rights and international humanitarian law in the wars in Syria and Yemen. Cases of extraterritorial complicity will be easier if the assisting state controls the relevant territory de facto, as was indeed the case in *Cyprus v Turkey*, the progenitor of the acquiescence or connivance test. But it again remains unclear whether the Court will be willing to go beyond that, to assistance provided without such territorial control. Consider, for example, the extraordinary rendition of Abdelhakim Belhaj and his pregnant wife to the Gaddafi regime in Libya,

[73] For example, a "softer" version of complicity could require only knowledge or some form of risk-based constructive knowledge on the part of the assisting state, while a "harder" version could be based on intent to assist, that is, connivance. Again, factoring in also the degree of causal contribution, ranging from the assistance substantially contributing to the human rights violation to it being a "but for" cause of the violation, the Court could conceivably make the "softer" version non-imputational and the "harder" one imputational. The risk-based "softer" complicity rule could be based on an analogy to state *non-refoulement* obligations in the context of torture and other forms of ill-treatment per *Soering v United Kingdom* App no 14038/88 (ECtHR, 7 July 1989) and its progeny. The prophylactic *Soering non-refoulement* rule is strictly speaking not one of complicity, since a violation of that rule occurs with the mere exposure of an individual to a real risk of harm, even if the risk itself does not subsequently materialize, that is, the further violation does not occur. See also Jørgensen, "Complicity in Torture" (n 40) 39 (distinguishing active from passive complicity); M Jackson, "Freeing *Soering*: The ECHR, State Complicity in Torture and Jurisdiction" (2016) 27 European Journal of International Law 817 (arguing for a *Soering* analogy).

[74] The state-to-state aid and assisting rule in art 16 of the ARSIWA would notably apply to *any* human rights violations across the board, so long as the states concerned are bound by the same substantive obligations. See also Jackson, "Freeing *Soering*" (n 73) 828–30 (arguing for a rule on complicity in torture, but noting that the normative argument could be equally valid for other human rights, especially the absolute ones).

committed by the CIA but initiated by the sharing of relevant intelligence by UK authorities, who arguably "connived" at Belhaj's rendition and without whose assistance the rendition would likely not have happened.[75] In all matters of substance except for extraterritoriality this does not seem to be a case that is distinguishable from *El-Masri*, yet we just cannot know how the Court would resolve it.[76]

One thing, however, is certain—cases based on allegations of wrongfully complicit behavior will keep coming to the Court, and will likely do so more and more frequently. A conceptually sound approach regarding complicity, which is reasonably clear, grounded in principle and avoids arbitrary line-drawing is needed with some urgency, and is probably not best built piecemeal.

[75] The domestic UK litigation initiated by Belhaj against the UK government was ultimately settled; the UK government issued a public apology to Belhaj and his wife and paid compensation without admitting legal liability. See "Britain apologises for 'appalling treatment' of Abdel Hakim Belhaj," *The Guardian*, 10 May 2018, at https://www.theguardian.com/world/2018/may/10/britain-apologises-for-appalling-treatment-of-abdel-hakim-belhaj; "Belhaj and Boudchar: Litigation Update," *The Hansard*, 10 May 2018, at https://hansard.parliament.uk/commons/2018-05-10/debates/B9AD50CD-9D54-41DA-A18B-1526E7658593/BelhajAndBoudcharLitigationUpdate.

[76] See Jackson, "Freeing *Soering*" (n 73) (arguing for an expansive approach to extraterritorial complicity); Milanovic, "Jurisdiction and Responsibility" (n 4) 124–26, 209–22 (discussing complicity scenarios, arguing that negative obligations should apply without any territorial limitation, including the obligation to refrain from complicity in violations committed by third parties).

13

A Comparison of the Rules of Attribution in the Law of State Responsibility, State Immunity, and Custom

*Christina Binder and Stephan Wittich**

1. Introduction

In general, attribution describes the process by which a specific fact is ascribed to a particular person. Any operation of attribution, and the rules governing that process, will be necessarily guided by the perception of reality. However, if we do not know as a matter of certainty a fact whose existence is legally relevant, we will have to resort to a presumption. Such a presumption will be based on proven facts or previous experience, through which we may substitute reality with our own subjective understanding of it. Alternatively, we may establish a fiction that attempts to reproduce reality as closely as possible.

For instance, if we do not know who has created a particular piece of art, for instance a painting, we may *attribute* it to an artist according to "objective" indicators that exist in reality, such as theme, style, use of colors and light, material, allegories, and so on. This process of attribution implies always an act of accountability for a certain fact or result, whatever the nature of the act to be attributed.

On that general basis, international law is full of rules of attribution, those in the law of state responsibility being the most prominent, but certainly not the only ones. Causation and evidence, some of the other topics dealt with in this volume, equally contain a number of rules that perform an attributive function in that they ascribe a specific result or effect to the conduct of a person or entity.

This chapter, in turn, will take a closer look at two further areas which contain attributive rules, that is, the law of state immunity and customary international law, and compare them with the well-known and recognized rules of the law of state responsibility. The rules of attribution in all three of these fields of international law deal with issues where the state acts through persons or entities.[1] With regard to

* The authors wish to thank Mag Isabella Brunner and Mag Koloman Roiger-Simek for valuable research assistance.

[1] See Chapter 1.

Christina Binder and Stephan Wittich, *A Comparison of the Rules of Attribution in the Law of State Responsibility, State Immunity, and Custom* In: *Secondary Rules of Primary Importance in International Law.* Edited by: Gábor Kajtár, Başak Çalı, and Marko Milanovic, Oxford University Press. © Christina Binder and Stephan Wittich 2022. DOI: 10.1093/oso/9780192869012.003.0013

state immunity, the question arises as to who is considered to be so closely linked up with the state that he, she, or it may reasonably benefit from rules of jurisdictional immunity.[2] In order for custom to emerge, both practice and *opinio juris* must be attributable to a state. Here as well, attributive rules determine which state actors are able to establish such *opinio juris* and state practice.

As we will show, all three fields—responsibility, immunities, and custom—show basic commonalities but also certain differences as to what is considered to be the state for the sake of attribution. One particularly interesting aspect of the rules of attribution in any of the fields mentioned is the fact that what or "who" is considered a state in terms of attribution has undergone certain changes over time, and the rules of attribution may well be deemed to reflect the overall changing international landscape to this effect. The rules of attribution may thus be considered a prism through which the state and its functions reflect the evolution of the international community.[3]

At the same time, the relevance of the nature of attributive rules varies. In the law of (state) responsibility, attribution is undoubtedly governed by secondary rules—if only because the law of responsibility in general is generally confined to stipulating secondary rules.[4] However, that type of distinction into primary and secondary rules has developed, and was devised, against the specific backdrop of the law of responsibility and cannot be transferred *tel quel* to the context of custom and state immunity. In fact, it is highly doubtful whether that distinction indeed makes sense, or can be reasonably used with regard to the two latter fields. It also follows that the question whether secondary rules have developed in a harmonized or standardized way that would allow them to apply in a broad manner to as many cases as possible within one of the fields examined, or whether the individual rules are tailor-made to specific circumstances and situations, does not arise. Unsurprisingly, the situation is different across the fields, given that the various rules of attribution in the areas of responsibility, immunity, and custom serve different purposes. There is no "one size fits all" set of attributive rules applying to each area. Finally, as is well known, the law of state responsibility allows for the possibility of displacing the existing set of rules by agreeing on a *lex specialis*,[5] and while this possibility also applies to the rules of attribution,[6] in practice there are hardly any *leges speciales* on

[2] See X Yang, *State Immunity in International Law* (CUP 2012) 230.

[3] In that context, see H Fox and P Webb, *The Law of State Immunity* (3rd edn, OUP 2013) 7 regarding state immunity: "[T]he doctrine provides a valuable case study of the present nature of the international community and in particular the interaction of international law and national law."

[4] ILC, (1970) II(2) Yearbook of the International Law Commission 306. See also L Condorelli and C Kress, "The Rules of Attribution: General Considerations" in J Crawford and others (eds), *The Law of International Responsibility* (OUP 2010) 221, 224–25.

[5] See art 55 of the UN ILC, "Draft Articles on Responsibility of States for Internationally Wrongful Acts, with Commentaries" (2001) GAOR 56th Session Supp. 10, 43 (ARSIWA).

[6] J Crawford, "First Report on State Responsibility" (1998) II(2) Yearbook of the International Law Commission 33 [154].

attribution.[7]

This chapter addresses, by way of comparison, the commonalities as well as the distinctions between the various rules of attribution in these areas. It begins by briefly explaining the nature and rationales behind the rules of attribution in the different fields (section 2). Section 3 then turns to structure and function as elements of attribution applicable to all fields, state responsibility, immunity, as well as custom. Section 4 compares the three areas of attribution in relation to specific issues, that is, attribution of conduct of private persons, *ultra vires* acts, as well as the nature of the respective acts. As mentioned earlier, the rules of attribution also reflect developments and conceptual shifts in international law more generally, which are examined in section 5.

As relevant yardsticks for the pertinent rules of attribution we will take a more in-depth look at the International Law Commission (ILC) Articles on State Responsibility for Internationally Wrongful Acts (ARSIWA),[8] the UN Convention on Jurisdictional Immunities of States and their Property (Jurisdictional Immunities Convention),[9] and the recent ILC Conclusions on the Identification of Customary International Law (ILC Conclusions).[10]

2. The Rationale Underlying the Rules of Attribution: General Remarks

Attribution is the process by which international law establishes whether the conduct of a natural person can be considered an act of state and thus ascribed to it.[11] In general, the nature or character of rules of attribution may be either normative/prescriptive or factual/descriptive. On the one hand, the normative approach would consider attribution as being based on criteria determined by law and require a legal assessment according to prescriptive legal norms and not of the mere recognition of a link of factual connection of causation. The descriptive or factual approach, on the other hand, would tie attribution to the factual perception of the person applying the law; in other words, it does not view attribution as a legal operation, but a simple empirical statement by the interpreter in question of a factual situation.[12]

[7] See Bruno Simma and Dirk Pulkowski, "Of Planets and the Universe: Self-contained Regimes in International Law" (2006) 17 European Journal of International Law 483, 488 (observing the general lack of a reference to special rules in state responsibility.

[8] UN ILC, "Draft Articles on Responsibility of States for Internationally Wrongful Acts, with Commentaries" (2001) (n 5).

[9] United Nations Convention on Jurisdictional Immunities of States and their Property, 2 December 2004, UN Doc A/RES/59/38.

[10] United Nations General Assembly (UNGA), "Text of the Draft Conclusions on Identification of Customary International Law" in Report of the International Law Commission (2018) GAOR 73rd Session Supp 10, UN Doc A/73/10 (ILC Conclusions).

[11] J Crawford, *State Responsibility: The General Part* (CUP 2013) 113.

[12] Condorelli and Kress, "The Rules of Attribution" (n 4) 226.

There is general agreement in the doctrine that rules of attribution in international law are normative or prescriptive rather than factual or descriptive. Whether for the purpose of establishing responsibility, immunity, or custom, the decisive criteria for attribution are assigned by international law in the first place, and do not follow from an empirical interpretation of facts that would establish a causal link between the act at issue and the state "behind" it.[13] This, of course, does not mean that attribution is detached from the factual circumstances or details of the particular case. Not only would this be in outright tension with the essential need that law shall govern or prescribe factual conduct; it would also ignore the fundamental idea that "normative processes must demonstrate sensitivity to the facts of each case."[14]

However, attributive rules frequently refer to domestic law and, as is well known, from the viewpoint of international law, domestic law is merely a fact.[15] This would strongly militate in favor of a factual construction of attributive rules. However, when the rules of attribution in the field of responsibility or of immunity refer to the status of an organ of the state under municipal law, it is precisely the *international* norm that provides for such reference as part of the operation of the process of attribution. Furthermore, we have to bear in mind that attribution always implies a strong element of representation and, within the conceptual framework of the *dédoublement fonctionnel*,[16] it will be first and foremost up to the state itself to determine which of its organs and agents shall be capable of acting on its behalf externally, even though such assessment will neither be exclusive nor exhaustive.

Turning now to the rationale behind attribution, this question cannot be entirely detached from the overall purpose of the field of law that the relevant attributive rules pertain to. In other words, and as mentioned above, the purpose of rules of attribution will follow the purpose of the area they are part of. Given the fact that the individual areas have different aims and purposes, the approach will necessarily differ between responsibility, immunity, and custom in relation to the state whose conduct is at issue.

For example, if a state is held accountable for internationally wrongful conduct, it will be burdened or encumbered if attribution is affirmed.[17] From the perspective

[13] The ILC commentaries make this clear by stating that "[t]he attribution of conduct to the State as a subject of international law is based on criteria determined by international law and not on the mere recognition of a link of factual causality": see ARSIWA Commentary (n NOTEREF _Ref21077667 \h* MERGEFORMAT 5, 38–39 (Part I, Chapter II, para 4). See also C Lehnardt, *Private Militärfirmen und völkerrechtliche Verantwortlichkeit* (Mohr Siebeck 2011) 124.

[14] Crawford, *State Responsibility: The General Part* (n 11) 114.

[15] *Certain German Interests in Polish Upper Silesia (Germany v Poland)* (Merits) 1926 PCIJ Series A no 7 at 19 (25 May 1926): "From the standpoint of International Law and of the Court which is its organ, municipal laws are merely facts which express the will and constitute the activities of States, in the same manner as do legal decisions or administrative measures."

[16] Georges Scelle, "Règles générales du droit de la paix" (1934) 46 Collected Courses of the Hague Academy of International Law 331.

[17] cf art 1 of the ARSIWA (n 5).

of the acting state, a restrictive approach to responsibility may thus be warranted to limit accountability as much as possible. Conversely, in the field of immunities, the state will benefit in case of attribution, as it will be protected against the exercise of another state's jurisdiction by the operation of immunity if the relevant act or organ can be attributed to it.[18] Therefore, the rules of attribution in the law of immunities perform a defensive function and aim at procuring a result clearly favored by the state involved. This setting will presumably call for an *extensive* or *inclusive* scope of the rules of attribution so as to cover as many persons, organs, agencies, entities, instrumentalities etc. of the state as possible. Customary international law for its part concerns the development of a new norm of international law. Based on the rules of attribution the state contributes to the formation of such a new norm, which may either impose upon the state an obligation, extend an existing one—and, in either case, limit that state's freedom to act—or it may grant that state a right. With regard to custom, therefore, the scope of the rules of attribution—extensive or restrictive—depends on the particular rule of customary law in the process of being formed.

Of course, what matters is not necessarily only the perspective of the acting state. The outcome may well be different if one takes other interests such as those of the victim state in the case state responsibility or of the individual in case of state immunity into account. As will be shown, this is also borne out by the subsequent analysis.

3. Structure and Function as Guiding Elements of the Rules of Attribution

3.1 General

In order to answer the question as to who is considered a state for the sake of attribution we will now turn to a more specific analysis of the rules of attribution. Looking at their general layout, two guiding elements can usually be discerned, namely structure and function. Structure here means the position, status, or rank of a person or entity within a state's internal organization, whereas function describes the role such a person or entity actually plays in the performance of state conduct.

[18] cf P-T Stoll, "State Immunity" in R. Wolfrum (ed), *Max Planck Encyclopedia of Public International Law (online ed.)* (2011) para 1.

3.2 Structure

The first element to be considered is that of structure. Attribution in the *law of state responsibility* crucially focuses on the status of the relevant organ within the structure of the state's internal organization as exemplified by article 4 of the ARSIWA.[19] The approach taken is comprehensive: given the diversity of international obligations, "virtually" any state organ, that is, any state organ acting in an official capacity, may be the author of an internationally wrongful act.[20] Similarly, and not very surprisingly, the UN Jurisdictional Immunities Convention ascribes immunity to "the State and its various organs of government."[21] As for *custom*, the ILC equally states that to "qualify as State practice, the conduct in question must be " 'of the State' ", meaning the conduct "of any State organ."[22]

The similarity between all three fields is quite striking, and it is telling that the ILC's commentaries to both the state immunity draft and the conclusions on the identification of custom refer to the wording of article 4 of the ARSIWA.[23] Dogmatically, this is a little perplexing because the Commentary to the ARSIWA seems to avoid, or even rule out, any such "reverse reference" when it states: "The question of attribution of conduct to the state for the purposes of responsibility is to be distinguished from other international law processes by which particular organs are authorized to enter into commitments on behalf of the state."[24] In any event, it follows for present purposes that, broadly speaking, the same concept of organ status as that employed in the law of state responsibility applies equally in the field of state immunity and custom. This includes particularly the following aspects:

[19] Article 4 of the ARSIWA (n 5) stipulates the following: "1. The conduct of any State organ shall be considered an act of that State under international law, whether the organ exercises legislative, executive, judicial or any other functions, whatever position it holds in the organization of the State, and whatever its character as an organ of the central Government or of a territorial unit of the State."

[20] ARSIWA Commentary (n5) 40 (art 4, para 5).

[21] See Jurisdictional Immunities Convention (n 9) art 2(1)(b).

[22] ILC Conclusions (n 10) 132.

[23] See ILC, Second Report on Identification of Customary International Law (Michael Wood, Special Rapporteur, 66th Session) (2014) UN Doc A/CN.4/672, 17, para 34: "As in other cases, such as State responsibility and subsequent practice in relation to the interpretation of treaties, for practice to be relevant for the formation of customary international law it must be attributable to the State. For this purpose, the actions of all branches of Government (whether exercising executive, legislative, judicial or other functions) may be relevant."

[24] ARSIWA Commentary (n 5) 39 (Pt I, Ch II, para 5), referring to the Vienna Convention on the Law of Treaties (VCLT) (27 January 1980) 1155 UNTS 331, (1980) 8 International Legal Materials 331. The Commentary continues to state that "the rules concerning attribution set out in [Chapter II of Part I] are formulated for this particular purpose [of responsibility], and not for other purposes for which it may be necessary to define the State or its government."

- irrelevance of whether the organ belongs to the executive, the legislative or the judiciary;[25]
- irrelevance of the position the organ holds in the organization of the state;[26]
- irrelevance of the organ's character as one of the central government or of a territorial units of the state.[27]

As already mentioned, this structural element invariably implies a reference to the organization of the state according to its own internal laws. Accordingly, we find in all three areas the general agreement that an organ includes any person or entity that has that status in accordance with the internal law of that state and acts in that capacity as an organ.[28] In addition, state responsibility, immunity, and custom have in common that the conduct of *de facto* organs is attributable to the state as well. The term *de facto* organ on this basis describes any person, agency, or other entity that is not bestowed as such in the formal sense under the internal law of the state, but that has the "factual status" to exercise government authority, or is otherwise controlled by the state on the basis of mere internal practice, and essentially acts in the same manner as a state organ having a formal status as such. This is recognized by the ARSIWA,[29] and while the UN Jurisdictional Immunities Convention primarily refers to municipal law in establishing the organ status,[30] it leaves room for relying on the internal practice of the forum state, at least in some matters.[31] The point here is that the state enjoys complete control over the person or entity concerned.[32]

[25] The concept of "separation of powers" is not relevant for attributing state responsibility, see art 4 of the ARSIWA (n 5). Regarding state immunity, see Fox and Webb, *The Law of State Immunity* (n 3) 347; Regarding customary international law, see ILC Conclusions (n 10) 132.

[26] Regarding state responsibility, see art 4 of the ARSIWA (n 5). Regarding state immunity, see Jurisdictional Immunities Convention (n 9) art 2(1)(b)(i). Regarding customary international law, see ILC Conclusions, (n 10) 135 (Commentary to Conclusions 7, para 2).

[27] Regarding state responsibility, see again art 4 of the ARSIWA (n 5). Regarding state immunity, see Jurisdictional Immunities Convention (n 9) art 2(1)(b)(ii). Regarding customary international law, this can be—again—deduced from ILC Conclusions, (n 10) 135 (Commentary to Conclusion 7, para 2), which takes into account "practice of all of the State's organs."

[28] Concerning state responsibility, see i.a. ARSIWA Commentary (n 5) 39 (Pt I, Ch II, para 6). Concerning customary international law, see BD Lepard, *Customary International Law: A New Theory with Practical Applications* (CUP 2010) 173. Concerning state immunity, see Fox and Webb, *The Law of State Immunity* (n 3) 335ff.

[29] ARSIWA Commentary (n 5) 42 (art 4, para 11): "In some systems the status and functions of various entities are determined not only by law but also by practice, and reference exclusively to internal law would be misleading."

[30] See T Grant, "Article 2(2)(*a*) and (*b*)" in R O'Keefe and CJ Tams (eds), *The United Nations Convention on Jurisdictional Immunities of States and Their Property: A Commentary* (2013) 40, 49.

[31] See eg art 2(2) referring to the practice of the forum state, albeit in the context of determining the commercial nature of an act.

[32] *Application of the Convention on the Prevention and Punishment of the Crime of Genocide (Bosnia and Herzegovina v Serbia and Montenegro)* (Merits) [2007] ICJ Rep 43 [392] (*Bosnian Genocide*); Crawford, "First Report" (n 6) 124–25. See also P Palchetti, "De Facto Organs of a State" in R Wolfrum (ed), *Max Planck Encyclopedia of Public International Law* (2017, online ed.) paras 5, 13; Marko Milanovic, "State Responsibility for Genocide" (2006) 17(3) European Journal of International Law 553, 582. Regarding customary international law, see ILC Second Report on Identification of Custom

Therefore, as regards attribution through structure, the basic rules are generally the same for all three fields: acts are attributed to a state when they originate from state organs including entities that are, very broadly, part of a state's structure.

3.3 Function

The second aspect is that of function, and a brief analysis yields a picture very similar to that of formal organ status: in all three areas it is recognized that the conduct of persons or entities who, while not having the formal status as an organ, are empowered to exercise elements of governmental control, is attributable to the state, provided that the person or entity is acting in that capacity in the particular instance. The relevant reference point here is article 5 of the ARSIWA, which relates to the situation where sovereign or governmental authority is delegated to an entity that is not a state organ, but a private party—a so-called "parastatal entity."[33] The underlying assumption is that states should not escape responsibility through outsourcing or representation.[34] Article 5 of the ARSIWA thus incorporates the "functional test of attribution" as compared to the "structural test" in article 4 of the ARSIWA.[35] Attribution accordingly is based on a dual criterion: internal law must authorize an entity to exercise some sort of governmental authority (formal criterion) and the relevant conduct must relate to governmental activity (not just some private or commercial activity).[36]

The obvious example from state immunity where the functional test is pivotal concerns entities, including private entities that are not established by the state as organs, but nonetheless endowed with governmental authority within the meaning of "State" in article 2(1)(b)(iii) of the Jurisdictional Immunities Convention.[37] Similar considerations apply to representatives of the state "acting in that capacity" in article 2(1)(b)(iv) of the Convention. In the law of state immunity, therefore, two requirements are to be met by an entity in order to be granted immunity, that is,

(n 23) 17–18, para 34. Regarding the concept of *de facto* organs and state immunity, cf Yang, *State Immunity* (n 2) 230–31.

33 See ARSIWA Commentary (n 5) 42–43 (art 5, para 1f).

34 ARSIWA Commentary (n 5) 43 (art 5, para 5): "The justification for attributing to the State under international law the conduct of 'parastatal' entities lies in the fact that the internal law of the State has conferred on the entity in question the exercise of certain elements of the governmental authority."

35 Crawford, *State Responsibility: The General Part* (n 11) 127.

36 ARSIWA Commentary (n 5) 42 f (art 5, paras 3, 7). Thus, art 5 is very narrow in its application.

37 According to art 2(1)(b) of the Jurisdictional Immunities Convention (n 9): " 'State' means: . . . agencies or instrumentalities of the State or other entities, to the extent that they are entitled to perform and are actually performing acts in the exercise of sovereign authority of the State." See also art 27 of the European Convention on State Immunity, 16 May 1972 (adopted 16 May 1972, entered into force 11 June 1976), (1972) 11 International Legal Materials 470.

that it is entitled to perform acts of governmental authority and that it is actually performing it in the particular case.

Finally, in customary international law, to qualify as state practice, "the conduct of a person or entity otherwise empowered by the law of the state to exercise elements of governmental authority is also conduct 'of the State,' provided the person or entity is acting in that capacity in the particular instance."[38] It is obvious here that the ILC just copied the text and the substance of the ARSIWA, particularly articles 4 and 5. Whether this self-referential approach is convincing, supported by practice, and theoretically sustainable is an altogether different question that cannot be addressed in the present context; it remains however a fact that the ILC expressly approved of that transferral of concepts.[39]

Thus, also in case of attribution through function, the basic rules are roughly the same for all three areas of law. The functional rules of attribution in the law of state responsibility, state immunity as well as in the emergence of custom consider entities to constitute a state to the extent that they are entitled to and actually perform acts of governmental authority.

3.4 Evaluation

Overall, all three areas rely on the same two elements for determining what constitutes a state and whether a specific conduct is indeed attributable to the state: structure and function. There are thus no real differences between the three fields as regards these general rules of attribution. These similarities are largely due to the fact that, as already mentioned, the materials of the codification processes of both the law of state immunity and the identification of customary law regularly invoke and refer to the law of state responsibility, which was a kind of blueprint with regard to the rules of attribution. As mentioned, one may validly doubt the conceptual justification for this but one motive for this kind of recursion may have been precisely to establish an element of consistency between these comparable areas.

In sum, the rules of state responsibility, immunity and custom rely on basically the same elements—structure and function—in general terms. They have also undergone a similar evolution during the respective drafting processes. While general elements are similar, differences relate in particular to issues that are more specific. This will be shown next.

[38] See ILC Conclusions (n 10) 132: to qualify as state practice, the conduct in question must be "of the State, provided the person or entity is acting in that capacity in the particular instance."

[39] The ILC Conclusions refer in fn 699 to Conclusion 5 to arts 4 and 5 of the ARSIWA, see ibid.

4. Specific Issues Concerning Attribution

The deeper one digs into specific questions of attribution, the more will differences between the areas under scrutiny surface. Of particular interest seem to be the following three points: first, the issue of attribution of conduct of private persons; second, the problem of *ultra vires* acts; and third, the nature of the act itself whose attribution is at issue. We will address these questions in turn.

4.1 Conduct of Private Persons

It is well recognized that in the law of state responsibility the conduct of private persons is, on certain conditions, attributable to the state. This is exemplified particularly by article 8, providing that the conduct of private entities or persons will be attributed to the state if they are controlled by that state,[40] and article 11 of the ARSIWA, providing that the conduct of private entities or persons will be attributed to the state if the conduct is adopted by that state as its own.[41]

The situation is different in the law of state immunity: there, conduct carried out by private individuals is not attributed to the state and, as a consequence, private persons do not benefit from the rules of immunity unless a "proper" rule of attribution applies, for example, because the individual or entity somehow exercises elements of governmental control and sovereign authority on behalf of the state.[42] The UN Convention, for instance, does not contain a rule of attribution of conduct by private persons similar to articles 8 or 11 of the ARSIWA. The definition of the term "State" in article 2(b) of the Jurisdictional Immunities Convention is limited to state organs in the structural or functional sense. No mention is made of private persons or entities unless of course they are entitled to exercise sovereign powers

[40] Article 8 of the ARSIWA (n 5), stipulates that "[t]he conduct of a person or group of persons shall be considered an act of a State under international law if the person or group of persons is in fact acting on the instructions of, or under the direction or control of, that State in carrying out the conduct."

[41] Article 11 of the ARSIWA stipulates that "[c]onduct which is not attributable to a State under the preceding articles shall nevertheless be considered an act of that State under international law if and to the extent that the State acknowledges and adopts the conduct in question as its own." Regarding the necessary degree of control for conduct to be attributed, the ICJ generally resorts to the "effective control" test: see *Case Concerning Military and Paramilitary Activities in and Against Nicaragua (Nicaragua v United States of America)* (Merits) [1986] ICJ Rep 14 [115]; *Bosnian Genocide* (n 32) [400]. For adoption of conduct, see *United States Diplomatic and Consular Staff in Tehran (United States of America v Iran)* (Merits) [1980] ICJ Rep 3 [74] (*Tehran Hostages*).

[42] cf Yang, *State Immunity* (n 2) 230–31; Palchetti, "De Facto Organs of a State" (32) para 5; cf also along that line art 27 of the European Convention on State Immunity (n 37): "For the purposes of the present Convention, the expression "Contracting State" shall not include any legal entity of a Contracting State which is distinct therefrom and is capable of being sued, even if that entity has been entrusted with public functions. 2. Proceedings may be instituted against any entity referred to in paragraph 1 before the courts of another Contracting State in the same manner as against a private person; however, the courts may not entertain proceedings in respect of acts performed by the entity in the exercise of sovereign authority (*acta jure imperii*)."

and actually perform acts under such powers.[43] This is supported by article 10(3) of the Jurisdictional Immunities Convention according to which the involvement of a state enterprise in a proceeding relating to a commercial transaction in which that enterprise is engaged does not affect the immunity of the state itself. In other words, the conduct of a state enterprise or entity established by the state with distinct legal personality, which is supposedly controlled by the state itself, is not attributable to the state and hence does not enjoy immunity unless it is entitled to perform acts in the exercise of sovereign authority and are actually performing such acts.[44]

In short, therefore, a state cannot invoke a private person's or entity's conduct with a view to extending state immunity to them, as the conduct strictly remains that person's or that entity's; as a result, they cannot claim state immunity in their own right. If, for example, a state official instructs or directs a private person to perform a certain act, both the state and the public official might arguably claim state immunity,[45] whereas the private person could most likely be sued abroad. Thus, attribution in the law of immunity is narrower than it is in the law of responsibility. This illustrates the rationale of establishing a high degree of accountability particularly from the perspective of an individual who should not be left without remedy.

With regard to custom, the picture is somewhat mixed. According to the traditional, state-centered view, as expressed most recently in the ILC Conclusions on the Identification of Custom, the main focus is on *state* practice.[46] Conclusion 4 para 1 states that "[t]he requirement of a general practice, as a constituent element of customary international law, refers *primarily to the practice of States* that contributes to the formation, or expression, of rules of customary international law." In a very cautious manner, the ILC recognizes that "[i]n certain cases, the practice of international organizations also contributes to the formation, or expression, of rules of customary international law."[47] However, when such a case arises, it will be the practice of the organization and, in terms of attribution, not that of any state. Such practice does not assume attributive value in relation to states unless it "is carried out on behalf of its member states or endorsed by them."[48] The ILC thus seems

[43] Whether the terms "acting in that capacity" in art 2(b)(iv) require an authorization by the state or not is disputed. For opposing views, see eg Fox and Webb, *The Law of State Immunity* (n 3) 368; and T Grant, "Article 2(1)(a) and (b)" in R O'Keefe and CJ Tams (eds), *The United Nations Convention on Jurisdictional Immunities of States and Their Property: A Commentary* (OUP 2013) 40, 52.

[44] However, this would already follow from art 2(b) at any rate. On the redundancy of art 10(3), see S Wittich, "Article 10" in R O'Keefe and CJ Tams (eds), *The United Nations Convention on Jurisdictional Immunities of States and Their Property: A Commentary* (OUP 2013) 167, 181.

[45] See eg *Jones v Saudi Arabia* [2007] 1 AC 270.

[46] See ILC Conclusions (n 10) (Conclusion 4).

[47] ibid 119 (Conclusion 4, para 2).

[48] ibid 131 (Commentary to Conclusion 4, para 7): "As a general rule, the more directly a practice of an international organization is carried out on behalf of its member States or endorsed by them, and the larger the number of such member States, the greater weight it may have in relation to the formation, or expression, of rules of customary international law."

to admit that endorsement similar to the provision in article 11 of the ARSIWA may play a role in attributing practice by an organization to states.

As regards private individuals, the ILC is even more cautious when it states that "[c]onduct of other actors is not practice that contributes to the formation, or expression, of rules of customary international law, but may be relevant when assessing the practice [of States and international organizations]."[49] This is understandable to the extent that from a factual point of view, private individuals hardly exert an influence in the sense of a generalizable pattern of conduct that could give rise to relevant practice. However, even pursuant to a conservative view, the state may arguably still render private practice into official state practice through some form of approval or endorsement. Assuming for instance that, prior to any official policy on the legal status of the continental shelf or the exclusive economic zone, private persons exploit these maritime zones for economic reasons, and assuming further that subsequently the state were to expressly acknowledge this private conduct as conforming to its official policy or views, would this not completely change the nature of the acts at issue and ultimately result in their attribution to the state at least for the purpose of establishing custom?

Indeed, this thought is reflected in the ILC Conclusions, which acknowledge that "the acts of private individuals may sometimes be relevant to the formation or expression of rules of customary international law, but only to the extent that states have endorsed or reacted to them."[50] While there is admittedly no discernible state practice to this effect, voices in the literature do draw the analogy here to article 11 of the ARSIWA.[51] It is argued that non-state actors may indirectly influence the development of custom through their practice when such practice is endorsed and adopted by states.[52] For example, captains of merchant or fishing vessels, commercial companies exploiting the seabed and fishermen, even if acting in their own name and interest, may indirectly contribute to the creation or development of international customs concerning the open sea, the territorial sea, or the continental shelf.[53]

Therefore, concerning the attribution of conduct of private individuals, custom aligns with responsibility whereas attribution in case of state immunity seems

[49] ibid 119 (Conclusion 4, para 3).

[50] ibid 132 (Commentary to Conclusion 4, para 8).

[51] See in more detail P Dumberry, *The Formation and Identification of Rules of Customary International Law in International Investment Law* (CUP 2016) 121ff.

[52] ibid 120–22: "The conduct of non-State actors may contribute to the customary process in its 'extended sense' when it is 'carried out on behalf of the State or adopted' by a State [...] Yet, [...] such practice should not be considered as constituting a *direct* source in the creation of custom, but rather as its 'material, historical or indirect' source [...] In that sense, it is undeniable that non-state actors 'can contribute *indirectly* to the formation' of custom." See also MH Mendelson, "The Formation of Customary International Law" 272 Collected Courses of the Hague Academy of International Law 203.

[53] Dumberry, *Formation and Identification* (n 51) 122 (quoting Karol Wolfke, *Custom in Present International Law* (2nd edn, Nijhoff 1993) 85). See also the Truman Declaration on the Continental Shelf (Presidential Proclamation No 2667) (28 September 1945).

to take a somehow more restrictive approach. Nonetheless, in all fields under examination there exists a need to at least consider the acts of private persons for means of attribution, whatever their value. That seems in line with the growing importance and influence of private persons on inter-state relations.[54]

4.2 *Ultra Vires* Acts

The second aspect to be looked at is that of *ultra vires* acts and it deals with the question whether the fact that the relevant conduct was carried out in violation of law, in contravention of instructions or outside the powers of the organ does have an impact on the attribution of that conduct. In the law of state responsibility, the answer is clear and straightforward: with regard to conduct of organs, the invocation of the *ultra vires* character is to no avail,[55] whereas in case of attribution of private conduct any excess of directions or instructions will prevent the conduct from being attributed.[56]

With regard to custom formation, there is no clear indication whether *ultra vires* acts should be attributable as relevant practice or *opinio juris*, and the matter is open to debate. On a strictly formal note, the considerations in the context of responsibility may well be viewed as "transferable," by way of analogy, to the field of custom. However, one must keep in mind that practice and *opinio juris* as elements of custom contribute to generating new law and thus may potentially result in new obligations reducing states' freedom of action. Under this premise, the analogy to treaty law would probably be more obvious and that would allow for a limited consideration of *ultra vires* acts as being irrelevant.[57]

For instance, one might draw an analogy to article 46 of the Vienna Convention on the Law of Treaties (VCLT): an organ *a priori* and clearly not competent to represent the state cannot produce state practice relevant to the establishment of custom. On the other hand, if the organ is in principle competent but exceeds its powers in the given case, the conduct may well be considered relevant state practice.[58] For example, a Justice Minister expressing a legal opinion concerning the state's reservations to human rights treaties would likely be considered as relevant

[54] See also section 5.2.

[55] See art 7 of the ARSIWA (n 5).

[56] See ARSIWA Commentary (n 5) 46 (art 7, para 7): "The central issues to be addressed in determining the applicability of article 7 to unauthorized conduct of official bodies is whether the conduct was performed by the body in an official capacity or not. Cases where officials acted in their capacity as such, albeit unlawfully or contrary to instructions, must be distinguished from cases where the conduct is so removed from the scope of their official functions that it should be assimilated to that of private individuals, not attributable to the State. In the words of the Iran–United States Claims Tribunal, the question is whether the conduct has been 'carried out by persons cloaked with governmental authority.'"

[57] See particularly arts 46 and 47 of the VCLT (n 24).

[58] See T Grant, "Article 2(1)(a) and (b)" in R O'Keefe and CJ Tams (eds), *The United Nations Convention on Jurisdictional Immunities of States and Their Property: A Commentary* (OUP 2013) 40, 52.

state practice, as such an act lies generally within a Justice Minister's portfolio, even when exceptionally—in accordance with a state's internal law—the Minister acts *ultra vires* (eg because he/she has no powers in external relations under domestic law).[59] Conversely, the same statement by a Minister of Education would not be considered as pertinent practice since it falls clearly outside his/her powers. While both act *ultra vires*, the statement of the former may count as relevant for the formation of custom whereas the statement of the latter will not.

With regard to state immunity, the question of whether the *ultra vires* character of acts might have a bearing on attribution is equally disputed. Again, practice is virtually non-existent, and the views in the doctrine diverge. On the one hand, it is argued that the view according to which individuals might benefit from state immunity where they have acted *ultra vires* is supported neither by principle nor by authority.[60] Indeed, for example, in *Pilger v United States Steel Corp*, the Public Trustee, which was a governmental agency, acted *ultra vires* by seizing the stock acquired by Pilger and continued to be "personally answerable for acts" committed beyond the scope of its authority.[61] However, a more balanced view argues that "State officials enjoy immunity *ratione materiae* in respect of acts performed in an official capacity since these acts are considered acts of the State, and these include unlawful acts and acts *ultra vires*."[62] This view clearly supports an analogy to the law of state responsibility. Much will depend, of course, on the particular circumstances of the given case, such as the type of person or entity or the particular character of the act at issue. In particular, it will make a great difference whether the immunity invoked is that of the state itself or that of a state organ (such as head of state, diplomat etc). With regard to the latter, examples from practice mentioned above indicate that the *ultra vires* nature of the act would do away with the entitlement to immunity, whereas the state itself would still enjoy immunity.[63] However,

[59] This was, for instance, the case in *Armed Activities on the Territory of the Congo (New Application: 2002) (Democratic Republic of the Congo v Rwanda)* (Jurisdiction and Admissibility) [2006] ICJ Rep 6, 27–28 [47]–[48], where the Court had to determine whether the Justice Minister was competent, under international law, to bind her state by her statements in respect of matters falling within her purview.

[60] Regarding *ultra vires* acts of state organs and state immunity, see M Tomonori, "The Individual as Beneficiary of State Immunity: Problems of the Attribution of *Ultra Vires* Conduct" (2001) 29 Denver Journal of International Law and Policy 101, 287: "If proceedings are brought against individuals who acted *ultra vires*, no room is left for state immunity to be granted."

[61] *Pilger v United States Steel Corp and Public Trustee*, Court of Errors and Appeals New Jersey, 1925; 130 Atl. 523 cited in Tomonori, "The Individual as Beneficiary" (n 60) 285.

[62] UNGA, "Report of the International Law Commission" (2011) GAOR 63rd Session Supp 10, UN Doc A/66/10, para 108. Regarding art 2(1)(b)(iv), see also Grant, "Article 2(1)(a) and (b)" (n 58) 52: "The conduct the subject of the proceeding instituted against the individual must have been performed in that individual's capacity as a representative of the State, not in a private capacity. This is not, however, the same as saying that the conduct must have been authorized or have been formally within the scope of the representative's official functions."

[63] *Anglo-Iberia Underwriting Management Co v Jamsostek*, 97 Civ 5116 (HB), 1998 US Dist. LEXIS 8181 (SDNY June 2, 1998) and 1999 US Dist. LEXIS 1563 (SDNY Feb. 10, 1999), as cited in Tomonori, "The Individual as Beneficiary" (n 60) 287. See also Fox and Webb, *The Law of State Immunity* (n 3) 345, stating that "the identification of an act as an act of State and its attribution to the State may not necessarily result in the grant of immunity to the organ or official which performs the act."

in view of the lack of practice with regard to the immunity of the state itself, a definite answer is impossible to give.

Overall, state responsibility seems to be most inclusive in terms of attribution of *ultra vires* acts whereas in customary law and the law of immunity the question whether to attribute such conduct is more controversial.

4.3 Nature of the Act: *Acta Iure Imperii* versus *Acta Iure Gestionis*

We will now turn to the last aspect, that is, the nature of the act. Here the question is whether the type of conduct—that is, whether it is, according to its nature, one in the exercise of governmental or sovereign authority, or whether the conduct involves purely commercial activities—has an influence on attribution.

The situation is clear in the law of state responsibility: for the purpose of attribution under article 4 of the ARSIWA, it does not matter whether or not, in the particular instance, the organ exercises sovereign powers or functions. The Commentary to article 4 leaves no doubt in this respect when it states that "[i]t is irrelevant for the purposes of attribution that the conduct of a State organ may be classified as 'commercial' or as '*acta iure gestionis*'."[64] Article 5 of the ARSIWA, for its part, takes up that distinction.[65] Again, the ILC Commentary makes that point clear: "If it is to be regarded as an act of the State for purposes of international responsibility, the conduct of an entity must accordingly concern governmental activity and not other private or commercial activity in which the entity may engage."[66] Therefore, under article 5, conduct is only attributed if and to the extent the private person or entity exercises sovereign authority.[67]

A largely identical approach to the attribution of commercial activities may be found with regard to the formation of custom:[68] commercial activities can be considered as state practice when exercised or authorized by state organs.[69] Especially

64 ARSIWA Commentary (n 5) 41 (art 4, para 6).

65 See art 5 of the ARSIWA (n 5), which stipulates: "The conduct of a person or entity which is not an organ of the State under article 4 but which is empowered by the law of that State to exercise elements of the governmental authority shall be considered an act of the State under international law, provided the person or entity is acting in that capacity in the particular instance."

66 ARSIWA Commentary (n 5) 43 (art 5, para 5).

67 Indeed, the distinction between *acta iure imperii* and *acta iure gestionis* matters in case of "parastatal" entities (ibid); these have to act in the exercise of governmental authority for their acts to be attributed to the state. On the concept of "governmental authority," see Crawford, *State Responsibility: The General Part* (n 11) 130: "[I]f a private person can perform the function without the government's permission, it is not to be considered governmental. According to the restrictive theory of state immunity, this manifests as the well-known distinction between *acta iure imperii*, which attract immunity, and *acta iure gestionis*, which do not."

68 Indeed, the ILC Conclusions (n 10) 132, fn 699 refer to arts 4 and 5 of the ARSIWA.

69 The ILC Commentary to Conclusion 5 (Conduct of the State as State practice) states in relation to relevant state practice: "In accordance with the principle of the unity of the State, this includes the conduct of any organ of the State forming part of the State's organization and acting in that capacity, whether in exercise of executive, legislative, judicial or "other" functions, such as commercial activities or the

the field of economic and trade law provides numerous examples where states have carried out commercial activities that ultimately generated customary rules. Thus, already the British Empire "used" the East India Company as a state organ to this effect,[70] other examples include the activities of resource exploitation by states in the various maritime zones, particularly the continental shelf,[71] or the development of the customary rules on the minimum standard or most favored nation treatment in international trade relations.[72]

In case of persons or entities otherwise empowered by the law of the state, the person or entity must act "in that capacity in the particular instance,"[73] that is, with sovereign authority, for conduct to be qualified as relevant state practice. Thus, the criteria for establishing customary international law mirror the approach of state responsibility as regards the relevance of the nature of the act for the sake of attribution.

With the gradual transition from absolute to restrictive immunity,[74] the distinction between sovereign acts and private or commercial acts has gained particular significance for the assessment or determination of attribution in the field of immunity. According to the well-known orthodox theory on restrictive immunity, the answer to the question whether a state enjoys immunity lies, contrary to the law of state responsibility,[75] in the distinction between *acta iure imperii* and *acta iure gestionis* and a state would only enjoy immunity for acts *iure imperii*.[76] Given the overall recognized rationale of that distinction under the traditional approach to state immunity, it is not surprising that article 5 of the ARSIWA was deliberately based on the model of this distinction to achieve consistency between these two areas of international law.[77] With the Jurisdictional Immunities Convention, however, the picture has become a little more fragmented as the Convention takes a much more nuanced approach. Article 10 for instance essentially provides that a state with all its subdivisions, including state enterprises, does not enjoy immunity in proceedings arising out of a commercial transaction, which is defined in article

giving of administrative guidance to the private sector." See ILC Conclusions (n 10) 132 (Commentary to Conclusion 5, para 1).

70 L Oppenheim (ed), *The Collected Papers of John Westlake on Public International Law* (CUP 2014) 196–97.

71 See eg ZJ Slouka, *International Custom and the Continental Shelf: A Study in the Dynamics of Customary Rules of International Law* (Martinus Nijhoff 1968).

72 See eg M Paparinskis, *The International Minimum Standard and Fair and Equitable Treatment* (OUP 2013).

73 ILC Conclusions (n 10) 132 (Commentary to Conclusions 5, para 2).

74 For a general overview over the transition from absolute to restrictive immunity as seen in (common and civil) case law, see Fox and Webb, *The Law of State Immunity* (n 3) 131ff.

75 See Jurisdictional Immunities Convention (n 9) art 2(2). There currently is, however, no precise definition of "commercial" and "non-commercial activity"; the decision to classify a certain transaction as "commercial" is thus left to the courts on a case-by-case basis: see Yang, *State Immunity* (n 2) 76ff.

76 J Crawford, *Brownlie's Principles of Public International Law* (OUP 2012) 471.

77 Crawford, *State Responsibility: The General Part* (n 11) 130.

2(1)(c) as any commercial, financial, or similar contract or transaction. Here, the old distinction into commercial and sovereign acts has become obsolete by definition since the "nature test" is embedded in the definition of article 2(1)(c) which means that any commercial transaction is not covered by immunity.[78]

Article 11, on the other hand, upholds the distinction between governmental and non-governmental employment contracts, by granting state immunity to those contracts of an employee who was recruited "to perform functions in the exercise of governmental authority." Here immunity is only to be enjoyed by the state if it has performed acts *jure imperii*.[79] Finally, article 12 of the Jurisdictional Immunities Convention, according to which a state cannot invoke immunity for injury inflicted on individuals abroad (territorial tort exception), again does not take up the distinction between private and sovereign acts; on its face, the wording would suggest that a state does not enjoy immunity for committing a tort abroad, even if the underlying conduct was carried out in the performance of sovereign acts. The ICJ for its part left the question open.[80] However, even this patchy picture illustrates that at least implicitly, the distinction between commercial or private acts and sovereign acts is of some relevance in the law of state immunity and that, for immunity purposes, only acts in the exercise of governmental authority are attributed to the state.[81] On that basis, it also follows that the law on state immunity is clearly narrower than the law on state responsibility in that not every act attributable to a state is also covered by state immunity.

5. Evolution Over Time of the Rules of Attribution

5.1 General

As a matter of course, the rules of attribution link a certain conduct to a state; it follows that if the state—its organization, structure, conception, function, or role—changes, these rules will transform accordingly in order to adapt to new exigencies and to accommodate changed political, societal, economic, and other necessities. One can give several examples of this flexibility of the rules of attribution. Most importantly, these relate to the change in state functions and the increasing importance of non-state actors, and they may again be discerned in all three areas under analysis.

[78] S Wittich, "Article 2(1)(c) and (2) and (3)" in R O'Keefe and CJ Tams (eds), *The United Nations Convention on Jurisdictional Immunities of States and Their Property: A Commentary* (OUP 2013) 54, 60.

[79] J Foakes/R O'Keefe, "Article 11" in ibid 183, 198 (n 78).

[80] *Jurisdictional Immunities of the State (Germany v Italy: Greece intervening)* (Judgment) [2012] ICJ Rep 99, 127–27 [65].

[81] See Fox and Webb, *The Law of State Immunity* (n 3) 345: "A progressive narrowing of the scope of 'acts in exercise of sovereign authority', for which immunity is accorded, rejects the equating of the scope of immunity afforded to acts with their attribution to the State."

5.2 Change in State Functions

At the beginning of the twentieth century, states increasingly engaged in business activities and entered into commercial transactions. This change in state behavior involved a rise in the various activities of states in spheres that were formerly reserved to private individuals and called for an establishment of accountability for such state activities in favor of their partners in commercial transactions. In turn, and at the expense of the state, this resulted in a restrictive effect on the rules of attribution in the law of state immunity. With the change from absolute to restrictive immunity, fewer acts are nowadays treated as ultimately leading to immunity even if they might in principle be attributed to the state.[82] In other words, what is considered to be the state that could benefit from international immunity has been gradually reduced.

In the law of state responsibility, the development is somewhat the opposite. The changed perception of the role of the state has brought about a retreat of governments from hitherto sovereign activities which were outsourced to private individuals and entities.[83] In order to maintain reasonable and effective accountability of the state, the ARSIWA took account of this growing practice of "subcontracting" and provide for the attribution of acts of private persons or entities, which may themselves not be state organs, but which are empowered to exercise governmental authority.[84] The delegation of state activities to private persons, companies, or other entities for acting on behalf of or under the control of the state has substantially transformed the nature of the attributive process, which thus has become more inclusive. This development has led to an effective expansion of state responsibility to cover also the conduct of private persons or entities.

Concerning customary law, the change in state functions has resulted in an extension of state activities which, in turn, has led to an increasing regulation and "juridification" in areas previously not covered by custom. Examples may include, for instance, the implementation of social welfare policies through the law or migration law where an expansion of state activities contributes to relevant state practice and *opinio iuris* and thus adds to the custom-related *corpus iuris* in these fields.

[82] See Yang, *State Immunity* (n 2) 8–12, on the change towards restrictive immunity: while granting absolute immunity was the prevailing position of international law during the nineteenth century, "[w]ith the steadily increasing volume of commercial and other dealings between States and foreign private persons on an equal footing, came the gradually diminishing justifiability of a State's assertion of immunity vis-à-vis a valid claim based on such dealings in a foreign court ... Allowing perhaps for some minor deviations, it can be safely asserted that restrictive immunity has now completely replaced absolute immunity with the conclusion of the UN Convention on State Immunity in 2004."

[83] eg private security firms being tasked with providing prison guards, or private airlines tasked with undertaking immigration controls: see ARSIWA Commentary (n 5) 43 (art 5, para 2).

[84] See art 5 of the ARSIWA (n 5).

5.3 Increasing Importance of Non-State Actors

On a more general level, this development reflects a broader shift in the status and role of states in different areas, as compared to non-state actors. The steady rise of the latter to the level of subjecthood in international law[85] has caused a blurring of the boundaries between state and non-state conduct and has rendered attribution in a given case a very delicate and complicated matter. On the one hand, the rules of attribution reflect the growing importance of non-state actors: conduct which is controlled or endorsed by a state is attributable.[86] At the same time, the rules of attribution struggle to accommodate this growing importance, particularly in the fields of state responsibility and custom.

In case of state responsibility, the insufficiency of the rules of attribution is illustrated, for example, in case of non-state actors, such as terrorists, residing in the territory of a state (the "harbouring" state) against which other states act in self-defense in response to a previous terrorist attack. A relevant example in point[87] is the US military intervention in Afghanistan post-9/11 in reliance on the right to self-defense. It showed that traditional categories/rules of attribution do not sufficiently account for armed attacks by non-state actors/terrorists harbored by a state. It proved difficult to attribute the armed attacks by Al-Qaeda to the Taliban Regime (Afghanistan).[88] Accordingly, it may be argued that the rules of attribution as enshrined in the ARSIWA are insufficient to reflect the full range of non-state actor activities without a significant relation to the state or where the relation can only be insufficiently established.

Similar observations may be made regarding the formation of customary international law. On the one hand, the rules of attribution reflect the growing importance of non-state actors. As we have seen above,[89] the ILC Conclusions attest the practice of non-state actors such as NGOs and Transnational Corporations (TNC)—though being "neither creative nor expressive of customary international law"[90]—at least an indirect role in the identification of customary law, particularly

[85] See eg A Alkoby, "Non-State Actors and the Legitimacy of International Environmental Law" (2003) 3 Non-State Actors and International Law 23, 26: "Nongovernmental organizations (NGOs), business corporations and other non-State entities have become increasingly influential in international environmental lawmaking processes."

[86] See section 4.1.

[87] This example is based on the assumption that the relevant rules of attribution concerning the use of force follow the secondary rules under the ARSIWA, but this is not uncontested. For the contrary view according to which attribution is governed by primary rule, see N Tsagourias, "Self-Defence against Non-state Actors: The Interaction between Self-Defence as a Primary Rule and Self-Defence as a Secondary Rule" (2016) 29 Leiden Journal of International Law 801–825, who considers it as in the scope of primary norms.

[88] The conduct was neither effectively controlled nor endorsed by Afghanistan/the Taliban regime (arts 8 and 11 of the ARSIWA); cf eg M Byers, "Terrorism, The Use of Force and International Law after 11 September" (2002) 51 International and Comparative Law Quarterly 401, 406.

[89] See section 4.1.

[90] ILC Conclusions (n 10) (Commentary to Conclusion 4, para 8.)

when it is endorsed by a state.[91] At the same time, it may be doubted whether this "soft" recognition of the role of non-state actors is adequate and whether the rules of attribution are sufficiently consistent and developed to reflect the increasing relevance of non-state actors.[92] Indeed, in times of interdependence and globalization, the influence of civil society has grown, and transnational corporations exercise significant political and economic influence,[93] on occasion even exceeding that of states. To accurately account for this influence, it might be necessary to recognize a more direct role for non-state actors, especially of NGOs and TNCs, in the formation of custom *de lege ferenda*.[94] True, numerous conceptual and normative difficulties, including the diversity of non-state actors and the identification of relevant practice, complicate such a development.[95] However, influential stakeholders themselves have voiced the need to take into account, if only residually, the practice of non-state actors in the process of forming customary law.

The most prominent example in this regard surely is the study on customary international humanitarian law of the International Committee of the Red Cross which has looked at the practice not only of international organizations, conferences, international case law and its own practice (the International Red Cross and Red Crescent Movement), but also that of armed opposition groups, statements of non-governmental organizations and other non-governmental sources. It is, of course, telling that this practice is mentioned under the label "other practice."[96] Therefore, while the state-centered approach towards custom still prevails today, the focus on state practice for the formation of custom might need to be further developed to live up to the reality of the international community as it stands today.

Perhaps the least need for alignment may be discerned in the field of immunities. It seems comparatively clear that, as we have noted earlier, states cannot immunize acts of individuals by adopting them as their own.

[91] ibid: "Paragraph 3 makes explicit that the conduct of entities other than States and international organizations—for example, non-governmental organizations (NGOs) and private individuals, but also transnational corporations and non-State armed groups—is neither creative nor expressive of customary international law. As such, their conduct does not contribute to the formation, or expression, of rules of customary international law, and may not serve as direct (primary) evidence of the existence and content of such rules. The paragraph recognizes, however, that such conduct may have an indirect role in the identification of customary international law, by stimulating or recording the practice and acceptance as law (*opinio juris*) of States and international organizations. For example, the acts of private individuals may sometimes be relevant to the formation or expression of rules of customary international law, but only to the extent that States have endorsed or reacted to them" (footnotes omitted).

[92] See section 4.1.

[93] cf K Nowrot, "New Approaches to the International Legal Personality of Multinational Corporations Towards a Rebuttable Presumption of Normative Responsibilities" Journal of Global Legal Studies 1, 2f <esil-sedi.eu/wp-content/uploads/2018/04/Nowrot.pdf>.

[94] For voices in the literature, see the references in Dumberry, *Formation and Identification* (n 51) 119–20.

[95] See the difficulties raised in the ILC Conclusions as regards the recognition of practice of international organizations: ILC Conclusions (n 10) 131 (Commentary to Conclusion 4, para 7).

[96] J-M Henckaerts and L Doswald-Beck (eds), *Customary International Humanitarian Law* (CUP 2005) vol I, xlii and vol II, Pt 1, xxv.

6. Conclusion

Where does that leave us with regard to a comparison of the rules of attribution in the law of responsibility, immunity and in the formation of custom? In all three fields, the rules of attribution follow basic similarities of structure and function. At the same time, all three fields display differences especially as regards the conduct of private actors and the qualification of *acta iure gestionis*. The rules of attribution in the law of state immunity, on the one hand, operate in a manner so as to produce the most restrictive result, that is, a limited scope of state immunity; on the other hand, those in the law of state responsibility apply in an expansive manner so as to include a broad spectrum of conduct attributable to the state. From the perspective of legal policy, both results are warranted as they establish comprehensive accountability regimes and avoid, as far as possible, accountability gaps. Therefore, it is not only the perspective of the state which matters but, more comprehensively, that of a rule based international community.

Finally, the rules of attribution in all three fields—while partly insufficiently—reflect the structural change of the international landscape, the growing importance of non-state actors and the change in state function, with states, for example, participating in economic activities. Thus, the "secondary rules" are of primary importance in giving an authentic picture of international law as it stands today. They can be viewed as a prism through which one may observe the gradual change of the structure of international law, particularly as illustrated by the enlargement of the circle of subjects of international law.

14

Untangling the Relationship Between Attribution and Due Diligence in International Investment Law and Beyond

Jure Zrilič[*]

1. Introduction

Due diligence is a substantive standard that requires a state to make a reasonable effort to prevent or mitigate harm to other states (and their nationals) in or from its territory.[1] It is a reflection of the principle of sovereignty: while states have a right to exercise sovereignty over objects and activities within their jurisdiction, they also have corresponding legal obligations. As articulated by the International Court of Justice (ICJ) in the *Corfu Channel* case, it is every state's "obligation not to allow knowingly its territory to be used for acts contrary to the rights of other states."[2] While the principle initially emerged in the context of the law of state responsibility for injury to aliens, its influence has quickly expanded to other fields of international law.[3] Its popularity can be explained by its flexible content; due diligence pertains to an obligation of conduct, which means that states are expected to strive towards accomplishing a certain goal, but are not obliged to guarantee it. Instead, they only have to do what could be reasonably expected from them in the given circumstances, with an aim to prevent or mitigate injury to another state. The open-endedness of this standard, reflected in its various designations such as "vigilance," "care," "best effort," or "feasible and practicable" arguably lessens the pressure on state sovereignty, and has consequently made it a preferred choice for regulating multiple challenges in modern society.[4]

[*] I would like to thank Gabor Kajtar, Marko Milanovic, and the anonymous peer reviewer for their insightful comments on the draft chapter, as well as to the organizers and participants of the 2019 ESIL–ELTE Joint Workshop, held on 16–17 May 2019, in Budapest. All errors are mine.

[1] International Law Association (ILA), Study Group on Due Diligence in International Law: Second Report (ILA, 2016) 3 (ILA Second Report).

[2] *Corfu Channel* (*United Kingdom v Albania*) [1949] ICJ Rep 4 at 22.

[3] ILA Second Report (n 1) (providing an overview of the application of due diligence across different disciplines of international law).

[4] ibid.

Jure Zrilič, *Untangling the Relationship Between Attribution and Due Diligence in International Investment Law and Beyond* In: *Secondary Rules of Primary Importance in International Law.* Edited by: Gábor Kajtár, Başak Çalı, and Marko Milanovic, Oxford University Press. © Jure Zrilič 2022. DOI: 10.1093/oso/9780192869012.003.0014

In international investment law, which has largely superseded in relevance the law of state responsibility for injury to aliens, the standard of due diligence has been commonly applied. As in the old jurisprudence dealing with the mistreatment of aliens, in most investment law cases the principle has been invoked in the context of a host state's failure to protect foreign investors against violent acts of non-state actors, such as rioters, terrorists, and revolutionists. In one conflict-related case, *AAPL v Sri Lanka*, however, the tribunal applied the standard with respect to the acts of the state's own security forces,[5] giving rise to confusion,[6] and prompting criticism.[7] Ultimately, scholars treated the case as an anomaly, decided on specific facts. The position that prevailed in the legal doctrine is that the application of due diligence is limited to prevention of harmful acts of private actors; in all other cases when harm is caused directly by the activity of state organs, the standard of diligence plays no role as the rules of attribution apply.[8]

This chapter questions this position. It examines why international tribunals and courts sometimes determine state responsibility for the wrongful activities of their own organs not on the basis of attribution of the actions violating a negative obligation, but rather on the ground of the breach of a positive obligation measured against the due diligence standard. In the law of state responsibility for injury to aliens, due diligence has often been conceptualized in relation to attribution, with the latter engaging state responsibility for actions of its own organs, and the due diligence rule constituting an exception to state non-responsibility when harm was caused by private individuals and a state failed to prevent the harmful event

[5] *Asian Agricultural Products Ltd (AAPL) v Republic of Sri Lanka* ICSID Case No ARB/87/3 (Award) (27 June 1990).

[6] Many scholars did not differentiate between the *AAPL* tribunal's application of due diligence and a standard measuring compliance with the obligation to protect from third parties, treating them as the same. See eg Eric De Brabandere, "Host States' Due Diligence Obligations in International Investment Law" (2015) 42(2) Syracuse Journal of International Law and Commerce 320, 356; H Bray "SOI: Save Our Investments! International Investment Law and International Humanitarian Law" (2013) 14(3) Journal of World Investment and Trade 578; S Alexandrov and J Robbins, "Proximate Causation in International Investment Disputes" in K Sauvant (ed), *Yearbook on International Investment Law and Policy 2008–2009* (OUP 2009) 317; K Greenman, "Aliens in Latin America: Intervention, Arbitration and State Responsibility for Rebels" (2018) (31)(3) Leiden Journal of International Law 617, 638.

[7] See eg J Gathii, "War's Legacy in International Investment Law" (2009) 11 International Community Law Review 353, 370, 382; M Sornarajah, *The International Law on Foreign Investment* (4th edn, CUP 2017) 252, 278; S Vasciannie, "Bilateral Investment Treaties and Civil Strife: The *AAPL/Sri Lanka* Arbitration" (1992) 39 Netherlands International Law Review 332; O Mayorga, "Arbitrating War: Military Necessity as a Defence to the Breach of Investment Treaty Obligations" (Policy Brief, August 2013) (Program on Humanitarian Policy and Conflict Research Harvard University) <https://www.hpcrresearch.org/sites/default/files/publications/081213%20ARBITRATING%20WAR%20%28final%29.pdf>; De Brabandere, "Host States" (n 6) 335; Greenman, "Aliens in Latin America" (n 6) 638. See also *AAPL* (n 5) (Dissenting Opinion of Samuel Asante).

[8] See R Pisillo-Mazzeschi, "The Due Diligence Rule and the Nature of the International Responsibility of States" (1992) 35 German Yearbook of International Law 9, 23–25; R Dolzer and C Schreuer, *Principles of International Investment Law* (2nd edn, OUP 2012) 162; H Zeitler, "Full Protection and Security" in S Schill (ed), *International Investment Law and Comparable Public Law* (OUP 2010) 191; De Brabandere, "Host States" (n 6) 333–34, 337. For the analysis of this orthodox doctrinal position, see section 3.

or adequately respond to it. This was especially evident in early attempts to codify state responsibility, in which due diligence was typically treated as a special case of attribution giving rise to a state's indirect responsibility. While the International Law Commission (ILC), following the mandate of the Special Rapporteur Crawford, eventually rejected the idea that due diligence should have a place in the ILC's Articles on State Responsibility (ARSIWA),[9] thus relegating it to the realm of primary rules, the arguments in doctrine still reflect the dichotomous understanding of attribution and due diligence. One area which is affected by the conflation between these two concepts and lack of clarity as to how the secondary rules of attribution interact with the due diligence standard, concerns the role of the latter in determining state responsibility for losses resulting from a state's own activity.

The chapter argues that departing from the binary view, that is, attribution-- harm from the state sphere versus due diligence--harm from the private sphere, allows for an analysis of due diligence that is truer to its nature and more aligned with its application across different fields of international law. To break this dichotomy, the chapter proposes to re-conceptualize due diligence through the rubric of risk and thus improve the understanding of the role of due diligence and enable a more nuanced assessment. Using the *AAPL* decision as a case study, it purports to show how risk-based due diligence provides a broad enough scope to accommodate the application of the standard with respect to activities of state organs as well. More specifically, it argues that due diligence cannot only be used to measure states' compliance with their positive obligations, but in some situations also as a standard of conduct in the context of assessing the compliance with negative obligations. It shows how this understanding is in line with the application of the standard in other fields of international law, in particular international humanitarian law (IHL) and international human rights law (IHRL).

Since the *AAPL* case, there has not been much opportunity for investment tribunals to apply the due diligence standard in such a manner. This has changed recently with a dramatic upsurge in claims for losses that investors have sustained in violent situations, in which they typically invoke the breach of the obligation of protection,[10] and which has resulted in a renewed interest in due diligence in

[9] ILC, Draft Articles on the Responsibility of States for Internationally Wrongful Acts with Commentaries, UN GAOR, 56th Sess, Supp 10, ch 4, UN Doc A/56/10 (2001).

[10] A great number of investment cases have been reported with respect to losses investors suffered in the midst of armed conflicts in Egypt, Libya, and Ukraine. See eg *Ampal v Arab Republic of Egypt* ICSID Case No ARB/12/11 (Decision on Liability and Heads of Loss) (21 February 2017); *Olin Holdings Ltd v Libya* ICC Case No 20355/MCP (Award) (25 May 2018); *Strabag SE v Libya* ICSID Case No ARB(AF)/15/1 (Award) (29 June 2020); *Cengiz Sanayi v Libya* ICC Case No 21537/ZF/AYZ (Award) (7 November 2018); *Oztas Construction v Libya* ICC Case No 21603/ZF/AYZ (Award) (14 June 2018); *Way2B ACE v Libya* (Award) (24 May 2018) (not public); *Guris v Libya* (Partial Award) (4 February 2020) (not public). See, however, D Charlotin, "Tribunal in *Guris v Libya* Award Draws Contrast with Cengiz Award on FPS Interpretation and Sides with Majority of Prior Libya Awards with Respect to War Losses Clauses" (*Investment Arbitration Reporter*, 5 March 2020) < https://www-iareporter-com.liverpool.idm.oclc.org/articles/analysis-tribunal-in-guris-v-libya-award-draws-contrast-with-cengiz-award-on-fps-int

international investment law.[11] In one of the awards emerging from Libya's Civil War, the tribunal thus reportedly confirmed that due diligence could be applied with respect to both actions of private individuals and a state's own forces.[12] In view of these developments, clarifying the role of the principle and the extent of its application is timely and relevant.

The chapter is structured as follows. Section 2 looks into the relationship between the rules of attribution and due diligence. It shows how due diligence was commonly conceptualized by contrast to the rules of attribution and how the concepts gradually grew apart in the ILC's process of codification of state responsibility. Section 3 shifts the focus on investment law's obligation to protect, as enshrined in investment treaties and the customary international minimum standard. It examines the decision of the *AAPL* tribunal, which applied due diligence in the context of a state's counterinsurgency operation. Departing from the doctrine, it argues that that application accurately reflected the scope of the relevant investment treaty obligation of protection, and further compares it with the application of due diligence to similar contexts in other fields of international law. Finally, section 4 introduces the concept of risk as a lens to better appraise the roles and scope of due diligence, and discusses the legal and policy justifications of a risk-based due diligence.

2. Attribution and Due Diligence: The Complicated Relationship

The relationship between attribution and due diligence has been traditionally shaped by the need to distinguish between the public and private sphere for the purpose of allocating international responsibility.[13] Accordingly, the rules of attribution ensure that state responsibility for an internationally wrongful act is engaged only as a result of a positive action or omission of individuals whose connection to the state apparatus is strong enough for the relevant conduct to be considered that of a state.[14] Conversely, while harmful conduct of private individuals,

erpretation-and-sides-with-majority-of-prior-libya-awards-with-respect-to-war-losses-clause/> accessed 15 February 2021.

[11] See eg J Zrilič, *The Protection of Foreign Investment in Times of Armed Conflict* (OUP 2019); K Fach Gomez and others (eds), "International Investment Law and the Law of Armed Conflict" European Yearbook of International Economic Law (Springer 2019).

[12] In *Guris v Libya*, the tribunal clarified that under the full protection and security standard of an investment treaty "the state was obliged to merely exercise due diligence in protecting investments, even from its own forces." Reported in *Investment Arbitration Reporter* (n 10).

[13] J Crawford, "First Report on State Responsibility" (1998) II(2) Yearbook of the International Law Commission, UN Doc A/CN.4/SER.A/1998/Add.1 1, 33–34 [154]; G Christenson, "Attributing Acts of Omission to the State" (1990) 12(2) Michigan Journal of International Law 312, 322.

[14] Christenson, "Attributing Acts" (n 13) 322.

that is, non-state actors, does not incur state responsibility, the latter may still emerge as a result of a state's failure to exercise due diligence in preventing or reacting to such conduct.[15] As such, due diligence has been understood to be a legal device for incurring state responsibility due to omission of conduct prescribed in an international obligation, which mostly concerns harmful activities stemming from the non-state sphere, either private individuals or public third parties like other states or international organizations.

This dichotomous but complementary understanding of the doctrines of attribution and due diligence was echoed in the early attempts to codify state responsibility, which, in view of the rich jurisprudence generated by the mixed claims commissions and arbitrations,[16] set to address the rules of attribution together with the treatment of aliens in a single document.[17] For example, in the Bases for Discussion drawn up in 1929 leading to the 1930 Hague Conference for the Codification of International Law, the due diligence rule was included as a special question, following the general rules on attribution, and covered the state responsibility "for damage caused by a private individual."[18] While the ILC's initial attempt to codify state responsibility followed a similar approach,[19] Special Rapporteur Ago departed from it by addressing first the rules for determining whether the state conduct exists before determining whether such conduct constitutes a breach of international obligation.[20] Ago introduced to the codification project the distinction between primary and secondary rules, whereby the ARSIWA would only address the latter.[21] Consequently, his proposal marked a shift towards objectification

[15] ibid 324. See also J Hessbruege, "The Historical Development of the Doctrines of Attribution and Due Diligence in International Law" (2004) 36 New York University Journal of International Law and Politics 265, 268.

[16] See eg *Sambiaggio Case* (*Italy v Venezuela*) (1903) 10 RIAA 499, 512–13. For an overview, see Zrilič, *The Protection* (n 11) ch 2.

[17] See eg Institute of International Law, Draft Resolution on "International Responsibility of States for Injuries on Their Territory to the Person or Property of Foreigners" (1927), arts III, VII (reproduced in ILC, (1956) II Yearbook of the International Law Commission, UN Doc A/CN.4/SER.A/1956/Add.1, 228); Harvard Draft on the Law of Responsibility of States for Damage Done in their Territory to the Person or Property of Foreigners (1929), arts 10–12, 14 (reproduced in ILC, (1956) II Yearbook of the International Law Commission, UN Doc A/CN.4/SER.A/1956/Add.1 229); Harvard Draft Convention on the International Responsibility of States for Injuries to Aliens (1961), arts 3, 13 (reproduced in ILC, (1956) II Yearbook of the International Law Commission, UN Doc A/CN.4/SER.A/1969/Add.1, 142, 145).

[18] Bases of Discussion Drawn up in 1929 by the Preparatory Committee of the Conference for the Codification of International Law (The Hague, 1930), Basis of Discussion No 7 (reproduced in ILC, (1956) II Yearbook of the International Law Commission, UN Doc A/CN.4/SER.A/1956/Add.1 223).

[19] Revised Draft on International Responsibility of the State for Injuries Caused in its Territory to the Person or Property of Aliens (1961), art 7; International Responsibility: Garcia Amador's Sixth Report on International Responsibility, ILC, (1961) II Yearbook of International Law Commission, UN Doc A/CN.4/SER.A/1961/Add.1, 47 (replacing the reference to due diligence with "manifest negligence in performance of the duty to protect").

[20] Report of the ILC to the General Assembly (1973) 163, 173, 179–84 (Draft Articles on State Responsibility, Commentary on art 3).

[21] R Ago, "Second Report on State Responsibility" Yearbook of the International Law Commission (1970) II, UN Doc A/CN.4/233, 178. See also E David, "Primary and Secondary Rules" in J Crawford and others (eds), *The Law of International Responsibility* (OUP 2010) 27.

of the regime of state responsibility by excluding an express reference to the responsibility for failing to exercise diligence in protecting aliens. Notwithstanding, Ago did not feel comfortable in completely abandoning the long tradition of addressing the special case of state responsibility for injuries caused by private persons.

In a proposed draft article 11, he thus restated that although conduct of private individuals acting in a private capacity is not considered to be an act of a state, any omission on the part of state organs, "where the latter ought to have acted to prevent or punish the conduct of individuals ... and failed to do so" is attributable to the state.[22] Although draft article 11 simply offered an example of attribution by omission, Ago justified its inclusion in the draft ARSIWA by arguing that the wrongfulness of the state conduct is closely connected to an act of the private individual and that such an act was "a condition for the existence of such responsibility acting externally as a catalyst on the wrongfulness of the conduct of the State organs."[23] The members of the ILC were divided on whether draft article 11 is needed, some finding it unacceptable, as it encroached on the primary rules of international law,[24] while others holding that although self-evident, the draft article had an important explanatory function and reaffirmed the responsibility by catalysis and the distinction between public and private conduct.[25]

The ILC decided to keep article 11 in the 1996 Draft Articles by reformulating it in an attempt to further remove it from the sphere of primary rules.[26] Referencing rich practice and jurisprudence in which state responsibility was established on the ground of lack of due diligence,[27] the ILC rationalized the placement of article 11 in the "attribution" chapter of the Draft Articles by reiterating Ago's arguments that acts of private individuals constitute "an external event" which is a "condition for the existence of [State] responsibility by acting from outside as a catalyst for the wrongfulness of the conduct of the State organs."[28] Article 11 would thus "prevent attempts by the State to evade the international responsibility which might be incurred as a result of conduct adopted by organs of the State" in relation to the acts of private individuals.[29]

[22] R Ago, "Fourth Report on State Responsibility" Yearbook of the International Law Commission (1972) II, UN Doc A/CN.4/SER.A/1972/Add.1, 126 [146].

[23] Ago, "Fourth Report" (n 22) 97 [65].

[24] See eg ILC, (1975) II Yearbook of the International Law Commission, UN Doc A/CN.4/SER.A/1975/Add.1, 1309th Meeting at 33 (Mr Hambro and Sir Vallat); 1311th Meeting at 38 (Mr Ustor).

[25] See eg ILC, (1975) II Yearbook of the International Law Commission, 1308th Meeting at 27 (Mr Yassen); 1309th Meeting at 31 (Mr Reuter and Mr Sahovic); 1310th Meeting at 37 (Mr Ramangasoavina).

[26] Draft Articles on State Responsibility with Commentaries thereto adopted by the International Law Commission on First Reading (1996) (1996 ILC Draft Articles). Draft art 11 stated: "The conduct of a person or a group of persons not acting on behalf of the State shall not be considered as an act of the State under international law. [...] Paragraph 1 is without prejudice to the attribution to the State of any other conduct which is related to that of the person or groups of persons referred to in that paragraph and which is to be considered as an act of the State by virtue of articles 5 to 10."

[27] ibid 53–61.

[28] ibid 51, fn 100.

[29] ibid 61.

Furthermore, due diligence implicitly featured in some other provisions of the 1996 Draft, in particular in article 23, which dealt with international obligations to prevent a given event. According to the ILC, such an obligation went beyond prevention of private harm inasmuch as the given event was an act of nature (eg a natural disaster), however, it excluded from its scope any act that involved action by the state.[30] Although the ILC, somewhat clumsily, tried to isolate the obligation of prevention from due diligence obligations,[31] the commentary centered on the situations when the "event" was "action of private individuals,"[32] replicating authorities discussed in the commentary to draft article 11, and thereby establishing a clear link between the two provisions.

The revised article 11 did not withstand the scrutiny of Special Rapporteur James Crawford, who held that it was superfluous and had no legal effect.[33] According to him, the responsibility by catalysis was not a rule of attribution. Notwithstanding the efforts of his predecessor to detach the article from the sphere of primary obligations, it was inherently linked to the content of the obligation of the state to prevent or respond to injurious acts.[34] Crawford acknowledged that in situations when state responsibility emerges in connection with the conduct of private individuals "there may be a close link between the basis of attribution and the particular primary rule which is said to have been breached," however, two elements were "analytically distinct."[35] Since the article did not reflect that, Crawford decided it should be deleted.[36] For similar reasons, he proposed deletion of draft article 23, arguing that the content of the obligation of prevention "depends on the interpretation of the relevant primary rule ... [which] falls outside the scope of the draft articles."[37] The members of the Commission were persuaded by the Special Rapporteur's arguments,[38] and consequently the "spirit of due diligence" was expelled from the ARSIWA.

[30] ibid 173.

[31] ibid 173, fn 396. This artificial distinction was later criticized as imprecise by Crawford, who held that the obligation of prevention were "inherently obligations to take all reasonable or necessary measures to ensure that the event does not occur": see J Crawford, "Second Report on State Responsibility" (1999) Yearbook of the International Law Commission, UN Doc A/CN.4/498, 27 [83]. See also comments by Mr Yamada, Mr Rao, and Mr Economides in the 2571st and 2573rd ILC meetings in ILC, (1999) I Yearbook of the International Law Commission, UN Doc A/CN.4/SER.A/1999, 31, 41; and ILC, (1999) II(2) Yearbook of the International Law Commission 62 [178] (noting that "obligations of prevention were often due diligence obligations.")

[32] 1996 ILC Draft Articles (n 26) 175, 176.

[33] Crawford, "First Report" (n 13) 48 [244]. Similar misgivings were expressed by the governments, holding that the article "adds nothing to the draft" (the United States) and was merely "a pedantic clarification" (Chile): ibid para 243.

[34] ibid.

[35] ibid [154]. In cases of a state's failure to prevent harm, attribution seems straightforward: the positive duty is to be fulfilled by the state, and typically its organs (military, police, authorities) fail to fulfill it. Due diligence falls within the scope of that duty.

[36] ibid [245].

[37] Crawford, "Second Report" (n 31) [90]. Similar arguments for deletion were expressed by France, Germany, and the UK: ibid para 84.

[38] Report of the ILC on the Work of its 50th Session (20 April–12 June and 27 July–14 August 1998) Official Records of the General Assembly, 53rd session, Supplement No 10, UN Doc No A/53/10,

The described development reveals that there was confusion as to the role of due diligence in particular in regard to two aspects. First, there was a disagreement as to whether due diligence belonged to the realm of secondary rules, and should thus be kept in the ARSIWA, or whether it was a part of some primary rules, like an obligation of a state to take reasonable care to protect foreign nationals from attack or harm and to apprehend and punish the offenders.[39] Second, due diligence was understood to form a special basis of attribution in cases of state omission where there was a duty to act related to harmful conduct of private individuals, and for a long time this appeared to have been the ILC's view, as demonstrated by the codification history leading to the 1996 Draft Articles. Although the express mention of due diligence in the text of the articles was removed early in the codification process, closer reading, in particular of the commentaries to draft articles 11 and 23, reveals that the exclusion was never total.[40]

This understanding blurred the relationship between the rules of attribution and due diligence. It gave rise to problematic concepts like indirect responsibility[41] or indirect attribution,[42] which attempted to conceptualize the difference between attribution and due diligence but have in fact only amplified confusion. While Ago brought some clarity by introducing the distinction between primary and secondary rules to the codification project, it was only after the deletion of his draft article on the "responsibility by catalysis" (and other articles that contained traces of due diligence like draft article 23) from the ARSIWA that any doubt was removed as to the actual role of the due diligence standard in international law. As stressed by Crawford, the duty of due diligence falls firmly within the ambit of primary rules (ie scope of the obligation) and does not constitute a special rule of attribution.[43]

85 [425]. The proposal to delete the distinction between obligations of conduct (draft art 20), which also implicated a due diligence standard, and obligations of result (draft art 21) generated more debate, but ultimately the view prevailed that this too fell within the realm of primary rules. See the discussion in the ILC 2573rd Meeting (18 May 1999) in ILC, (1999) I Yearbook of the International Law Commission 41; ILC, (1999) II(2) Yearbook of the International Law Commission 59–62.

[39] This disagreement was most clearly evidenced in the ILC discussion with respect to draft art 31 on *force majeure*, with Simma and Hafner, arguing that due diligence is a secondary rule, and Economides and Pellet among others, holding it is a primary rule. See comments in the ILC 2592nd Meeting in ILC, (1999) I Yearbook of the International Law Commission 176–83.

[40] Simma made a similar observation during the ILC discussion of Crawford's Second Report. See ILC, (1999) I Yearbook of the International Law Commission 176.

[41] Ago, "Fourth Report" (n 22) 127; ILC, (1975) Yearbook of the International Law Commission 23 [5], 73 [11]; Crawford, "First Report" (n 13) [49]. See also Christenson, "Attributing Acts" (n 13) 349–51; Hessbruege, "Historical Development" (n 15) 268.

[42] V Tzevelekos, "Reconstructing the Effective Control Criterion in Extraterritorial Humans Rights Breaches: Direct Attribution of Wrongfulness, Due Diligence, and Concurrent Responsibility" (2014) 36(1) Michigan Journal of International Law 129.

[43] J Crawford, *Brownlie's Principles of Public International Law* (8th edn, OUP) 543; Crawford, "First Report" (n 13) [44].

Notwithstanding the clarity brought by the final ARSIWA, the tradition of conceptualizing due diligence as a special case of attribution has had another consequence. It has solidified the doctrinal conviction that the due diligence standard can be only utilized for attributing wrongful conduct in cases when immediate harm was caused by private individuals, and consequently a state has no duty to exercise due diligence with respect to the activities of their own organs. Section 3 turns to discussing this argument.

3. Scope of the Due Diligence Standard in International Investment Law

In international investment law, the responsibility of host states for failing to exercise requisite diligence in protecting foreign investors, has been mostly addressed on the basis of the investment treaty provision that emerged from the customary international minimum standard and is known under the name full protection and security (FPS).[44] The provision, which has become part of most investment treaties,[45] is typically worded succinctly and stipulates that the "[i]nvestments by nationals or companies of either Contracting Party shall enjoy full protection and security in the territory of the other Contracting Party."[46] Arbitral tribunals have applied the provision in a number of cases where investors sustained injuries as a result of physical violence. They have held that under the FPS standard, the host state is obliged to provide protection and security against the actions of both its own organs and third parties.[47] In the latter case, state liability can emerge from the failure to exercise due diligence in protecting investors from the violent acts of non-state actors as well as the obligation to apprehend and punish those responsible for the harm.[48] In contrast, when it comes to actions of its own organs, the impairment to the investor is caused directly by state organs or through their

[44] For more on the FPS standard, see C Schreuer, "Full Protection and Security" (2010) 1(2) Journal of International Dispute Settlement 6; G Cordero Moss, "Full Protection and Security" in A Reinisch (ed), *Standards of Investment Protection* (OUP 2008); Zeitler, "Full Protection" (n 8); Zrilič, *The Protection* (n 11) ch 4.

[45] According to the United Nations Conference on Trade and Development (UNCTAD), the FPS provision has been included in 84% of 2,577 mapped investment treaties: see UNCTAD, International Investment Agreements Navigator <https://investmentpolicyhub.unctad.org/IIA/mappedContent> accessed 28 April 2020.

[46] See eg Germany–Mali Bilateral Investment Treaty (BIT) (1977), art 4.

[47] Schreuer, "Full Protection and Security" (n 44) 2–5; K Vandevelde, *Bilateral Investment Treaties: History, Policy, and Interpretation* (OUP 2010).

[48] See eg *American Manufacturing & Trading Inc (AMT) v Republic of Zaire* ICSID Case No ARB/93/1 (Award) (21 February 1997); *Pantechniki SA Contractors & Engineers v Republic of Albania* ICSID Case No ARB/07/21 (Award) (30 July 2009); *Joseph Houben v Republic of Burundi* ICSID Case No ARB/13/17 (Award) (20 May 2013) [167], [178]; *Bernhard von Pezold v Zimbabwe* ICSID Case No ARB/10/15 (Award) (28 July 2015) [585], [597]; *Ampal* (n 10) [290]; *Strabag* (n 10) [345]; *Cengiz* (n 10) [450]; *Oztas* (n 10) [162]; *Way2Be* (n 10); *Guris* (n 10).

contribution.[49] The responsibility emerges from the breach of the obligation to refrain from such wrongful interference and is attached to the host state through the attribution of the positive actions of its organs. Although this distinction between private violence and the violence of state organs may seem obvious, its treatment in doctrine and jurisprudence has been unsatisfactory, in particular with respect to the question as to whether the due diligence standard can be used for determining state responsibility in situations when the harm has been caused by state organs.[50]

In one case, an investment tribunal has answered in the affirmative. *AAPL v Sri Lanka* concerned a Sri Lankan counterinsurgency operation against the Liberation Fighters of Tamil Elaam.[51] In January 1987, a Sri Lankan Special Task Force launched a forceful attack on the Serendib Shrimp Farm, co-owned by a Hong Kong company called AAPL, which resulted in the death of more than twenty AAPL employees and the destruction of the farm's property, leading to the termination of the farm's operations.[52] The tribunal applied the obligation to protect as enshrined in customary standard under the law of state responsibility for injury to aliens and the FPS provision in article 2.2 of the UK–Sri Lanka Bilateral Investment Treaty (BIT),[53] and found Sri Lanka liable for not taking certain precautions in the planning of its military operation (eg issuing warnings before the attack, conducting judicial investigations against the suspected persons, and taking measures to peacefully remove the suspected persons from the farm) that were "essential to minimise the risks of killings and destruction."[54] The tribunal held that Sri Lanka's inaction and omission was a violation of "its due diligence obligation which requires undertaking [of] all possible measures that could reasonably [be] expected to prevent the eventual occurrence of killing and property destruction."[55] In other words, the tribunal decided that the obligation of protection and security does not require the exercise of due diligence only with respect to violent actions of private individuals and insurrectional movements, but also with respect to the operations of its own organs, such as police and military forces.

The position of the *AAPL* tribunal is in contrast with the dominant view of scholars who have written on due diligence, who argued that the duty of due diligence never applies in situations when harmful activity was carried out by state organs themselves. The essence of this argument is that the conduct of state organs does not need to be measured against the due diligence standard, since it is already

[49] See eg *Cengiz* (n 10) [450]; *Biwater Gauff Ltd v United Republic of Tanzania* ICSID Case No ARB/05/22 (Award) (24 July 2008) [730]; *Frontier Petroleum Services v Czech Republic* UNCITRAL (Award) (12 November 2010) [261]; *Parkerings-Compagniet AS v Republic of Lithuania* ICSID Case No ARB/05/8 (Award) (11 September 2007) [355].

[50] Zrilič, *The Protection* (n 11) 96.

[51] *AAPL* (n 5).

[52] For a detailed analysis of the case, see Zrilič, *The Protection* (n 11) ch 6.

[53] *AAPL* (n 5) [67], [70], [78].

[54] ibid [85(b)].

[55] ibid. The dissenting arbitrator disagreed and argued there is no such due diligence obligation in launching military attacks.

directly attributed to the state. This position was most prominently articulated by Pisillo-Mazzeschi in his seminal article on due diligence published in 1992. Having examined the practice of state responsibility for injury to aliens, he argued that "the due diligence rule does not play any role" with respect to the actions of competent state organs as "such actions are attributed to the State."[56] Reflecting the view that was at the time popular with the ILC,[57] the due diligence concept was to be utilized only with respect to the obligation to protect from private conduct.[58] This understanding has been carried into the investment law scholarship. For example, the most authoritative textbook in the field written by Dolzer and Schreuer, clarifies that the issue of due diligence will not arise in situations when "state organs themselves act in violation of the [FPS] standard ... because the state will then be held directly responsible."[59] Other investment law textbooks do not seem to make a departure from this position.[60] Similarly, in the oft-cited academic work on the FPS standard, Zeitler distinguished between situations when harm was caused by state actors and those when it was caused by private actors, whereby the state owed due diligence to prevent and investigate only in the latter case.[61]

More specifically in the context of state forceful actions, De Brabandere, who was one of the members of the International Law Association's (ILA) Study Group on Due Diligence in International Law, argued that the due diligence test is irrelevant for determining responsibility of a state when the harm results from the action of its organs, since the wrongful conduct (eg unlawful killing or destruction) itself is attributable to the state.[62] According to him, the *AAPL* tribunal did not apply the due diligence standard to the conduct of state organs, since it was not proved that the killing of investor staff and destruction of property was caused by the state forces.[63] This observation does not accurately reflect the tribunal's decision, in which the application of due diligence was discussed specifically and expressly with regard to state conduct, that is, the planning and execution of the military counterinsurgency operation which resulted in investor losses. Moreover, the conduct that was attributable was wrongful precisely because of lack of the state's diligence (ie failure to take adequate precautions). Berkes, defending the same general position, observed more broadly that the due diligence obligation cannot be applied to the conduct of the state's own agents, since their wrongful act is "automatically

[56] Pisillo-Mazzeschi, "The Due Diligence Rule" (n 8) 23.
[57] See section 2.
[58] Pisillo-Mazzeschi, "The Due Diligence Rule" (n 8) 23–24.
[59] Dolzer and Schreuer, *Principles* (n 8) 162.
[60] The textbooks in the field limit discussion of due diligence only to prevention of actions of third parties. See eg A Newcombe and L Paradell, *Law and Practice of Investment Treaties* (Kluwer 2009) 246; CL Lim and others, *International Investment Law and Arbitration* (CUP 2018) 278; Y Radi, *Rules and Practices of International Investment Law and Arbitration* (CUP 2020) 106.
[61] Zeitler, "Full Protection" (n 8) 191.
[62] De Brabandere, "Host States" (n 6) 334.
[63] ibid 335.

attributable to the state."[64] He noted that, in the context of military operations, the state's armed forces incur the state responsibility "not because of the breach of a due diligence obligation (primary norm), but on the basis of the attribution of the conduct of its agents to the state (secondary norm)."[65]

There is no doubt that the conduct of armed forces as a whole is attributable to a state. This rule is well established in the ARSIWA and confirmed in practice.[66] The state conduct, however, encompasses both the acts (eg wanton destruction of property, deliberate killing) and omission (eg lack of due care in exercising official powers) of state agents. While the cited commentators generally agree that due diligence is a primary norm, their arguments, commonly contrasting due diligence with "direct responsibility" and "automatic attribution,"[67] still signal a binary understanding of the concepts of attribution and due diligence. These views are influenced by the above-described understanding of due diligence as a special case of attribution concerning conduct of third persons, often conceptualized as indirect responsibility or indirect attribution. This position does not adequately account the fact that in both cases, when the perpetrator of the injury is a state organ or a private entity, state responsibility will be direct and automatic following the breach of the primary obligation by its agents. In all these instances, the state accepts a duty to prevent an outcome irrespective of whether that restrains the conduct of state organs or private actors—due diligence simply helps shape the scope of that obligation. The support for this claim can be found in the practice of due diligence application in other sub-fields of international law. As concluded in the Second ILA Report on Due Diligence, there are no contradictions between a general standard of due diligence and its specific manifestations in different branches of international law.[68] Thus, drawing analogies with other areas of international law is not only justified but also necessary for determining accurately the nature and scope of due diligence.

First, some evidence of applying a due diligence standard to public conduct can be found already in the cases of the old post-conflict commissions applying the law of state responsibility for injury to aliens. For example, in the *Garcia and Garza* case,[69] the US–Mexican Commission held that while a state has a due diligence obligation to prevent crime and apprehend criminals, it must also act diligently in discharging that duty.[70] This duty of care that state officials needed to exercise

[64] A Berkes, "The Standard of 'Due Diligence' as a Result of Interchange between the Law of Armed Conflict and General International Law" (2018) 23(3) Journal of Conflict and Security Law 433, 440.
[65] ibid 443.
[66] See ARSIWA, art 4; *Armed Activities on the Territory of Congo* (*DRC v Uganda*) [2005] ICJ Rep 251 [243].
[67] See eg Dolzer and Schreuer, *Principles* (n 8) 162; De Brabandere, "Host States" (n 6) 359; Berkes (n 64), "The Standard" 440.
[68] ILA Second Report (n 1) 6.
[69] *Garcia and Garza Case (Mexico v USA)* (1926) 4 RIAA 119.
[70] ibid 121 (and authorities cited therein).

in regard of their own forceful action in order to prevent injury to others would entail considering less harmful alternatives and undertaking "sufficient precaution."[71] In another post-conflict case, *In re Rizzo*, which concerned the sequestration of Italian property by the French government, the Conciliation Commission held that the wrongful act was not sequestration itself but rather "an alleged lack of diligence on the part of the French State ... in the execution of the said measure."[72] Some leading international law scholars have confirmed such use of a due diligence standard.[73]

More relevant to the context of state security operations, this understanding of due diligence is in line with its application in the law of armed conflict. For example, the rules of IHL impose on the parties to armed conflict the obligation to exercise due diligence with respect to not only the opposite belligerent party and private persons (eg armed opposition groups and rebels) but also the action of its own soldiers.[74] In *DRC v Uganda*, the ICJ confirmed this, finding Uganda responsible for breaching its duty of vigilance by failing to take "adequate measures to ensure that its military forces did not engage in the looting, plundering and exploitation of the DRC's natural resources."[75] The revised Commentaries to the Geneva Conventions have identified several examples where due diligence is to be applied with respect to a party's own soldiers in complying with the obligation to protect wounded and sick.[76] More pointedly, in the context of the law of targeting, which regulates a situation analogous to the one from which the *AAPL* case emerged, the IHL requires parties to take certain precautions in attack. Article 57 of Additional Protocol I (AP I) thus specifies that parties must exercise constant care in the conduct of military hostilities and take certain feasible precautions in the planning and deciding of the military operations, including in the choice of the means and methods of attack with an aim to avoid or minimize incidental losses to civilian lives and property.[77] It is widely accepted that this obligation is assessed

[71] ibid. See also *Lillie Kling v Mexico* (1930) 4 RIAA 575, 579, 580 (and authorities cited therein).

[72] *In re Rizzo* (1955) 22 ILR 317, 322.

[73] Crawford, *Brownlie's Principles* (n 43) 559; I Brownlie, *State Responsibility: Part I* (OUP 1983) 46 (and other authorities cited in fn 65).

[74] See eg International Committee of the Red Cross (ICRC, 2016), Revised Commentary to Common Article 1 of the Geneva Conventions, paras 118–19, 126.

[75] *Armed Activities* (n 66) 252 [246)], 253 [250].

[76] See eg ICRC, Commentary to Geneva Convention I (2016) art 12, paras 1360–61 (specifying that the obligation to protect wounded and sick requires the exercise of due diligence in preventing harm caused by, among others, party's own soldiers). Similarly, ICRC, Commentary to Geneva Convention I (2016) art 15, para 1499; ICRC, Commentary to Geneva Convention II (2017) art 12, para 1407. See also Hague Convention VIII relative to Laying of Automatic Submarine Contact Mines (1907), arts 3, 4.

[77] Additional Protocol I to the Geneva Conventions (AP I), art 57, paras 1, 2. The obligation to take precautions in attack is customary and also applies to non-international armed conflict. See J-M Henckaerts and L Doswald-Beck, *International Committee of the Red Cross, Customary International Humanitarian Law, vol I, Rules* (CUP 2005) (ICRC Study) 58–65, Rules 15–21; International Institute of Humanitarian Law, *Manual on the Law of Non-International Armed Conflict* (IIHL, 2006) 25 [2.1.2]; *Western Front, Aerial Bombardment and Related Claims, Eritrea's Claims 1, 3, 5, 9–13, 14, 21, 25, and 26* (Partial Award of 19 December 2005) (2005) 26 RIAA 291, 327 [95].

against the due diligence standard,[78] as implied by the use of word "feasible," which denotes "everything that [is] practicable or practically possible, taking into account all circumstances at the time of attack."[79]

In IHRL, a similarly open approach towards the use of due diligence for determining state responsibility has been signaled in the First Report of the ILA Study Group on Due Diligence in International Law. The human rights law section of the Report specifies that in exceptional cases, states must exercise due diligence to protect persons from their own organs, for example, when the latter deploy justifiable lethal force that may result in harm to innocent bystanders.[80] In practice, however, the due diligence standard has been generally applied restrictively. Human rights bodies have traditionally relied on due diligence when assessing whether a state has breached its positive obligation to protect human rights against the infringements of non-state actors.[81] On the other hand, with respect to the harm caused by the activity of its own security forces, diligence was factored in the assessment of violations of the negative obligation, which were imputable to a state. In other words, human rights courts have considered state police and military organs' duty of care as part of the proportionality analysis of the measures those organs had taken. Specifically in the context of planning and executing forceful operations, on a number of occasions they have found that states failed to exercise requisite care or failed to take requisite precaution, which amounted to the breach of a negative obligation.[82]

Following this overview, it is safe to conclude that the *AAPL* tribunal adhered to the approach firmly established in the IHL as well as the IHRL. Admittedly, the tribunal was not clear and specific enough in explaining the manner in which it

[78] Y Dinstein, *The Conduct of Hostilities under the Law of International Armed Conflict* (3rd edn, CUP 2016) 165; W Boothby, *The Law of Targeting* (OUP 2012) 122, 177; M Bothe, "Legal Restraints on Targeting: Protection of Civilian Population and the Changing Faces of Modern Conflicts" (2001) 31 Israel Yearbook on Human Rights 35, 45; K Trapp, "Great Resources Mean Great Responsibility: A Framework of Analysis for Assessing Compliance with API Obligations in the Information Age" in D Saxon (ed), *International Humanitarian Law and the Changing Technology of War* (Martinus Nijhoff 2013) 153, 156.

[79] ICRC Commentary to art 57(2)(a)(i) of AP I, para 2198. Such circumstances comprise humanitarian and military considerations, as well as means available to the state and the level of technological development (eg states' surveillance and networking capabilities). See ICRC Study, 131, 174; Trapp, "Great Resources" (n 78) 163–64.

[80] ILA, Study Group on Due Diligence in International Law: First Report (ILA, 2014) 15–16 (ILA First Report).

[81] *Osman v United Kingdom* (2000) 29 EHRR 245, para 116; *Ituango Massacres v Colombia* (Judgment) IACtHR Series C no 148 (1 July 2006) [132]–[135]; IACHR, Annual Report of the Inter-American Commission on Human Rights 1996 (17 March 1997) OEA/Ser.L/V/II.95, Doc 7, rev, para 80; UN Human Rights Committee, "Concluding Observations on Algeria" (5 August 1998) UN Doc CCPR/C/79/Add.95, para 6.

[82] See eg *McCann v United Kingdom* App no 18984/91 (ECtHR, 27 September 1995), para 149; *Ergi v Turkey* App no 23818/94 (Judgment) (ECtHR, 28 July 1998), para 79; *Isayeva, Yusupova, and Bazayeva v Russia* App nos 57947/00, 57948/00, and 57949/00 (Judgment) (ECtHR, 24 February 2005), para 199; *Isayeva v Russia* App no 57950/00 (Judgment) (ECtHR, 24 February 2005), paras 187, 191; *Santo Domingo Massacre v Colombia* (Judgment) IACtHR Series C no 259 (30 November 2012) [226], [228], [229].

deployed due diligence and the legal basis for doing it, which has given rise to erroneous interpretations of the tribunal's application of the standard and led to unjustified criticism of the decision.[83] First, the tribunal did not use due diligence in the traditional sense, that is, as a standard measuring the compliance with the positive obligation to protect investors from rebels. This understanding of the *AAPL* award has been fostered by many academics in support of the critique that the due diligence standard tends to extend host states' responsibility in situations which are outside their control such as armed conflicts.[84]

Second, although the cursory reading of the award may suggest otherwise, the legal basis for the decision was not a standalone due diligence obligation that states have with respect to their own agents. Due diligence was used as a standard of conduct in the context of compliance with the negative obligation in the same manner the cognate concepts like diligence, care and feasibility have been used as part of the justification analysis for violations of negative obligations in IHL and IHRL. In other words, had there been no attack against the *AAPL* farm which resulted in destruction and killing, there would have been no violation of the positive obligation to take precautions. Conversely, once the attack had been launched, the government could have escaped responsibility for the losses if it had proved that the measures had been justified and it had fulfilled its positive obligations (eg proper planning and precautions) assessed against due diligence.

To better understand the implication of and the rationale for this aspect of the due diligence standard, section 4 proposes to conceptualize it through the prism of risk.

4. Due Diligence as a Tool for Managing Risks

Over the past years, international law has become increasingly open to deploying the lens of risk for examining and regulating the conduct of states in various types of situations.[85] While the exact meaning of risk differs, depending on the context, it can be described as a "possibility of something bad happening,"[86] and thus consisting of two elements: probability of a certain event happening and the harm

[83] See text and references set out at nn 6 and 7.

[84] Based on this understanding, a number of scholars inaccurately argued that the *AAPL* tribunal applied the objective standard of due diligence, thus not sufficiently taking into account the circumstances of a state in armed conflict. See eg De Brabandere, "Hosts States" (n 6) 356; Bray, "Save Our Investments" (n 6) 591; and other authorities set out at nn 6 and 7.

[85] S Townley, "The Rise of Risk in International Law" (2018) 18(2) Chicago Journal of International Law 594, 602; M Ambrus, R Rayfuse, and W Werner, "Risk and International Law" in Mónika Ambrus, Rosemary Rayfuse, and Wouter Werner (eds), *Risk and the Regulation of Uncertainty in International Law* (OUP 2017) 1, 5.

[86] M Ambrus, "The European Court of Human Rights as Governor of Risk" in Mónika Ambrus, Rosemary Rayfuse, and Wouter Werner (eds), *Risk and the Regulation of Uncertainty in International Law* (OUP 2017) 100.

resulting from it.[87] The probability of the negative event occurring in the future enables a state to adopt certain measures for preventing or mitigating harm, and thereby manage or control the risk.[88] Scholars have noted that international law and institutions have embraced such measures, which is reflected in the increasing application of the rules on prevention and precautions beyond the field of international environmental law,[89] within which they have been traditionally discussed.[90] As accurately noted by one commentator, due diligence is a vital aspect of this equation, since it acts as a "standard of conduct for the implementation of prevention rules."[91] While this is not a novel finding in international investment law, the concept of risk can improve the understanding of the multifaceted nature of due diligence and the roles it performs.

As part of the obligation of protection and security, due diligence has a dual role: risk allocation (*ex post* assessment) and risk management (*ex ante* assessment). As a tool for risk allocation, due diligence is used by adjudicators to ascertain whether a state has breached its obligation of prevention. It is a tool for determining state responsibility but also serves as defense against the claim of responsibility. In the latter sense, it performs a similar role to the defense of *force majeure*, allocating the risk by taking account of its characteristics (eg unforeseeability, irresistibility, uncontrollability), and thus rendering *force majeure* as a secondary "defense" norm irrelevant for the obligation of prevention.[92]

On the other hand, the risk management role shifts the focus from dispute resolution to the proactive and anticipatory state conduct before the harmful event

[87] Townley, "The Rise of Risk" (n 85) 597 (arguing that a "threat" is also a form of risk, assessed on individual rather than statistical basis); N Tsagourias, "Risk and the Use of Force" in Mónika Ambrus, Rosemary Rayfuse, and Wouter Werner (eds), *Risk and the Regulation of Uncertainty in International Law* (OUP 2017) (arguing that these two elements do not need to be symmetrical and thus risk can be both, a less probable but more harmful event as well as more probable but less harmful event); A Trouwborst, "Prevention, Precaution, Logic and Law" (2009) Erasmus Law Review 105, 117.

[88] Ambrus, "Governor of Risk" (n 86) 101 (deploying the term "risk governance").

[89] In international environmental law, there is a distinction between preventative and precautionary measures, whereby the latter are taken in situations of scientific uncertainty. Scholars have noted that the two concepts have effectively merged, and precautions constitute a form of prevention. See eg Trouwborst, "Prevention" (n 87); Townley, "The Rise of Risk" (n 85). This is certainly true in investment law, in which the two notions have often been used interchangeably, or precautions have been referred to as a form of prevention.

[90] Due diligence featured prominently in the ILC discussions on draft articles on prevention of transboundary damage from hazardous activities. See eg PS Rao, "Second Report on International Liability for Injurious Consequences Arising Out of Acts Not Prohibited by International Law (Prevention of Transboundary Damage from Hazardous Activities)" in ILC, (1999) I Yearbook of the International Law Commission 237–45. See also Ambrus, "Governor of Risk" (n 86); Townley, "The Rise of Risk" (n 85) 598–99 (noting how the prevention rules have been used widely across different disciplines of international law, including regulation of cyberspace, business activities, security measures, etc).

[91] Townley, "The Rise of Risk" (n 85) 598.

[92] For more on the relationship between *force majeure* and due diligence, see J Zrilič, "Armed Conflict as Force Majeure in International Investment Law" (2019) 16(1) Manchester Journal of International Economic Law 28.

occurs.[93] It facilitates prudence and requires the state to engage in certain proactive, future-oriented behavior in order to prevent the harm or mitigate the risk thereof. This is the aspect that further removes due diligence from the traditional conceptualization as a rule of attribution for conduct of non-state actors. Rather, due diligence is part of certain risk-based primary norms and as such a legal device for managing and controlling risks regardless of whether they stem from the private or public sphere.[94] This understanding has become well embedded in international environmental law, where international courts and tribunals have held that a state has an obligation to exercise due diligence in preventing transboundary environmental harm not only with respect to activities of industrial actors on their territory but also more generally with respect to their own activities.[95] This obligation entails a duty to take certain precautionary measures (eg to conduct environmental impact assessment) when there is a risk of significant transboundary harm emerging from the planned activities. In a similar vein, there seems to be a trend to apply the due diligence standard in cyberspace "with respect to both government and private cyber infrastructure on, and cyber activities emanating from, their territory," regardless of the attributability of the acts in question to a state.[96]

The risk-oriented concept of due diligence provides for a more complete understanding of the scope of the investment obligation to protect. Accordingly, a host state not only has a due diligence duty to protect investors from external risks (eg when the catalyst for state responsibility is private violence),[97] but also from the harm that might result from the actions of its own organs, especially when the latter are not *prima facie* wrongful and involve a heightened risk of incidental injuries.[98] This will be the case if the state undertakes a harmful or inherently risky

[93] For more on "proactive law," see G Berger-Walliser and P Shrivastava, "Beyond Compliance: Sustainable Development, Business, and Proactive Law" (2015) 46 Georgetown Journal of International Law 417, 438; Townley, "The Rise of Risk" (n 85) 639 (observing a "shift toward *ex ante* compliance rather than *ex post* reparation").

[94] This is not to say that there is no difference in how different types of risks are expected to be managed. The issue is what is reasonably expected, which will depend on the circumstances of the case and the degree of state control over such risks. For example, when state agents use force, the acceptance of permissible risks will be much lower than in situations when states are expected to prevent private violence.

[95] *Certain Activities Carried Out By Nicaragua in the Border Area (Costa Rica v Nicaragua)* and *Construction of a Road in Costa Rica Along the San Juan River (Nicaragua v Costa Rica)* (Judgment) [2015] ICJ Rep 665, 706 [104], 720–21 [153–57]; *Pulp Mills on the River Uruguay (Argentina v Uruguay)* (Judgment) [2010] ICJ Rep 14, 79 [197], 83 [204]; *Responsibilities and Obligations of States Sponsoring Persons and Entities with Respect to Activities in the Area* ITLOS Case No 17 (Advisory Opinion) (1 February 2011) [131]. See also Pisillo-Mazzeschi, "The Due Diligence Rule" (n 8) 38, 40 (stating that such application of the due diligence rule reflects customary environmental law).

[96] See Michael N Schmitt (ed), *Tallinn Manual on the International Law Applicable to Cyber Warfare* (CUP, 2013) r 5, comment 1; M Schmitt, "In Defense of Due Diligence in Cyberspace" (2015) 125 Yale Law Journal: Forum 68, 70; K Bannelier-Christakis, "Cyber Diligence: A Low-Intensity Due Diligence Principle for Low-Intensity Cyber Operations?" (2014) 14 Baltic Yearbook of International Law 1, 4, 8.

[97] That is, the obligation to protect from harmful acts of non-state actors, and the obligation to investigate and apprehend the wrong-doers.

[98] See *McCann* (n 82).

but justifiable activity that included diligent planning and measures to avert or minimize the harm, for example, targeting operations conducted by enforcement and military organs.[99] While there is no general obligation to abstain from legitimate targeting operations, diligence is required in the planning and execution thereof with a view to avoid or minimize the harm.[100] Finding the state responsible would thus depend on the assessment of whether the state organs exercised requisite care, that is, on whether they adequately evaluated the risks and took necessary measures for minimizing them to the extent possible.[101]

There are compelling legal, policy, and practical reasons underpinning the risk-based concept of due diligence. First, the risk-based due diligence analysis enables tribunals to avoid making potentially controversial pronouncements on the legitimacy and legality of state actions while still finding a state liable on a different, less contentious, ground. Thus, basing state responsibility on omission and due diligence could be a desirable option when the alternative ground for responsibility, for example, finding that state forces committed a war atrocity, would bear negative policy implications for the state, increase the likelihood of the state resisting the enforcement of the decision, and potentially give rise to an attack on the legitimacy of the tribunal. Investment tribunals, primarily tasked to apply and interpret investment treaties, may be in particular sensitive to this aspect, as they have been often criticized for expansively interpreting their mandate.[102]

For example, one can speculate that *AAPL* tribunal's choice to base its decision on due diligence could be motivated by policy considerations. While the tribunal questioned the credibility of the military reports and found many inconsistencies in the Government's account of the combat action,[103] it was careful to note that the counterinsurgency operation was a legitimate act of a sovereign government.[104] In another conflict-related case, *AMT v Zaire*, the tribunal similarly held the state responsible on the basis of due diligence, despite the fact that losses were caused through the looting and destruction of Zairean soldiers.[105] The perception of responsibility based on due diligence as a "lesser" form of responsibility is based on policy grounds.[106] Politically, it may be less detrimental for a government to be

[99] Zrilič, *The Protection* (n 11) 96.

[100] ibid.

[101] ibid. See also *AAPL* (n 5) [85(b)].

[102] Sornarajah, *The International Law on Foreign Investment* (n 7) 252 (arguing that investment tribunals were not designed to deal with such political issues as the legality of force used to suppress an insurrection, etc).

[103] More than ten years later, Human Rights Watch reported that army personnel in the area where the investor's farm was located, admitted to their involvement in destruction and killing. See Human Rights Watch, *World Report: Events of 2001* (HRW, 2002) 255.

[104] *AAPL* (n 5) [85B]; *AAPL* (Dissenting Opinion) (n 5) 592.

[105] *AMT* (n 48).

[106] This perception of the due diligence is related to the distinction between direct and indirect responsibility, with the latter term used by states to signal a "lesser degree of culpability." See Christenson, "Attributing Acts" (n 13) 350–51 (referring to the report of the Israeli Commission of Enquiry which investigated the 1982 massacre of Palestinian civilians in a refugee camp and found that Israel bore

found responsible for failing to take precautions in launching a legitimate security operation, than for wanton destruction and deliberate killing, as the claim was formulated in the *AAPL* case. Legally, however, a state is responsible for all the damage caused by its omission to prevent the harmful act, which, in practice, will often be calculated as equivalent to the damage caused by the immediately harmful act.[107] This notwithstanding, a politically more acceptable ground of responsibility could facilitate compliance with the final award.[108]

Second, as stated above, risk-based due diligence promotes caution in state operations involving high levels of risk. Risk can be the basis for obligation or authorization.[109] Investment treaties accommodate risk as authorization in several of their provisions that permit the state to take action, which may encroach on investor rights, with an aim to prevent or address certain risks (eg security threats). These include security exceptions,[110] "necessity of the situation" exemptions in advanced armed conflict clauses,[111] and justification on the level of substantive standards such as the police powers doctrine.[112] Within due diligence, risk is relevant as both obligation and authorization. When exercised against the conduct of non-state actors, due diligence obliges the state to prevent private violence and injuries stemming therefrom, but also authorizes it to exercise its sovereign powers for maintaining public order and safety, or in other words, measures necessary for establishing a precautionary regime.[113] If left unsupervised, such authorizations could give rise to abuses under the guise of protecting national security or compliance with the FPS standard.[114] This prompts the question of what are the limits of risk as authorization.[115] Due diligence with respect to actions of state

"indirect responsibility" for allowing the militiamen to enter the refugee camp); Hessbruege, "Historical Development" (n 15) 268.

[107] While the compensation awarded for breach of an obligation of prevention should not be automatically equated with the damages caused by the harmful act, in practice there will often be no difference between the two. For example, the *AAPL* tribunal calculated the compensation based on the evaluation of losses the investor suffered by the destruction of the property: see *AAPL* (n 5) [88]. For a view that the compensation for the breach of due diligence should be calculated differently than simply accounting the damage caused by the harmful act, see *Spanish Zone of Morocco* (*Great Britain v Spain*) (1924) 2 RIAA 615 [709]–[710]; *Janes* (*US v Mexico*) (1926) 4 RIAA 82 [89].

[108] The *AAPL* award was paid without delay.

[109] Townley, "The Rise of Risk" (n 85) 630.

[110] See eg art IX of the US–Ukraine BIT (1994).

[111] See eg art 5(2) of the UK–Ukraine BIT (1993).

[112] Zrilič, *The Protection* (n 11).

[113] *AAPL* (n 5) [85(b)] (noting that precautionary measures are part of "governmental inherent power" that can be exercised against non-state actors in security sensitive areas); *Garcia and Garza* (n 69).

[114] A similar observation in the context of cybersecurity was noted by Bannelier-Christakis, who cautioned that due diligence could become a "Trojan horse to eroding civil liberties": see Bannelier-Christakis, "Cyber Diligence" (n 97) 12.

[115] The question can emerge as to how much force a state must deploy to meet its due diligence obligation of protection in, for instance, suppressing violent riots, demonstrations in opposition to an investor, etc. See eg *Pezold* (n 48) [590]; *Autopista Concesionada v Republic of Venezuela* ICSID Case No ARB/00/5 (Award) (23 September 2003) [124].

organs presents a needed counterpart by establishing a new form of accountability based on "precautions against the precautionary politics of arbitrary decisions,"[116] thereby permitting greater scrutiny of state conduct which is justified by risk as authorization.

Third and finally, the broader understanding of due diligence helps to avoid potential normative conflicts between different subfields of international law. As described in this chapter, the standard and its various manifestations has been applied across different branches of international law with no contradictions.[117] Risk-based due diligence embodies this generality and helps discrete legal regimes, which regulate similar situations, communicate better, thus avoiding potential norm conflicts.[118] For example, the *AAPL* tribunal applied investment law to a situation of military targeting, which is primarily regulated in the IHL rules; however, by using risk as justification it ultimately arrived at a finding which was in line with the IHL.

5. Conclusion

This chapter has sought to show how a due diligence standard is not limited to the prevention of harm by non-state actors but can sometimes be applied with respect to the activity of a state's own organs, as a standard of conduct measuring compliance with negative obligations. While in international investment law practice, this understanding has thus far not been commonly accepted, and moreover, has been misunderstood and critiqued in the literature, the chapter aimed to clarify the legal basis and justifications for, what is otherwise considered, a pragmatic judicial solution to an exceptional predicament. Moving away from the rubric of attribution to the rubric of risk, it has been argued that due diligence has a greater potential than being limited to prevention and punishment of private violence, and permits much room for norm development.

[116] See C Aradau and R Van Munster, "Governing Terrorism through Risk: Taking Precautions, (un) Knowing the Future" (2007) 13(1) European Journal of International Relations 89.

[117] ILA, *Second Report* (n 1) 6.

[118] See ILC Study Group, Fragmentation of International Law: Difficulties Arising from the Diversification and Expansion of International Law (2006) UN Doc A/CN.4/L.682, 211 [421].

15
Fragmentation of Attribution in International Law

*Gábor Kajtár**

1. Introduction

Much has been said in scholarly literature about fragmentation and unity of international law. Some express deep concerns about the phenomenon of fragmentation,[1] while others do not conceive it as a defining challenge in international law.[2] The present author subscribes to a view which falls in between these two extremes. This chapter will argue that even though some forms of fragmentation are indeed inevitable in international law, certain types of it are not only unnecessary, but also ought to be avoided, as they undermine the systemic nature of international law. This chapter will focus on the latter, unwelcome form of fragmentation among attribution standards in international law. The analysis will focus on the jurisprudence of international courts and tribunals in the fields of *jus ad bellum*, *jus in bello*, and investment law. It will present a plea for making a strict analytical distinction between attribution tests of specialized fields of international law both in terms of theory and in judicial practice.

This chapter will first examine the practice of international courts and tribunals and will contend that adjudicators, consciously or unconsciously, use the notion of attribution in a narrow and in a broad sense. Attribution tests in the narrow sense are drawn from the International Law Commission's (ILC) Articles on Responsibility of States for Internationally Wrongful Acts (ARSIWA) and are applied in the context of establishing the international responsibility of states. Whereas broad sense attribution concepts serve a variety of other legal purposes. This phenomenon will be termed here as the fragmentation of attribution, which will form the main concern of this study (see section 2). The chapter will then

* The author would like to thank André Nollkaemper and Marko Milanovic for their thought-provoking comments on earlier and on the present version of this research. The author is also very grateful to the anonymous reviewer for their insightful remarks.

[1] See eg Speech by his Excellency Judge Gilbert Guillaume, President of the International Court of Justice, to the Sixth Committee of the General Assembly of the United Nations (31 October 2001) https://www.icj-cij.org/public/files/press-releases/5/2995.pdf (accessed 21 July 2022).

[2] See eg Martti Koskenniemi and Päivi Leino, "Fragmentation of International Law? Postmodern Anxieties" (2002) 15 Leiden Journal of International Law 553.

Gábor Kajtár, *Fragmentation of Attribution in International Law* In: *Secondary Rules of Primary Importance in International Law.* Edited by: Gábor Kajtár, Başak Çalı, and Marko Milanovic, Oxford University Press.
DOI: 10.1093/oso/9780192869012.003.0015

map various attribution concepts used in the fields of *jus ad bellum*, *jus in bello*, and international investment law in adjudicatory practice and scholarship. By identifying their proper legal purpose and nuanced content, the chapter will distinguish attribution concepts that are used in the broad as well as in the narrow sense (see section 3). Finally it will point out some doctrinal inconsistencies arising from the judicial use of different attribution tests in an interchangeable way and call for doctrinal scrutiny and methodological consistency in dealing with secondary rules of international law (see section 4).

2. On the Notion of Attribution in a Broad and Narrow Sense

It appears to be a widely held view that attribution is exclusively a state responsibility concept, which serves for imputing internationally wrongful acts to states.[3] According to the most frequently used narrow definition, attribution stands for "the process by which international law establishes whether the conduct of a natural person or other such intermediary can be considered an 'act of state' and thus give rise to state responsibility."[4] Yet, I will argue here that attribution is in fact a much broader notion, which may carry different legal meanings and serve different purposes across different subfields of international law. Put differently, the term "attribution" covers a host of imputability criteria across various specialized fields that ought not to be used interchangeably.

Given that states are abstract legal entities, they do not exist in the physical world as actors. As the Permanent Court of International Justice (PCIJ) has famously stated: "States can act only by and through their agents and representatives."[5] This statement has broader and more significant legal consequences than usually appreciated. Contrary to the general understanding, agency is not solely necessary in the context of committing an internationally wrongful act. If understood properly, the PCIJ's statement in fact implies that every act, whether lawful or unlawful, which one seeks to link to a state for legal purposes, has to be attributed to that state.

The commentary to the ARSIWA also reaffirms that the question of attribution as contained in the ARSIWA is limited to answering the question what constitutes an organ or otherwise an agent of a state *for purposes of* establishing its responsibility.[6] At the same time, the commentary implicitly recognizes that attribution may serve other purposes beyond state responsibility as well:

[3] See eg Alexander Kees, "Responsibility of States for Private Actors" in Rüdiger Wolfrum (ed), *Max Planck Encyclopedia of Public International Law* (OUP 2011).

[4] James Crawford, *State Responsibility: The General Part* (CUP 2014) 113.

[5] *Questions relating to Settlers of German Origin in Poland* (Advisory Opinion) 1923 PCIJ Series B no 6 at 22 (10 September 1923).

[6] International Law Commission (ILC), "Articles on Responsibility of States for Internationally Wrongful Acts, with Commentaries" (2001) II(2) Yearbook of the International Law Commission 38–39.

> The question of attribution of conduct to the State for the purposes of responsibility is to be distinguished from other international law processes by which particular organs are authorized to enter into commitments on behalf of the State. Thus the Head of State or Government or the minister of foreign affairs is regarded as having authority to represent the State without any need to produce full powers. Such rules have nothing to do with attribution for the purposes of State responsibility ... Thus, the rules concerning attribution set out in this chapter are formulated for this particular purpose, and not for other purposes for which it may be necessary to define the State or its Government.[7]

The definition of Condorelli and Kress also explicitly confirms that attribution is a much wider notion than a ground for imputing only wrongful acts to states:

> "Attribution" (or "imputation") is the term used to denote the legal operation having as its function to establish whether given conduct of a physical person, whether consisting of a positive action or an omission, is to be characterized, from the point of view of international law, as an "act of the State." In other words by the term "attribution," reference is made to the body of criteria of connection and the conditions which have to be fulfilled, according to the relevant principles of international law, in order to conclude that it is a State (or other subject of international law) which has acted in the particular case.[8]

Even more explicitly, Nollkaemper argues that attribution is relevant in practically all fields of international law and that the test applied can vary from field to field. His words are worth being reproduced in full here:

> Attribution plays an essential function in the definition and application of mutual obligations of states in a variety of fields of international law, including the law of state responsibility, the law of treaties, the formation of customary law, the law of diplomatic representation and ... the law of self-defence. The fact that the principle of attribution is used in several parts of international law does not necessarily mean that its contents in each of these fields is identical.[9]

Against this background, this contribution will examine in detail the exact contexts in which the notion of attribution is relied on in various fields of international

[7] ibid 39.

[8] Luigi Condorelli and Claus Kress, "The Rules of Attribution: General Considerations" in James Crawford and others (eds), *The Law of International Responsibility* (OUP 2010) 221.

[9] André Nollkaemper, "Attribution of Forcible Acts to States: Connections Between the Law on the Use of Force and the Law of State Responsibility" in Niels M Blokker and Nico Schrijver (eds), *The Security Council and the Use of Force: Theory and Reality—A Need for Change?* (Martinus Nijhoff 2005) 133, 140.

law, well beyond the scope of establishing state responsibility. Furthermore, section 3 will also show how the notion of attribution attracts different legal tests in disputes concerning the use of force, international humanitarian law (IHL), and international investment protection, giving rise to the fragmentation of the notion of attribution in international adjudication. We shall now turn to addressing the variety of legal contents and meanings clothed as "attribution" in different branches of international law.

3. Mapping the Fragmentation of Attribution

Chronologically first in line, in the 1980s competing interpretations of attribution appeared in the field of *jus ad bellum* in the aftermath of the International Court of Justice's (ICJ) judgment in *Nicaragua*. This was followed, in the 1990s, with the confusion of different attribution tests in IHL as a consequence of the *Tadić* judgment. In the last two decades, the same conceptual debate surfaced in the burgeoning practice of investment arbitration tribunals. These will be addressed here as separate stages of the fragmentation of attribution.

3.1 Attribution Requirements in the Field of *jus ad bellum*

Ian Brownlie has already in the 1950s pointed out the inconsistent application of attribution standards in the field of use of force against non-state actors.[10] The reasoning of the ICJ in *Nicaragua* has been the source of many misunderstandings in scholarly literature. What is often overlooked by commentators is that the Court has applied two different attribution standards when assessing the conduct and responsibility of the United States (US). First, the ICJ emphasized that "[t]he question of the degree of control of the *contras* by the United States Government is relevant to the claim of Nicaragua attributing responsibility to the United States for activities of the contras whereby the United States has, it is alleged, violated an obligation of international law not to kill, wound or kidnap citizens of Nicaragua."[11] Thus, the Court employed the effective control and the complete dependence tests in a purely state responsibility context.[12] Secondly, when assessing the armed attack condition of self-defense, the Court intentionally applied article 3(g) of UNGA Resolution 3314 on the Definition of Aggression,[13] namely the "sending by or on

[10] Ian Brownlie, "International Law and the Activities of Armed Bands" (1958) 7 International and Comparative Law Quarterly 712, 713.

[11] *Military and Paramilitary Activities in and against Nicaragua (Nicaragua v United States of America) (Merits)* [1986] ICJ Rep 14 [113] (*Nicaragua*).

[12] ibid [115]–[116].

[13] United Nations General Assembly (UNGA) Resolution 3314 on the Definition of Aggression (XXIX).

behalf" criterion.[14] Emphatically, the ICJ did not apply the effective control test in *Nicaragua* when it decided on use of force, and more specifically, self-defense issues. The well known effective control test was therefore used in a state responsibility context in 1986.

As opposed to this, many scholars interpreted *Nicaragua* as if the content of the "sending" criteria of article 3(g) of UNGA Resolution 3314 on the Definition of Aggression was equal to the effective control test, by making no distinction between *jus ad bellum* attribution and state responsibility attribution standards.[15] Consequently, authors have criticized the ICJ for mandating a too strict armed attack attribution condition and argued for a substantial broadening of the effective control test.

In a similar vein, by conceptualizing attribution as a single concept applicable invariably across specialized fields of international law, the International Criminal Tribunal for the Former Yugoslavia (ICTY) famously discerned a tendency in *Tadić*[16] broadening the scope of the attribution requirement, which was also followed by several commentators.[17]

The present author suggests that is appears to be a misinterpretation of the Nicaragua judgment to suggest that the effective control test was applied in a *jus ad bellum* context to appraise the legality of self-defense claims. Such a reading of the ICJ's judgment has led to filling the notion of attribution with divergent legal contents, many requiring looser control between imputable acts and the respective state. Post-9/11, even looser tests have emerged in the literature such as planning, authorization, support, or harboring. More recently, the unable or unwilling theory[18] is relied on, where the failure of prevention or the absence of cooperation with the victim state or the international community render the acts of irregular forces to be practically attributable to the territorial state, enabling the exercise of self-defense against them. This theory broadens the attribution requirement

[14] *Nicaragua* (n 11) [194]–[195].

[15] Jan Klabbers, *International Law* (CUP 2016) 195; Giuliana Ziccardi Capaldo, "Providing a Right of Self-Defense Against Large-Scale Attacks by Irregular Forces: The Israeli–Hezbollah Conflict" (2007) Harvard International Law Journal Online 101, 105; Christian J Tams, "The Use of Force against Terrorists" (2009) 20 European Journal of International Law 359–97, 368; Y Arai-Takahashi, "Shifting Boundaries of the Right of Self Defence" (2002) 36 International Lawyer 1081, 1097; Stefan Kirchner, "Third Party Liability for Hezbollah Attacks Against Israel" (2006) 7 German Law Journal 777, 783; Christopher Greenwood, "International Law and the Pre-emptive Use of Force: Afghanistan, Al-Qaida, and Iraq" (2003) 4 San Diego International Law Journal 7, 24.

[16] *Prosecutor v Tadić* ICTY Case No IT-94-1-A (Appeals Chamber) (Judgment of 15 July 1999) [131] (*Tadić (A)*).

[17] See eg Yoram Dinstein, *War, Aggression and Self-Defence* (OUP 2005) 203–04; Theresa Reinhold, "State Weakness, Irregular Warfare, and the Right to Self-Defense Post-9/11" (2011) 105 American Journal of International Law 244, 250; Capaldo, "Providing a Right" (n 15) 105; Sean Murphy, "Terrorism and the Concept of 'Armed Attack' in Article 51 of the UN Charter" (2002) 43 Harvard International Law Journal 41, 50.

[18] Ashley Deeks, "'Unwilling or Unable': Toward a Normative Framework for Extraterritorial Self-Defense" (2012) 52 Virginia Journal of International Law 483.

to such an extent that it virtually rules out any attribution requirement in the traditional sense.

Based on these various understandings of the concept of attribution, we may depict a fictitious scale of attribution standards, which on one end begins with the effective control test, continues with the concept of the overall control test, and leads to factual circumstances set out in the ARSIWA that are satisfied with even looser notions of attribution, like article 11.[19] Approaching the other end of the imaginary spectrum, one may find even looser tests, such as planning, authorization, support, or harboring.[20] On the other extreme, lies the unable or unwilling doctrine, eliminating the traditional attribution requirement between non-state actors and the territorial state.

3.1.1 The original attribution requirement of the right to self-defense

In contrast to the above understandings of attribution that are met by looser forms of control or even in the absence of it, the wording, spirit, and entire logic of the UN Charter appear to suggest that a close control of the state over the actors in question is a strict condition for exercising self-defense against a state. Attribution has been consistently viewed as an immanent criterion of the right of self-defense since 1945. According to the original interpretation of article 51 of the UN Charter, an armed attack has to directly or indirectly emanate from a state.[21] The structural interpretation of article 51, read in conjunction with article 2(4) of the UN Charter[22] and the established case law of the ICJ[23] confirms that some degree of state involvement is required for establishing an armed attack. Besides the wording, spirit, and entire logic of the UN Charter, this attribution requirement is further confirmed by UNGA Resolution 3314 on the Definition of Aggression. The Resolution explicitly provides that "Aggression is the use of armed force by a State against the sovereignty, territorial integrity or political independence of another State."[24] Such

[19] "Conduct which is not attributable to a State under the preceding articles shall nevertheless be considered an act of that State under international law if and to the extent that the State acknowledges and adopts the conduct in question as its own." (ARSIWA art 11)

[20] Benjamin Langille, "It's 'Instant Custom': How the Bush Doctrine Became Law after the Terrorist Attacks of September 11, 2001" (2003) 26 International and Comparative Law Review 145.

[21] Hans Kelsen, *The Law of the United Nations* (Stevens & Sons 1951) 798–800; Josef L Kunz, "Individual and Collective Self-Defense in Article 51 of the Charter of the United Nations" (1947) 41 American Journal of International Law 876; Benjamin B Ferencz, "Defining Aggression: The Last Mile" (1973) 12 Columbia Journal of Transnational Law 431.

[22] The main prohibition bans the use or threat of force between states. The well-established exception to this prohibition can possibly not be broader than the main prohibition rule.

[23] *Nicaragua* (n 11) [195]; *Case Concerning Oil Platforms (Islamic Republic of Iran v United States of America)* (Judgment of 6 November 2003) [2003] ICJ Rep 161 [64]; *Case Concerning Armed Activities on the Territory of the Congo (Democratic Republic of the Congo v Uganda)* (Judgment of 19 December 2005) [2005] ICJ Rep 168 [146]; *Legal Consequences of the Construction of a Wall in the Occupied Palestinian Territory* (Advisory Opinion) [2004] ICJ Rep 136 [139].

[24] See also Olivier Corten, "The 'Unwilling or Unable' Test: Has It Been, and Could It Be, Accepted?" (2016) 29 Leiden Journal of International Law 777, 795.

an immanent attribution requirement regarding article 51 of the UN Charter has been widely supported by eminent scholars as well.[25]

More specifically, notable scholars in the field consider either "sending" and/or "substantial involvement" as a special *jus ad bellum* attribution test, which diverges from the ARSIWA rules governing the imputability of attacks by non-state actors against states. Thus, "substantial involvement" and "sending" may serve as a special *jus ad bellum* attribution test on the level of primary norms,[26] that is, as a *lex specialis* attribution standard.[27] According to Ruys, "[t]he concept of the 'sending by or on behalf of a State' of armed bands is generally considered to convey this idea of imputability/attributability."[28] Gray reaffirms this reading by arguing that "[s]tates do not today challenge the view that actions by irregulars can constitute armed attack; the controversy centres on the degree of state involvement that is necessary to make the action attributable to the state and to justify action in self-defence in particular cases."[29]

Furthermore, the Independent International Fact-Finding Mission on the Conflict in Georgia (IIFFMCG) also supports the reading that the "sending" and "substantial involvement" requirements function as attribution tests.[30] These authorities all suggest that attribution is required in the *jus ad bellum* regime for a lawful exercise of self-defense.

3.1.2 Recent attempts at changing the attribution requirement: the unable or unwilling doctrine

More recently, the fight against the Islamic State (ISIL) provided states and international law scholars alike[31] with an opportunity for challenging and radically expanding the attribution requirement of the right of self-defense. The present author has examined in detail elsewhere the battle of competing interpretations on the scope of article 2(4) of the UN Charter and the requirements of the right to self-defense in scholarly debates and in states' positions.[32] Suffice it to underline

[25] Christine Gray, *International Law and the Use of Force* (OUP 2018) 132; James Crawford, *Brownlie's Principles of Public International Law* (OUP 2012) 747; Olivier Corten, *The Law Against War: The Prohibition on the Use of Force in Contemporary International Law* (Hart 2010) 443–70; Tom Ruys, *"Armed Attack" and Article 51 of the UN Charter: Evolutions in Customary Law and Practice* (CUP 2013); Jörg Kammerhofer, *Uncertainty in International Law: A Kelsenian perspective* (Routledge 2011) 44. See also Separate Opinion of Judge Kooijmans in the *Palestinian Wall* (Advisory Opinion) admitting that the criterion that an armed attack has to emanate from another state "has been the generally accepted interpretation for more than 50 years": see *Palestinian Wall* (Advisory Opinion) (n 23) [35].

[26] Nollkaemper, "Attribution" (n 9) 147, 170.

[27] Corten, *The Law Against War* (n 25) 468. See also ibid 445–46, 450.

[28] Ruys, *"Armed Attack"* (n 25) 408, 414.

[29] Gray, *Use of Force* (n 25) 137.

[30] Independent International Fact-Finding Mission on the Conflict in Georgia (IIFFMCG), *Report on the Conflict*, vol II (2009) 259.

[31] Ashley Deeks, "'Unwilling or Unable': Toward a Normative Framework for Extraterritorial Self-Defense" (2012) 52 Virginia Journal of International Law 483.

[32] For more details, see Gabor Kajtar, "Use of Force Against ISIL in Iraq and Syria: A Legal Battlefield" (2017) 34 Wisconsin International Law Journal 535.

here that some of the intervening states, such as the US,[33] the UK,[34] Australia,[35] and Canada[36] relied on a novel legal basis for claiming self-defense alleging that Syria was unable or unwilling to fight ISIL effectively. What is most relevant for the present analysis is that this unable or unwilling doctrine rules out any attribution requirement under article 51 of the UN Charter. Yet the practice of states is not uniform in this respect as neither Germany,[37] Denmark,[38] Norway,[39] nor Belgium[40] based their justifications for using force against ISIL on the unable and/or unwilling doctrine. Hence, in light of a survey of the actual practice of states, the present author finds it difficult to accept that the unable and/or unwilling test has found its way into customary international law. Although on its face the unable or unwilling test may sound very persuasive, legal scholarship is rightfully very critical about its capacity to provide a new legal basis for using force or to serve as a test that substantially lowers the threshold of attribution and therefore broadens the right to self-defense under article 51 of the UN Charter.[41]

State practice suggests that *jus ad bellum* still mandates attribution for a territorial state in order to legitimately invoke self-defense against non-state actors. Importantly, even if we accept that using force in Syria was lawful based on article 51, it is not necessary to subscribe either to exercising self-defense without any attribution requirement and, thus, directly against non-state actors, nor to the vague unable and/or unwilling doctrine abolishing the attribution requirement. The inability or unwillingness of a state could be interpreted as the content of the "allowing its territory to be used for perpetrating an act of aggression" traditional

[33] UN Doc S/2014/695, 165 (23 September 2014). For a more detailed description of the US position, see Brian Egan (US State Department Legal Advisor), Speech at ASIL (1 April 2016).

[34] Permanent Representative of Great Britain to the UN, Letter dated 7 September 2015 from the Permanent Representative of the United Kingdom of Great Britain and Northern Ireland to the United Nations addressed to the President of the Security Council, UN Doc S/2015/688 (8 September 2015); Permanent Representative of Great Britain to the UN, Letter dated 3 December 2015 from the Permanent Representative of the United Kingdom of Great Britain and Northern Ireland to the United Nations addressed to the President of the Security Council, UN Doc S/2015/928 (3 December 2015).

[35] UN Doc S/2015/693, 106 (9 September 2015).

[36] UN Doc S/2015/221, 106 (31 March 2015).

[37] UN Doc S/2015/946, 179 (10 December 2015).

[38] UN Doc S/2016/34 (13 January 2016).

[39] UN Doc S/2016/513 (3 June 2016).

[40] UN Doc S/2016/523 (9 June 2016).

[41] Kevin Jon Heller, "Do Attacks on ISIS in Syria Justify the 'Unwilling or Unable' Test?" *Opinio Juris* (13 December 2014) <http://opiniojuris.org/2014/12/13/attacks-isis-syria-justify-unwilling-unable-test/> accessed 6 June 2022; Paulina Starski, "Right to Self-Defense, Attribution and the Non-State Actor: Birth of the 'Unable or Unwilling' Standard?" (2015) 75 Zeitschrift für ausländisches öffentliches Recht und Völkerrecht 455; Tom Ruys and Luca Ferro, "Divergent Views on the Content and Relevance of the *Jus Ad Bellum* in Europe and the United States? The Case of the US-Led Military Coalition Against 'Islamic State'" in Chiara Giorgetti and Guglielmo Verdirame (eds), *Concepts on International Law in Europe and the United States* (CUP 2021) 231–264; Monica Hakimi, "Defensive Force against Non-State Actors: The State of Play" (2015) 91 International Law Studies 1; Kinga Tibori-Szabó, "The 'Unwilling or Unable' Test and the Law of Self-Defence" in Christophe Paulussen and others (eds), *Fundamental Rights in International and European Law* (Springer 2016) 73; Corten, "The 'Unwilling or Unable' Test" (n 24) 777.

attribution scenario, enshrined in article 3(f) of UNGA Resolution 3314 on the Definition of Aggression.[42] Under such a reading, being unwilling or unable to prevent attacks from a state's territory results *de facto* in allowing its territory to be used for perpetrating an act of aggression.

By distinguishing between the rules of attribution in *jus ad bellum* and state responsibility contexts, one may acknowledge that some slight modifications may have indeed occurred on account of repeated claims of states. State practice may allow for more flexible attribution standards in terms of exercising the right of self-defense, yet these modifications are only possible within the limits provided by the UN Charter that still requires attributing the armed attack to the territorial state.

3.2 Attribution Rules in International Humanitarian Law

The field of international humanitarian law (IHL) also sees different strict sense attribution rules of the ARSIWA transported to and applied in cases governed by the law of armed conflict. The forthcoming analysis will therefore provide another illustration for the fragmentation of attribution concepts and the judicial confusion of different standards across specialized fields of international law.

3.2.1 Conflict classification versus law of international responsibility

Ever since the *Tadić* judgment of the ICTY the content of the correct attribution test for determining the nature of an armed conflict has been subject to extensive judicial and scholarly debate. Importantly, in an IHL context attribution rules determine the nature of an armed conflict, which in turn determines the applicable law. In *Tadić*, the ICTY had to establish whether there had been an international armed conflict (IAC), giving rise to the grave breaches regime on account of the relationship between the Yugoslav National Army and the Bosnian Serb Army (VRS). The ICTY announced that a non-international armed conflict (NIAC) may become international if another state intervenes in that conflict through its troops, or if some of the participants in the internal armed conflict "act on behalf of that other State."[43]

To decide about the applicable attribution test, the Tribunal famously examined whether the VRS could be regarded as a *de facto* state organ of Yugoslavia, and it did so by applying the ARSIWA attribution standards originally designed to govern state responsibility.[44] In the Tribunal's interpretation, attribution is a

[42] "The sending by or on behalf of a State of armed bands, groups, irregulars or mercenaries, which carry out acts of armed force against another State of such gravity as to amount to the acts listed above, or its substantial involvement therein." See UNGA Res 3314 (n 13) art 3(g).

[43] *Tadić (A)* (n 16) [84].

[44] *Prosecutor v Tadić* ICTY Case No IT-94-1-T (Trial Chamber Opinion and Judgment) (7 May 1997) [585]–[587], [595] (*Tadić (T)*).

homogeneous concept, which can be applied outside the ARSIWA as well, and it crafted the overall control test to fulfill the attribution requirement in the material case. The incorrect nature of such an interpretation, that is, using the ARSIWA attribution tests of state responsibility for conflict classification purposes was expressly denounced by the ICJ in *Bosnian Genocide*, where the Court stressed that state responsibility for acts of non-state actors is to be governed by the effective control test under article 8 of the ARSIWA and not by the overall control test.[45]

Despite the clear and authoritative judicial distinction made between attribution rules of state responsibility and those of IHL in *Bosnian Genocide*, the overall control test has made its way into surprisingly different legal contexts. It has been proposed as the correct attribution test for state responsibility[46] and even that of *jus ad bellum* questions,[47] thereby blurring the dividing line between the various primary and secondary rules of international law, as well as distinct attribution standards.

Some of the more recent applications of the overall control test confirm its continuing relevance in international law. The Trial Chamber of the International Criminal Court (ICC) in *Prosecutor v Thomas Lubanga Dyilo*[48] applied the test for conflict classification purposes,[49] similarly to Trial Chamber II, which did so in the *Katanga and Prosecutor v Jean-Pierre Bemba Gombo* cases in 2014 and in 2016, respectively.[50] The IIFFMCG applied this test for classifying the conflict between Georgia and the armed forces of Abkhazia and South Ossetia.[51] Similarly, the Prosecutor of the ICC relied on the overall control test when examined the nature of the conflict between the Ukrainian forces and the rebels in 2017 and 2018.[52]

The above overview sought to lay ground for the proposition that attribution rules of conflict classification and those of state responsibility ought to be analytically distinguished. Yet, the question still remains what is the correct attribution

[45] *Application of the Convention on the Prevention and Punishment of the Crime of Genocide (Bosnia and Herzegovina v Serbia and Montenegro)* (Judgment of 26 February 2007) [2007] ICJ Rep XXX [406]–[407] (*Bosnian Genocide*).

[46] Helen Duffy, *The "War on Terror" and the Framework of International Law* (CUP 2015) 75–116; Jens David Ohlin, "Control Matters: Ukraine and Russia and the Downing of Flight 17" *Opinio Juris* (23 July 2014) <http://opiniojuris.org/2014/07/23/control-matters-ukraine-russia-downing-flight-17/ > accessed 6 June 2022.

[47] Yoram Dinstein, *The Conduct of Hostilities under the Law of International Armed Conflict* (CUP 2016) 35–36.

[48] *Prosecutor v Thomas Lubanga Dyilo* (Decision on the Confirmation of Charges) ICC-01/04-01/06 (29 January 2007) [210]–[211]. See also *Prosecutor v Thomas Lubanga Dyilo* (Judgment) ICC-01/04-01/06-2842 (14 March 2012) [541].

[49] Thomas R Liefländer, "The *Lubanga* Judgment of the ICC: More than Just the First Step?" (2012) 1 Cambridge Journal of International and Comparative Law 191.

[50] *Prosecutor v Germain Katanga* ICC-01/04-01/07 (7 March 2014) [1177]–[1178]; *Prosecutor v Jean-Pierre Bemba Gombo* (Trial Chamber Judgment) ICC-01/05-01/08 (21 March 2016) [130].

[51] IIFFMCG, *Report* (n 30) 302

[52] Office of the Prosecutor (ICC), *Report on Preliminary Examination Activities* (ICC, 2017) [95]. See also Office of the Prosecutor (ICC), *Report on Preliminary Examination Activities* (ICC, 2018) [73].

test in an IHL context? What is the legal basis and the precise content of the overall control test? Section 3.2.2 will provide answers to these queries.

3.2.2 What is the correct attribution test for conflict classification?

There are a host of divergent theories as to the applicable test for conflict classification in the context of IHL, proposing different origins, scope, and implications for the correct attribution standard. Major propositions are the following:

- Some are of the view that the Appeals Chamber's decision was correct: the overall control test is applicable both for conflict classification purposes and for establishing international responsibility of states.[53]
- Others agree with this conclusion with a caveat emphasizing that the overall control test is not irreconcilable with the effective control test as the former constitutes a *lex specialis* to the latter in the context of humanitarian law compared to the general rule of effective control within the meaning of article 55 of the ARSIWA.[54]
- A third view holds that the language of "acting on behalf of a party" mandates a strict twofold test requiring, on the one hand, that the group accepts the control of that state and shares its goals and policies. On the other hand, it is also necessary that the state in question regards the group as an entity that acts under its control.[55] For finding the requisite link between the entity and the state, it is sufficient to establish a *de facto* consent or even an explicit understanding between the two to that effect.[56]
- Yet another group of scholars proposes that the IHL regime needs an even more autonomous attribution test for conflict classification purposes. Some even call for two separate standards to distinguish the involvement of a state in IACs depending on whether the state's support was the triggering event for the armed conflict, or it only internationalized an already on-going (internal) armed conflict.[57]

[53] Marina Spinedi, "On the Non-Attribution of the Bosnian Serbs' Conduct to Serbia" (2007) 5 Journal of International Criminal Justice 829. For a similar position, see ICRC Commentary of 2016, GC I, art 2, paras 265–273, Commentary on the First Geneva Convention (CUP 2016) <https://assets.cambridge.org/97811071/70100/frontmatter/9781107170100_frontmatter.pdf>.

[54] Remy Jorritsma, "Where General International Law Meets International Humanitarian Law: Attribution of Conduct and the Classification of Armed Conflicts" (2018) 23 Journal of Conflict and Security Law 405. See also Akande, who raises this theoretical possibility however dismisses it in the same vain: Dapo Akande, "Classification of Armed Conflict: Relevant Legal Concepts" in Elizabeth Wilmshurst (ed), *International Law and the Classification of Conflicts* (OUP 2012) 32, 61.

[55] Nordic Experts, "The Requirement of Belonging to a Party to the Conflict" (1970) 40 Nordic Journal of International Law 54.

[56] Katherine Del Mar, "The Requirement of 'Belonging' under International Humanitarian Law" (2010) 21 European Journal of International Law 105.

[57] Djemila Carron, "When Is a Conflict International? Time for New Control Tests in IHL" (2016) 98 International Review of the Red Cross 1019.

- Others suggest that there is no need for a separate IHL attribution standard for determining the nature of an armed conflict, because jus ad bellum tests can be properly applied in this context as well.[58]
- Finally, some claim that the body of IHL is capable of having its own attribution standard,[59] in line with the finding of the ICTY Appeals Chamber, derived from the wording "belonging to" enshrined in article 4 of the Third Geneva Convention.[60]

The present author agrees with the last position, as this not only appears to be correct from a doctrinal point of view but is also justified on pragmatic grounds, and it adequately reflects the fragmented nature of attribution concepts across different fields of international law. On a pragmatic level, differentiating between the attribution tests of state responsibility and those of IHL seems also to be necessary to align with the general understanding of states.[61]

3.2.3 The interplay between attribution concepts in case of an armed conflict

The confusion around applicable attribution tests in case of an armed conflict, as addressed above, is not very surprising considering that various attribution rules may be applicable in the judicial and scholarly evaluation of a given armed conflict for appraising different legal aspects of the same set of facts. The interplay of different rules of attribution will now be illustrated through some typical scenarios.

First, the ARSIWA attribution tests can solely be applied to establish the intervening states' international responsibility. Yet, if the responsibility of an intervening state is based on articles 4, 5, or 8 of the ARSIWA, it is very likely that an IAC would also be established given that these attribution grounds mandate stricter control than the attribution test of IHL. For the same reason, this hypothetical situation would also find an armed attack to have occurred provided that the attack in question met the requisite *jus ad bellum* standard of gravity.

However, a situation may also arise where the responsibility of an intervening state may not be established, yet there would still be an IAC. This is owing to the fact that the attribution test properly used for conflict classification purposes is more lenient than the one used for establishing international responsibility of states. Moreover, there may be other cases where *vice versa* this would be true, that

[58] See Separate Opinion of Judge Shahabuddeen *Prosecutor v Tadic*, Appeal Judgement, IT-94-1-A, 15 July 1999, paras [7]–[14], 150. See also Akande, "Classification of Armed Conflict" (n 54) 61–62.

[59] Marko Milanovic, "The Applicability of the Conventions to Transnational and Mixed Conflicts" in Andrew Clapham and others (eds), *The 1949 Geneva Conventions: A Commentary* (OUP 2015) 27, 37. See also Christopher Greenwood, "International Humanitarian Law and the *Tadić* Case" (1996) 7 European Journal of International Law 265.

[60] *Tadić (A)* (n 16) [95]–[96].

[61] Suffice it to refer to the fact that normally states do not accept responsibility for acts beyond their effective control. Thus attribution based on control for purposes of state responsibility is necessarily much stricter than for purposes of conflict classification where state practice is more lenient in terms of the required level of control.

is the responsibility of an intervening state could be established, yet there would be no IAC. This may typically be the case if the responsibility of a state is established based on article 11 of the ARSIWA.[62]

Moreover, attribution tests of *jus ad bellum* (eg "sending by or on behalf" or "substantial involvement" standards) establish whether there was an armed attack committed by a state. If this test is met, an IAC for purposes of IHL is also established, however, this will not necessarily trigger the intervening state's international responsibility (eg in cases where effective control cannot be established).

Lastly, the overall control test might be fulfilled by the concept of "belonging to" as enshrined in article 4(2) of the Third Geneva Convention. This term entails the most lenient attribution test, meaning that even if it is met in a particular case, there would be no armed attack, and neither could the responsibility of the intervening state be established.[63]

To summarize the above, different attribution tests might be used for different purposes and scenarios. The content and stringency of these attribution standards vary; for this reason, they can only be applied in their own context and their practical impact on each other is rather limited.

3.3 The Fragmentation of Attribution in Investment Law

The notion of attribution is directly relevant in the field of investment arbitration given that the rules as enshrined in Part 1 of the ARSIWA are applicable in the context of disputes between states and non-state subjects of international law.[64] Suffice it to refer to the fact that more than 60% of attribution-related international disputes were brought before investment arbitration panels.[65]

In this specific context too, attribution questions can be classified into two distinct groups. On the one hand, investor-state disputes raise classic attribution issues, which are decided under relevant provisions of the ARSIWA, set forth typically in article 4 (*de jure* and *de facto* state organ),[66] article 5 (exercise

[62] In this scenario the subsequent acknowledgement and adoption of an internationally wrongful act by a state does not transform a NIAC into an IAC.

[63] Clapham proposes a system with four tests. However, this is unlikely to shed more light on this complex issue as these tests contain attribution and intensity elements at the same time: see Andrew Clapham, "The Concept of International Armed Conflict" in Andrew Clapham and others (eds), *The 1949 Geneva Conventions: A Commentary* (OUP 2015) 1, 19.

[64] James Crawford, "Investment Arbitration and the ILC Articles on State Responsibility" (2010) 25 ICSID Review: Foreign Investment Law Journal 127, 132.

[65] ibid 128.

[66] See eg *Compañía de Aguas del Aconquija SA and Vivendi Universal SA v Republic of Argentina (I)* ICSID Case No ARB/97/3 (Award) (21 November 2000) [49] (Buergenthal, Trooboff, Rezek); *Eureko BV v Poland*, Partial Award and Dissenting Opinion, IIC 98 (2005), 19th August 2005, Ad Hoc Tribunal (UNCITRAL); *Kristian Almås and Geir Almås v Republic of Poland* PCA Case No 2015-13 (27 June 2016) [207]–[213] (Mestad, Reinisch, Crawford); *Noble Ventures Inc v Romania* ICSID Case No ARB/01/11 (Award) (12 October 2005) [68]–[80] (Böckstiegel, Lever, Dupuy); *Generation Ukraine Inc v Ukraine* ICSID Case No ARB/00/9 (16 September 2003) [10] (Salpius, Voss, Paulsson); *Jan de Nul*

of governmental authority),[67] and article 8 (instruction, direction or control).[68] Ample case practice illustrates the complex and fragmented nature of attribution even within its strict sense aiming to establish the responsibility of a state for an international wrongful act.

On the other hand, rules of attribution are also used in a broad sense, covering a host of legal concepts having different scope, aim, and purpose than strict sense attribution standards. Such attribution issues, understood in a broad sense are, for example, as follows:

- the preliminary question to establish the jurisdiction of the given investment tribunal;
- questions arising under the umbrella clause of a bilateral investment treaty (BIT);
- issues of representation, that is, who may conclude a treaty on behalf of a state.

Such broader application of attribution has already been noted in the scholarly literature.[69] Yet this doctrinal distinction between attribution in the traditional sense (ie state responsibility) and attribution in a much broader sense has not received a universal acceptance among investment arbitration tribunals, which still tend to apply the ARSIWA rules of attribution for scenarios beyond the scope of state responsibility.

The ensuing sections will illustrate the diversity of wider attribution-based legal questions in the law of investment arbitration. It will be argued that although many tribunals apply the ARSIWA attribution standards in the above contexts as well, such issues have different aims and scope than attribution rules as envisaged by the ILC in the ARSIWA, and hence, ought not to be used interchangeably.

3.3.1 Attribution to establish jurisdiction over an investment dispute

The International Centre for Settlement of Investment Disputes (ICSID) Convention contains a special rule of attribution to decide whether a given

NV and Dredging International NV v Arab Republic of Egypt ICSID Case No ARB/04/13 (Award) (6 November 2008) [158]–[162] (Kaufmann-Kohler, Mayer, Stern).

[67] See eg *EnCana Corp v Republic of Ecuador* LCIA Case No UN3481 (Award) (3 Februrary 2006) [154] (Crawford, Naón, Thomas); *Gustav FW Hamester GmbH & Co KG v Republic of Ghana* ICSID Case No ARB/07/24 (Award) (18 June 2010) [189] (Stern, Cremades, Landau); *Almås* (n 66) [214]–[267]; *Jan de Nul NV* (n 66) [163]–[171].

[68] See eg *Almås* (n 66) [268]–[272]; *Jan de Nul NV* (n 66) [172]–[173]; *Gustav FW Hamester GmbH* (n 67) [256].

[69] For the distinction of attribution tests in situations regarding internationally wrongful acts and acts which, *per se*, do not establish a violation, see Csaba Kovács, *Attribution in International Investment Law* (Wolters Kluwer 2018). See also Jürgen Kurtz, "The Paradoxical Treatment of the ILC Articles on State Responsibility in Investor-State Arbitration" (2010) 25 ICSID Review: Foreign Investment Law Journal 200, 201.

dispute may be brought before an ICSID tribunal. Under article 25 of the ICSID Convention, the jurisdiction of ICSID extends to any legal dispute arising directly out of an investment between a Contracting State (or any constituent subdivision or agency of a Contracting State designated to the ICSID by that state) and a national of another Contracting State. Despite this apparently clear wording, it is far from settled how to identify the agencies the conduct of which are attributable to a state in this specific jurisdictional context. Investment tribunals have recurrently decided this question under the ARSIWA.[70] This is all the more remarkable considering that at the stage of establishing jurisdiction, the international responsibility of the respondent state has not yet even been examined.

The *Maffezini v Spain* case provides an apt illustration of the variety of attribution concepts implicated in such an assessment. The tribunal applied articles 4 and 5 of the ARSIWA to rule on its own jurisdiction. Yet even the adjudicators acknowledged that whether the Spanish state organ was responsible for the acts complained of, whether they were wrongful, whether they were governmental rather than commercial in character, and whether they can be attributed to the Spanish state are distinct questions from the jurisdiction of the tribunal and have to be decided in the merits phase.[71] It follows from acknowledging the different aim and nature of attribution rules applicable to establishing the jurisdiction of a tribunal that it is problematic to use the ARSIWA's attribution tests for such an entirely different legal context.[72]

3.3.2 Umbrella clause: the law of contract versus the law of treaty

Umbrella clauses of bilateral investment treaties (BIT) are special catch-all clauses that bring obligations and commitments of the host state in connection with a foreign investor under the protective "umbrella" of the BIT.[73] Investment panels interpret such clauses in a surprisingly different way as to their nature and effect.[74] Even though there is by now a scholarly consensus that the scope of umbrella clauses may extend to all kinds of legal obligations of the host state undertaken under domestic contracts,[75] arbitration practice does not reflect such a uniform

[70] See eg *Emilio Agustin Maffezini v Kingdom of Spain* ICSID Case No ARB 97/7 (Decision of the Tribunal on Objections to Jurisdiction) (25 January 2000) [71]–[89]; *Salini Costruttori SpA and Italstrade SpA v Morocco* ICSID Case No ARB/00/4 (Decision on Jurisdiction) (23 July 2001) [28]–[35] (Briner, Cremades, Fadallah).

[71] *Maffezini* (n 70) [89].

[72] Simon Olleson, "Attribution in Investment Treaty Arbitration" (2016) 31 ICSID Review 457–83, 467; Rudolf Dolzer and Chrisoph Schreuer, *Principles of International Investment Law* (OUP 2012) 227.

[73] See eg United Kingdom–Argentina BIT (11 December 1990) art 2(2); United States–Argentina BIT (14 November 1991) art II(2)(c); Italy–Jordan BIT (21 July 1996) art 2(2); Greece–Mexico BIT (30 November 2000) art 19(2); Germany–Pakistan BIT (1 December 2009) art 7(2).

[74] Anthony Sinclair, "Bridging the Contract/Treaty Divide" in Christina Binder and others (eds), *International Investment Law for the 21st Century: Essays in Honour of Christoph Schreuer* (OUP 2009) 92–104.

[75] For a detailed analysis of the correct interpretation of umbrella clauses, see Hege Elisabeth Kjos, *Applicable Law in Investor-State Arbitration: The Interplay Between National and International Law* (OUP 2013) 247–53.

understanding.[76]

This results in a fragmented application and interpretation of attribution issues in investment disputes. Certain tribunals are of the view that the existence of an umbrella clause in an international treaty, that is, in the BIT, entails that any breach of the underlying domestic contract shall be evaluated according to the law of international responsibility of states.[77] While others arrive at an opposite conclusion by distinguishing the law of (domestic) contract from the law of (international) treaty.[78] The Panel in *Noble Ventures* rightly recalled the established rule of international law that "in normal circumstances *per se* a breach of a contract by the State does not give rise to direct international responsibility on the part of the State."[79]

Thus, it is far from being established what type of law and what specific attribution test should be applied to the attribution questions of a breach of municipal contracts. Scholars are also divided on this issue. Some hold a view[80] that such situations are governed by the ARSIWA. Others[81] argue that the umbrella clause raises separate issues from state responsibility and therefore distinct legal tests ought to be applied for such an assessment.[82]The present author argues that a clear dividing line has to be drawn between municipal and international law.[83] Such an interpretation is supported by the language of article 3 of the ARSIWA, the case law of the PCIJ,[84] as well as the ICJ.[85]

[76] See CMS Gas v Argentina, Decision on Annulment (Guillaume, Elaraby, Crawford), 2007, para 95; *MTD Equity v Chile* ICSID Case No ARB/01/7 (Award) (25 May 2004) [187] (Sureda, Lalonde, Blanco); *Marion Unlaube v Costa Rica* ICSID Case No ARB/01/8 (Award) (16 May 2012) [190] (Kessler, Berman, Cremades).

[77] See eg the reasoning of the *SGS v Pakistan* tribunal to that effect concerning the interpretation of an umbrella clause in art 11 of the Switzerland–Pakistan BIT. See *SGS Société Générale de Surveillance SA v Islamic Republic of Pakistan* ICSID Case No ARB/01/13 (Decision on Objections to Jurisdiction) (6 August 2003) [166]–[173] (Feliciano, Faurès, Thomas).

[78] *SGS Société Générale de Surveillance SA v Republic of the Philippines* ICSID Case No ARB/02/6 (Decision of the Tribunal on Objections to Jurisdiction) (29 January 2004) [115]–[128] (El-Kosheri, Crawford, Crivellaro). For a detailed critique of the decision, see Stanimir A Alexandrov, "Breaches of Contract and Breaches of Treaty: The Jurisdiction of Treaty-Based Arbitration Tribunals to Decide Breach of Contract Claims in *SGS v Pakistan* and *SGS v Philippines*" (2004) 5 Journal of World Investment and Trade 555–77.

[79] *Noble Ventures* (n 66) 53.

[80] Georgios Petrochilos, "Attribution" in Katia Yannaca-Small (ed), *Arbitration Under International Investment Agreements: A Guide to the Key Issues* (OUP 2010) 287–322, 316; Kaj Hobér, "State Responsibility and Attribution" in Peter T Muchlinski and others (eds), *The Oxford Handbook of Investment Law* (OUP 2008) 549–83, 582.

[81] Michael Feit, "Attribution and the Umbrella Clause: Is There a Way Out of the Deadlock?" (2012) 21 Minnesota Journal of International Law 21–41, 38; Shotaro Hamamoto, "Parties to the 'Obligations' in the Obligations Observance ('Umbrella') Clause" (2015) 30 ICSID Review 449–64, 459.

[82] Hamamoto argues for applying the test of representation: see Hamamoto, "Parties" (n 81) 463. Feit proposes the test of apparent authority: see Feit, "Attribution and the Umbrella Clause" (n 81) 38.

[83] See also Kjos, *Applicable Law in Investor-State Arbitration* (n 75) 171–76.

[84] *Payment of Various Serbian Loans Issued in France (France v Yugoslavia)* 1929 PCIJ Series A no 20 [41] (12 July 1929).

[85] *Elettronica Sicula SpA (ELSI)* (Judgment) [1989] ICJ Rep 15 [73], [124].

According to this understanding, a state may breach a BIT even without violating a municipal contract (eg a concession agreement) and, *vice versa*, a breach of the latter does not necessarily engage the state's international responsibility for infringing the BIT.[86] In other words, these arguably form two separate legal issues and each has to be decided according to its own governing law. On the one hand, a state will be internationally responsible for breaching a BIT if relevant bases of attribution, as set forth in the ARSIWA, are met. On the other hand, the state is not necessarily responsible for breaching a municipal contract provided that the breach was made by a state entity that has, under rules of domestic law, separate legal personality triggering its own responsibility for not performing its contractual obligations.[87]

For all these reasons, a nuanced analysis of attribution issues in investment arbitration reveals that the classic concept of attribution is an entirely separate legal inquiry from the question of responsibility for breaches of domestic law.[88] The ARSIWA attribution tests can only be applied where the inquiry directly concerns a breach of an international obligation, typically that of the BIT or general international law. All other matters are to be governed by the law of the contract, that is, domestic law.

4. Conclusion

The above mapping of the different specialized rule-systems suggests that the divergence of attribution standards across different fields of international law has been an overlooked aspect of judicial practice and scholarly literature. Recognizing the fragmented nature of the notion of attribution entails first and foremost that different tests operate across different rule-systems of international law, which cannot be used outside their original legal context. In other words, attribution is not a single concept, which is readily transferrable into other sub-systems, as for instance the ICTY has contended in *Tadić*. Quite the contrary, different attribution tests are tied to their specific purpose, and hence they can only be applied appropriately in that specific subsystem of international law.

[86] See eg *Compañiá de Aguas del Aconquija SA and Vivendi Universal SA v Argentina* ICSID Case No ARB/97/3 (Decision on Annulment) (3 July 2002) [95] (Fortier, Crawford, Rozas).

[87] See ibid [96]; CMS Gas Transmission Co v Argentina ICSID Case No ARB/01/8 (Decision on Annulment) (25 September 2007) [95] (Guillaume, Elaraby, Crawford).

[88] James Crawford, "Treaty and Contract in Investment Arbitration" (2008) 24 Arbitration International 351; James Crawford and Paul Mertenskötter, "The Use of the ILC's Attribution Rules in Investment Arbitration" in Meg Kinnear and others (eds), *Building International Investment Law: The First 50 Years of ICSID* (Kluwer 2015) 27–42. See also the detailed analysis in *Bayindir Insaat Turizm Ticaret Ve Sanayi AS v Pakistan* ICSID Case No ARB/03/29 (Award) (27 August 2009) [111]–[139] (Gabrielle Kaufmann-Kohler, Berman, Böckstiegel).

It flows from the above that the notion of attribution is relevant in various legal regimes, besides its original, classical state responsibility context. This calls for distinguishing attribution in the narrow sense, serving to establish the responsibility of states, from attribution understood in the broad sense, where this notion serves other legal purposes.

The above analysis showed that attribution in the narrow sense specifies the person/entity whose conduct may engage the responsibility of the state or international organization (or any other subject of international law) for a breach of an international obligation. Importantly, these attribution tests come into play only with regard to internationally wrongful acts. In every instance, when attribution concepts relate to other acts of states, attribution is used in the broad sense, and it may serve various purposes from conflict classification in IHL, through the power to validly represent a state while signing a contract to marking the boundaries of exercising self-defense in the *jus ad bellum* regime. These attribution standards operate in their own specific fields of international law and replacing them with the ARSIWA attribution tests would result in an erroneous application of the law.

Admittedly, these attribution rules do not coexist side by side in "splendid isolation" of each other. They may be closely related to, and sometime even overlapping with, attribution standards of neighboring fields. Bearing in mind the fragmented nature of attribution standards, this chapter argued for a more nuanced legal appreciation of complex factual matters. This analysis has demonstrated several of the possible interrelations between attribution standards belonging to neighboring legal regimes, some of which are worth being reiterated here to illustrate the practical implications of making a thorough analytic distinction between attribution rules.

There may be situations when an armed attack has occurred that satisfies the attribution test of *jus ad bellum*, and at the same time the responsibility of the state for using illegal force is also engaged under attribution standards of the ARSIWA. Yet, *jus ad bellum* and state responsibility attribution do not necessarily go hand in hand in every scenario. For instance, the existence of state responsibility under article 11 of the ARSIWA on account of a subsequent adoption of conduct does not necessarily mean that an armed attack has occurred in the material case due to the difference between applicable attribution standards.[89] Moreover, satisfying the attribution requirement of an armed attack also does not automatically offer a ground for attribution in a state responsibility context as the ARSIWA tests are usually stricter than *jus ad bellum* attribution standards.

[89] The subsequent adoption of a conduct according to art 11 of the ARSIWA cannot render an attack retroactively attributable to the same state in a jus of force sense. The (armed) attack has to be attributable to the attacking state at the time of the attack, otherwise all other criteria of a lawful self-defense (imminence, proportionality, and necessity) are being hollowed out.

The same logic applies to the field of investment arbitration. Merely accepting state responsibility for an unlawful act against an investor does not entail that the same state was a party to the concession contract, too. Moreover, the ARSIWA attribution tests cannot be relied on to determine whether a state was a party to a concession contract as this is to be judged under municipal law.

As is clear from the forgoing analysis, the web of attribution concepts creates a matrix of primary and secondary norms, the complexity of which may explain the inclination of adjudicators to substitute the widely known ARSIWA attribution standards for the attribution test of other legal subsystems. Yet such a confusion of attribution standards, as has been argued in this chapter, is ought to be avoided in order to safeguard against an erroneous interpretation of secondary norms of international law.

Index of Authorities

Books

Agamben G, *Karman: breve trattato sull'azione, la colpa e il gesto* (Bollati Boringhieri 2017)

Altwicker T, *Menschenrechtlicher Gleichheitsschutz. Zugl.: Mannheim, Univ. Diss* (Springer 2010)

Arai-Takahashi Y, *The Margin of Appreciation Doctrine and the Principle of Proportionality in the Jurisprudence of the ECHR* (Intersentia 2002)

Aust HP, *Complicity and the Law of State Responsibility* (CUP 2011) <http://ebooks.cambridge.org/ref/id/CBO9780511862632> accessed 23 May 2019

Baade B, *Der Europäische Gerichtshof für Menschenrechte als Diskurswächter: Zur Methodik, Legitimität und Rolle des Gerichtshofs im demokratisch-rechtsstaatlichen Entscheidungsprozess (Beiträge zum ausländischen öffentlichen Recht und Völkerrecht* (Springer 2017)

Barry B, *Culture and Equality: An Egalitarian Critique of Multiculturalism* (HUP 2002)

Becroft R, *The Standard of Review in WTO Dispute Settlement* (Elgar 2012)

Benvenisti E, *Sharing Transboundary Resources: International Law and Optimal Resource Use* (CUP 2002)

Benvenisti E and Downs GW, *Between Fragmentation and Democracy: The Role of National and International Courts* (CUP 2017) <http://ebooks.cambridge.org/ref/id/CBO9781108236607> accessed 23 May 2019

Besson S, *La due diligence en droit international*(2020) 409 Recueil des cours de l'Académie du droit international de La Haye 153–398

Birkmeyer K, *Über Ursachenbegriff und Kausalzusammenhang im Strafrecht* (Wentworth Press 1885)

Blanco SM, *Full Protection and Security in International Investment Law* (Springer 2018)

Bogdandy A and Venzke I, *In Whose Name?: A Public Law Theory of International Adjudication (International Courts and Tribunals Series* (OUP 2016)

Boothby W, *The Law of Targeting*, vol 122 (OUP 2012)

Brownlie I, *State Responsibility, Part I* (OUP 1983)

——— *Principles of Public International Law* (7th edn, OUP 2008)

Cairney P, Studlar D, and Mamudu HM, *Global Tobacco Control: Power, Policy, Governance and Transfer* (Palgrave McMillan 2012)

Canadian Cancer Society, Cigarette Package Health Warnings: International Status Report (7th edn, September 2021)

Carper D, McKinsey J, and West B, *Understanding the Law* (5th edn, Thomson 2008)

Collected Edition of the "Travaux Préparatoires" of the European Convention on Human Rights, vol I (Martinus Nijhoff 1975)

——— vol IV (Martinus Nijhoff 1977)

——— vol IV (Martinus Nijhoff 1979)

——— vol V (Martinus Nijhoff 1979)

Corten O, *The Law Against War: The Prohibition on the Use of Force in Contemporary International Law* (Hart Publishing 2010)

Crawford J, *The International Law Commission's Articles on State Responsibility: Introduction, Text and Commentary* (OUP 2002)
——— *Brownlie's Principles of Public International Law* (8th edn, OUP 2012)
——— *State Responsibility: The General Part* (CUP 2013)
Cryer R, *An Introduction to International Criminal Law and Procedure* (CUP 2007)
Daly P, *A Theory of Deference in Administrative Law: Basis, Application and Scope* (CUP 2012)
DeNicola DR, *Understanding Ignorance: The Surprising Impact of What We Don't Know* (MIT Press 2017)
Dinstein Y, *War, Aggression and Self-Defence* (4th edn, CUP 2005)
———, *The Conduct of Hostilities under the Law of International Armed Conflict* (3rd edn, CUP 2016)
Dolzer R and Schreuer C, *Principles of International Investment Law* (2nd edn, OUP 2012)
Duffy H, *The "War on Terror" and the Framework of International Law* (CUP 2015)
Dumberry P, *The Formation and Identification of Rules of Customary International Law in International Investment Law* (CUP 2016)
Dupuy P-M and Vinuales JE, *International Environmental Law* (CUP 2018)
Ely JH, *Democracy and Distrust* (HUP 1981)
Fahner JH, *Judicial Deference in International Adjudication: A Comparative Analysis* (Hart 2020)
Foster CE, *Science and the Precautionary Principle in International Courts and Tribunals* (CUP 2011)
Fox H and Webb P, *The Law of State Immunity* (3rd edn, OUP 2013)
Friedmann W, *The Changing Structure of International Law* (Stevens & Sons 1964)
Gerards J, *General Principles of the European Convention on Human Rights* (CUP 2019)
Gerards J and Brems E (eds), *Procedural Review in European Fundamental Cases* (CUP 2017)
Gomez KF, Gourgourinis A, and Titi C (eds), *International Investment Law and the Law of Armed Conflict* (Springer 2019)
Gray C, *International Law and the Use of Force* (4th edn, CUP 2018)
Gruszczynski L and Werner W (eds), *Deference in International Courts and Tribunals: Standard of Review and Margin of Appreciation* (OUP 2014)
Hart HLA, *The Concept of Law* (2nd edn, OUP 1994)
——— *The Concept of Law* (3rd edn, OUP 2012)
Hart HLA and Honoré T, *Causation in the Law* (2nd edn, OUP 1985)
Henckaerts J-M and Doswald-Beck L, *Customary International Humanitarian Law* (CUP 2005)
Henckels C, *Proportionality and Deference in Investor-State Arbitration: Balancing Investment Protection and Regulatory Autonomy* (CUP 2015)
Honoré T, *Responsibility and Fault* (Hart 1999)
Hume D, *An Enquiry Concerning Human Understanding* (LA Selby-Bigge ed, 1st edn, OUP 1975)
International Criminal Court, *Elements of Crimes* (International Criminal Court 2011) <https://www.refworld.org/docid/4ff5dd7d2.html> (accessed 22 July 2022)
International Institute of Humanitarian Law, *Manual on the Law of Non-International Armed Conflict* (IIHL, 2006)
Jackson M, *Complicity in International Law* (OUP 2015)
Jarman H, *The Politics of Trade and Tobacco Control* (Palgrave Macmillan 2015)
Jarrett M, *Contributory Fault and Investor Misconduct in Investment Arbitration* (CUPP 2019)
Kammerhofer J, *Uncertainty in International Law: A Kelsenian Perspective* (Routledge 2011)
Kelsen H, *The Law of the United Nations* (Stevens & Sons 1951)

Kiss A, *Abus de droit en droit international* (Librairie générale de droit et de jurisprudence 1952)
Kjos HE, *Applicable Law in Investor-State Arbitration: The Interplay Between National and International Law* (OUP 2013)
Klabbers J, *International Law* (CUP 2016)
Kokoff J, *The Burden of Proof in Comparative and International Human Rights Law* (Kluwer 1998)
Korenica F, *The EU Accession to the ECHR: Between Luxembourg's Search for Autonomy and Strasbourg's Credibility on Human Rights Protection* (Springer 2015)
Kovács C, *Attribution in International Investment Law* (Wolters Kluwer 2018)
Kulesza J, *Due Diligence in International Law* (Brill 2016)
Lanovoy V, *Complicity and Its Limits in the Law of International Responsibility* (Hart 2016)
Latour B, *We Have Never Been Modern* (Harvester Wheatsheaf 1993)
Lauterpacht H, *The Function of Law in the International Community* (2nd edn, OUP 2011)
Legg A, *The Margin of Appreciation in International Human Rights Law: Deference and Proportionality* (OUP 2012)
Lehnardt C, *Private Militärfirmen und völkerrechtliche Verantwortlichkeit* (Mohr Siebeck 2011)
Lepard BD, *Customary International Law: A New Theory with Practical Applications* (CUP 2010)
Letsas G, *A Theory of Interpretation of the European Convention on Human Rights* (OUP 2007)
Lim CL, *International Investment Law and Arbitration* (CUP 2018)
Lo C-F, Nakagawa J, and Chen T-F, *The Appellate Body of the WTO and Its Reform* (Springer 2020)
Mackie JL, *The Cement of the Universe* (OUP 1974)
Mayorga O, *Arbitrating War: Military Necessity as a Defence to the Breach of Investment Treaty Obligations* (Policy Brief 2013)
Mbengue MM, *Essai sur une theorie du risque en droit international public: l'anticipation du risque environnemental et sanitaire* (Pedone 2009)
Mendelson MH, *The Formation of Customary International Law* (1998)
Milanovic M, *Extraterritorial Application of Human Rights Treaties: Law, Principles, and Policy* (OUP 2011)
Mill JS, *A System of Logic Ratiocinative and Inductive* (JM Robinson ed, Routledge 1973)
Mitchell A, Sheargold E, and Voon T (eds), *Regulatory Autonomy in International Economic Law: The Evolution of Australian Policy on Trade and Investment* (Edward Elgar 2017)
Montt S, *State Liability in Investment Treaty Arbitration: Global Constitutional Law and Administrative Law in the BIT Generation* (Hart 2009)
Moon G and Toohey L (eds), *The Future of International Economic Integration. The Embedded Liberalism Compromise Revisited* (CUP 2018)
Moore M, *Causation and Responsibility: An Essay in Law, Morals, and Metaphysics* (OUP 2009)
Newcombe A and Paradell L, *Law and Practice of Investment Treaties* (Kluwer 2009)
Nollkaemper A and Plakokefalos I, *Principles of Shared Responsibility in International Law: An Appraisal of the State of the Art* (CUP 2014)
Oesch M, *Standards of Review in WTO Dispute Resolution* (OUP 2003)
Ollino A, *Due Diligence Obligations in International Law: A Theoretical Study* (CUP 2021)
Olson M, *The Logic of Collective Action* (HUP 1965)

Oppenheim L (ed), *The Collected Papers of John Westlake on Public International Law* (CUP 2014)
Paparinskis M, *The International Minimum Standard and Fair and Equitable Treatment* (OUP 2013)
Pasqualucci JM, *The Practice and Procedure of the Inter-American Court of Human Rights* (2nd edn, CUP 2013)
Peel J, *Science and Risk Regulation in International Law* (CUP 2010)
Pirker B, *Democracy and Distrust in International Law: The Procedural Democracy Doctrine and the Standard of Review Used by International Courts and Tribunals* (OUP 2014)
Pisillo-Mazzeschi R, *Due diligence e responsabilitá internazionale degli Stati* (Giuffré 1989)
Pollack F, *The Law of Torts* (6th edn, Stevens & Sons 1901)
Radi Y, *Rules and Practices of International Investment Law and Arbitration* (CUP 2020)
Rescher N, *Presumption and the Practices of Tentative Cognition* (CUP 2006)
Rotsch T, *"Einheitstäterschaft" statt Tatherrschaft: Zur Abkehr von einem differenzierenden Beteiligungsformensystem in einer normativ-funktionalen Straftatlehre* (Mohr Slebeck 2009)
Ruys T, *"Armed Attack" and Article 51 of the UN Charter: Evolutions in Customary Law and Practice* (CUP 2013)
Sahabi B, *Compensation and Restitution in Investor-State Arbitration: Principles and Practice* (OUP 2011)
Salmond J, *The Law of Torts* (6th edn, Sweet & Maxwell 1924)
Scelle G, « Règles générales du droit de la paix », RCADI, vol 46, 1933-IV, 327–703
Schauer F, *Playing by the Rules: A Philosophical Examination of Rule-Based Decision-Making in Law and in Life* (OUP 1993)
Michael N Schmitt (ed), *Tallinn Manual on the International Law Applicable to Cyber Warfare* (CUP 2013)
Schwarzenberger G and Brown E, *A Manual of International Law* (6th edn, Milton 1976)
Shany Y, *Assessing the Effectiveness of International Courts* (OUP 2014)
Shirlow E, *Judging at the Interface: Deference to State Decision-Making Authority in International Adjudication* (CUP 2021)
Slouka ZJ, *International Custom and the Continental Shelf: A Study in the Dynamics of Customary Rules of International Law* (Martinus Nijhoff 1968)
Sornarajah M, *The International Law on Foreign Investment* (4th edn, CUP 2017)
Sourgens FG, Duggal K, and Laird IA, *Evidence in International Investment Arbitration* (OUP 2018)
Stern B, *Le préjudice dans la théorie de la responsabilité internationale* (Pedone 1973)
Sulyok K, *Science and Judicial Reasoning: The Legitimacy of International Environmental Adjudication* (CUP 2021)
Vadi V, *Proportionality, Reasonableness and Standards of Review in International Investment Law and Arbitration* (Edward Elgar 2018)
Vandevelde K, *Bilateral Investment Treaties: History, Policy, and Interpretation* (OUP 2010)
Walton D, *Burden of Proof, Presumption and Argumentation* (CUP 2014)
Wiessman R, *International Trade Agreements and Tobacco Control: Threats to Public Health and the Case for Excluding Tobacco from Trade Agreements* (Essential Action 2003)
Wolfke K, *Custom in Present International Law* (2nd edn, Martinus Nijhoff 1993)
Yang X, *State Immunity in International Law* (CUP 2012)
Zrilič J, *The Protection of Foreign Investment in Times of Armed Conflict* (OUP 2019)

Chapters in Edited Books

Abbott FM, "The Evolution of Public Health Provisions in Preferential Trade and Investment Agreements of the United States" in Pedro Roffe and Xavier Seuba (eds), *Current Alliances in International Intellectual Property Lawmaking: The Emergence and Impact of Mega-Regionals, Global Perspectives for the IP System* (CEIPI-ICTSD 2017)

Akande D, "Classification of Armed Conflict: Relevant Legal Concepts" in Elizabeth Wilmshurst (ed), *International Law and the Classification of Conflicts* (OUP 2012)

Alemanno A, "EU Risk Regulation and Science: The Role of Experts in Decision-Making and Judicial Review" in Ellen Vos (ed), *European Risk Governance Its Science, its Inclusiveness and Its Effectiveness* (University of Mannheim 2008)

Alexandrov S and Robbins J, "Proximate Causation in International Investment Disputes" in K Sauvant (ed), *Yearbook on International Investment Law and Policy 2008–2009* (OUP 2009)

Alvarez JE, "The Public International Law Regime Governing International Investment" *Collected Courses of the Hague Academy of International Law*, vol 344 (Brill Nijhoff 2011)

Ambrus M, "The European Court of Human Rights as Governor of Risk" in Mónika Ambrus, Rosemary Rayfuse, and Wouter Werner (eds), *Risk and the Regulation of Uncertainty in International Law* (OUP 2017)

Ambrus M, Rayfuse R, and Werner W, "Risk and International Law" in Mónika Ambrus, Rosemary Rayfuse, and Wouter Werner (eds), *Risk and the Regulation of Uncertainty in International Law* (OUP 2017)

Bentes P, "In Search of a 'Genuine and Substantial' Cause: The Analysis of Causation in Serious Prejudice Claims" in Marion Jansen, Joost Pauwelyn, and Theresa Carpenter (eds), *The Use of Economics in International Trade and Investment Disputes* (CUP 2017)

Benvenisti E, "Customary International Law as a Judicial Tool for Promoting Efficiency" in Eyal Benvenisti and Moshe Hirsch (eds), *The Impact of International Law on International Cooperation* (CUP 2004)

——— "Community Interests in International Adjudication" in Eyal Benvenisti and Georg Nolte (eds), *Community Interests Across International Law* (OUP 2018)

Besson S, "Sovereignty", *Max Planck Encyclopaedia of Public International Law* (OUP 2011)

Bohanes J and Lockhart N, "Standard of Review in WTO Law" in Daniel Bethlehem and others (eds), *The Oxford Handbook of International Trade Law* (OUP 2009)

Brown C, "Inherent Powers in International Adjudication" in Cesare PR Romano, Karen J Alter, and Yuval Shany (eds), *The Oxford Handbook of International Adjudication* (OUP 2014)

Burke-White WW and Staden A, "The Need for Public Law Standards of Review in Investor-State Arbitrations" in SW Schill (ed), *International Investment Law and Comparative Public Law* (OUP 2010)

Busuioc EM, "Blurred Areas of Responsibility: European Agencies' Scientific 'Opinions' under Scrutiny" in Monika Ambrus and others (eds), *The Role of "Experts" in International and European Decision-Making Processes* (CUP 2014)

Caflisch L, "Règles générales du droit des cours d'eau internationaux" (1989) 219 Recueil Des Cours 9–226

Çalı B and Hatas K, "History as an Afterthought: The (Re)Discovery of Article 18 in the Case Law of the European Court of Human Rights" in Helmut Aust and Esra Demir-Gürsel (eds), *The European Court of Human Rights: Current Challenges in Historical Perspective* (Edward Elgar 2021)

Cannizzaro E, "Margin of Appreciation and Reasonableness in the ICJ's Decision in the Whaling Case" in Pierre d'Argent, Beatrice Bonafé, and Jean Combacau (eds), *The Limits of International Law: Essays in Honour of Joe Verhoeven* (Bruylant 2015)

Clapham A, "*The Concept of International Armed Conflict*" in Andrew Clapham, Paola Gaeta, Marco Sassòli (eds), The 1949 Geneva Conventions: A Commentary (OUP 2015)

Cohen HG, "Legitimacy and International Courts: A Framework" in Harlan Grant Cohen (ed), *Legitimacy and International Courts* (CUP 2018)

Condorelli L and Kress C, "The Rules of Attribution: General Considerations" in James Crawford and others (eds), *The Law of International Responsibility* (OUP 2010)

Cot J-P, "The Law of the Sea and the Margin of Appreciation" in Tafsir Malick Ndiaye and Rüdiger Wolfrum (eds), *Law of the Sea, Environmental Law and Settlement of Disputes: Liber Amicorum Judge Thomas A Mensah* (Martinus Nijhoff 2007)

Crawford J and Keene A, "The Structure of State Responsibility under the European Convention on Human Rights" in Anne van Aaken and Iulia Motoc (eds), *The European Convention on Human Rights and General International* (OUP 2018)

Crawford J and Mertenskötter P, "The Use of the ILC's Attribution Rules in Investment Arbitration" in Meg Kinnear (ed), *Building International Investment Law: The First 50 Years of ICSID* (Kluwer 2015)

Dąbrowska-Kłosińska P, "Risk, Precaution and Scientific Complexity before the Court of Justice of the European Union" in Lukasz Gruszczynski and Wouter Werner (eds), *Deference in International Courts and Tribunals: Standard of Review and Margin of Appreciation* (OUP 2014)

David E, "Primary and Secondary Rules" in James Crawford (ed), *The Law of International Responsibility* (OUP 2010)

Davis M, "Identity, Power, and Rights: The State, International Institutions, and Indigenous Peoples in Canada" in Suzana Sawyer and Edmund T Gomez (eds), *The Politics of Resource Extraction* (Palgrave Macmillan 2012)

Durling JP and McCullough MP, "Teaching Old Laws New Tricks: The Legal Obligation of Non-Attribution and the Need for Economic Rigour in Injury Analyses Under US Trade Law" in EK Choi and J Hartigan (eds), *Handbook of International Trade*, vol II (OUP 2005)

Elliott M, "Proportionality and Deference: The Importance of a Structured Approach" in Christopher Forsyth and others (eds), *Effective Judicial Review: A Cornerstone of Good Governance* (OUP 2010) 272–77

Fahner J, "The Margin of Appreciation in Investor-State Arbitration: The Prevalence and Desirability of Discretion and Deference" in Nikos Lavranos and Ruth Kok (eds), *Hague Yearbook of International Law 2013* (Brill Nijhoff 2014)

Flett J, "The Client's Perspective" in Marion Jansen, Joost Pauwelyn, and Theresa Carpenter (eds), *The Use of Economics in International Trade and Investment Disputes* (CUP 2017)

Foakes J and O'Keefe R, "Article 11" in Christian J Tams and Roger O'Keefe (eds), *The United Nations Convention on Jurisdictional Immunities of States and Their Property: A Commentary* (OUP 2013)

Foster CE, "Methodologies and Motivations: Was Japan's Whaling Programme for Purposes of Scientific Research?" in Malgosia Fitzmaurice and Dai Tamada (eds), *Whaling in the Antarctic: The Significance and the Implications of the ICJ Judgment* (Brill Nijhoff 2016)

Gattini A, "Breach of International Obligations" in André Nollkaemper and Ilias Plakokefalos (eds), *Principles of Shared Responsibility in International Law* (CUP 2014)

Giuliani A, "Civilian Treatises on Presumptions, 1580–1620" in Richard H Helmholz and WDH Sellar (eds), *The Law of Presumptions: Essays in Comparative Legal History No 27* (Duncker & Humboldt 2009)

Grant TD, "Article 2(1)(a) and (b)" in Roger O'Keefe, Christian J Tams, and Antonios Tzanakopoulos (eds), *The United Nations Convention on Jurisdictional Immunities of States and Their Property: A Commentary* (OUP 2013)

Gruszczynski L, "Standard of Review of Health and Environmental Regulations by WTO Panels" in Geert Van Calster and Denise Prévost (eds), *Research Handbook on Environment, Health and the WTO* (Edward Elgar 2014)

—— "The Role of IEL Dispute Settlement Bodies in Reinforcing the Sovereign Rights of the States in the Field of Tobacco Control" in Marie EC Gispen and Brigit Toebes (eds), *Human Rights and Tobacco Control* (Edward Elgar 2020)

Gruszczynski L and Werner WG, "Introduction" in Lukasz Gruszczynski and Wouter G Werner (eds), *Deference in International Courts and Tribunals: Standard of Review and Margin of Appreciation* (OUP 2014)

Haas PM, "Ideas, Experts and Governance" in Monika Ambrus and others (eds), *The Role of "Experts" in International and European Decision-Making Processes* (CUP 2014)

Halberstam D, "Constitutional Heterarchy: The Centrality of Conflict in the European Union and the United States" in Jeffery L Dunoff and Joel P Trachtman (eds), *Ruling the World?: Constitutionalism, International Law, and Global Governance* (CUP 2009)

Hamamoto S, "From the Requirement of Reasonableness to a 'Comply and Explain' Rule: The Standard of Review in the Whaling Judgment" in Malgosia Fitzmaurice and Dai Tamada (eds), *Whaling in the Antarctic Significance and Implications of the ICJ Judgment*, vol 23 (Brill Nijhoff 2016)

Henckels C, "The Role of the Standard of Review and the Importance of Deference in Investor-State Arbitration" in Lukasz Gruszczynski and Wouter G Werner (eds), *Deference in International Courts and Tribunals: Standard of Review and Margin of Appreciation* (OUP 2014)

Hobér K, "State Responsibility and Attribution" in Peter T Muchlinski (ed), *The Oxford Handbook of Investment Law* (OUP 2008)

Ioannidis M, "Beyond the Standard of Review: Deference Criteria in WTO Law and the Case for a Procedural Approach" in Lukasz Gruszczynski and Wouter Werner (eds), *Deference in International Courts and Tribunals: Standard of Review and Margin of Appreciation* (OUP 2014)

Jasanoff S, "*Ordering Knowledge, Ordering Society*", *States of Knowledge - The Co-Production of Science and Social Order* (Routledge 2004)

Kapla S, "Injury and Causation in USITC Antidumping Determinations: Five Recent Approaches" in PKM Tharakan (ed), *Policy Implications of Antidumping Measures* (Elsevier Science 1991)

Kees A, "Responsibility of States for Private Actors" in Rüdiger Wolfrum (ed), *Max Planck Encyclopedia of Public International Law* (OUP 2011)

Kiss A, "Abuse of Rights", *The Max Planck Encyclopedia of Public International Law* (2019)

Kohr M, "Rethinking Liberalization and Reforming the WTO", *Jane Kelsey (Ed.), International Economic Regulation* (Routledge 2017)

Leibniz GW, "Elementa Juris Naturalis, Variants, A VI, 2, No 12 (Quote Taken from Andreas Blank, 'Presumptions and Cognitive Simplicity in Leibniz and Early Modern Legal Theory' in Tilmann Altwicker, Francis Cheneval, and Matthias Mahlmann (eds), *Rechts- und Staatsphilosophie bei G. W. Leibniz* (Mohr Siebeck 2020)

Martin, EA and Law J (eds) Oxford Dictionary of Law (OUP 2006)

Milanovic M, "The Applicability of the Conventions to Transnational and Mixed Conflicts" in Andrew Clapham, Paola Gaeta, and Marco Sassòli (eds), *The 1949 Geneva Conventions: A Commentary* (OUP 2015)

——— "Jurisdiction and Responsibility: Trends in the Jurisprudence of the Strasbourg Court" in Anne van Aaken and Iulia Motoc (eds), *The European Convention on Human Rights and General International Law* (OUP 2018)

Moss GC, "Full Protection and Security" in A Reinisch (ed), *Standards of Investment Protection* (OUP 2008)

Nollkaemper A, "Attribution of Forcible Acts to States: Connections Between the Law on the Use of Force and the Law of State Responsibility" in Niels M Blokker and Nico Schrijver (eds), *The Security Council and the Use of Force: Theory and Reality—A Need for Change?* (Martinus Nijhoff 2005)

Orford A, "Trade, Human Rights and the Economy of Sacrifice" in Anne Orford (ed), *International Law and Its Others* (CUP 2006)

Owen DG, "Philosophical Foundations of Fault in Tort Law" in David G Owen (ed), *The Philosophical Foundations of Tort Law* (OUP 1997)

Paine J, "Standard of Review (Investment Arbitration" in Hélène Ruiz Fabri (ed), *Max Planck Encyclopedia of International Procedural Law* (OUP 2019)

Palchetti P, "De Facto Organs of a State" in Rüdiger Wolfrum (ed), *Max Planck Encyclopedias of International Law* (2017)

Pearsall PW and Heath JB, "Causation and Injury in Investor-State Arbitration" in Christina L Beharry (ed), *Contemporary and Emerging Issues on the Law of Damages and Valuation in International Investment Arbitration* (Brill Nijhoff 2018)

Perez-Leon-Acevedo J-P, "International Human Rights Law in the Reparation Practice of the Extraordinary Chambers in the Courts of Cambodia" in Giuliana Z Capaldo (ed), *The Global Community Yearbook of International Law and Jurisprudence 2017* (OUP 2018)

Petrochilos G, "Attribution: State Organs and Entities Exercising Elements of Governmental Authority" in K Yannaca-Small (ed), *Arbitration Under International Investment Agreements* (2nd edn, OUP 2018)

Puig S, "The Role of Procedure in the Development of Investment Law: The Case of Section B of Chapter 11 of NAFTA" in Chester Brown and Kate Miles (eds), *Evolution in Investment Treaty Law and Arbitration* (CUP 2011)

Quadri R, "Cours général de droit international public", *Recueil de Cours de l'Académie de Droit International*, vol 113 (1964)

Ragni C, "Standard of Review and the Margin of Appreciation before the International Court of Justice" in Lukasz Gruszczynski and Wouter G Werner (eds), *Deference in International Courts and Tribunals: Standard of Review and Margin of Appreciation* (OUP 2014)

Rayfuse R, "Standard of Review in the International Tribunal for the Law of the Sea" in Lukasz Gruszczynski and Wouter G Werner (eds), *Deference in International Courts and Tribunals* (OUP 2014)

Rimmer M, "Plain Packaging for the Pacific Rim: Tobacco Control and the Trans-Pacific Partnership" in Tania Voon (ed), *Trade Liberalisation and International Co-operation: A Legal Analysis of the Trans-Pacific Partnership Agreement* (Edward Elgar 2013)

Ruys T and Ferro L, "Divergent Views on the Content and Relevance of the Jus Ad Bellum in Europe and the United States? The Case of the US-Led Military Coalition Against 'Islamic State'" in Chiara Giorgetti and Guglielmo Verdirame (eds), *Concepts on International Law in Europe and the United States* (CUP 2021)

Sajó A, "Abuse of Fundamental Rights or the Difficulties of Purposiveness" in András Sajó (ed), *Abuse: The Dark Side of Fundamental Rights* (Eleven International 2006)

Sena PD, “La «due diligence» et le lien entre le sujet et le risqué qu’il faut prévenir: quelques observations” in Sarah Cassella (ed), *Le standard de due diligence et la responsabilité internationale* (Pedone 2018)
Sinclair A, “Bridging the Contract/Treaty Divide” in Christina Binder (ed), *International Investment Law for the 21st Century: Essays in Honour of Christoph Schreuer* (OUP 2009)
Stapleton J, “Causation in the Law” in Helen Beebee, Christopher Hitchcock, and Peter Menzies (eds), *The Oxford Handbook of Causation* (OUP 2009)
Stern B, “The Elements of An Internationally Wrongful Act” in James Crawford, Alain Pellet, and Simon Olleson (eds), *The Law of International Responsibility* (CUP 2010)
——— “The Obligation of Reparation” in James Crawford, Alain Pellet, and Simon Olleson (eds), *The Law of International Responsibility* (OUP 2010)
Stoll P-T, “State Immunity” in Rüdiger Wolfrum (ed), *Max Planck Encyclopedia of Public International Law* (OUP 2011)
Tallent K, “The Tractor in the Jungle: Why Investment Arbitration Tribunals Should Reject a Margin of Appreciation Doctrine” in Ian Laird and Todd Weiler (eds), *Investment Treaty Arbitration and International Law* (Jurisnet 2010)
Tibori-Szabó K, “The ‘Unwilling or Unable’ Test and the Law of Self-Defence” in Christophe Paulussen (ed), *Fundamental Rights in International and European Law* (Asser Press 2016)
Tienhaara K, “Regulatory Chill and the Threat of Arbitration: A View from Political Science” in Chester Brown and Kate Miles (eds), *Evolution in Investment Treaty Law and Arbitration* (CUP 2011)
Trapp K, “Great Resources Mean Great Responsibility: A Framework of Analysis for Assessing Compliance with API Obligations in the Information Age” in D Saxon (ed), *International Humanitarian Law and the Changing Technology of War* (Martinus Nijhoff 2013)
Tsagourias N, “Risk and the Use of Force” in Mónika Ambrus, Rosemary Rayfuse, and Wouter Werner (eds) Risk and the Regulation of Uncertainty in International Law (OUP 2017)
Vasani S, “Bowing to the Queen: Rejecting the Margin of Appreciation Doctrine in International Investment Arbitration” in Ian Laird and Todd Weiler (eds), *Investment Treaty Arbitration and International Law* (Jurisnet 2010)
Vos E, “The European Court of Justice in the Face of Scientific Uncertainty and Complexity” in Mark Dawson, Bruno De Witte, and Elise Muir (eds), *Judicial Activism at the European Court of Justice* (Edward Elgar 2013)
Vylder H and Haeck Y, “The Duty of Cooperation of the Respondent State During the Proceedings Before the European Court of Human Rights” in Yves Haeck and Eva Brems (eds), *Human Rights and Civil Liberties in the 21st Century* (Springer 2014)
Waldron J, “Moments of Carelessness and Massive Loss” in David G Owen (ed), *The Philosophical Foundations of Tort Law* (OUP 1995)
Wittich S, “Article 2(1)(c), (2) and (3)” in R O’Keefe and CJ Tams (eds), *The United Nations Convention on Jurisdictional Immunities of States and Their Property: A Commentary* (OUP 2013)
——— “Article 10” in R O’Keefe and CJ Tams (eds), *The United Nations Convention on Jurisdictional Immunities of States and Their Property: A Commentary* (OUP 2013)
Wright RW, “The Nightmare and the Noble Dream: Hart and Honoré on Causation and Responsibility” in Matthew H Kramer (ed), *The Legacy of HLA Hart: Legal, Political, and Moral Philosophy* (OUP 2008)

—— "Causation: Metaphysics or Intuition?" in Kimberly Kessler Ferzan and Stephen J Morse (eds), *Legal, Moral, and Metaphysical Truths: The Philosophy of Michael S Moore* (OUP 2016)
Zeitler H, "Full Protection and Security" in S Schill (ed), *International Investment Law and Comparable Public Law* (OUP 2010)

Journal Articles

Ackerman BA, "Beyond 'Carolene Products'" (1985) 98 Harvard Law Review 713
Ahn D and Moon WJ, "Alternative Approach to Causation Analysis in Trade Remedy Investigations: 'Cost of Production' Test" (2010) 44 Journal of World Trade 1023
Alexandrov SA, "Breaches of Contract and Breaches of Treaty: The Jurisdiction of Treaty-Based Arbitration Tribunals to Decide Breach of Contract Claims in SGS v Pakistan and SGS v Philippines" (2004) 5 Journal of World Investment and Trade 555
Alkoby A, "Non-State Actors and the Legitimacy of International Environmental Law" (2003) 3 Non-State Actors and International Law 23
Andia T and Chorev N, "Making Knowledge Legitimate: Transnational Advocacy Networks' Campaigns Against Tobacco, Infant Formula and Pharmaceuticals" (2017) 17 Global Networks 255
Aradau C and Munster RV, "Governing Terrorism through Risk: Taking Precautions, (Un) Knowing the Future" (2007) 13 European Journal of International Relations 89
Arai-Takahashi Y, "Shifting Boundaries of the Right of Self Defence" (2002) 36 International Lawyer 1081
Arato J, "The Margin of Appreciation in International Investment Law" (2014) 54 Virginia Journal of International Law 545
Ballantyne N, "Epistemic Trespassing" (2019) 128 MIND 367
Bannelier-Christakis K, "Cyber Diligence: A Low-Intensity Due Diligence Principle for Low-Intensity Cyber Operations?" (2014) 14 Baltic Yearbook of International Law 1
Bartels L, "The Chapeau of the General Exceptions in the WTO GATT and GATS Agreements: A Reconstruction" (2015) 109 American Journal of International Law 105
Baumberg B and Andreson P, "Trade and Health: How World Trade Organization Law Affects Alcohol and Public Health" (2008) 103 Addiction 1952
Beale JH, "The Proximate Consequences of an Act" (1920) 33 Harvard Law Review 633
Benvenisti E, "Exit and Voice in the Age of Globalization" (1999) 98 Michigan Law Review 167
—— "Margin of Appreciation, Consensus, and Universal Standards" (1999) 31 New York University Journal of International Law and Politics 843
—— "Sovereigns as Trustees of Humanity: On the Accountability of States to Foreign Stakeholders" (2013) 107 American Journal of International Law 295
—— "Democracy Captured: The Mega-Regional Agreements and the Future of Global Public Law" (2016) 23 Constellations 58
—— "The Margin of Appreciation, Subsidiarity and Global Challenges to Democracy" (2018) 9 Journal of International Dispute Settlement 240
Benvenisti E and Downs GW, "The Empire's New Clothes: Political Economy and the Fragmentation of International Law" (2007) 60 Stanford Law Review 595
Benzing M, "Community Interests in the Procedure of International Courts and Tribunals" (2006) 5 The Law and Practice of International Courts and Tribunals 369

Berger-Walliser G and Shrivastava P, "Beyond Compliance: Sustainable Development, Business, and Proactive Law" (2015) 46 Georgetown Journal of International Law 417
Berkes A, "The Standard of 'Due Diligence' as a Result of Interchange between the Law of Armed Conflict and General International Law" (2018) 23 Journal of Conflict and Security Law 433
Berman A, "The Role of Domestic Administrative Law in the Accountability of Transnational Regulatory Networks: The Case of the ICH" (2012) 22 IILJ Emerging Scholars Paper 22
Berry SE, "A 'Good Faith' Interpretation of the Right to Manifest Religion? The Diverging Approaches of the European Court of Human Rights and the UN Human Rights Committee" (2017) 37 Legal Studies 672
Bjorge E, "Been There, Done That: The Margin of Appreciation and International Law" (2015) 4 Cambridge International Law Journal 181
Bjorklund A, "Causation, Morality, and Quantum" (2009) 32 Suffolk Transnational Law Review 435
Bodansky DM and Crook JR, "Symposium on the ILC's State Responsibility Articles: Introduction and Overview" (2002) 96 American Journal of International Law 773
Bogdandy A and Venzke I, "On the Functions of International Courts: An Appraisal in Light of Their Burgeoning Public Authority" (2013) 26 Leiden Journal of International Law 49
Born G, Morris D, and Forrest S, "'A Margin of Appreciation': Appreciating Its Irrelevance in International Law" (2020) 61 Harvard Journal of International Law 65
Bothe M, "Legal Restraints on Targeting: Protection of Civilian Population and the Changing Faces of Modern Conflicts" (2001) 31 Israel Yearbook on Human Rights 35
Boutin B, "Attribution of Conduct in International Military Operations: A Causal Analysis of Effective Control" (2017) 18 Melbourne Journal of International Law 154
Brabandere D, "Host States' Due Diligence Obligations in International Investment Law" (2015) 42 Syracuse Journal of International Law and Commerce 320
Bray H, "SOI: Save Our Investments! International Investment Law and International Humanitarian Law" (2013) 14 Journal of World Investment and Trade 578
Brems E and Lavrysen L, "Procedural Justice in Human Rights Adjudication: The European Court of Human Rights" (2013) 35 Human Rights Quarterly 176
Brewer S, "Scientific Expert Testimony and Intellectual Due Process" (1998) 107 Yale Law Journal 1535
Brower C, "Evidence before International Tribunals: The Need for Some Standard Rules" (1994) 28(1) International Lawyer 47–58
Brower CN and Schill SW, "Is Arbitration a Threat or a Boon to the Legitimacy of International Investment Law? Investment Law?" (2009) 9 Chicago Journal of International Law 471
Brownlie I, "International Law and the Activities of Armed Bands" (1958) 7 International and Comparative Law Quarterly 712
Burke-White WW and Staden A, "Private Litigation in a Public Law Sphere: The Standard of Review in Investor-State Arbitrations" (2010) 35 Yale Journal of International Law 283
Byers M, "Abuse of Rights: An Old Principle, a New Age" (2002) 47 McGill Law Journal 389
Byers M, "Terrorism, The Use of Force and International Law after 11 September" (2002) 51 International and Comparative Law Quarterly 401
Calabresi G, "Concerning Cause and the Law of Torts: An Essay for Harry Kalven, Jr" (1975) 43 University of Chicago Law Review 69
Çalı B, "Coping with Crisis: Whither the Variable Geometry in the Jurisprudence of the European Court of Human Rights" (2018) 35 Wisconsin International Law Journal 237

Callard C, Chitanondh H, and Weissman R, "Why Trade and Investment Liberalization May Threaten Effective Tobacco Control Efforts" (2001) 10 Tobacco Control 68

Cannizzaro E, "Proportionality and Margin of Appreciation in the Whaling Case: Reconciling Antithetical Doctrines?" (2016) 27 European Journal of International Law 1061

Capaldo GZ, "Providing a Right of Self-Defense Against Large-Scale Attacks by Irregular Forces: The Israeli-Hezbollah Conflict" (2007) Harvard International Law Journal Online 101

Carpenter CE, "Workable Rules for Determining Proximate Cause" (1932) 20 California Law Review 229

Carron D, "When Is a Conflict International? Time for New Control Tests in IHL" (2016) 98 International Review of the Red Cross 1019

Christenson G, "Attributing Acts of Omission to the State" (1990) 12 Michigan Journal of International Law 312

Clark RS, "The Mental Element in International Criminal Law: The Rome Statute of the International Criminal Court and the Elements of Offences" (2002) 12 Criminal Law Forum 291

Combacau J and Alland D, "'Primary' and 'Secondary' Rules in the Law of State Responsibility Categorizing International Obligations" (1985) 16 Netherlands Yearbook of International Law 81–109

Condon BJ, "Treaty Structure and Public Interest Regulation in International Economic Law" (2014) 17 Journal International Economic Law 333

Corten O, "The 'Unwilling or Unable' Test: Has It Been, and Could It Be, Accepted?" (2016) 29 Leiden Journal of International Law 777

Crawford J, "The ILC's Articles on Responsibility of States for International Wrongful Acts: A Retrospect" (2002) 96 American Journal of International Law 874

——— "Treaty and Contract in Investment Arbitration" (2008) 24 Arbitration International 351

——— "Investment Arbitration and the ILC Articles on State Responsibility" (2010) 25 ICSID Review: Foreign Investment Law Journal 127

Croley SP and Jackson JH, "WTO Dispute Procedures, Standard of Review and Deference to National Governments" (1996) 90 American Journal of International Law 193

Crosbie E and Thomson G, "Regulatory Chills: Tobacco Industry Legal Threats and the Politics of Tobacco Standardised Packaging in New Zealand" (2018) 131 New Zealand Medical Journal 25

Dannenbaum T, "Translating the Standard of Effective Control into a System of Effective Accountability: How Liability Should Be Apportioned for Violations of Human Rights by Member State Troop Contingents Serving as United Nations Peacekeepers" (2010) 51 Harvard International Law Journal 157

D'Aspremont J and Mbengue MM, "Strategies of Engagement with Scientific Fact-Finding in International Adjudication" (2014) 5 Journal of International Dispute Settlement 240

Deeks A, "Unwilling or Unable: Toward a Normative Framework for Extraterritorial Self-Defense" (2012) 52 Virginia Journal of International Law 483

Diependaele L, Ville FD, and Sterckx S, "Assessing the Normative Legitimacy of Investment Arbitration: The EU's Investment Court System" (2019) 24 New Political Economy 37

Dorlach T and Mertenskötter P, "Interpreters of International Economic Law: Corporations and Bureaucrats in Contest over Chile's Nutrition Label" (2020) 57 Law and Society Review 571

Douglas Z, "International Responsibility for Domestic Adjudication: Denial of Justice Deconstructed" (2014) 63 International and Comparative Law Quarterly 867
Drope J and Lencucha R, "Tobacco Control and Trade Policy: Proactive Strategies for Integrating Policy Norms" (2013) 34 Journal of Public Health Policy 153
Dupuy P-M, "Reviewing the Difficulties of Codification: On Ago's Classification of Obligations of Means and Obligations of Result in Relation to State Responsibility" (1999) 10 European Journal of International Law 371
Durkee MJ, "Astroturf Activism" (2017) 69 Stanford Law Review 201
Edgerton H, "Legal Cause" (1924) 72 University of Pennsylvania Law Review 211
Esty DC, "Good Governance at the World Trade Organization: Building a Foundation of Administrative Law" (2007) 10 Journal of International Economic Law 509
Feit M, "Attribution and the Umbrella Clause: Is There a Way out of the Deadlock?" (2012) 21 Minnesota Journal of International Law 21
Ferencz BB, "Defining Aggression: The Last Mile" (1973) 12 Columbia Journal of Transnational Law 431
Føllesdal A, "Subsidiarity and International Human-Rights Courts: Respecting Self-Governance and Protecting Human Rights—Or Neither?" (2016) 79 Law and Contemporary Problems 147
Fontanelli F and Busco P, "The Function of Procedural Justice in International Adjudication" (2016) 15 Law and Practice of International Courts and Tribunals 1
Foster CE, "Adjudication, Arbitration and the Turn to Public Law 'Standards of Review': Putting the Precautionary Principle in the Crucible" (2012) 3 Journal of International Dispute Settlement 525
——— "International Adjudication—Standards of Review and Burden of Proof: Australia-Apples and Whaling in the Antarctic" (2012) Review of European Community and International Environmental Law 80
Fukunaga Y, "Standard of Review and 'Scientific Truths' in the WTO Dispute Settlement System and Investment Arbitration" (2012) 3 Journal of International Dispute Settlement 559
——— "Margin of Appreciation as an Indicator of Judicial Deference: Is It Applicable to Investment Arbitration?" (2019) 10 Journal of International Dispute Settlement 69
Gaja G, "Primary and Secondary Rules in the International Law on State Responsibility" (2014) 97 Rivista di Diritto Internazionale 981
Gardbaum S, "Comparative Political Process Theory" (2020) 8 I-CON 1
Garrido-Munoz A, "Managing Uncertainty: The International Court of Justice, 'Objective Reasonableness' and the Judicial Function" (2017) 30 Leiden Journal of International Law 457
Gathii J, "War's Legacy in International Investment Law" (2009) 11 International Community Law Review 353
Gattini A, "Breach of the Obligation to Prevent and Reparation Thereof in the ICJ's Genocide Judgment" (2007) 18 European Journal of International Law 695
Gilles S, "Negligence, Strict Liability, and the Cheapest Cost-Avoider" (1992) 78 Vanderbilt Law Review 1291
Gogarty B and Lawrence P, "The ICJ Whaling Case: Missed Opportunity to Advance the Rule of Law in Resolving Science-Related Disputes in Global Commons?" (2016) 77 Heidelberg Journal of International Law 161
Gourgourinis A, "General/Particular International Law and Primary/Secondary Rules: Unitary Terminology of a Fragmented System" (2011) 22 European Journal of International Law 993

Gragl P, "An Olive Branch from Strasbourg? Interpreting the European Court of Human Rights' Resurrection of Bosphorus and Reaction to Opinion 2/13 in the Avotiņs Case" (2017) 13 European Constitutional Law Review 551
Greenman K, "Aliens in Latin America: Intervention, Arbitration and State Responsibility for Rebels" (2018) 31(3) Leiden Journal of International Law 617
Greenwood C, "International Humanitarian Law and the Tadic Case" (1996) 7 European Journal of International Law 265
——— "International Law and the Pre-Emptive Use of Force: Afghanistan, Al-Qaida, and Iraq" (2003) 4 San Diego International Law Journal 7
Grüning T, "Tobacco Industry Attempts to Influence and Use the German Government to Undermine the WHO Framework Convention on Tobacco Control" (2012) 21 Tobacco Control 30
Gruszczynski L, "How Deep Should We Go: Searching for an Appropriate Standard of Review in the SPS Cases" (2011) 2 European Journal of Risk Regulation 111
——— "Australia Plain Packaging Law, International Litigations and Regulatory Chilling Effect" (2014) 5 European Journal of Risk Regulation 160
Gutteridge HC, "Abuse of Rights" (1933) 5 Cambridge Law Journal 22
Guzman AT, "Determining the Appropriate Standard of Review in WTO Disputes" (2009) 42 Cornell International Law Journal 45
Hakimi M, "Defensive Force against Non-State Actors: The State of Play" (2015) 91 International Law Studies 1
Hamamoto S, "Parties to the 'Obligations' in the Obligations Observance ('Umbrella') Clause" (2015) 30 ICSID Review 449
Hamer D, "'Factual Causation' and 'Scope of Liability': What's the Difference?" (2014) 77 Modern Law Review 155
Harten G and Loughlin M, "Investment Treaty Arbitration as a Species of Global Administrative Law" (2006) 17 European Journal of International Law 121
Heath JB, "The New National Security Challenge to the Economic Order" (2019) 129 Yale Law Journal 1020
Henckels C, "Balancing Investment Protection and the Public Interest: The Role of the Standard of Review and the Importance of Deference in Investor-State Arbitration" (2013) 4 Journal of International Dispute Settlement 197
Hessbruege J, "The Historical Development of the Doctrines of Attribution and Due Diligence in International Law" (2004) 36 New York University Journal of International Law and Politics 265
Hill TE, "Moral Purity and the Lesser Evil" (1983) 66 The Monist 213
Howse R, "Democracy, Science, and Free Trade: Risk Regulation on Trial at the World Trade Organization" (1999) 98 Michigan Law Review 2329
——— "The World Trade Organization 20 Years On: Global Governance by Judiciary" (2016) 27 European Journal of International Law 9
Howse R and Levy PI, "The TBT Panels: US-Cloves, US-Tuna, US-COOL" (2013) 12 World Trade Review 327
Hutchinson MR, "The Margin of Appreciation Doctrine in the European Court of Human Rights" (1999) 48 International and Comparative Law Quarterly 638
Iluyomade BO, "Scope and Content of Abuse of Right" (1975) 16 Harvard International Law Journal 47
Irwin DA, "Causing Problems? The WTO Review of Causation and Injury Attribution in US Section 201 Cases" (2003) 2 World Trade Review 297

Jachtenfuchs M and Krisch N, "Subsidiarity in Global Governance" (2016) 79 Law and Contemporary Problems 1
Jackson JH, "Remarks by John H Jackson" (1994) 88 Proceedings of the ASIL Annual Meeting 136
Jackson M, "Freeing Soering: The ECHR, State Complicity in Torture and Jurisdiction" (2016) 27 European Journal of International Law 817
Jørgensen N, "Complicity in Torture in a Time of Terror: Interpreting the European Court of Human Rights Extraordinary Rendition Cases" (2017) 16 Chinese Journal of International Law 11
Jorritsma R, "Where General International Law Meets International Humanitarian Law: Attribution of Conduct and the Classification of Armed Conflicts" (2018) 23 Journal of Conflict and Security Law 405
Kajtar G, "Use of Force against ISIL in Iraq and Syria: A Legal Battlefield" (2017) 34 Wisconsin International Law Journal 535
Katselas AT, "A Comparative Analysis of the US Administrative Procedure Act's Arbitrary and Capricious Standard of Review and the Fair and Equitable Treatment and Arbitrary or Discriminatory Measures Treaty Standards" (2012) 34 Michigan Journal of International Law 87
Keller H and Heri C, "Selective Criminal Proceedings and Article 18 ECHR: The European Court of Human Rights Untapped Potential to Protect Democracy" (2016) 37 Human Rights Law Journal 1
Kelly K, "The Analysis of Causality in Escape Clause Cases" (1988) 37 Journal of Industrial Economics 187
Kelsen H, "Causality and Imputation" (1950) 61 Ethics 1
Keohane RO, Macedo S, and Moravcsik A, "Democracy-Enhancing Multilateralism" (2009) 63 International Organization 1
Kirchner S, "Third Party Liability for Hezbollah Attacks Against Israel" (2006) 7 German Law Journal 777
Klarman M, "An Interpretive History of Modern Equal Protection" (1991) 90 Michigan Law Review 213
Kleinlein T, "The Procedural Approach of the European Court of Human Rights: Between Subsidiarity and Dynamic Evolution" (2019) 68 International and Comparative Law Quarterly 91
Koskenniemi M and Leino P, "Fragmentation of International Law? Postmodern Anxieties" (2002) 15 Leiden Journal of International Law 553
Kunz JL, "Individual and Collective Self-Defense in Article 51 of the Charter of the United Nations" (1947) 41 American Journal of International Law 876
Kurtz J, "The Paradoxical Treatment of the ILC Articles on State Responsibility in Investor-State Arbitration" (2010) 25 ICSID Review: Foreign Investment Law Journal 200
Lang A, "The Judicial Sensibility of the WTO Appellate Body" (2016) 27 European Journal of International Law 1095
Langille B, "It's 'Instant Custom': How the Bush Doctrine Became Law after the Terrorist Attacks of September 11, 2001" (2003) 26 International and Comparative Law Review 145
Lanovoy V, "Causation in the Law of State Responsibility" (2022) British Yearbook of International Law 1
Liberman J and Mitchell A, "In Search of Coherence Between Trade and Health: Inter-Institutional Opportunities" (2010) 25 Maryland Journal of International Law 143
Liefländer TR, "The Lubanga Judgment of the ICC: More than Just the First Step?" (2012) 1 Cambridge Journal of International and Comparative Law 191

Linderfalk U, "State Responsibility and the Primary-Secondary Rules Terminology: The Role of Language for an Understanding of the International Legal System" (2009) 78 Nordic Journal of International Law 53

Lopert R and Gleeson D, "The High Price of 'Free' Trade: US Trade Agreements and Access to Medicines" (2013) 41 Journal of Law, Medicine and Ethics 199

Vagias M and Ferencz J, "Burden and Standard of Proof in Defence Challenges to the Jurisdiction of the International Criminal Court" (2015) 28 Leiden Journal of International Law 133

Mamudu HM and Glantz S, "Civil Society and the Negotiation of the Framework Convention on Tobacco Control" (2009) 4 Global Public Health 150

Mamudu HM, Hammond R, and Glantz S, "Tobacco Industry Attempts to Counter the World Bank Report Curbing the Epidemic and Obstruct the WHO Framework Convention on Tobacco Control" (2008) 67 Social Science and Medicine 1690

——— "Project Cerberus: Tobacco Industry Strategy to Create an Alternative to the Framework Convention on Tobacco Control" (2008) 98 American Journal of Public Health 1630

Mar KD, "The Requirement of 'Belonging' under International Humanitarian Law" (2010) 21 European Journal of International Law 105

McCrudden C and O'Leary B, "Courts and Consociations, or How Human Rights Courts May De-Stabilize Power-Sharing Settlements" (2013) 24 European Journal of International Law 477

McGoldrick D, "A Defence of the Margin of Appreciation and an Argument for Its Application by the Human Rights Committee" (2016) 65 International and Comparative Law Quarterly 21

McGrath S, "Causation by Omission: A Dilemma" (2005) 123 Philosophical Studies 125

Mensah TA, "Provisional Measures in the International Tribunal for the Law of the Sea (ITLOS)" (2002) 62 Zaörv 43

Milanovic M, "State Responsibility for Genocide" (2006) 17 European Journal of International Law 553

Mitchell AD and Voon T, "Someone to Watch Over Me: Use of FOI Requests by the Tobacco Industry" (2014) 22 Australian Journal of Administrative Law 18

Moore M, "The Metaphysics of Causal Intervention" (2000) 88 California Law Review 827

Murphy S, "Terrorism and the Concept of 'Armed Attack' in Article 51 of the UN Charter" (2002) 43 Harvard International Law Journal 41

Newcombe A, "The Boundaries of Regulatory Expropriation in International Law" (2005) 20 ICSID Review: Foreign Investment law journal 1

Nollkaemper a and jacobs d, "shared responsibility in international law: a conceptual framework" (2013) 34 michigan journal of international law 359

Nordic Experts, "The Requirement of Belonging to a Party to the Conflict" (1970) 40 Nordic Journal of International Law 54

Oduntan G, "The Demarcation of Straddling Villages in Accordance with the International Court of Justice Jurisprudence: The Cameroon–Nigeria Experience" (2006) 5 Chinese Journal of International Law 79

Olleson S, "Attribution in Investment Treaty Arbitration" (2016) 31 ICSID Review 457

Ollino A and Puma G, "La causalità e il suo ruolo nella determinazione dell'illecito internazionale" (2022) 105 Rivista di diritto internazionale 313

Paul V, "The Abuse of Rights and Bona Fides in International Law" (1977) 28 Österreichische Zeitschrift für Öffentliches Recht und Völkerrecht 121

Peat D, "The Use of Court-Appointed Experts by the International Court of Justice" (2014) 84 British Yearbook of International Law 271
Pellet VA, "Remarques sur une révolution inachevée. Le projet d'Articles de la CDI sur la responsabilité des États" (1996) 42 Annuaire Française de Droit International 4
Petroski K, "The Public Face of Presumptions" (2009) 5 Episteme 388
Pisillo-Mazzeschi R, "The Due Diligence Rule and the Nature of the International Responsibility of States" (1992) 35 German Yearbook of International Law 9
Plakokefalos I, "Causation in the Law of State Responsibility and the Problem of Overdetermination: In Search of Clarity" (2015) 26 European Journal of International Law 471
Politis N, "Le Problème des limitations de la souveraineté et la théorie de l'abus des droits dans les rapports internationaux" (1925) 6 Collected Courses of the Hague Academy of International Law 1
Pozen DE, "Constitutional Bad Faith" (2016) 129 Harvard Law Review 885
Simma B and Pulkowski D, "Of Planets and the Universe: Self-Contained Regimes in International Law" (2006) 17 European Journal of International Law 483
Raz J, "Responsibility and the Negligence Standard" (2010) 30 Oxford Journal of Legal Studies 1
Reinhold S, "Good Faith in Public International Law" (2013) 2 UCL Journal of Law and Jurisprudence 40
Reinhold T, "State Weakness, Irregular Warfare, and the Right to Self-Defense Post-9/11" (2011) 105 American Journal of International Law 244
Roberts A, "The Next Battleground: Standards of Review in Investment Treaty Arbitration" (2011) 16 International Council for Commercial Arbitration Congress Series 170
Saliternik M, "Perpetuating Democratic Peace: Procedural Justice in Peace Negotiations" (2016) 27 European Journal of International Law 617
Sartorio C, "Moore on Doing versus Allowing Harm" (2011) 42 Rutgers Law Journal 435
Saul M, "The European Court of Human Rights' Margin of Appreciation and the Processes of National Parliaments" (2015) 15 Human Rights Law Review 745
Scheppele KL, "The Rule of Law and the Frankenstate: Why Governance Checklists Do Not Work" (2013) 26 Governance 559
Schill SW, "Deference in Investment Treaty Arbitration: Re-Conceptualizing the Standard of Review" (2012) 3 Journal of International Dispute Settlement 577
Schill SW and Briese R, "'If the State Considers': Self-Judging Clauses in International Dispute Settlement" (2009) 13 Max Planck Yearbook of United Nations Law 61
Schmitt M, "In Defense of Due Diligence in Cyberspace" (2015) 125 Yale Law Journal Forum 68
Schreuer C, "Full Protection and Security" (2010) 1 Journal of International Dispute Settlement 6
Schwarzenberger G, "Uses and Abuses of the 'Abuse of Rights' in International Law" (1956) 42 Transactions of the Grotius Society 147
Scott J and Sturm S, "Courts as Catalysts: Re-Thinking the Judicial Role in New Governance" (2007) 13 Columbia Journal of European Law 565
Shaffer E, "International Trade Agreements: A Threat to Tobacco Control Policy" (2005) 14 Tobacco Control 19
Shaffer G, "A Tragedy in the Making? The Decline of Law and the Return of Power in International Trade Relations"(2019) 44 Yale Journal of International Law (Online) 37
Shany Y, "Toward a General Margin of Appreciation Doctrine in International Law?" (2005) 16 European Journal of International Law 907

Shelton D, "Righting Wrongs: Reparations in the Articles on State Responsibility" (2002) 96 American Journal of International Law 833
Shlomo-Agon S and Benvenisti E, "The Law of Strangers: The Form and Substance of Other-Regarding International Adjudication" (2018) 68 University of Toronto Law Journal 598
Sloane R, "On the Use and Abuse of Necessity in the Law of State Responsibility" (2012) 106 American Journal of International Law 447
Smith J, "Legal Cause in Actions of Tort" (1911) 25 Harvard Law Review 103
——— "Legal Cause in Actions of Tort [Concluded]" (1912) 25 Harvard Law Review 303
Sousa Mendes P, "A Semantic Model for Causation in Criminal Law and the Need of Logico-Legal Criteria for the Attribution of Causation" (2013) Law, Probability and Risk 207
Spielmann D, "Allowing the Right Margin: The European Court of Human Rights and the National Margin of Appreciation Doctrine: Waiver or Subsidiarity of European Review?" (2012) 14 Cambridge Yearbook of European Legal Studies 381
Spinedi M, "On the Non-Attribution of the Bosnian Serbs' Conduct to Serbia" (2007) 5 Journal of International Criminal Justice 829
Staden A, "The Democratic Legitimacy of Judicial Review Beyond the State: Normative Subsidiarity and Judicial Standards of Review" (2012) 10 I-CON 1023
Stapleton J, "Law, Causation and Common Sense" (1988) 8 Oxford Journal of Legal Studies 111
——— "Legal Cause: Cause-in-Fact and the Scope of Liability for Consequences" (2001) 54 Vanderbilt Law Review 941
——— "Factual Causation" (2010) 38 Federal Law Review 467
——— "An 'Extended But-For' Test for the Causal Relation in the Law of Obligations" (2015) 35 Oxford Journal of Legal Studies 697
Starski P, "Right to Self-Defense, Attribution and the Non-State Actor: Birth of the 'Unable or Unwilling' Standard?" (2015) 75 ZaörV 455
Steel S, "Defining Causal Counterfactuals in Negligence" (2014) 130 Law Quarterly Review 564
Stern B, "Civil Society's Voice in the Settlement of International Economic Disputes" (2007) 22 ICSID Review: Foreign Investment Law Journal 280
Stewart RB, "Remedying Disregard in Global Regulatory Governance: Accountability, Participation, and Responsiveness" (2014) 108 American Journal of International Law 211
Stoyanova V, "Causation between State Omission and Harm within the Framework of Positive Obligations under the European Convention on Human Rights" (2018) 18 Human Rights Law Review 309
Straus M, "Causation as an Element of State Responsibility" (1984) 16 Law and Policy in International Business 893
Tams CJ, "The Use of Force against Terrorists" (2009) 20 European Journal of International Law 359
Taylor GDS, "Content and Rule against Abuse of Rights in International Law" (1972) 46 British Yearbook of International Law 323
Teitelbaum R, "Recent Fact-Finding Developments at the International Court of Justice" (2007) 6 Law and Practice of International Courts and Tribunals 119
Thomas CA, "Of Facts and Phantoms: Economics, Epistemic Legitimacy, and WTO Dispute Settlement" (2011) 14 Journal of International Economic Law 295
Tienhaara K, "Regulatory Chill in a Warming World: The Threat to Climate Policy Posed by Investor-State Dispute Settlement" (2018) 7 Transnational Environmental Law 229

Tomonori M, "The Individual as Beneficiary of State Immunity: Problems of the Attribution of Ultra Vires Conduct" (2001) 29 Denver Journal of International Law and Policy 101
Townley S, "The Rise of Risk in International Law" (2018) 18 Chicago Journal of International Law 594
Trouwborst A, "Prevention, Precaution, Logic and Law" (2009) 105 Erasmus Law Review 117
Tsagourias N, "Self-Defence against Non-State Actors: The Interaction between Self-Defence as a Primary Rule and Self-Defence as a Secondary Rule" (2016) 29 Leiden Journal of International Law 801
Tyler TR, "Procedural Justice and the Courts" (2007) 44(1/2) Court Review The Journal of the American Judges Association 26–31
Tzevelekos V, "Reconstructing the Effective Control Criterion in Extraterritorial Humans Rights Breaches: Direct Attribution of Wrongfulness, Due Diligence, and Concurrent Responsibility" (2014) 36 Michigan Journal of International Law 129
Vasciannie S, "Bilateral Investment Treaties and Civil Strife: The AAPL/Sri Lanka Arbitration" (1992) 39 Netherlands International Law Review 332
Weimer M, "Reconciling Regulatory Space with External Accountability through WTO Adjudication: Trade, Environment and Development" (2017) 30 Leiden Journal of International Law 901
Wright R, "Once More Into the Bramble Bush: Duty, Causal Contribution, and the Extent of Legal Responsibility" (2001) 54 Vanderbilt Law Review 1071
Wright RW, "Causation in Tort Law" (1985) 73 California Law Review 1735
——— "Causation, Responsibility, Risk, Probability, Naked Statistics, and Proof: Pruning the Bramble Bush by Clarifying the Concepts" (1988) 73 Iowa Law Review 1001
Wright RW and Puppe I, "Causation: Linguistic, Philosophical, Legal and Economic" (2016) 91 Chicago-Kent Law Review 461
Yach D, "The Origins, Development, Effects, and Future of the WHO Framework Convention on Tobacco Control: A Personal Perspective" (2014) 383 Lancet 1771
Ziegler DW, "International Trade Agreements Challenge Tobacco and Alcohol Control Policies" (2006) 25 Drug and Alcohol Review 567
Zipursky BC, "Foreseeability in Breach, Duty and Proximate Cause" (2009) 44 Wake Forest Law Review 1247
Zrilič J, "Armed Conflict as Force Majeure in International Investment Law" (2019) 16 Manchester Journal of International Economic Law 28

United Nations Documents

General Assembly (UNGA)

UNGA "Report of the Human Rights Committee" (2019) UN Doc A/74/40
——— "Report of the Committee on the Elimination of Discrimination against Women" (2018) UN Doc A/73/38
——— Possible Reform of Investor-State Dispute Settlement (ISDS): Note by the Secretariat, UN Doc A/CN.9/WG.III/WP.166
——— Resolution 3314 "Definition of Aggression" (XXIX), UN Doc A/RES/3314

Security Council (UNSC)

Permanent Representative of Great Britain to the UN, Letter dated 3 December 2015 from the Permanent Representative of the United Kingdom of Great Britain and Northern

Ireland to the United Nations addressed to the President of the Security Council, UN Doc S/2015/928 (2015)
Permanent Representative of Great Britain to the UN, Letter dated 7 September 2015 from the Permanent Representative of the United Kingdom of Great Britain and Northern Ireland to the United Nations addressed to the President of the Security Council, UN Doc S/2015/688 (2015)
UN Doc S/2014/695 (Sept. 23, 2014)
UN Doc S/2015/221 (Mar. 31, 2015)
UN Doc S/2015/693 (Sept. 9, 2015)
UN Doc S/2015/946 (Dec. 10, 2015)
UN Doc S/2016/34 (Jan. 13, 2016).
UN Doc S/2016/513 (June 3, 2016)
UN Doc S/2016/523 (June 9, 2016)

International Law Commission (ILC)

2571st and 2573rd ILC Meetings in (1999) I Yearbook of the International Law Commission, UN Doc A/CN.4/SER.A/1999, 31, 41
Ago R, "First Report on State Responsibility" (1989) II(2) Yearbook of the International Law Commission 139
—— "Second Report on State Responsibility" (1970) II Yearbook of the International Law Commission, UN Doc A/CN.4/233
—— "Fourth Report on State Responsibility" (1972) II Yearbook of the International Law Commission, UN Doc A/CN.4/SER.A/1972/Add.1
—— "Seventh Report on State Responsibility" (1978) II(2) Yearbook of the International Law Commission 31
—— "Sixth Report on State Responsibility" (1977) II(1) Yearbook of the International Law Commission 3
Articles on Responsibility of States for Internationally Wrongful Acts, with commentaries (2001) II(2) Yearbook of the International Law Commission
Crawford J, "First Report on State Responsibility" (1998) II(2) Yearbook of the International Law Commission, UN Doc A/CN.4/SER.A/1998/Add.1
—— "Second Report on State Responsibility" (1999) II(2) Yearbook of the International Law Commission, UN Doc A/CN.4/498/Add.1
Draft Articles on Prevention of Transboundary Harm from Hazardous Activities, with commentaries (2001) II(2) Yearbook of the International Law Commission
Draft Articles on the Responsibility of International Organizations (2011) II(2) Yearbook of the International Law Commission
Draft Articles on the Responsibility of States for Internationally Wrongful Acts, Report of the ILC on the Work of its 53rd Session, UN GAOR, 56th Sess, Supp No 10, p 43, UN Doc A/56/10 (2001).
Draft On "International Responsibility Of States For Injuries On Their Territory To The Person Or Property Of Foreigners" Prepared By The Institute Of International Law (1927) – in ILC, *Yearbook of the International Law Commission, 1956, Volume II,* UN Doc A/CN.4/SER.A/1956/Add.1, 228
Gaetano Arangio-Ruiz, "Second report on State Responsibility" (1989) II(2) Yearbook of the International Law Commission
García Amador, "Sixth Report on State Responsibility" (1961) II(2) Yearbook of the International Law Commission, UN Doc A/CN.4/SER.A/1961/Add.1

Office of the United Nations High Commissioner for Human Rights (OHCHR)

United Nations Commission on International Trade Law (UNCITRAL)

Human Rights Committee

World Health Organization (WHO)

Documents of International Courts, Tribunals, and Organizations

Council of Europe—European Court of Human Rights (ECtHR)

Rules of the Court, European Court of Human Rights, new edition of the Rules of Court, entry into force 3 June 2022 <https://www.echr.coe.int/documents/rules_court_eng.pdf> accessed 22 July 2022.

Guide by the Council of Europe on the Criminal Limb of Article 6 ECHR (updated on 30 April 2022) <https://www.echr.coe.int/Documents/Guide_Art_6_criminal_ENG.pdf> accessed 22 July 2022

Council of Europe, Guide on Article 1 of the European Convention on Human Rights: Obligation to respect human rights—Concepts of "jurisdiction" and imputability of 30 April 2022 <https://www.echr.coe.int/Documents/Guide_Art_1_ENG.pdf> accessed 22 July 2022

Inter-American Commission on Human Rights (IACHR)

Annual Report of the Inter-American Commission on Human Rights 1996 (17 March 1997) OEA/Ser.L/V/II.95, Doc 7, rev

Rules of Procedure of the Inter-American Commission on Human Rights (entry into force 1 August 2013) <http://www.oas.org/en/iachr/mandate/basics/rulesiachr.asp> accessed 26 April 2019

Others

Administrative Tribunal of the International Monetary Fund, Statute

Commentary to Geneva Convention II (2017)

ICRC Commentary to AP I

ICRC Commentary to Geneva Convention I

ICRC Revised Commentary to Common Article 1 of the Geneva Conventions

International Criminal Court, Report on Preliminary Examination Activities 2018

International Criminal Court, The Office of the Prosecutor: Report on Preliminary Examination Activities 2017

International Labour Organization Administrative Tribunal, Statute

International Tribunal for the Law of the Sea, Statute

Permanent Court of Arbitration, "Annual Report" (2016) https://docs.pca-cpa.org/2017/03/ONLINE-PCA-Annual-Report-2016-28.02.2017.pdf (accessed 22 July 2022)

United Nations Appeals Tribunal, Rules of Procedure

United Nations Appeals Tribunal, Statute

World Bank Administrative Tribunal, Statute

Websites

Çalı B, "No Going Nuclear in Strasbourg" (*Verfassungsblog*, 30 May 2019) <https://verfassungsblog.de/no-going-nuclear-in-strasbourg/> accessed 27 August 2019

Charlotin D, "Tribunal in Guris v Libya Award Draws Contrast with Cengiz Award on FPS Interpretation and Sides with Majority of Prior Libya Awards with Respect to War Losses Clauses" (*Investment Arbitration Reporter*, 5 March 2020) <https://www.iareporter.com/articles/analysis-tribunal-in-guris-v-libya-award-draws-contrast-with-cengiz-award-on-fps-interpretation-and-sides-with-majority-of-prior-libya-awards-with-respect-to-war-losses- clause/> (accessed 22 July 2022)

Heller KJ, "Do Attacks on ISIS in Syria Justify the 'Unwilling or Unable' Test?" (*Opinio Juris*, 13 December 2014) http://opiniojuris.org/2014/12/13/attacks-isis-syria-justify-unwilling-unable-test/ (22 July 2022)

Nollkaemper A, "The ECtHR Finds Macedonia Responsible in Connection with Torture by the CIA, but on What Basis?" (*EJIL:Talk!*, 24 December 2012) <https://www.ejiltalk.org/the-ecthr-finds-macedonia-responsible-in-connection-with-torture-by-the-cia-but-on-what-basis/> (22 July 2022)

Miscellaneous

Ian Cobain, Owen Bowcott, Pippa Crerar and Kareem Shaheen: "Britain Apologises for 'Appalling Treatment' of Abdel Hakim Belhaj" (*The Guardian*, 10 May 2018) https://www.theguardian.com/world/2018/may/10/britain-apologises-for-appalling-treatment-of-abdel-hakim-belhaj (22 July 2022)

"Copenhagen Declaration on the Reform of the European Convention of Human Rights System", 13 April 2018 https://rm.coe.int/copenhagen-declaration/16807b915c (22.07.2022)

"Speech of Brian Egan, State Department Legal Advisor at ASIL" (1 April 2016) <https://2009-2017.state.gov/s/l/releases/remarks/255493.htm> (22 July 2022)

ILA Study Group on Due Diligence in International Law, First Report (7 March 2014) <https://www.ila-hq.org/index.php/study-groups?study-groupsID=63> (22 July 2022)

Speech by his Excellency Judge Gilbert Guillaume, President of the International Court of Justice, to the Sixth Committee of the General Assembly of the United Nations (31 October 2001) <https://www.icj-cij.org/public/files/press-releases/5/2995.pdf (22 July 2022)

The ILA Study Group on Due Diligence in International Law, "Due Diligence in International Law: Second Report" (Johannesburg 2016) <https://www.ila-hq.org/index.php/study-groups?study-groupsID=63> (22 July 2022)

Human Rights Watch, *World Report: Events of 2001* (HRW 2002) 255

UNCTAD, International Investment Agreements Navigator <https://investmentpolicyhub.unctad.org/IIA/mappedContent> accessed 28 April 2020

Independent International Fact-Finding Mission on the Conflict in Georgia (IIFFMCG), Report on the Conflict, vol II, 2009 <https://www.mpil.de/files/pdf4/IIFFMCG_Volume_II1.pdf> (22 July 2022)

"Belhaj and Boudchar: Litigation Update" (*Hansard*, 10 May 2018) https://hansard.parliament.uk/commons/2018-05-10/debates/B9AD50CD-9D54-41DA-A18B-1526E7658593/BelhajAndBoudcharLitigationUpdate (22 July 2022)

Index

For the benefit of digital users, indexed terms that span two pages (e.g., 52–53) may, on occasion, appear on only one of those pages.

Figures are indicated by *f* following the page number